Proceedings

IEEE Workshop on FPGAs for Custom Computing Machines

FPGAs for Custom Computing Machines

Proceedings

IEEE Workshop on FPGAs for Custom Computing Machines

April 10 - 13, 1994

Napa Valley, California

Edited by

Duncan A. Buell

Kenneth L. Pocek

Sponsored by

IEEE Computer Society

Technical Committee on Computer Architecture

IEEE Computer Society Press

Los Alamitos, California

Washington • Brussels • Tokyo

IEEE Computer Society Press
10662 Los Vaqueros Circle
P.O. Box 3014
Los Alamitos, CA 90720-1264

IEEE Computer Society Press Order Number 5490-02
Library of Congress Number 93-80746
IEEE Catalog Number 94TH0611-4
ISBN 0-8186-5490-2 (paper)
ISBN 0-8186-5491-0 (microfiche)
ISBN 0-8186-5492-9 (case)

Additional copies may be ordered from:

IEEE Computer Society Press
Customer Service Center
10662 Los Vaqueros Circle
P.O. Box 3014
Los Alamitos, CA 90720-1264
Tel: +1-714-821-8380
Fax: +1-714-821-4641
Email: cs.books@computer.org

IEEE Service Center
445 Hoes Lane
P.O. Box 1331
Piscataway, NJ 08855-1331
Tel: +1-908-981-1393
Fax: +1-908-981-9667

IEEE Computer Society
13, Avenue de l'Aquilon
B-1200 Brussels
BELGIUM
Tel: +32-2-770-2198
Fax: +32-2-770-8505

IEEE Computer Society
Ooshima Building
2-19-1 Minami-Aoyama
Minato-ku, Tokyo 107
JAPAN
Tel: +81-3-3408-3118
Fax: +81-3-3408-3553

Editorial production by Regina Spencer Sipple and Edna Straub
Cover design by Joseph Daigle/Schenk-Daigle Studios
Printed in the United States of America by Braun-Brumfield, Inc.

The Institute of Electrical and Electronics Engineers, Inc.

Table of Contents

Committees vii

A Field Programmable Multi-Chip Module (FPMCM) 1
J. Darnauer, P. Garay, T. Isshiki, J. Ramirez, and W.W.-M. Dai

Pin Assignment for Multi-FPGA Systems 11
S. Hauck and G. Borriello

Emulation of the Sparcle Microprocessor with the MIT Virtual Wires Emulation System 14
M. Dahl, J. Babb, R. Tessier, S. Hanono, D. Hoki, and A. Agarwal

The Nano Processor: A Low Resource Reconfigurable Processor 23
M.J. Wirthlin, B.L. Hutchings, and K.L. Gilson

DPGA-Coupled Microprocessors: Commodity ICs for the Early 21st Century 31
A. DeHon

Field Programmable Gate Array Based Reconfigurable Preprocessor 40
B. Box

Virtual Hardware for Graphics Applications Using FPGAs 49
S. Singh and P. Bellec

A Reconfigurable Monte-Carlo Clustering Processor (MCCP) 59
C.P. Cowen and S. Monaghan

CAFCA (Compact Accelerator for Cellular Automata): The Metamorphosable Machine 66
P. Marchal and E. Sanchez

Global Control Synthesis for an MIMD/FPGA Machine 72
P. Dhaussy, J.-M. Filloque, B. Pottier, and S. Rubini

Hardware-Software Codesign of Multidimensional Programs 82
W. Luk, T. Wu, and I. Page

A Reconfigurable Compute Engine for Real-Time Vision Automata Prototyping 91
G.M. Quénot, I.C. Kraljić, J. Sérot, and B. Zavidovique

An Asynchronous Approach to Efficient Execution of Programs on Adaptive Architectures Utilizing FPGAs 101
L. Agarwal, M. Wazlowski, and S. Ghosh

A Case Study on Hardware/Software Partitioning 111
A. Jantsch, P. Ellervee, J. Öberg, and A. Hemani

From High Level Programming Model to FPGA Machines 119
J.P. Banâtre, D. Lavenier, and M. Vieillot

Behavioral Synthesis for FPGA-Based Computing 125
H. Schmit, L. Arnstein, D. Thomas, and E. Lagnese

PAM Programming Environments: Practice and Experience 133
P. Bertin and H. Touati
A Reconfigurable Data-Driven ALU for Xputers 139
R.W. Hartenstein, R. Kress, and H. Reinig
Compiling to the Gate Level for a Reconfigurable Co-Processor 147
D. Wo and K. Forward
Finding Lines and Building Pyramids with Splash 2 155
A.L. Abbott, P.M. Athanas, L. Chen, and R.L. Elliott
Comparing the Performance of FPGA-Based Custom Computers with General-Purpose Computers for DSP Applications 164
N.W. Bergmann and J.C. Mudge
An FPGA-Based Custom Coprocessor for Automatic Image Segmentation Applications 172
G.J. Gent, S.R. Smith, and R.L. Haviland
Density Enhancement of a Neural Network Using FPGAs and Run-Time Reconfiguration 180
J.G. Eldredge and B.L. Hutchings
FPGA-Based Stochastic Neural Networks — Implementation 189
S.L. Bade and B.L. Hutchings

Author Index 199

Committees

Conference Co-Chairs

Duncan A. Buell
Kenneth L. Pocek

Finance Chair

Kenneth L. Pocek

Steering Committee Members

Duncan A. Buell, *Supercomputing Research Center*
Kenneth L. Pocek, *Intel*
Jeffrey M. Arnold, *Supercomputing Research Center*
Peter M. Athanas, *Virginia Polytechnic Institute*
Tom Kean, *Xilinx*
Hervé Touati, *DEC — Paris Research Center*
Jonathon Rose, *University of Toronto*
Wayne Luk, *University of Oxford*
Pak Chan, *University of California, Santa Cruz*

A Field Programmable Multi-chip Module (FPMCM) *

Joel Darnauer, Porfirio Garay, Tsuyoshi Isshiki,
John Ramirez, Wayne Wei-Ming Dai

Computer Engineering, UC Santa Cruz,
Santa Cruz, CA 95064
Internet: ce.ucsc.edu

Abstract

Multi-chip module (MCM) packaging can reduce the cost and increase the utility of field programmable systems. We are currently developing a first generation Field Programmable Multi-chip Module (FPMCM) as a test vehicle for a particular MCM technology. We present the advantages of MCM for field programmable systems and develop analytical models for estimating the capacity of FPMCM architectures based on Rent's Rule. These models are used to generate the architecture of our first generation prototype which employs smaller FPGA die and a mixture of direct and switched interconnect. We conclude with a discussion of the challenges and opportunities that FPMCMs face.

1 MCM Benefits Field Programmable Systems

Field programmable systems (FPS) combining large numbers of field programmable gate arrays (FPGAs) and field programmable interconnect (FPIC) have the potential to revolutionize computing [CSM92] [BRV92] [Arn93] [dB93]. Current implementations typically consist of large ICs in single chip packages mounted on one or more multilayer circuit boards. These systems are often bulky, expensive and slow, because the inherently low integration density of FPGAs forces a large part of the system interconnect to be carried in the upper levels of the packaging hierarchy, such as printed wiring boards (PCBs) and backplanes, rather than in the more cost effective integrated circuit technology. We believe there are substantial cost and performance advantages to introducing an intermediate layer in the packaging hierarchy.

Dobbleare and El Gamal first proposed to apply Multichip Module (MCM) technology to FPGAs by adding additional switchboxes and special drivers to the IO structures of standard FPGAs [DGHK92]. Applying other integration techniques like wafer-scale integration to FPS has also been noted [Cas93]. We present justification for the application of MCM technology to field programmable systems and discuss our original work on the actual implementation of a Field Programmable Multi-Chip Module (FPMCM).

*This work supported in part by ARPA under ONR Grant N00014-93-1-1334.

1.1 Overview of MCM

A Multi-chip Module (MCM) is a device in which several ICs are attached to a single substrate and then packaged as a unit [Bak89]. There are many types of MCM technologies that use different materials for the substrate including silicon, ceramics and epoxy based laminates. There are also many types of chip to module attachment, such as traditional wirebonding, TAB, and flip chip. In this paper, we will focus on the particular process in use at AT&T which uses silicon substrates, aluminum interconnect, polyimide dielectrics, and flip-chip attachment. This type of process is often referred to as MCM-D.

The AT&T process uses a degenerately doped silicon substrate with three layers of aluminum. One aluminum layer is used for power, the remaining two layers contain interconnections, and the substrate acts as a ground plane. If desired, additional process steps can be added to fabricate resistors, capacitors [FTLL92], and bipolar transistors [DHT+94] directly on the substrate. Conventional ICs, sometimes post-processed to meet flip-chip assembly requirements, are bumped, diced, and tested. They are then attached face-down on the the substrate with solder bumps in a manner similar to surface mount on a printed circuit board. The resulting assembly is attached, wirebonded, and encapsulated in a traditional package such as a pin or ball grid array. Figure 1 shows a cross sectional view of a typical MCM assembly. Key features of the AT&T process that make it suitable for FPMCM are flip-chip die attach and high performance, high density interconnect. The process has been carefully optimized to minimize cost without sacrificing the performance of digital circuits [Fry93].

1.2 Advantages of MCM

MCMs have many advantages over traditional packaging: lower electrical parasitics between packages, smaller size, increased interconnect resources, and reduced packaging cost. The MCM packaging technology can provide value to a system producer in two ways: by providing the

0-8186-5490-2/94 $03.00

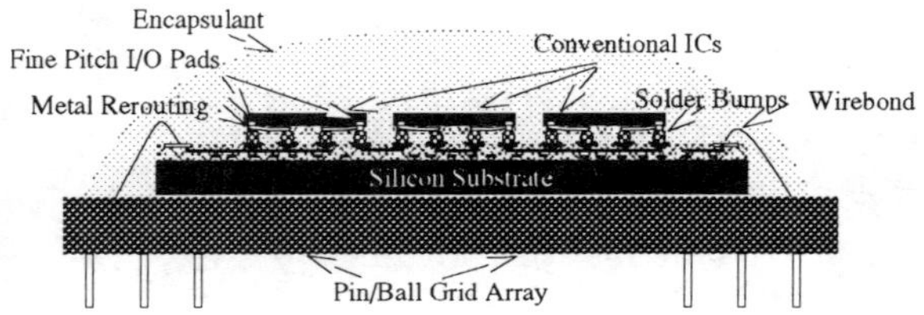

Figure 1: Cross Section of a Flip Chip Assembly

means to produce the same product at a lower cost or by yielding a product, which has a higher value for the same cost. It should be stressed that while increasing system performance and decreasing size was the original motivation for much work on MCM, practical FPMCMs must also provide significant cost advantages. In the following sections, we explore the chief benefits of MCM technology.

1.2.1 MCM Reduces Size

Reducing system size is the fundamental advantage that MCMs have over printed wire board (PWBs)—most of the other advantages of MCM technology stem from this fact. As an example, figure 2 shows a comparison of the area occupied by the devices in our first generation FPMCM, FPMCM-I, and the packages that they would need to be in on a PWB based system. Most of the area of the PWB system is taken up by the IC packages. The cost, mass, and electrical parasitics of the IC packages only detract from the assembled system's value. In contrast, the area of the FPMCM is limited mostly by the size of the ICs themselves. Despite these other important factors, reduced size has several advantages in and of itself. This is best seen in the next generation personal computer in which component size must be kept small because portability has become a valuable feature. If field programmable systems, such as reconfigurable co-processors, are to be a key component in this area then FPS size must be greatly reduced. One way of achieving this is by using FPMCMs.

1.2.2 MCM Reduces Power Consumption

Lower capacitive loads of shorter MCM interconnections provide substantial power savings. The power used by MCMs is typically about fifty percent of conventional packaging. This power savings increases dramatically when the drivers are specifically designed for the MCM interconnects [Fry93].

Low power is an important feature of MCMs for several reasons. Most important is that the power density in an MCM can quickly exceed the ability of most materials to carry heat away from components, resulting in decreased reliability and lifetime. Secondly, components that have large transient power needs increase the complexity and cost of the system power distribution network. In addition,

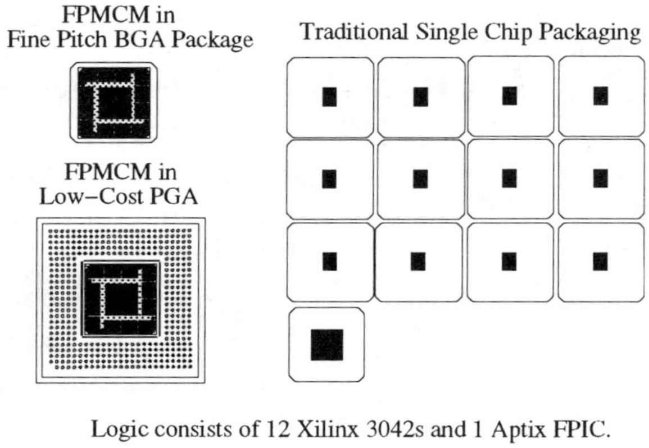

Figure 2: Size Comparison of Packaging for ICs in FPMCM-I

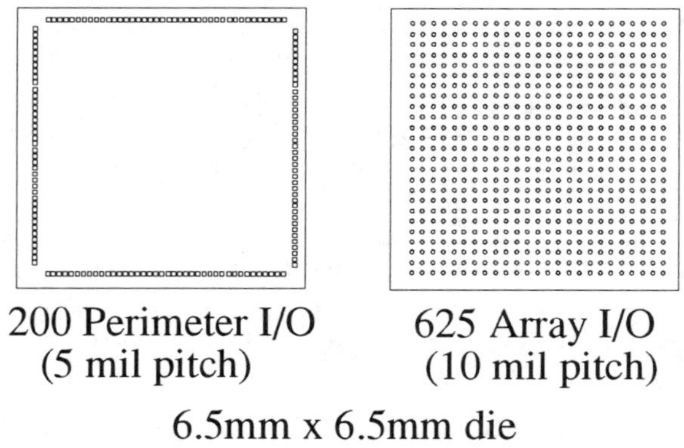

Figure 3: Comparison of Perimeter and Array IO

portable systems and add-on cards have stringent limits on total power consumption.

1.2.3 MCM Increases Flexibility

A big advantage for a FPMCM is that the solder bumps used for flip-chip attachment can be placed over the entire surface of the FPGA, rather than just at the die periphery. See figures 3 and 4. Pin limitations for FPGAs have often been observed to be a limiting factor in FPS [BTA93]. In systems where each FPGA is a small part of the total logic and the pattern of interconnections is random, the number of IO needed by an FPGA often increases faster than the square root of the size of the device. This phenomenon is governed by a relationship known as *Rent's Rule*, which states that the number of pins, p, required by a small portion of a larger system is often determined by the number of blocks, b, in the cluster and two system dependent parameters :

$$p \approx kb^r \tag{1}$$

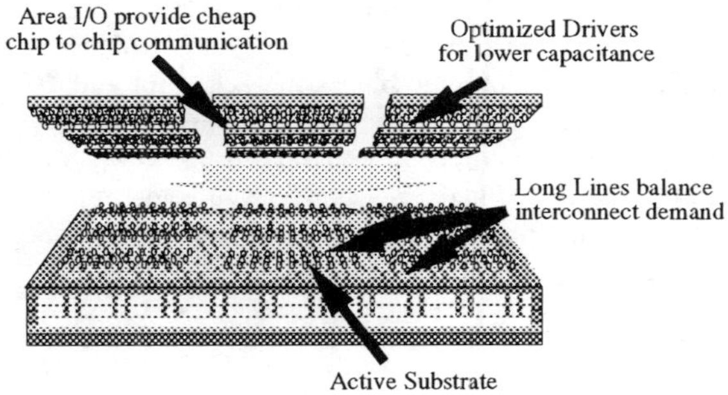

Figure 4: FPMCM as a giant FPGA

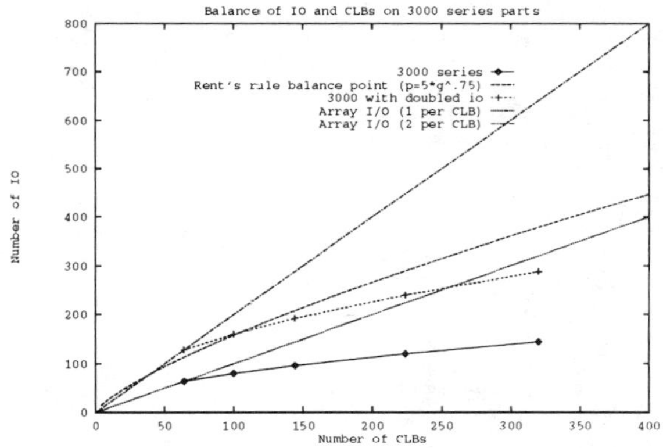

Figure 5: Array-IO vs. Perimeter IO. The number of array-IO grows linearly with chip size, satisfying Rent's rule, while the number of perimeter IO grow more slowly, causing congestion at chip boundaries in a multi-chip system. Based on chip sizes, the technologies corresponding to the array-IO use bump pitches of 20 mils and 14 mils respectively – both readily manufacturable.

Here k is the mean number of pins per block and r is a design dependent parameter between 0 and 1 known as the *Rent Exponent*. Past literature has reported Rent exponents in or around the neighborhood of 0.75, depending on the parallelism or complexity of the logic [LR71]. This large exponent does not apply to specially designed circuits such as systolic arrays that effectively serialize the communication but has been observed consistently in control and other random logic.

While the number of IO that are needed on a given FPGA grow faster than the square root of the number of logic elements, the number of perimeter bond pads that can fit along the die periphery only grow as the square root of the area. This means that for a given pad pitch and logic element pitch, there will be a die size beyond which the demand for IO far far exceeds the supply, in which case the device is pin limited. Experience with the X3090 shows that existing FPGA families have already encountered that problem—large numbers of logic elements are essentially wasted, resulting in low silicon efficiency and high cost per usable logic element. With flip-chip, the number of IO can increase more or less linearly with the die area, leaving the architect free to balance the supply of IO and logic blocks on each die. If the substrate wiring pitch and bump pitch are sufficiently small, it becomes possible for the substrate to provide effectively seamless integration between separate FPGA die, in which case the FPMCM resembles a giant chip made up of separately manufactured and separately tested tiles (Figure 4).

1.2.4 MCM Reduces Packaging Cost

MCMs also offer cost savings by moving interconnections from expensive interconnection media high in the packaging hierarchy to inexpensive media in lower levels of the hierarchy. For example, a common rule-of-thumb is that the cost of packages and interconnections at the printed wiring board level will cost a few cents per pin including the cost of the wirebond, lead frame, package, pin, and board trace. The cost per interconnection in MCM technology can be quite a bit lower. If combining devices into an MCM reduces the total number of terminals at the board level, there can be substantial cost reduction. This effect is especially pronounced if the application of MCMs allows the system designer to wholly eliminate one level of packaging—in other words, replacing a cabinet with a single card or a circuit card with a single module.

2 Architecture Estimation

Although the motivation for FPMCM is compelling, the decision to design and build an FPMCM raises many questions that are not easy to answer. What set of devices should be used as components? How large should they be and how many IO should they have? How should the logic devices be interconnected?

The utility or value of field programmable devices is usually measured along two dimensions: capacity and clock frequency. In order to provide value above that offered by existing single chip devices, the FPMCM must have a capacity significantly larger than other devices. In this section, we focus on the question: *Given a particular architecture, what capacity can we expect it to have?*

To simplify the analysis, we will use Rent's rule and assume that it accurately describes the relationship between the number of utilized logic blocks and pins on a FPGA. We also assume that Rent's rule relates the number of MCM pins and total utilized logic blocks across all FPGAs. We use "average" Rent parameters of $k = 5$ and $r = 0.75$ and do not restrict ourselves to currently available FPIC or FPGA sizes.

2.1 Tree Architecture

We based our FPMCM-I architecture on a simple *tree architecture*, which is shown in Figure 6. The tree architec-

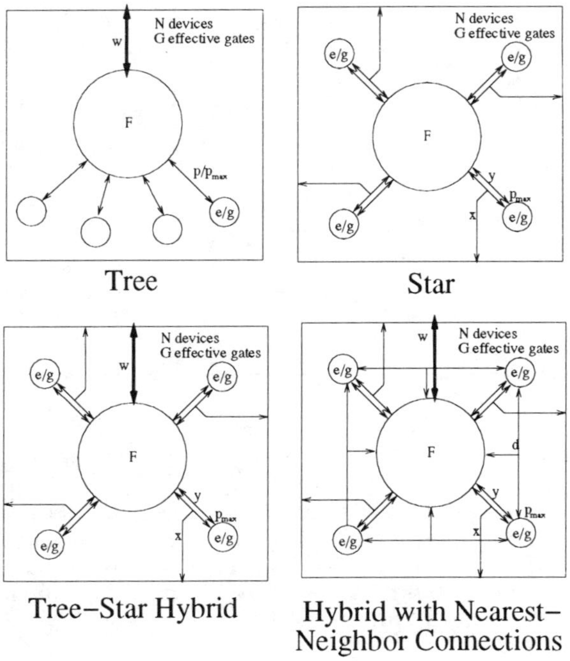

Figure 6: FPMCM Architectures

ture served as a theoretical starting point for FPMCM-I. Although practical limitations restricted us from implementing such an scheme in our MCM, we think it is important that early analysis of the tree architecture be discussed.

A tree consists of N logic devices connected to a central switching network, which has F pins. All of the MCM IO passes through a bus of w lines that forms the trunk of the tree. A single FPIC device [Apt93] or a collection of smaller switches [VBB93] [CS93] comprise the switching network. For purposes of this paper, we do not concern ourselves with the construction of the switching network, which we assume to be a single device and a near-perfect crossbar.

Since all of the IO for the module first pass through the switch, there is no need to worry about assignment of pins. This makes the architecture quite flexible, allowing the partitioner a great deal of freedom. In addition, each net on the device is observable from the central switch and each logic device is independently controllable, making the module testing very simple. The problem is that any signal going on or off the device must be driven through the switch and the switch pins quickly become quite scarce.

How many usable logic blocks, G, might we expect a particular tree architecture to provide? To answer this question, we use Rent's Rule and pin limitations to formulate a system of integer inequalities. The architecture can be described by the following parameters: F, the number of pins on the switching network, w, the number of IO, p_{max}, the number of pins on each logic device, p, the number of pins actually connected to the central switch, g, the maximum number of logic blocks in each chip, and N, the number of logic chips. Now let the expected number of logic blocks that we can fit into each device be e and the expected number of logic blocks over the whole module be G (Figure 6). To a first order, the following inequalities must hold:

$$
\begin{aligned}
G &\leq Ne &(2)\\
G &\leq (w/k)^{1/r} &(3)\\
F &\leq Np + w &(4)\\
e &\leq \alpha\, g &(5)\\
e &\leq (p/k)^{1/r} &(6)\\
p &\leq p_{max} &(7)
\end{aligned}
$$

Statements 2 and 3 stipulate that the total number of logic elements are limited by either the number of gates that fit in each of the N logic chips or by the total number of pins on the module. Note that statement 3 may be overly conservative if the FPMCM contains an entire system because Rent's rule only applies to small parts of a larger design. Statement 4 states that the number of interconnections to the central switch cannot exceed F, and statements 5 and 6 limit the number of logic blocks in each die by the lower of the pin and block limitations. Statement 5 expresses the inherent inefficiency of partitioning. When circuits are partitioned based on pin limitations some clusters will be larger than others; chips with small partitions will have some fraction of unused logic blocks. The software-dependent term $\alpha \in [0, 1]$ has been observed to be around one-half for a particular partitioner [LR71]. Statement 7 allows the number of pins on each logic device to exceed that actually connected to the switch.

Assuming that α,k and r are known, then there are eight unknowns $G, F, N, e, g, p, w, p_{max}$. If we decide that the architecture will have no left over pins or other unutilized resources, we can convert each of the inequalities into an equality. The resulting system has six equations and eight unknowns but since we are trying to maximize G, we really only have a single degree of freedom. The key equation is:

$$G = N \left(\frac{F}{k(N^r + N)} \right)^{1/r} \qquad (8)$$

G is monotonically increasing with respect to F for fixed N, and monotonically decreasing with respect to N for fixed F. This would seem to imply that the ideal FPMCM architecture consists of a single very large logic device—not a multi-chip module at all! The reason for this degeneracy is that the capacity model does not consider the cost of the logic devices. One approach would be to constrain the size of g by an upper limit on die size, g_{max}, to force a

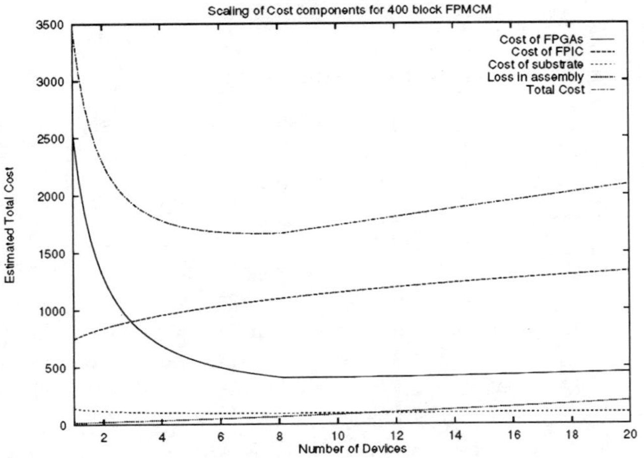

Figure 7: Scaling of cost components vs. number of FPGA in 400 block architectures

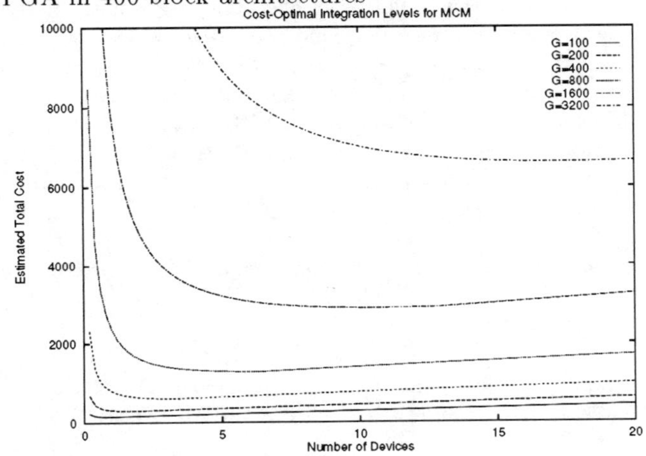

Figure 8: Optimal integration levels for FPMCM with various capacity targets.

multiple chip solution. A more useful approach would be to formulate an expression for the dollar cost of a architecture based on the die size, g, the number of pins, p, switch size, F, and the number of devices, N. We could then set G at a target capacity and optimize the architecture for cost. Figure 8 shows how the cost-optimal integration count (number of FPGA die on the MCM) varies as the system capacity target from cost models obtained by fitting exponential functions plus a fixed cost to the die size for the FPGAs. In agreement with common sense, the larger the system, the more pieces it must be broken into to achieve minimal cost.

The scaling of cost components is shown in figure 7. Here we see that for the 400 block architecture, the cost of the system is dominated either by the cost of the FPGAs or the cost of the FPIC depending on the number of FPGA used. The minimum cost architecture has around 6 to 8 FPGAs.

2.2 Star Architecture

The next step in the evolution of the FPMCM-I was to to consider the *star architecture*, with direct IO, as shown in Figure 6. The star architecture attracted us because it reduced demand on the F pins of the central switch, which seemed to be the limiting resource.

In the star architecture the central switch is mostly used in chip to chip communication and the IO are distributed among the logic device. y pins on each logic device touch only the switch and x pins on each logic chip touch both the switch and an external pad (Figure 6). This allows signals to travel from the device pin to the module pad without traveling though the switch at all, resulting in faster IO without losing the option of routing the IO to multiple logic devices at the same time. Some inefficiency is introduced, however; if all of the IO pins are used, it is unlikely that all of the IO signals will be connected to the particular logic device that they need to communicate with. In the event that a pin does not connect to the logic device it is wired to, we detour the signal through the FPIC to its destination. The net effect of the detour is to waste one IO pin on one of the logic devices, and one pin on the switch.

The architecture is constrained as follows:

$$G \leq Ne \quad (9)$$

$$G \leq (Nx/k)^{1/r} \quad (10)$$

$$F \leq N(x+y) \quad (11)$$

$$e \leq \alpha\ g \quad (12)$$

$$e \leq ((\beta\ x + y/k)^{1/r} \quad (13)$$

$$x+y \leq p_{max} \quad (14)$$

The relationships are essentially the same, with the introduction of the software-dependent parameter β to characterize the efficiency of the pin assignment algorithm. β is simply the fraction of pins that use the direct IO instead of detouring through the FPIC. By converting the inequalities to equalities, as in the previous section, six equations with eight unknowns result. Boiling away the dependent terms gives:

$$G = N\left(\frac{F}{k((1-\beta)N^r + N)}\right)^{1/r} \quad (15)$$

Comparing this to equation 8 shows that in the case where $\beta = 0$ the capacities for a given F and N will be identical, although the star architecture will have larger FPGAs because of the many wasted pins on the logic devices. As β increases, however, the capacity increases as well, to a limit of $G_{max} = N(F/kN)^{1/r}$. The actual value of β encountered will depend on whether the pins were assigned before or after placement, and whether any effort was taken to balance them across the logic devices. If the pins are assigned after the placement has been done, it can be shown that $\beta \geq x/(x+y)$. If, on the other hand, the module pin assignments are fixed before placement can begin, we can imagine that β might be close to 0, depending on how much weight the placement routine gives to the IO assignments. The star-tree hybrid architecture in figure 6 suggests a way of reducing wasted pins without depending on the switch for all of the off-module communication. Allowing direct communication between logic devices further alleviates the demand for FPIC pins.

The preceding discussion shows how various architectures can be roughly compared using some simple assumptions. In the next section we discuss some of the practical limitations we encountered in our first generation design and how they affected our architectural choices.

3 FPMCM-I

We have designed and are in the process of fabricating a first generation FPMCM. The purpose of the first generation device is to fully exercise the MCM fabrication and assembly technology, familiarize ourselves with the technical problems of FPMCM design, uncover any pitfalls, and try out an initial architecture. As a consequence of our goals the architecture is far from optimal. However, we do believe that this architecture demonstrates some innovative and useful features that will become a part of future FPMCM designs.

3.1 Objectives

When we began the design, our objective was to produce a device that exceeded the logic capacity of any single chip FPGA. In order to accomplish this goal we needed to exceed the 400 CLB capacity of the Xilinx 4010, the most current Xilinx 4000 part at the time. In addition, we were designing the device to be a stand-alone component, so we knew that it would also need a large number of pins.

3.2 Constraints

There were a number of constraints that impacted our architectural decisions that would not be present if we were not developing a prototype:

- The entire substrate could not be larger than 1.25" on a side.
- We could only use devices that were already solder bumped or could be obtained in whole wafers for later bumping.
- Our package needed to be zero insertion force (ZIF) socket compatible and have a low NRE cost.
- All the nets in the substrate had to be part had to be observable and controllable for fault-diagnosis.

Fault diagnosis and budgeting limits had a strong impact on the final design.

3.3 Design Process

This section details the process by which we arrived at our final design.

3.3.1 Device Selection

When we were selecting devices for the FPMCM-I we were constrained by what parts were available for MCM assembly. We needed uncut FPGA wafers to solder bump for flip-chip assembly. At the time, Xilinx was just beginning to sell bare die and whole tested wafers were not available. As a result, we were limited to the X3000 series devices from AT&T Microelectronics. We needed to use some dedicated interconnect on the module because the X3000 FPGAs could not provide the interconnect resources we needed. We decided to use the Aptix FPIC-D because it was designed for flip-chip.

Before selecting a particular FPGA we used cost data (Table 1) and applied previously discussed capacity models to the devices in the X3000 series. The results are presented in tables 2 and 3. In each case, for a given switch size, maximization of the module capacity demands that we use the largest FPGA available. We observe that the tree architecture cannot accommodate our target capacity of 400 usable CLBs because the FPIC doesn't have enough pins. If we use a star architecture, with a β of 0.5, we can achieve a capacity of 420 CLBs because the star architecture places less demand on the FPIC pins. Note that the architecture estimates in tables 2 and 3 assume that the IO requirements are given by Rent's rule. We can exceed the 400 CLB target by adding more FPGAs if we are willing to trade off the module IO.

Although the larger devices do have a larger effective capacity, the cost required to achieve it is significantly larger. We see immediately that a CLB in an X3042 costs 50% less than a CLB in a X3090, presumably because of the lower yield of the larger die. It seems the cost effective solution, given our design targets, is the X3064. Yet, we use the X3042 for its high internal routability. We based this decision on routability experiments, which indicate that the X3064 and X3090 occasionally have trouble routing designs. It is possible that pin limits of the devices might limit on-chip logic before the routing becomes a limiting factor. However, we thought it better not to take unnecessary chances.

If smaller devices exhibit better routability, why not choose a X3020? There are several reasons. First the MCM yield is, to a first order, exponentially related to the number of components in the assembly. This means the likelihood of the MCM failing goes up as more parts are put in it. Secondly, each die has a small fixed cost for configuration logic and for inter-chip spacing which takes up otherwise useful IO and real estate. Thirdly, the significant performance penalties going from chip to chip motivates more logic to be placed in a single chip. Finally, multiple chip systems with fewer components do have an advantage in partitioning if the FPMCM is used to hold a complete design, because Rent's rule overstates the pins needed when the clusters are fewer than about ten. Considering all of these factors, we think that the X3042 is a good compromise position.

3.3.2 Interconnect Architecture

After looking at the star architecture we wanted to experiment with nearest neighbor interconnect. This arose after looking at how a two point net travels from one logic device to another. The connection uses *two* pins on the FPIC, while a nearest neighbor wire would use none. In addition, the signal delay is longer because the path travels though the routing of the FPIC to reach an IC which is physically only a millimeter away! Routing connections to a neighbor through the central switch is a big disadvantage for applications such as systolic arrays that don't really need the flexibility of the FPIC but do need a few fast paths to communicate.

We altered the star architecture by creating a ring of direct interconnections d bits wide between nearest neighbors. Since each 3042 has 96 pins and approximately ten neighbors with whom to talk, we calculated that, on average, each device would have about eight signals going to each FPGA. We believe that the placement can be done in such a way that a small direct bus does not interfere with the routability of the FPMCM.

For testability, we connected each of the direct interconnect lines to the FPIC at a cost of one FPIC pin for each direct net. Although we initially chose the number of nearest neighbor connections to be 8, we found that we could fit two additional X3042s on the module if we raised the width of the nearest neighbor bus to 12. We also added four global nets for clock and global control signals and connected left-over pins on the FPIC to the FPMCM pads to enable probing. The overall interconnect architecture for the FPMCM-I is a hybrid between the star and tree architectures and includes direct interconnect in addition to switched interconnect on the substrate.

3.3.3 Module IO

Since the MCM is large (30mm on a side), we could have accommodated up to 1000 wire bonds fairly easily. Applying Rent's Rule to the FPMCM as a whole implies an IO demand of around 340 IO. Although ball-grid array (BGA) technology is now progressing to the point where such a large pin count is not unreasonable, for this generation we did not want to invest in a surface mount package—our applications do not require the high IO. What limits the MCM IO is the size of the pin grid array which is feasible to fabricate and socket to a board. For us, a 25x25 array was the limit for PGA outlines. Our FPMCM-I design includes 476 bondpads, 171 power and ground pins, and 305 signals. This gives us a comfortable 10 mil bond pitch. Because of prototyping limitations, however, only 204 of the user IO are routed to the package pins.

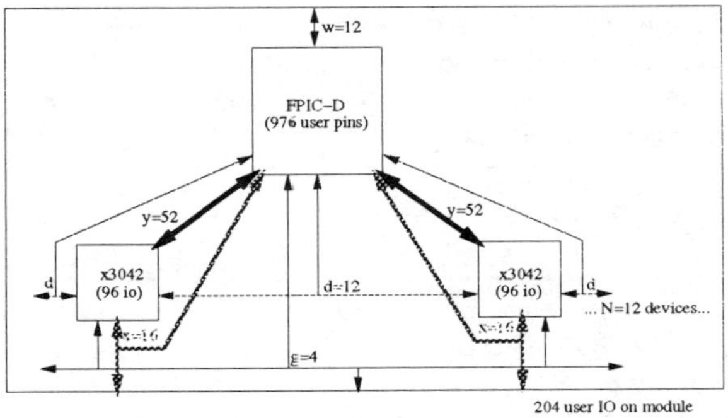

Figure 9: FPMCM-I Architecture: w is the number of direct IO from the PIC, y is the number of connections between each X3042 and the PIC, x is the number of direct IO for each FPGA. g is some number of global lines. d is the number of direct neighbor interconnections. Configuration and control pins are not shown. All nets touch the PIC for testability.

3.3.4 Physical Design

The layout of the system is shown in figure 10. The interconnect underneath the central FPIC is about twice as dense as the minimum density fanout pattern in order to distribute the IO of each FPGA evenly over the FPIC device. Distributing FPGA IO over the FPIC helps with the FPIC routability. We note that the high interconnect density of the FPIC *requires* the high interconnect density provided by MCM-D technology.

3.4 Final Design

The final FPMCM-I consists of 12 X3042's encircling an Aptix FPIC-D [Apt93]. Four surface mount chip capacitors provide power decoupling on the substrate. See Figure 10. Each FPGA has 12 pins connecting to each nearest neighbor in the ring and 22 pins connecting to external bondpads. Four global signals (clocks) are shared by all FPGAs. For testability purposes every signal net on the MCM substrate connects to a PIC pin. There are a small number of direct connections from the pins of the MCM to the PIC for diagnostic purposes; this is in addition to the connections needed for the configuration and control lines. The FPMCM-I has 204 user IO, in addition to power, ground and control signals. The resulting architecture is shown in figure 9.

4 Challenges of FPMCM

Because the first generation device is mainly a prototype FPMCM, it will be used primarily as a learning device. From our preliminary work we have identified several challenges that future FPMCMs must address.

4.1 System Optimization

Careful co-design of the MCM substrate and ICs can provide increased flexibility, performance, and reliability.

Redesign of the FPGA die for an MCM environment involves moving from perimeter to array-IO structures and resizing the drivers to deal with the smaller thin film interconnects on the MCM.

4.1.1 Area-IO

Perhaps the biggest opportunity for FPMCM is that flip-chip allows the use of area-IO. As previously mentioned, perimeter IO constrain FPGA integration. With area-IO, the number of IO can increase linearly with the die area, leaving the architect free to balance the supply of IO and CLBs. In addition, placing IO in the center of the die instead of at the periphery may reduce the overall wire-length, resulting in increased routability and decreased on-chip delays. Another motive for using area-IO on MCMs is that the post-process step needed to reroute the perimeter pads for flip chip assembly is no longer needed. Since this additional layer of interconnect adds manufacturing and design steps, decreases reliability, and adds additional electrical parasitics to the system, removing the rerouting layer will result in a decrease in the cost of the FPMCM.

4.1.2 Driver Optimization

Driver optimization is another area that can increase the performance of field programmable systems. Since MCMs form an enclosed electrical environment, many of the FPGA IO will not contact external MCM pins. Because of this, they are far less susceptible to electro-static discharge (ESD) or other forms of damage so much of the costly input protection circuitry can be reduced or eliminated. In addition, since traces on an MCM have far less capacitance than longer PCB traces, the drivers and receivers do not need to be as large [GFK+93]. In large systems, this power savings is critical because it means less noise on the power rails during IO switching and less heat to dissipate.

4.2 Technological Problems

The effort to produce a first generation FPMCM has uncovered the following technological and infrastructure challenges that must be addressed before the full potential of FPMCM can be realized.

MCM Infrastructure Availability of speed-tested bare die is critical for FPMCM success. Until state-of-the-art bare die and wafers are widely available from vendors, MCM architectures will be artificially constrained. A second concern is that the operating frequency of the FPMCM is limited by the slowest die in the assembly, so speed testing of the die needs to be done before assembly. Advances are being made in this area, but as of this writing, no adequate solution is widely available.

Thermal Management Although MCM designs typically have lower power consumption than a counterpart with traditional packaging, the power density and flux can be quite high, requiring robust materials with low thermal resistances, careful design, or expensive heat removal schemes in order to guarantee reasonable system reliability. This cost can be alleviated by employing ICs with lower-power drivers or by using low-voltage low-power ICs.

Ground Bounce One problem all large systems must contend with is the danger of simultaneous switching noise of the FPGA outputs. To counteract this affect in FPMCM-I, we placed four ceramic chip capacitors on the MCM substrate and provided one pair of power/ground bonds for every 3.25 user IO. This reduces the inductance of the power and ground planes. However, even steps like this cannot not fully eliminate the hazards of simultaneous switching, since users are free to build pathological applications that strain the limits of any power supply network.

Performance Limits In the past, MCM technology was motivated by the desire to reduce transmission line length and the capacitive loading of interconnects, resulting in a decrease in propagation delays and a net increase in clock frequency [RKT93]. Smaller inductances and lower capacitive loading on signal lines also allow drivers to switch faster without increasing noise or power. Although performance increases remains a definite advantage in FPMCM, since much of the delay in a field programmable system is taken up by programmable interconnects within a single IC, it is not certain that MCMs will provide more than a marginal benefit in this area with current FPGA families. Redesign of the FPGA IO buffers for the smaller capacitive loads of thin film MCM is needed to realize substantial improvements over current FPS.

Second-Level Packaging Although most MCM applications are able to enclose enough logic that their pin counts are reasonable, it is not clear that FPMCMs in a field programmable system will be able to escape the requirements of Rent's rule. Second-level packages which have more than a few hundred pins are technically feasible but add to the system cost.

5 Conclusions

We have presented the case for application of MCM technology in field programmable systems. MCM offers the advantages of small size, low power, architectural improvements, and lower overall system cost. We have used Rent's Rule to characterize some simple architectures in terms of capacity and used economic data to compare the cost of various alternatives. This analysis lead to the design of our first generation FPMCM, FPMCM-I. Our architecture is novel in that it employs smaller devices to save on silicon cost and uses a combination of direct and switched interconnections between FPGAs. This exercise has identified several challenges for future FPMCM architectures, including parametric yield, interconnect density, thermal dissipation and second level packaging. Future generations will deliver higher gate counts and increased performance by employing area-IO and the interconnect resources of the substrate to create a "giant" FPGA.

Acknowledgments

The authors wish to thank AT&T Bell Laboratories, Aptix Corporation, Quickturn, ARPA, and Xilinx for providing material and technical support of this project.

References

[Apt93] Aptix. Aptix field programmable interconnect data book, 1993.

[Arn93] Jeffrey M. Arnold. The splash 2 software environment. In *IEEE Workshop on FPGAs for Custom Computing Machines*, 1993.

[Bak89] H.B. Bakoglu. *Circuits, Interconnections and Packaging for VLSI.* Addison-Wesley Publishing Company, 1989.

[BRV92] P. Bertin, D. Roncin, and J. Vuillemin. Programmable active memories - performance measurements. In *ACM/SIGDA Workshop on Field Programmable Gate Arrays*, 1992.

[BTA93] J. Babb, R. Tessier, and A. Agarwal. Virtual wires: overcoming pin limitations in fpga-based logic emulators. In *Proceedings IEEE Workshop on FPGAs for Custom Computing Machines*, pages 142–51, 1993.

[Cas93] Steve Casselman. White paper on virtual computing. In *IEEE Workshop on FPGAs for Custom Computing Machines*, 1993.

[CS93] Pak K. Chan and Martine Schlag. Architectural tradeoffs in field-programmable-device-based computing systems. In *IEEE Workshop on FPGAs for Custom Computing Machines*, pages 152–61, 1993.

[CSM92] Pak Chan, Martine Schlag, and Marcelo Martin. Borg: A reconfigurable prototyping board using field programmable gate arrays. In *ACM/SIGDA Workshop on Field Programmable Gate Arrays*, 1992.

[dB93] D.E. Van den Bout. The anyboard: Programming and enhancements. In *IEEE Workshop on FPGAs for Custom Computing Machines*, 1993.

[DGHK92] I. Dobbelare, A. El Gamal, D. How, and B. Kleveland. Field programmable mcm systems- design of an interconnection frame. In *Proceedings of the IEEE 1992 Custom Integrated Circuits Conference*, pages 15.1/1–6, 1992.

[DHT+94] R.L Day, C.D. Hruska, K.L. Tai, R.C. Frye, M.Y. Lau, and P.A. Sullivan. A silicon-on-silicon technology with integrated bipolar components in the substrate. In *IEEE Multichip Module Conference*, pages 64–67, 1994.

[Fry93] Robert C. Frye. Balancing performance and cost in cmos-based thin film multichip modules. In *IEEE Multichip Module Conference*, pages 6–11, 1993.

[FTLL92] R.C. Frye, K.L Tai, M.Y. Lau, and A.W.C. Lin. Low-cost silicon-on-silicon mcms with integrated passive components. In *IEPS. Proceedings of the Technical Conference. 1992 International Electronics Packaging Conference.*, volume 1, page 343, 1992.

[GFK+93] T. Gabara, W. Fischer, S. Knauer, R. Frye, K. Tai, and M. Lau. A i/o cmos buffer set for silicon multi-chip modules. In *IEEE Multichip Module Conference*, pages 147–152, 1993.

[LR71] Bernard Landman and Roy Russo. On the pin versus block relatitionship for partitions of logic graphs. *IEEE Transactions on Computers*, C-20(12):1469–1479, December 1971.

[RKT93] Frye R.C., Tai K.L., and Lau M.Y. Gabara T.J. Trends in silicon-on-silicon multichip modules. *IEEE Design and Test of Computers*, 10(4):8–17, December 1993.

[VBB93] J. Varghese, M. Butts, and J. Batcheller. An efficient logic emulation system. *IEEE Transactions on Very Large Scale Integration Systems*, 1(2):171–174, June 1993.

[Xil93] Xilinx. Prices for unpackaged die in volume, September 1993.

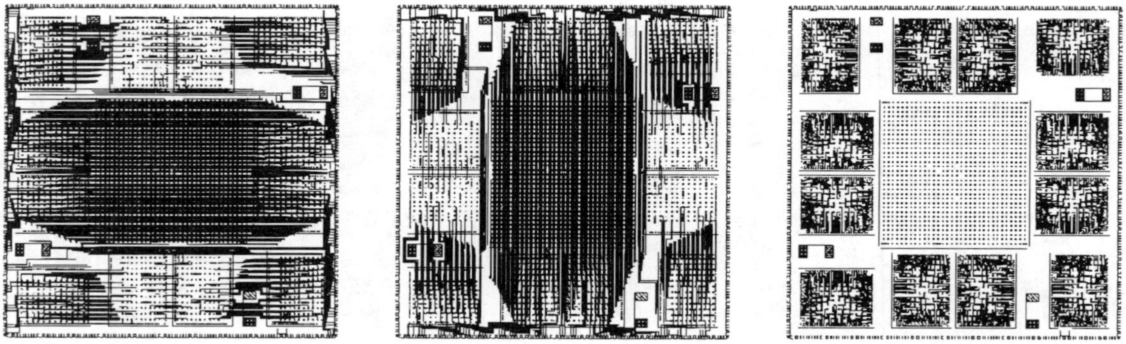

Figure 10: Physical Design First Generation FPMCM. Outer dimensions of the module are 30.6 mm square. The device contains 12 X3042's and a single Aptix FPIC. Four ceramic chip capacitors are provided to stabilize the module power and ground planes. The figure shows the three metal routing layers. The first two (X and Y) layers shown are on the silicon substrate, while the third consists of a IO redistribution pattern for each X3042 die that is necessary because the bond pad pitch on the devices series is too small for inexpensive flip chip assembly.

Device	CLBs (g)	IO (p_{max})	Usable CLBs (e)	Cost [Xil93]	Cost/ Usable CLB
3020	64	64	30	\$28.15	\$0.94
3030	100	80	40	\$38.30	\$0.96
3042	144	96	51	\$51.75	\$1.01
3064	224	120	68	\$88.80	\$1.30
3090	320	144	87	\$135.85	\$1.54

Table 1: Cost comparison of usable CLBs in the 3000 series

Device	N	p	w	G	Cost/CLB
3020	10	63	350	284	\$0.99
3030	8	77	368	304	\$1.01
3042	7	87	377	313	\$1.16
3064	5	118	340	335	\$1.32
3090	4	144	358	349	\$1.54

Table 2: Part Comparison for Tree Architectures, F=1000. Cost/CLB is the cost of the FPGA per usable logic element. Capacity goals favor a small number of large devices, though costs rise for larger devices.

Device	N	y	x	e	G	Cost/CLB
3020	15	38	26	22	332	\$1.27
3030	12	46	34	29	352	\$1.30
3042	10	54	42	37	369	\$1.40
3064	8	65	55	49	391	\$1.82
3090	7	75	66	60	420	\$2.25

Table 3: Part Comparison for Star Architecture, $\beta = 0.5$. Cost/CLB is the cost of the FPGA per usable logic element. For a given capacity, the star architecture is slightly more cost effective than the tree architecture - though the small β shows a clear source of inefficiency in the design.

Pin Assignment for Multi-FPGA Systems[1] (Extended Abstract)

Scott Hauck, Gaetano Borriello
Department of Computer Science and Engineering
University of Washington
Seattle, WA 98195

Abstract

There is currently great interest in using systems of FPGAs for logic emulators, custom computing devices, and software accelerators. An important step in making these technologies more generally useful is to develop completely automatic mapping tools from high-level specification to FPGA programming files. In this paper we examine one step in this automatic mapping process, the selection of FPGA pins to use for routing inter-FPGA signals. We present an algorithm that greatly increases mapping speed while also improving mapping quality.

Introduction

There is great interest in using multiple-FPGA systems for such tasks as logic emulation, software acceleration, and custom-computing devices. Many such systems are discussed elsewhere in these proceedings. An important aspect shared by all of these systems is that they harness multiple FPGAs, connected in a fixed routing structure, to perform their tasks. While the FPGAs themselves can be routed and rerouted, the wires moving signals between FPGA pins are fixed by the routing structure on the implementation board.

While some very impressive results have been achieved by hand-mapping of algorithms and circuits to FPGA systems, developing a completely automatic system for mapping to these structures is important to achieving more widespread utility. In general, an automatic mapping approach will go through five phases, in the following order: Synthesis, Partitioning/Global Placement, Global Routing, FPGA Place, FPGA Route. During the Synthesis step, the circuit to be implemented is converted from its source format into a netlist appropriate for implementation in FPGAs, possibly after several optimization steps. Partitioning and Global Placement breaks this mapping into subcircuits that will fit into the individual FPGAs, and determines which FPGAs a given subcircuit will occupy. Signals that connect logic in different FPGAs are then routed during the Global Routing step, which determines both which intermediate FPGAs a signal will move through (if any), as well as what FPGA I/O pins it will use. With the logic assigned and the inter-FPGA signals routed, standard FPGA Place and Route software can then produce programming files for the individual FPGAs.

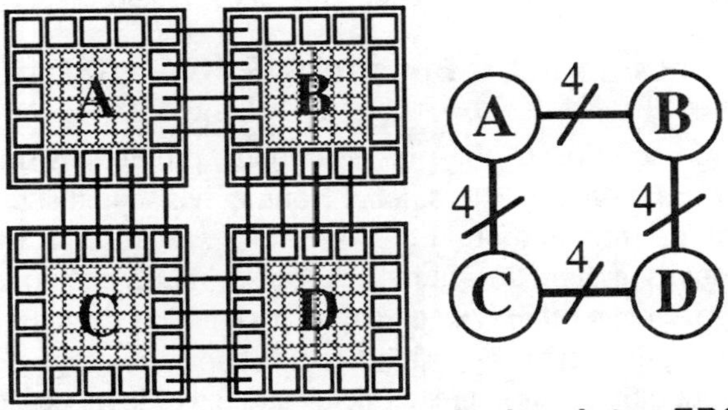

Figure 1. Two views of the inter-FPGA routing problem: As a complex graph including internal resources (left), and an abstract graph with FPGAs as nodes (right).

The Global Routing phase of mapping to multi-FPGA systems bears a lot of similarity to routing for individual FPGAs, and hopefully similar algorithms can be applied to both problems. Just as in single FPGAs, Global Routing needs to route signals on a fixed topology, with strictly limited resources, while trying both to handle high-density mappings and minimize clock periods. The obvious method for applying single-FPGA routing algorithms to multi-FPGA systems is to view the FPGAs as complex entities, explicitly modelling both internal routing resources and pins connected by individual external wires (figure 1 left). A standard routing algorithm would then be used to determine both which intermediate FPGA to use for long distance routing (i.e., a signal from FPGA A to D would be assigned to use either FPGA B or C), as well as which individual FPGA pins to route through. Unfortunately, this apprcach will not work. The problem is that although the logic has been already assigned to FPGAs during partitioning, the placement of logic into

0-8186-5490-2/94 $03.00 © 1994 IEEE

individual logic blocks will not be done until the next step, FPGA placement. Thus, since there is no specific source or sink for the individual routes, standard routing algorithms cannot be applied.

The approach we take here is to abstract entire FPGAs into single nodes in the routing graph, with the arcs between the nodes representing bundles of wires. This solves the unassigned source and sink problem mentioned above, since while the logic hasn't been placed into individual logic blocks, partitioning has assigned the logic to the FPGAs. It also simplifies the routing problem, since the graph is much simpler, and similar resources are grouped together (i.e. all wires connecting the same FPGAs are grouped together into a single edge in the graph). Unfortunately, the routing algorithm can no longer determine the individual FPGA pins a signal should use, since those details have been abstracted away. It is this problem, the assignment of interchip routing signals to FPGA I/O pins, that the rest of this paper addresses.

Pin assignment for multi-FPGA systems

One solution to the pin assignment problem is quite simple: ignore it. After Global Routing has routed signals through intermediate FPGAs, those signals are then randomly assigned to individual pins. While this simple approach can quickly generate an assignment, it gives up some optimization opportunities. A poor pin assignment can not only result in greater delay and lower logic density, but can also slow down the place and route software, which must deal with a more complex mapping problem.

A second solution is to use a topology that simplifies the problem. Specifically, topologies such as bipartite graphs only connect logic-bearing FPGAs with routing-only FPGAs. In this way, the logic-bearing FPGAs can be placed initially, and it is assumed that the routing-only FPGAs can handle any possible pin assignment. More details on such an approach can be found in [1]. However, it is important to note that these approaches only apply to topologies such as bipartite graphs and partial crossbars, topologies where logic-bearing FPGAs are not directly connected.

A third approach is to allow the FPGA placement tool to determine its own assignment. This requires that the placement tool allow the user to restrict the locations where an I/O pin can be assigned (e.g., Xilinx APR and PPR placement and routing tools [4]). With such a system, I/O signals are restricted to only those pin locations that are wired to the proper destinations. Once the placement tool determines the pin assignment for one FPGA, this assignment is propagated to the attached FPGAs. It is important to note that this does limit the number of placement runs that can be performed in parallel. Specifically, since the assignment from one FPGA is propagated to adjacent FPGAs only after that entire FPGA has been placed, no two adjacent FPGAs can be placed simultaneously. Since the placement and routing steps can be the most time-consuming steps in the mapping process, achieving the greatest parallelism in this task can be critical. Also, while the iterative placement approach can optimize locally, creating good results in a single FPGA, it ignores more global optimization opportunities. Finally, there are some topologies for which iterative placement may be unable to determine a correct pin assignment, because the placement of one FPGA may use up resources required in another FPGA.

Force-directed pin assignment for multi-FPGA systems

As we have discussed, pin assignment via sequential placement of individual FPGAs can be slow, cannot optimize globally, and may not work at all for some topologies. What is necessary is a more global approach which optimizes the entire mapping, while avoiding sequentializing the placement step. Intuitively, the best approach to pin assignment would be to simultaneously place all FPGAs, with the individual placement runs communicating with each other to balance the pin assignment demands of each FPGA. In this way a global optimum could be reached, and the mapping of all FPGAs would be completed as quickly as any single placement could be accomplished. Unfortunately, tools to do this do not exist, and the communication necessary to perform this task could become prohibitive. Our approach is similar to simultaneous placement, but we will perform the assignment on a single machine within a single process. Obviously, with the placement of a single FPGA consuming considerable CPU time, complete placement of all FPGAs simultaneously on a single processor is impractical, and thus simplification of the problem will be key to a workable solution.

Our approach is to use force-directed placement of the individual FPGAs [3]. In force-directed placement, the signals that connect logic in a mapping are replaced by springs between the signal's source and each sink, and the placement process consists of seeking a minimum net force placement of the logic. By finding this minimum net force configuration, we expect to minimize wirelength in the resulting mapping. To find this configuration, the software randomly chooses a logic block and moves it to its minimum net force location. This hill-climbing process continues until a local optimum is found, at which point the software accepts the current configuration.

Force-directed placement may seem a poor choice for pin assignment, and is generally felt to be inferior to simulated annealing for FPGA placement. Two reasons for this are the difficulty force-directed placement has with optimizing for goals other than wirelength, and the inaccuracy of the spring approximation to routing costs. However, force-directed placement can handle all of the optimization tasks involved in pin assignment, and the spring metric is the key to efficient handling of multi-FPGA systems.

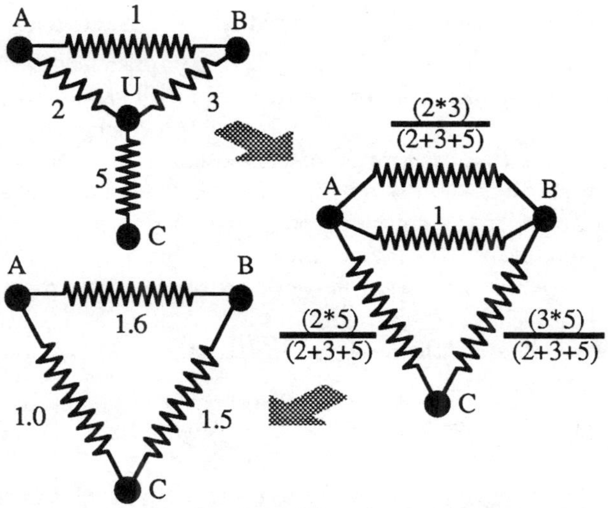

Figure 2. Example of spring simplification rules. Source circuit at top has node U replaced at middle, and any springs created in parallel to others are merged at bottom.

As implied earlier, we will not simply place individual FPGAs, but will in fact use force-directed placement simultaneously on all FPGAs in the system. To make this tractable, we can simplify the mapping process. Specifically, since we are only performing pin assignment, we do not care where the individual logic blocks are placed. Thus, we can examine the system of springs built for the circuit mapping, and use the laws of physics to remove nodes corresponding to FPGA logic blocks, leaving only I/O pins. As shown in the example of figure 5, the springs connected between an internal logic node and its neighbors can be replaced with a set of springs connected between the node's neighbors while maintaining the exact same forces on the other nodes. By repeatedly applying these simplification rules to the logic nodes in the system, we end up with a mapping consisting only of I/O pins, with spring connections that act identically to the complete mapping they replace. In this way, we simplify the problem enough to allow the pin assignment of a large system of FPGAs to be performed efficiently.

We have performed comparisons of our force-directed approach with iterative placement approaches, as well as random pin assignments, on several current multi-FPGA systems. The results have shown that the force directed approach is faster than all other alternatives, including random, by up to almost a factor of ten. It also produces higher-quality results than the other approaches, yielding up to an 8.5% decrease in total wirelength in the system. Our algorithm works on arbitrary topologies, including those for which iterative placement approaches generate incorrect results. Complete results, along with a more thorough discussion of this topic, can be found in [2].

[1] This paper is an extended abstract of University of Washington, Dept. of Computer Science & Engineering Technical Report #94-04-01, April 1994.

References

[1] P. K. Chan, M. D. F. Schlag, "Architectural Tradeoffs in Field-Programmable-Device-Based Computing Systems", *IEEE Workshop on FPGAs for Custom Computing Machines*, pp. 152-161, 1993.

[2] S. Hauck, G. Borriello, "Pin Assignment for Multi-FPGA Systems", University of Washington, Dept. of Computer Science & Engineering Technical Report #94-04-01, April 1994.

[3] K. Shahookar, P. Mazumder, "VLSI Cell Placement Techniques", *ACM Computing Surveys*, Vol. 23, No. 2, pp. 145-220, June 1991.

[4] Xilinx Development System Reference Guide and The Programmable Logic Data Book, Xilinx, Inc., San Jose, CA, 1993.

Emulation of the Sparcle Microprocessor with the MIT Virtual Wires Emulation System

Matthew Dahl[1], Jonathan Babb[1], Russell Tessier, Silvina Hanono, David Hoki, and Anant Agarwal

MIT Laboratory for Computer Science
Cambridge, MA 02139

Abstract

We describe a complete FPGA-based emulation software system using *Virtual Wires* technology and present the results of emulating an 18K-gate ASIC implementation of a modified Sparc microprocessor. Virtual Wires overcomes the pincount limitation that formerly restricted the efficiency of FPGA-based logic emulators. The MIT Virtual Wires softwire compiler accepts a netlist description of the system to be emulated and produces programming information for the FPGA hardware, an inexpensive ($3000) board designed for Virtual Wires in-circuit emulation. The compiler also provides an interface to standard logic simulator tools for hardware accelerated simulation. We discuss innovative features of the compiler system and knowledge gained during its construction. A comparison is made of different implementations of the on-chip Virtual Wires circuitry synthesized by the compiler. Several enhancements to the original Virtual Wires concept are presented that will further emulation speed and FPGA utilization.

Keywords: FPGA, logic emulation, prototyping, reconfigurable technologies, static routing, Virtual Wires.

1 Introduction

Introduced at last year's IEEE FPGA Workshop, *Virtual Wires* [4] overcome the pincount limitation that restricts the efficiency of current FPGA-based logic emulators. Existing systems dedicate each FPGA pin to a single emulated signal, rapidly consuming pins and limiting utilization of available FPGA gates to typically 10 to 20 percent. Virtual Wires intelligently multiplex pins to allow each pin to support multiple emulated signals. In addition to improving gate utilization to greater than 50 percent, Virtual Wires can speed emulation by decreasing the size of the FPGA array and the length of communication paths.

The MIT Virtual Wires softwire compiler has been constructed using a combination of off-the-shelf commercial CAD products and internally developed modules. A netlist description of the system to be emulated is first divided into multiple FPGA-sized partitions. The core of the softwire compiler, referred to as the *Virtual Wires Kernel*, produces a pipelined, statically-routed communication network to connect the partitions. Technology-mapping and FPGA place-and-route software reduce the networked partitions to FPGA programming data.

The compiler has been used to configure a Virtual Wires emulation circuit board [13] for use as an in-circuit hardware emulator and as a hardware accelerator of software logic simulation. The board uses low-cost, low-pinout FPGAs and a simple mesh interconnect topology. An interface to popular logic simulators has been developed using multiple communication interfaces between the Virtual Wires hardware and a host computer. We have compared several possible implementations of the embedded Virtual Wires circuitry for speed and use of FPGA resources.

An example application of the Virtual Wires system is described: emulation of Sparcle [2], an 18K-gate ASIC implementation of the Sparc microprocessor with added multiprocessing support. The system has been used both for hardware-accelerated simulation and full hardware emulation of the Sparcle chip in a test bed system. Clocking and input/output timing methodologies for hardware emulation are presented, and the use of the SRAMs in the Virtual Wires hardware for emulation of Sparcle's on-chip memory is outlined. Correct operation has been verified by loading a multiprocessor operating system kernel and execution of system diagnostics.

In Section 2 of this paper we focus on the kernel of the Virtual Wires software. In Section 3 we compare several specific circuit topologies for the embedded Virtual Wires logic. Section 4 summarizes the rest of the Virtual Wires software system and the insights gained

[1] Currently with Virtual Machine Works, Inc., Cambridge, MA 02139

0-8186-5490-2/94 $03.00 © 1994 IEEE

during its development. In Section 5 we describe the methodology used to emulate the Sparcle microprocessor and present emulation results. Section 6 presents conclusions and topics of ongoing research.

2 The Virtual Wires Kernel

The core of the Virtual Wires compiler is a set of software modules that read a partitioned netlist and produce an inter-partition communication network using Virtual Wires (Figure 1). The initial stages of this process have been discussed previously [3] [4]. Here we summarize these steps, then concentrate on the communication circuitry produced by the compiler.

2.1 Static Timing Analysis

In order to schedule the mapping of physical wires between partitions onto virtual wires, a timing analysis of the partitioned netlist is performed. The timing information allows inputs to individual partitions to be scheduled for propagation before the outputs dependent upon them, thus recreating the normal flow of signal values through the original network.

2.2 Global Placement

A global placement module arranges the partitions within the physical FPGA array to minimize the communication distances and corresponding latency. When necessary, partitions containing hardware interface logic are placed in fixed locations within the array to communicate with external interface hardware, SRAMs, and other localized resources.

2.3 Global Routing

A global routing module assigns inter-partition signals to Virtual Wires evaluation timeslots based on their dependency information and determines the routing of Virtual Wires signals through the FPGA network. Signals with the greatest number of dependencies, i.e. most critical, are routed first. Each signal is assigned a shortest-path route through the FPGA network over a single physical connection. In addition to inter-partition signals, Virtual Wires-specific global and control signals are also routed at this time.

2.4 Embedding of Virtual Wires Logic

The router's signal routing and timing results are used by an embedder module that generates a new top-level netlist for the partitioned network containing all necessary Virtual Wires communication logic. New network modules are produced, each of which encapsulates a previously generated partition and completes the description of an FPGA in the array. The embedder synthesizes shift registers, multiplexing and control logic for each FPGA pin, and any necessary Virtual Wires sequencing logic. Some logic implementation decisions are made at this point in order to use to best advantage limited FPGA resources such as tristate busses and combinatorial logic blocks.

Low-level assignment of specific FPGA physical pins is made at this time. To reduce the use of on-chip routing resources for Virtual Wires signals being routed across multiple FPGAs, a pin permutation algorithm [7] [13] is used. Groups of four adjacent FPGA pins are connected to each of the FPGA's north, south, east, and west neighbors. Thus a multi-chip path proceeding in any direction can be created by making local connections within each pin grouping. The embedder attempts to keep routed-through signals confined to a single pin group whenever possible by assigning multi-chip path pins before other pins.

The embedder also allows any external network connection to be assigned to any FPGA pin on the periphery of the network. In the current Virtual Wires hardware, some of these pins connect to external interface hardware for communication with a logic simulator or other control program. Other pins provide global clocks and sequencing signals. Additional features support in-circuit emulation; these are discussed in Section 5.2.

3 Embedded Virtual Wires Communication Logic

3.1 Basic Concepts

The design goals of the logic added to implement Virtual Wires are compactness and speed. Note that no custom FPGA hardware is required for Virtual Wires; the Virtual Wires logic is simply added to the partitioned design netlist and compiled into the FPGAs along with it. Several different Virtual Wires logic designs have been implemented; these are presented and compared.

The current Virtual Wires logic evaluates in a phase-oriented fashion (Figure 2). The evaluation period of the system being emulated, termed the *emulation clock* period, is broken into several phases by the global routing program. During each phase, a single static routing of connections is established across the FPGA array, and multiple emulated signals are multiplexed

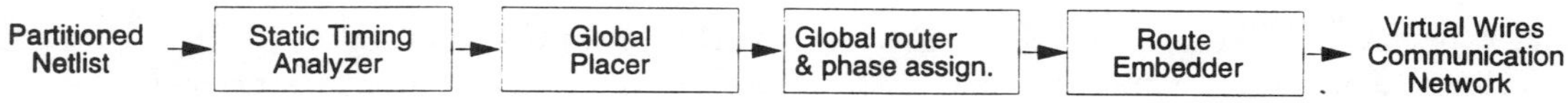

Figure 1: Virtual Wires Software Compiler Kernel

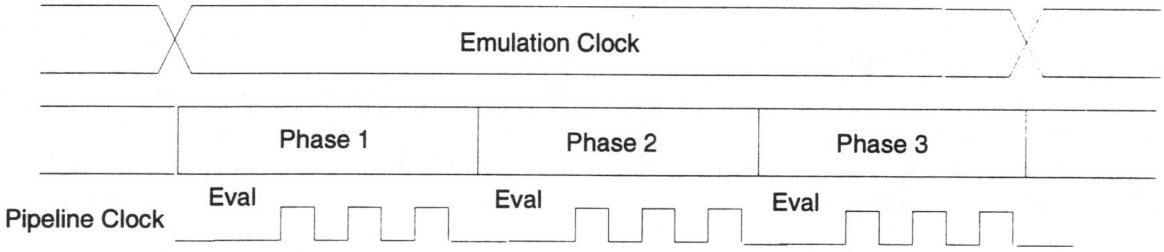

Figure 2: Virtual Wires Clocking Scheme

onto each of these connections. The multiplexing is driven by a *pipeline clock* which typically runs close to the maximum clocking frequency of the FPGA. As the phase clock advances, new routings are set up, and new groups of emulated signals are propagated. After all emulated signals have been communicated, the emulation clock is ticked, typically updating the state of registers in the emulated circuit, and the Virtual Wires evaluation process repeats. A small sequencer module is embedded in each FPGA to generate the Virtual Wires phases and other control signals.

3.2 Full Shift Register Architecture

The original Virtual Wires logic implementation consists of input and output shift registers, termed *shift loops* (Figure 3), together with routing and control logic. Output shiftloops load emulated signal states at the beginning of each phase and shift these states out serially onto a routed physical connection at the pipeline clock rate. At the end of each connection, corresponding input shiftloops demultiplex and latch the emulated signals and drive them into the emulated logic. Note that the input shiftloops (at least) must store their state so that all emulated logic inputs are available for subsequent evaluation. This storage mode is made less expensive in the Xilinx architecture by use of the clock-enable input of each register bit, which is connected to the phase control signal in which the input shift group is loaded. Output shiftgroup logic, however, can be reused for multiple groups of emulation signals in different phases.

For connections requiring multiple hops, a one-bit shift register is placed in each intermediate FPGA, forming a shift register pipeline between source and destination. In such cases, the number of emulated signals being transmitted in a phase must be reduced to allow for the added connection latency.

To implement the per-phase routing, each inter-FPGA I/O pad is preceded by a multiplexer that enables each connection output routed through that pad in its active phase. Pads are allowed to be bidirectional - phases in which a pad is an output are ORed together to form the pad driver enable signal. However, the embedder module tries to group inputs and outputs to reduce the number of bidirectional pads and associated enable logic. In the original implementation, the pad multiplexors were constructed of normal FPGA combinatorial logic, but in more recent versions the tristate-driver MUXes available in the Xilinx FPGA architecture have been used. These tristate drivers are typically unused by the technology mapping software, but their use does consume FPGA routing resources.

3.3 Gated Shift Register Architecture

Other architecture-specific FPGA features have been used to reduce the consumption of core FPGA resources by Virtual Wires logic. In the low-cost, low-pinout FPGA parts used in the current Virtual Wires emulation board, many of the I/O pads are not connected to pins, and their registers can be concatenated to form Virtual Wires shift registers (Figure 4). Due to pad configuration constraints, these shift registers cannot be parallel-loaded, so they are not usable for output shiftgroups. Input shiftgroups and intermediate hop shift registers can be placed here, however. Since input shiftgroups must hold the emulated signal state after receiving it, and these I/O registers do not have clock enables, a gated pipeline clock is generated and distributed. This clock is frozen during the portions of the Virtual Wires cycle in which the emulated logic is being evaluated. In addition, the length of these input shiftgroup shift registers is adjusted to divide evenly into the number of pipeline clocks between evaluation periods so that the state in these registers can recirculate yet be unchanged during each evaluation period. In

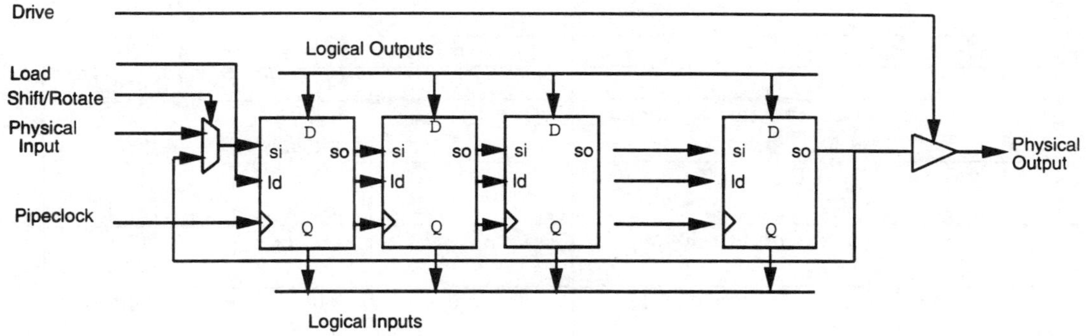

Figure 3: Full Shift Register Shift Loop Architecture

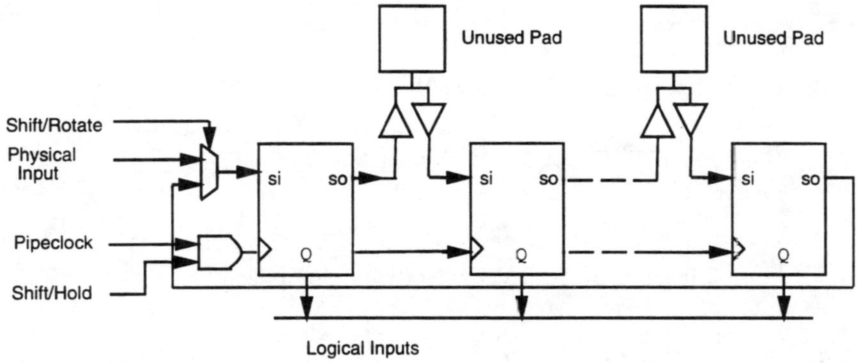

Figure 4: Gated Shift Registers Using Pad Registers

the Xilinx 4005, 84-pin-package FPGA currently used, 102 input and hop shift register bits can be recovered in this manner. However, the pipeline clocking speed is somewhat slower due to clock gating and the slower timing of the I/O pad registers.

Other implementation architectures for the Virtual Wires logic are also possible, but we do not discuss them here due to space limitations.

3.4 Comparisons

We compare these embedded logic architectures in terms of speed, logic overhead, and routing overhead (Table 1). The numbers presented are the result of compiling Palindrome-128, a 14K-gate systolic circuit, onto the 16-FPGA Virtual Wires emulation board using the Virtual Wires compiler. Raw speed is measured in terms of the pipeline clock speed, although the number of pipeline clock ticks required per emulation clock also determines the ultimate emulation speed. It must be noted that FPGA clock speeds are often strongly dependent on the quality of the on-chip routing performed by the APR software, which is in turn dependent on the packing density of logic on each FPGA. Logic overhead is measured in terms of packed Xilinx configurable logic blocks (CLBs) compared with a non-Virtual Wires (hard wire) compilation of the same partitions onto high-pincount FPGAs. Usage of individual logic lookup tables and CLB flipflops is also broken out to further distinguish the architectures. Routing overhead is difficult to measure directly; an rough estimate can be made from the routing resource usage statistics reported by the APR program. Xilinx programmable interconnect points (PIPs) are compared here.

We see that the full shift register implementation (Figure 3) is relatively fast but has significant overhead. The gated shift register architecture using the I/O pad flip flops (Figure 4) is somewhat slower due to the reduced speed of these flip flops. This version does use fewer of the core flip flops, but routing overhead is higher (probably because of the greater wiring distances covered between the pad flip flops and the core logic).

Characteristic	*Emulated Logic*	*Virtual Wires Architecture*	
		Figure 3	Figure 4
Logic Blocks (packed Xilinx CLBs)	54	79 (46%)	80 (48%)
Combinatorial Logic (function generators)	115	165 (43%)	167 (45%)
Sequential Logic (core flip flops)	74	141 (91%)	102 (38%)
Routing Resources (Xilinx PIPs)	1009	1729 (71%)	1948 (93%)
Average Resource Usage per FPGA (Virtual Wires Overhead)			
Virtual Wires Pipeline Clock Speed		33 MHz	24 MHz
Emulation Clock Speed		1.22 MHz	0.89 MHz

Table 1: Comparison of Embedded Virtual Wires Logic Architectures

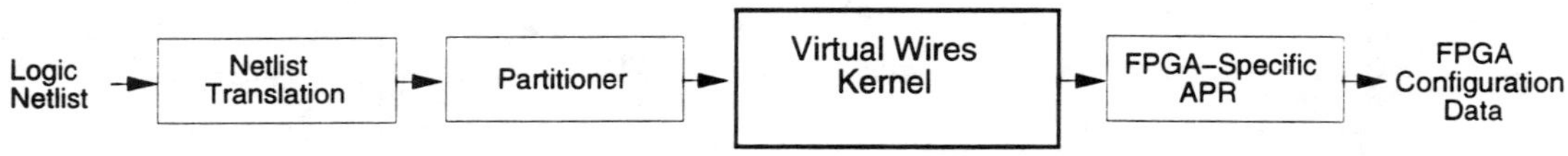

Figure 5: Virtual Wires Softwire Compiler Flow

4 Virtual Wires Softwire Compiler Construction

4.1 Introduction

The goal of the Virtual Wires softwire compiler is to convert the user's circuit description into a hardware programming file with little or no human intervention. Beginning with a netlist description of the user's system and hardware description files, the software performs the following procedures (Figure 5):

1. Technology mapping of system structures to FPGA primitives
2. Partitioning the netlist into per-FPGA sections (partitions)
3. Virtualization of inter-FPGA connections using the Virtual Wires kernel
4. Backend compilation of the virtualized netlist into FPGA programming data

Additional files and information are generated to support the logic simulator interface to the Virtual Wires hardware, to allow debugging of the Virtual Wires system, and to provide compilation statistics.

The current prototype Virtual Wires software system's operation is driven by a set of scripts for the Unix make and shell utilities. The make utility's dependency checking is used to enforce ordering of the steps of the build process and allow incremental changes to portions of the system without requiring a complete recompilation.

4.2 Emulated System Description

The Virtual Wires software system requires a netlist description of the system to be emulated. The netlist format used is the LSI Logic Network Description Language [9]. The netlist primitives currently used are the LSI Logic LCA100K gate array technology [11]. Other system description formats (e.g. Verilog [5] or other hardware description languages) can be converted to LSI format by logic synthesis or simple format translation. Other primitive libraries can be mapped to LSI100K or used directly if an appropriate description is available for the technology mapping process.

4.3 Initial Technology Mapping

The conversion of the emulated system description to the target FPGA technology is performed in two stages: replacement or encapsulation of complex or pathological structures, and straightforward mapping of low-level primitives. High-level structures such as RAM are replaced with groups of simpler primitives that can be mapped directly to FPGAs. Some network features may require special handling in order to operate in the Virtual Wires environment.

4.3.1 Memory Structure Replacement

Large memory arrays in the input netlist are mapped to SRAM chips attached to each FPGA in the Virtual Wires hardware. While small RAM/ROM structures (typically 16-256 bits) can be constructed from the lookup tables used in some FPGA architectures [14], large register files and caches would be extremely expensive to implement using FPGA logic. These large arrays must be identified and their organization rearranged to fit in one or more of the 64K by 4 bit SRAMs available in the hardware. Appropriate address and sequencing logic is needed to emulate wide, multiport, or content-addressable memories. Such logic is synthesized and, together with primitive representations of the SRAMs, is used to replace the memories in the original design. These new structures are then mapped to FPGA logic, placed in any of the FPGAs with attached SRAMs, and connected using Virtual Wires as part of the normal compilation process.

The current Virtual Wires software system supports the use of the hardware SRAMs in this fashion, but the actual mapping from the original netlist to the SRAMs must be manually generated. An automatic memory compiler is being developed that will deduce the structure of memories in the design to be emulated and generate the appropriate control logic and SRAM references without assistance.

4.3.2 Handling of Special Network Structures

Certain structures in the emulated system may require special attention to operate in the Virtual Wires environment. For example, asynchronous logic cannot be routed using Virtual Wires and must either be confined to single partitions or routed using hardwires. The Virtual Wires software system allows specific modules to be declared non-partitionable to confine them to a single FPGA. Alternatively, these structures can be placed in dedicated FPGAs that will not be used by the Virtual Wires software. The Virtual Wires simulator interface module, which operates outside of normal Virtual Wires timing, is handled in this manner.

4.3.3 Low-Level Technology Mapping

Once all high-level transformations of the emulated system have been performed, generic technology mapping of primitive gates to FPGA technology is typically done. It is desirable to do this mapping prior to partitioning the netlist, since accurate partition gate counts are needed to allow maximal use of each FPGA without risk of overfilling. Logic minimization can also be done during the technology mapping process to further increase the packing density of emulated gates. Both mapping and minimization can be performed simultaneously by tools such as the Synopsys FPGA Compiler [12].

In order to develop a working system as quickly as possible, we have chosen to defer technology mapping until after partitioning and the embedding of Virtual Wires communication logic. While this choice reduces FPGA packing density somewhat, it allows the Virtual Wires structures to be built using a generic technology and then mapped to specific FPGAs along with the emulated system logic.

4.4 Partitioning

After preliminary technology mapping, the emulated netlist is partitioned into per-FPGA sections. The InCA Concept Silicon partitioner [8] is currently used; it employs clustering and mincut methods to reduce connections between partitions while maintaining acceptable gate counts. The gate count limit used includes both the emulated logic in each partition and an estimate of the Virtual Wires logic that will be added later. In addition, a script-driven method is used to allocate the SRAM control logic to separate partitions so that no more than the one SRAM attached to each FPGA is required per partition. Non-partitionable structures are declared as network primitives for partitioning; they are then left unaltered by the partitioner.

4.5 Per-FPGA Backend Processing

The remaining stages of the Virtual Wires compilation process are largely FPGA technology-specific. In the present Virtual Wires software system, technology mapping and logic optimization is performed at this stage using the Synopsys FPGA Compiler. Even when pre-partitioning technology mapping is implemented, a second backend pass of logic minimization may still be desirable to take advantage of local optimizations possible in the embedded Virtual Wires logic. The Synopsys compiler allows constraints to be specified to direct the optimization process, and the Virtual Wires software provides multiple options to allow the user to trade off among compile time, emulation speed, and FPGA utilization.

The FPGA place-and-route program and other backend software is then invoked for each chip. This, together with the technology mapping/logic optimization process, is the most time-consuming portion of the Virtual Wires compilation process. The Sparcle emulation described in this paper requires 4 to 6 cpu-hours on a Sparc-10 workstation, although the degree of optimization requested has a large effect on compile time (as much as a factor of two in the case of Sparcle). The

Xilinx place-and-route program has options to select timing-driven routing versus high-density route-at-any-cost operation; the Virtual Wires compiler allows these to be selected as well.

4.6 Debugging Support

Simulation netlists are generated at various points in the build process to verify Virtual Wires correctness. Partition I/O logical values of virtualized and hard-wired netlist can be compared at the end of each emulation clock cycle to confirm the operation of the Virtual Wires communication between partitions. This capability has been instrumental in debugging the Virtual Wires embedder module and testing new embedded logic architectures.

Statistic	Palindrome	Sparcle
LSI Gate Count	14,241	17,252
Element Count	4,623	4,802
Element Complexity	3.1	3.6
Memory Bit Count	0	4,352
Net Count	4,626	5,094
Pins per Net	2.900	3.484
FPGAs	16	20
Avg. Gates / partition	890	868
Avg. IO / partition	45	126
Mesh Emulation Speed (MHz)	1.00	0.12

Table 2: Hardware Statistics for Simulation Acceleration

5 Virtual Wires Emulation of the Sparcle Microprocessor

We have used the Virtual Wires softwire compiler and hardware prototype to emulate several designs, including Sparcle [2], an 18K-gate ASIC implementation of the Sparc microprocessor with enhanced multiprocessor support. We have demonstrated both hardware-accelerated simulation and full hardware emulation of the Sparcle chip in a test bed system. Correct operation has been verified by executing multiprocessor system diagnostics.

5.1 Simulation Accelerator Support

We have implemented an interface between the Virtual Wires emulator hardware and popular logic simulators (Verilog, LSI Logic) to support hardware-accelerated simulation [6] [13]. A serial link is currently being used to exchange vector data between the emulator module and a host computer. Client/server software modules permit the simulator to be run on a separate computer if desired. The Virtual Wires compiler synthesizes an I/O logic module that maps the top-level connections of the emulated design to the interface hardware. The compiler also provides support files to couple the client side of the interface to the simulator. To increase simulation speed, the emulator module also provides an Sbus parallel interface to the host. Software support for simulation acceleration via the Sbus interface has been developed and is currently being tested.

The Sparcle hardware simulation accelerator is driven by a behavioral model test shell running in the LSI Logic MBSIM simulator [10] via the simulation interface. The test shell includes a memory system and program loader so that standard Sparcle diagnostics can be executed on the accelerator. The simulation interface speed is currently restricted by the serial link used between the hardware and the host computer, but the Sbus interface will remove this restriction. Since the Virtual Wires accelerator's maximum emulation clock rate is over 100 KHz, Sparcle test vectors can potentially be processed at speeds exceeding 100K vectors/second, subject to the speed limitations of the simulator or other host software.

Table 2 presents speed and resource statistics for the Sparcle simulation accelerator, as well as for the systolic circuit Palindrome-128 that was used in section 3.4 for architecture comparison.

5.2 Hardware Emulation Methodology

The Sparcle hardware emulator substitutes for the Sparcle CPU chip in a testbed board developed for the Alewife multiprocessor project [1]. The emulator system plugs directly into the Sparcle chip PGA socket using a commercially-built interface pod (Figure 6). The pod signals are connected to FPGA pins at the edges of the FPGA mesh interconnect of the Virtual Wires emulator board. The emulator synchronizes automatically to the Sparcle system clock and control signals. Therefore, no modifications to the target system are needed other than slowing the system clock. The emulated Sparcle has executed Alewife system test programs successfully at speed, including booting of the prototype Alewife operating system.

The Virtual Wires softwire compiler includes several features to support hardware emulation. The embedder module allows any external network connection to be assigned to any FPGA pin on the periphery of the network. In the current Virtual Wires hardware, some of these pins connect to external interface hardware for communication with a logic simulator or other control

Statistic	Sparcle
FPGAs	24
Avg. Gates / partition	718
Avg. IO / partition	119
Mesh Emulation Speed (MHz)	0.18

Table 3: Hardware Statistics for In-circuit Emulation

program. Other pins provide global clocks and sequencing signals. For hardware emulation, most of the edge pins are brought out to connectors for interfacing with an external emulation pod. The embedder generates input/output buffers with optional bidirectional control for these pins. Registering and retiming with internal control signals is also provided for timing-critical emulation pins. This retiming feature was used to correct the timing of Sparcle write data which, unlike most Sparcle outputs, is driven on the falling edge of the emulation clock.

The Sparcle register file is emulated by the on-board SRAM available on the Virtual Wires prototype board. A replacement cell for the 136 word by 32 bit, triple-ported register file was written in Verilog. This replacement contains a sequencer to emulate multi-port operation using the single-ported SRAMs, address decoding, and instantiations of several of the SRAMs themselves. A gate-level equivalent was synthesized, and this module replaced the original register file in the Sparcle netlist. Inputs from the Virtual Wires control logic trigger the memory sequencer's operations at the appropriate time in each Virtual Wires emulation cycle.

5.3 Emulation Results

Table 3 lists statistics for the Sparcle hardware emulator. We chose to use a relatively large number of FPGA partitions in order to reduce FPGA packing and obtain higher clock rates. We expect FPGA density to improve with the implementation of front-end technology mapping.

6 Future Research

While the current partitioning subsystem performs adequately, a replacement partitioner is envisioned with greater comprehension of system characteristics. For example, timing-driven partitioning would reduce the splitting up of long critical paths of logic evaluation, thus increasing the speed of the emulated system. Finally, certain structures may require more Virtual Wires logic overhead, which a more sophisticated partitioner could make allowance for.

Other improvements to the Virtual Wires compiler are under development to improve mapping efficiency and support larger, more sophisticated designs. Technology mapping before partitioning will give more accurate gate counts and allow larger partitions to be used. An automatic memory compiler will deduce the structure of memories in the design to be emulated and generate the appropriate control logic and SRAM references without assistance. Multiple-edged clocks will be a requirement in complex designs and will be supported in the next revision of the Virtual Wires kernel.

References

[1] A. Agarwal et al. The MIT Alewife machine: A large-scale distributed memory multiprocessor. In *Scalable Shared Memory Multiprocessors*. Kluwer Academic Press, 1991.

[2] A. Agarwal, J. Kubiatowicz, D. Kranz, B.-H. Lim, D. Yeung, G. D'Souza, and M. Parkin. Sparcle: An Evolutionary Processor Design for Multiprocessors. *IEEE Micro*, 13(3):48–61, June 1993.

[3] J. Babb. Virtual Wires: Overcoming Pin Limitations in FPGA-based Logic Emulators. Master's thesis, EECS Department, MIT, Nov. 1993.

[4] J. Babb, R. Tessier, and A. Agarwal. Virtual Wires: Overcoming Pin Limitations in FPGA-based Logic Emulators. In *Proceedings, IEEE Workshop on FPGA-based Custom Computing Machines*, pages 142–151, Napa, CA, April 1993. IEEE. Also as MIT/LCS TM-491, January 1993.

[5] D. Thomas and P. Moorby. *The Verilog Hardware Description Language*. Kluwer Academic Publishers, Boston, 1991.

[6] S. Hanono. LSI and Verilog Serial Interface to FPGA Board. Alewife Systems Memo 39, MIT Computer Architecture Group, Oct. 1993.

[7] S. Hauck, G. Boriello, and C. Ebeling. Mesh Routing Topologies For FPGA Arrays (advance copy). In *Advance Proceedings, IEEE Workshop on FPGA-based Custom Computing Machines*. IEEE, 1994.

[8] InCA Inc. *Concept Silicon Reference Manual*, Nov. 1992. Version 1.1

[9] LSI Logic Corporation, 1551 McCarthy Blvd., Milpitas, California, 95035. *Network Description Language Reference*, Sept. 1988.

[10] LSI Logic Corporation, 1551 McCarthy Blvd., Milpitas, California, 95035. *User's Guide for The Multi-Chip Logic Simulation Programs*, Oct. 1989.

[11] LSI Logic Corporation, 1551 McCarthy Blvd., Milpitas, California, 95035. *LCA100K Products Databook*, May 1990.

[12] Synopsys, Inc. *4000 Series (Xilinx) Interface Using FPGA Compiler*, feb 1993.

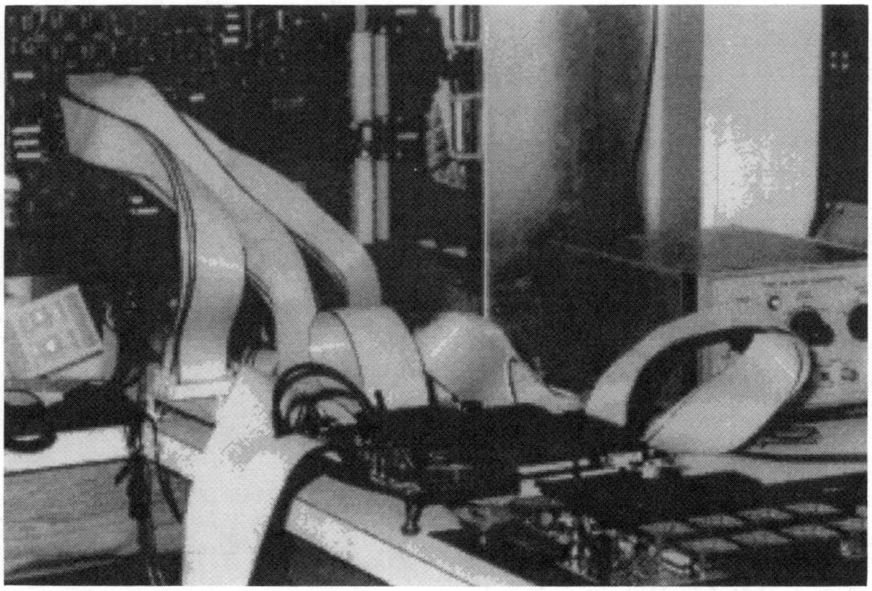

Figure 6: Sparcle Hardware Emulation Setup

[13] R. Tessier, J. Babb, M. Dahl, S. Hanono, and A. Agarwal. The Virtual Wires Emulation System: A Gate-Efficient ASIC Prototyping Environment. In *Submitted to 1994 ACM International Workshop on Field-Programmable Gate Arrays*, Berkeley, CA, February 1994. ACM.

[14] XILINX, Inc., 2100 Logic Drive, San Jose, California, 95214. *The XC4000 Data Book*, Aug. 1992.

The Nano Processor: a Low Resource Reconfigurable Processor

Michael J. Wirthlin and Brad L. Hutchings
Dept. of Electrical and Computer Eng.
Brigham Young University
Provo, UT 84602

Kent L. Gilson
National Technology Inc.
9500 South 500 West Suite #104
Sandy, UT 84070

Abstract

Reconfigurable logic systems approach the performance of Application-Specific Integrated Circuits (ASICs) while retaining much of the generality of conventional computing systems through reconfiguration. Unfortunately, the development of these systems, unlike conventional software systems, is hardware intensive, requiring significant hardware development time. One way to introduce a more flexible development approach is to implement a customizable stored-program *processor. For a given application, the designer can develop customized hardware to increase performance and then control the sequencing and operation of this hardware with software. Development time can be significantly reduced because conventional software development tools, e.g., assemblers and compilers, can be used to quickly develop new applications on the customized processor. This paper presents the Nano Processor (nP), a fully customizable reconfigurable processor, together with its integrated assembler, that has been successfully implemented on the Xilinx 3000 series Field Programmable Gate Array (FPGA).*

1 Introduction

In order to obtain substantial speed up for computationally intensive algorithms, developers rely on ASICs. These systems use fully hardwired control and specialized functional units to increase performance. ASICs are often employed in Digital Signal Processing (DSP), image processing, and other highly computational applications. Although hardwired ASICs provide excellent performance, they have two important disadvantages. First, the inability to modify an ASIC after development makes them inflexible. Second, the high development costs makes them expensive for low volume implementations. These disadvantages prevent many applications from exploiting ASIC capabilities.

Technology improvements in FPGAs opens new avenues for implementing application specific circuits without the non-recurring engineering costs associated with ASICs. Lower development costs allow custom circuits with low volume implementations to become economically feasible. In addition, the dynamic reconfigurability of FPGAs allows more than one custom circuit to run on a given piece of hardware. The hardwired circuit developed for one application can be replaced with the circuit for a new application. Therefore, reconfigurable logic systems can approach the performance of custom ASICs *without the inflexibility of custom silicon.* This combination of custom hardware and flexible configurability has also been shown to outperform large scale general purpose computing systems [1, 2]. Thus, reconfigurable logic systems have the potential to bring application-specific performance to general purpose computing systems.

In order for reconfigurable systems to become general purpose computing systems, they must be easy to program and use. Although some early work has been done on automated software/hardware co-synthesis [3], most reconfigurable systems are programmed using conventional hardware development techniques such as schematic capture or hardware description languages [2]. As the number of FPGAs in reconfigurable systems increases, the task of developing custom circuits for each FPGA in the system becomes enormous. In addition, the knowledge and tools necessary to develop reconfigurable applications further hinders general purpose implementation. A strong background in hardware development is required as well as expensive CAD and synthesis tools. Until reconfigurable systems address the deficiencies of large scale application development, reconfigurable logic will remain in the application-specific realm.

One way to reduce the problem of realizing custom circuitry on reconfigurable hardware systems is implementing or adapting a general purpose processor in reconfigurable hardware. This paper will discuss background research in reconfigurable processors, introduce the Nano Processor, and provide a design example.

2 Reconfigurable Stored-Program Processor Architectures

A number of reconfigurable stored-program processors have been implemented on reconfigurable systems. Although each system has a unique hardware architecture and software implementation, all utilize a reconfigurable platform to implement application-specific hardware in conjunction with a general purpose processor.

2.1 Background

The PRISM architecture is based on a standard microprocessor closely coupled with a reconfigurable hardware platform [3, 4]. The microprocessor implements standard functions, and executes application-specific instructions on the reconfigurable platform. The advantage of PRISM is that the integrated compiler generates both the hardware image of the unique instructions and the source code for the microprocessor. With little or no hardware background, users can generate a hardware configuration and software executable for the integrated system through high a level

0-8186-5490-2/94 $03.00

programming language.

The Spyder processor uses an array of FPGAs to implement a reconfigurable VLIW processor [5]. The processor has multiple execution units, dual register banks and a host computer interface. Application specific functionality is implemented in custom execution units. The large array allows a complex multiprocessing system to be implemented. Currently, the execution units are hand made with conventional schematic entry tools.

An 8-bit Reconfigurable Microprocessor (RM) has been developed that includes a complete instruction set [6]. In addition, a cross-assembler was developed to port C code to the processor. This single FPGA reconfigurable processor is intended for low-volume custom processor applications. Using a FPGA for this processor allows for easy testing and modification.

Each of these systems mix the more conventional form of computing, using a stored-program, with the use of application specific hardware computing. Similar to DSP processors, each unique reconfigurable processor becomes a special-purpose processor unique to its own class of problems. Low-volume, special-purpose processors become economically feasible.

2.2 Advantages

A major advantage of mixing a stored-program architecture with reconfigurable logic is that it maintains both programmability and application-specific performance. Although hardwired logic may achieve a higher level of performance, introducing programmability makes it possible to reuse hardware and reduce development time. With this approach, the reconfigurable system becomes reconfigurable at two levels. First, the processor hardware can be reconfigured to adapt its register file, instruction set, and data paths to a specific application class. Second, the executable software program can be modified to change the behavior of the processor. Such a paradigm gives more flexibility and adaptability.

Implementing a custom processor in reconfigurable hardware adds the ability to interface application-specific hardware with high level programming languages. The large set of software development tools available for standard stored-program processors become usable on reconfigurable systems.

Another advantage of a reconfigurable processor is that it allows users without a hardware background to program the hardware. Users with a programming background and an understanding of the custom functionality in the reconfigurable processor can program such machines like other conventional processors. They do not need the expensive schematic entry or synthesis tools necessary to develop custom applications. They only need custom software compilers to port their code to the custom processor. With a reconfigurable processor, the number of hardware configurations can be reduced or replaced with software modules that are easier to develop.

Once a hardware reconfigurable processor is made, multiple software modules can be executed. Software modules are developed to control the custom hardware according to the application needs. The software modules can be used to implement a variety of algorithms on the same hardware configuration. Unique hardware is not required for every custom processor application.

In addition, custom functionality developed for one processor can be used in another processor with different requirements. This custom functionality, usually implemented in custom instructions, can be archived in a custom instruction library. As more custom modules are made for the library, processors are built by simply choosing custom instructions from the library. Custom processors are built by packaging custom functionality into one design and routing the design for a particular part or family.

3 Nano Processor - a Low Resource Stored-Program Processor

The Nano Processor (nP) is a stored-program processor that achieves application-specific performance with general purpose programmable control. The nP implements application-specific functionality through the development of custom instructions. An integrated assembler generates the program data necessary to convert custom assembly instructions into executable code.

Similar to the Reconfigurable Microprocessor[6], the nP implements the processor control within a FPGA instead of using a standard microprocessor. Not only does this reduce the part count, but it allows full control over processor operation. As with PRISM, the nP offers available reconfigurable logic for implementing application-specific hardware to achieve application-specific performance. And, as Spyder allows the development of custom execution units, the nP offers the ability to develop custom hardware modules for each individual processor.

Yet, unlike other reconfigurable processors that require extensive FPGA resources, *the nP requires only a fraction of the resources available in a moderate sized FPGA*. Minimizing the control logic, registers and busses frees the logic and routing resources necessary to implement application-specific hardware in a single FPGA. With most of the FPGA resources dedicated to application-specific hardware, the nP can approach the performance achieved by application-specific hardware systems.

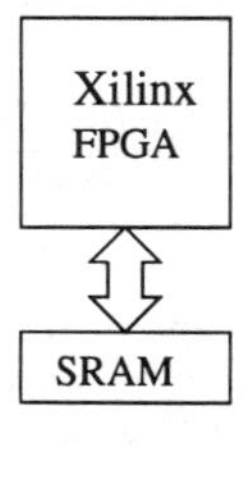

Figure 1: Nano Processor Implementation.

The nP is currently implemented on any of the Xilinx 3000 series parts [7] in conjunction with a variable size 8-bit static RAM (Figure 1). Many Xilinx device specific features are implemented to minimize

FPGA resource utilization, but the architecture can be adapted to other FPGA families with similar results. Multiple Nano Processors can be implemented on relatively small printed circuit boards to obtain a low-cost reconfigurable multiprocessing system.

The nP contains an inner core that serves as the hardware basis for each custom processor. This core implements six instructions using 21 IOBs, and 40 CLBs of any part in the Xilinx 3000 series FPGA family. Depending on the amount of custom hardware needed, any of the 3000 parts can be chosen (Table 1). Resources available after implementing the nP core vary from 24 CLBs when using the XC3020 to 444 CLBs when using the XC3195.

Part	3020	3030	3042	3064	3090	3195
CLBs	64	100	144	244	320	484
nP Size	40	40	40	40	40	40
Available	24	60	104	204	280	444
% Available	38%	60%	72%	84%	88%	92%

Table 1: Resource utilization of Nano Processor on various Xilinx 3000 series FPGAs.

3.1 Processor Organization

The nP is organized with several hierarchical levels as indicated in Figure 2.

3.1.1 nP Core

The inner most processor level is the nP core. This core is a general purpose processor that has been carefully developed to accommodate a wide range of custom instructions and is not intended to be modified. The core contains six essential instructions, and can operate without any customization. In fact, several designs have been implemented on smaller FPGAs with little or no customization.

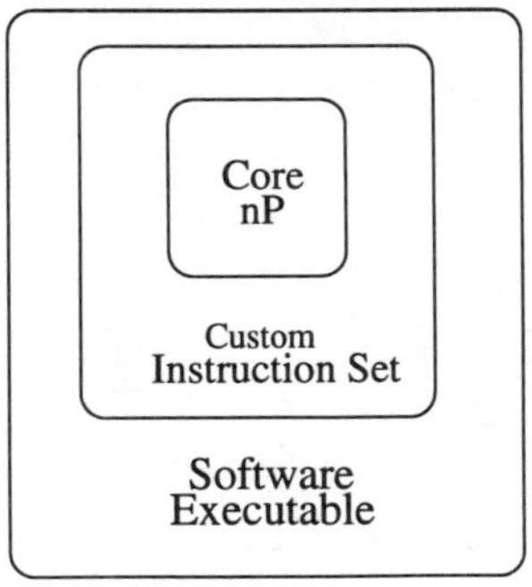

Figure 2: Nano Processor Organization.

3.1.2 Custom Instruction Set

The next processor level is the custom instruction set. With the core nP design minimized, most of the FPGA resources are available for application-specific hardware in the form of a custom instruction set.

An instruction set is built by choosing instructions from an instruction library or designing new instructions. New instructions are currently developed with standard schematic entry or high level synthesis tools. After a new custom instruction has been designed and verified, it is placed in the instruction library of nP custom instructions. This allows custom functions to be reused - *unique operations and instructions only have to be made once.* As more and more special-purpose instructions are developed, it becomes much easier to develop high speed custom processors.

Implementing special-purpose functionality in the form of an instruction allows quick and easy control of the custom functionality. Custom logic of nearly any form can be encapsulated in a custom instruction to provide easy interfacing and control. The instruction can become an active member of the processor, and operate in parallel with other events in the processor. Custom instructions can also take over the functions of dedicated logic in conventional computer systems.

As an example, a special-purpose data sorting processor could be built with high-speed, hardware sorting algorithms. Without any custom instructions, the nP core could perform simple sorting algorithms. But, like most processors, it must proceed byte by byte through the data structure and perform individual comparisons on the data set. A custom sort instruction could be developed that, when given two address pointers, would read the values, compare, and swap if necessary. Much of the overhead in data calculation and instruction processing would be removed. If additional reconfigurable logic is available, a more complex sorting algorithm could be implemented. A "sort_block" instruction could be developed that loads several bytes of data into custom registers, performs a hardware sort, and writes the block back to memory in sorted order. Such instruction modules may require much more logic than simple compare and swap instructions, but they could dramatically improve performance. Custom instructions can remove much of the overhead associated with general purpose computing algorithms by encapsulating time consuming activities within dedicated logic.

Once the instruction set of a processor has been chosen, the processor must be mapped to a specific FPGA device. Using manufacturer tools, the netlists of the nP core and the custom instructions are flattened and converted to a vendor specific netlist. Using place and route tools, the custom processor netlist is implemented.

3.1.3 Software Executable

The software executable is the outermost level of the processor. Users program the nP in assembly language using any of the core nP instructions or custom instructions specified in the processor definition.

Hardware processors for a class of applications can be reused so users do not have to create a custom processor for each application. This gives users the ability to develop custom applications without any understanding of the hardware in the special-purpose processor. When writing applications on a custom processor, no extra tools are required except the nP assembler.

In summary, the multi-level organization of the nP provides users with the flexibility necessary to reconfigure the processing environment at two levels - hardware and software.

3.2 nP Core Architecture

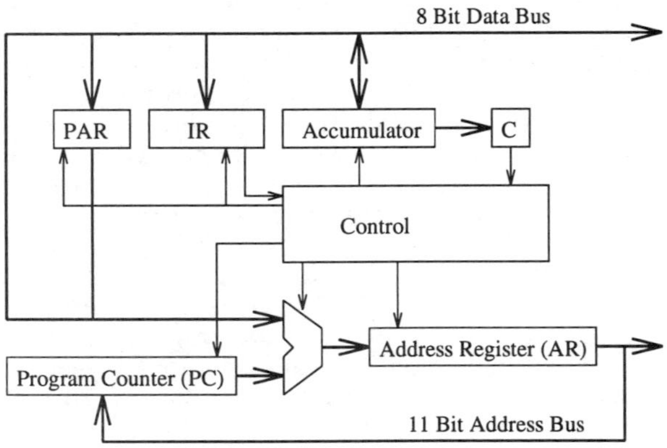

Figure 3: Nano Processor Core Architecture.

The data path size for the nP core is eight bits - the width of the attached SRAM. The various register sizes are established as a result of this 8-bit data width.

The nano processor consists of five registers:

- Instruction Register (**IR**),
- Page Address Register (**PAR**),
- Program Counter (**PC**),
- Address Register (**AR**),
- Accumulator (**A**).

To conserve resources, the **IR**, **PAR**, and the **AR** are all stored in Xilinx IOB flip-flops (Figure 3). Under the current architecture, the **IR** contains five bits and the **PAR** contains three bits. Five **IR** bits allows up to 32 unique instructions, and three **PAR** bits allows up to eight different pages (256-byte pages). For the Xilinx implementation, both registers can be mapped into IOBs to conserve available registers and logic.

The program counter (**PC**) and the address register (**AR**) are both eleven bits wide allowing for a 2K addressing space. The **PC** controls the program flow as in conventional processors, and is often loaded into the **AR**. The **AR** is the final register that addresses external memory.

The arithmetic capabilities are contained in the single data register of the processor, the accumulator (**A**). The accumulator is eight bits wide with a single carry bit. Under the current implementation, the accumulator can perform addition, and subtraction. All other logical functions are possible, but limiting functionality to these two instructions insures that each bit fits within a single CLB for single level logic performance. Additional functionality should be performed in custom instructions.

The internal data paths of the processor include the 8-bit data bus and the 11-bit address bus. The bi-directional data bus is used to load the **IR**, **PAR**, **A**, and **AR** registers. This bus is coupled with the external SRAM. The address bus is used to address the external SRAM, and to load the program counter. The **AR** can be loaded by multiplexing between the **PC**, and a combination of the **PAR** and the data bus. The limited bus connections allows for easy FPGA routing.

The control circuitry for the processor is hardwired in the control module. This module controls the latches, multiplexers, and global clocking.

Resource	**IOB**	**CLB**
Address Register	11	
Instruction Register	5	
Page Address Register	3	
Address Multiplexer		11
Program Counter		12
Accumulator		9
Control Logic	2	8
Total	21	40

Table 2: Resource Utilization of Nano Processor Core.

As stated previously, the core nP consumes 40 Xilinx CLBs with resources divided among the functional units as described in Table 2. The goal in this design is to minimize the logic necessary for control in order to leave valuable reconfigurable logic for custom hardware.

3.3 Instruction Set

As stated previously, the nP core instruction set consists of six standard instructions. To simplify execution, the nano processor has fixed instruction lengths of two bytes. Each instruction contains only two parts: an instruction opcode, and one operand reference. The operand reference is split into two parts: the page address (3-bits) that specifies which of the eight 256-byte pages the reference belongs, and the page offset, an eight bit offset value within the specified page.

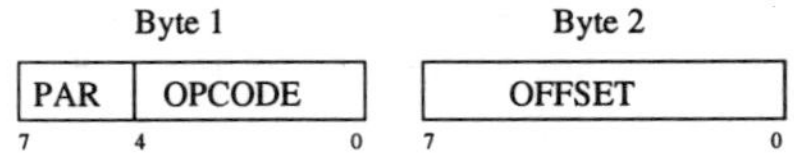

Figure 4: Nano Processor Instruction.

The first byte contains the instruction opcode in the lower five bits, and the page address in the upper three bits. The second byte contains the page offset (Figure 4).

STore Accumulator to memory	STR	mem[AR] <- A
LoaD accumulator from memory	LD	A <- mem[AR]
LoaD accumulator from memory + C	LDC	A <- mem[AR]+C
ADd memory to accumulator with Carry	ADC	A <- A+C+mem[AR]
SuBtract memory from accumulator - C	SBB	A <- A-C-mem[AR]
Jump to new location at No Carry	JNC	PC <- AR (if C=0)

Table 3: EX stage for Nano Processor instructions.

The nano processor has a three-stage instruction cycle.

- Instruction Fetch (**IF**)
- Instruction Decode (**ID**)
- Execution cycle (**EX**)

The **IF** stage performs two primary operations. First, it loads the instruction register and the page address register with the first byte of the instruction specified by the **PC**. Second, it increments the program counter.

```
stage IF:

     IR  <- mem[PC],0-4
     PAR <- mem[PC],5-7
     PC  <- PC + 1
```

The **ID** stage fetches the second byte of the instruction word (page offset) and calculates the address of the referenced operand (specified by the **PAR** and the page offset). In addition, it increments the **PC** to prepare for the next instruction.

```
stage ID:

     AR <- mem[PC] + PAR
     PC <- PC + 1
```

The **EX** stage performs the desired function on the operand specified by the opcode. Although five instruction register bits allow for 32 unique instructions, the core nP implements only six instructions and leaves the extra instruction slots available for custom instructions. The basic operation of the **EX** stage is as follows:

```
stage EX:

     A <- A op mem[AR]
```

The six basic instructions are described in Table 3. This limited instruction set contains all the necessary features to implement a larger and more complicated instruction set, while minimizing the required control logic.

```
; SAMPLE INSTRUCTION DEFINITION FILE
; test.inc
;
;     .INST = COMPILER DIRECTIVE
;       (INSTRUCTION DEFINITION)
;     .INST "<name>", <opcode>, <opcode length>
      .INST      "STR", 0x07, 0x0001
      .INST      "LD",  0x02, 0x0001
      .INST      "LDC", 0x03, 0x0001
      .INST      "ADC", 0x01, 0x0001
      .INST      "SBB", 0x00, 0x0001
      .INST      "JNC", 0x05, 0x0001
```

Figure 5: Example Instruction Definition.

3.4 Instruction Set Augmentation

As stated earlier, custom functionality for the nP is provided through custom instructions. The custom instructions, along with the six instructions provided with the core nP, provides a custom instruction set for each nP. Although a nP can operate without any custom instructions, the nP is intended to be extended with custom instructions on the available reconfigurable hardware.

Custom instructions are developed as separate modules using conventional schematic entry or synthesis methods. Instruction modules interface with the nP core by having access to nP core registers and control signals. Each custom instruction module must decode the **IR** register during the **ID** stage to detect the instruction reference. During the **EX** stage, the instruction may make use of operand reference on the 8-bit data bus.

With the instruction set defined, the nano assembler is used to generate the program files. The nano assembler is a flexible assembler that includes instruction definition support for custom instructions. Before any program can be written, the instruction definitions must be built. The instructions are defined using the .INST assembler directive. Although the instructions can be defined in each program, it is best to write an include file that has all unique instruction definitions for an individual nP configuration. This insures that all instruction calls for the same configuration are the same. The following parameters for each instruction must be defined: instruction name, opcode, and instruction length. An example instruction definition for the core nP instructions defined above is seen in Figure 5.

After the instructions are defined, a conventional assembly language program can be written for the new processor. Conventional assembler directives, labels, macros and commands can then be added to obtain a functional program. Figure 6 is a code segment that shows how the defined instructions are used to implement a simple counter.

```
; program test.nsm
.include test.inc

:loop_back
     ld temp
     adc one
     str temp
     sbb count
     jnc stop
     adc zero
     jnc loop_back
stop:
    jnc stop

; data definitions
one:     .db 0x01
zero:    .db 0x00
count:   .db 0xdd
temp:    .db 0x00
```

Figure 6: Sample nP Code.

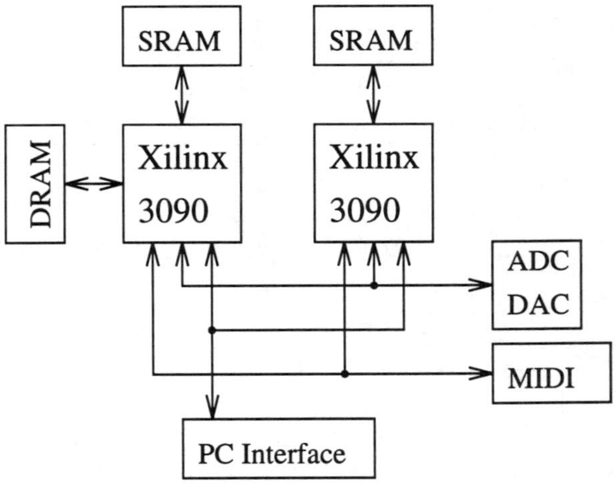

Figure 7: X2 Layout.

3.5 Performance

In order to optimize performance, the design goal was to minimize the system cycle time. Because of the synchronous nature of the design, the cycle speed is limited by the slowest unit in any of the three cycles. Using the - 125 speed grade and Xilinx's APR with no optimizations, the slowest signal in the control logic is approximately 30 ns for a system cycle speed of 33 MHz. The nP will operate at 11 MIPS under this configuration. Maximum system clock is estimated at 75 MHz using -230 speed grade parts and routing optimizations.

4 Nano Processor Applications

A number of custom Nano Processors have been implemented on reconfigurable systems with encouraging results. A good example of how the Nano Processor operates on a reconfigurable system is the National Technologies Inc., X2 sound card. The X2 is a small reconfigurable logic system with the external components necessary to implement a 16-bit stereo sound card on a PC system. Specifically, the card includes two Xilinx 3090 FPGAs, two 32K x 8 SRAMs, 1 Mb DRAM, a 16-bit stereo Codec, and a PC interface (Figure 7).

Although the X2 offers two reprogrammable FPGAs for general purpose reconfigurable systems, it was specifically designed for a versatile PC sound card system. The on-board FPGAs allow for multiple hardware realizations of sound related algorithms as well as control over the data acquisition. Currently, a number of unique configurations run on the system for a wide variety of audio applications. A subset of these configurations include those using the Nano Processor as the core processing unit (Figure 8).

The audio interface is a Nano Processor configuration that implements custom instructions and logic to interface 48 kHz stereo audio data to and from the PC as well as asynchronous MIDI (Musical Instrument Digital Interface) data. It includes several software modules that change the functionality of the interface system. The saturating mixer is a Nano Processor configuration that mixes multiple audio data files. Running on the X2 sound card, the saturating mixer executes 240 times faster than a 486-33 PC. This configuration is used with special audio editing tools to speed up audio editing features. A number of other audio editing effects and acquisition configurations are under development that take advantage of nP versatility. Each custom processor has the same core instruction set yet employs different custom instructions unique to its application. The audio interface processor has custom instructions to efficiently handle audio data transfers as well as external device control. The saturating mixer includes a custom multiply and accumulate instruction and other special-purpose signal processing functionality.

4.1 Audio Interface

The audio interface is a custom nP configuration designed to control a complex multi-media sound card. The card has three major functions that must be carefully integrated:

- Transfer of stereo 48kHz PCM audio data between ADC/DAC and PC,
- Handle all asynchronous data transfer to and from the external MIDI port,
- Control external synthesis engine.

To appropriately handle the data transfer and Codec control, five modules were added to the core nP (Figure 9):

- MIDI Interface,
- Codec Interface,
- PC Interface,

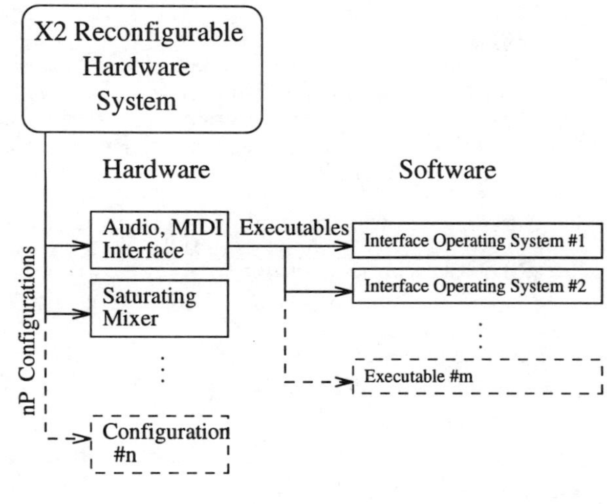

Figure 8: X2 Nano Processor Configurations.

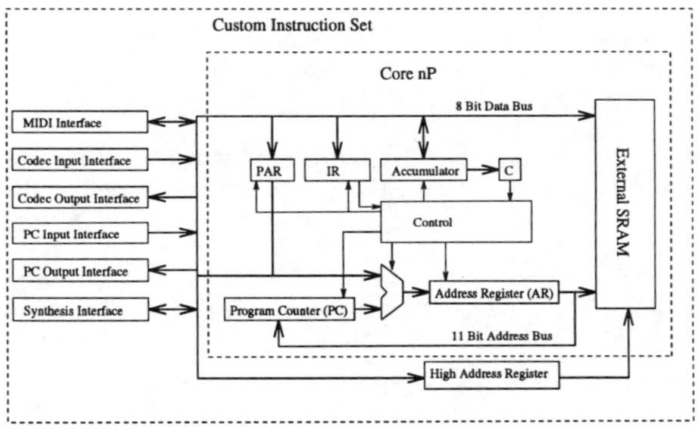

Figure 9: X2 Audio Interface Configuration.

- Synthesis Interface,
- Memory Interface.

Each module interfaces with an external device attached to the nP, and contains the custom functionality necessary to independently handle the interface. Associated with each hardware module is a set of instructions used to control and read the interface.

The MIDI interface handles the interface to the serial UART used for MIDI data transfer. The interface must be responsible for receiving and transmitting asynchronous data at 32 kbits/sec. The interface implements a custom UART that operates independently of the nP. The nP includes instructions to poll the incoming data port, send a data byte, and control the function of the MIDI interface. All overhead associated with the interface is encapsulated in the MIDI hardware module.

The Codec interface must control the external ADC/DAC and send it the appropriate data. This interface implements eight input ports dedicated to the ADC/DAC. Four 8-bit registers buffer the two incoming 16-bit audio data bytes, and four 8-bit registers buffer the two outgoing audio data bytes. The interface must have the ability to change the various modes of the ADC/DAC, and adjust dataflow appropriately.

The PC interface must handle PC requests for data in a timely fashion, and receive data from the PC at audio data rates. Similar to the Codec interface, the PC interface uses four 8-bit input registers and four 8-bit output registers. Custom port read and write instructions automatically control a six-byte FIFO that is used to buffer data to and from the PC. Interfacing with these ports requires only simple PC port-read and port-write functions.

The Synthesis interface controls the operation of the wavetable synthesis engine. The wavetable load instruction used for this interface automatically loads a specific wavetable in the DRAM with an incoming data packet. In addition, special-purpose control registers are used to modify the synthesis behavior.

The memory interface buffers incoming and outgoing audio data on the 32k x 8 SRAM used for the nP program memory. Because the nP core can only address 2K, an extra high address register is added to address higher pages in memory. The nP program is stored in the low 2k, and the upper 30k is used for audio data buffering. Custom instructions are available that set this high address register, and access data using this high address register.

The individual interfaces allow custom control for each module in the system. Unique control of these interfaces is available through unique custom instructions. The operation of these interfaces is dependent upon the software system associated with it. This allows for flexible control over the interface without redesigning the nP.

4.2 Interface Operating System

The audio interface nP offers all the hardware capability necessary to control the external devices simultaneously. Although the hardware for the interfaces is available, software modules must be present to control each interface. Software modules allow custom control of the interfaces to tailor the hardware to the specific needs of the user.

Currently, there are five software modules that run on the audio interface. Other software modules may be available in the future to allow further control over the processor. The five software modules differ in the control over the PC and Codec interfaces. For varying audio data formats, each interface must transfer data differently. Each of the five software modules changes the control of the interfaces to adapt the card to the appropriate data format. The five data formats are as follows:

- 16-bit stereo (in/out),
- 16-bit mono (in/out),
- 8-bit stereo (in/out),
- 8-bit mono (in/out),
- dual channel 16-bit mono (in/out).

Using a custom program for custom interfacing provides exceptional flexibility in controlling the audio interface. Adding other software modules will provide further flexibility and customization of the X2 sound system.

The X2 reconfigurable sound system is a good example of how the nP can be implemented to take advantage of customization at two levels of development. Multiple nP hardware configurations optimize hardware resources to maximize performance for application-specific algorithms and control. In addition, multiple software executable modules for the various hardware nP configurations reuse carefully designed application-specific functionality while customizing these resources to unique algorithms.

5 Conclusion

We have found that the Nano Processor, a low resource reconfigurable stored-program processor, is an effective tool for implementing reconfigurable logic systems. Its low resource utilization frees essential reconfigurable hardware needed to implement high performance application-specific hardware. Custom instructions have been implemented that take advantage of application-specific hardware to produce exceptional results not available on general purpose processors.

Future research with the Nano Processor includes tools that allow higher levels of development and abstraction. These include a C compiler to generate the nP assembly code, and hardware compilers for higher levels of custom instruction definition. In addition, more complex Nano Processor cores are being developed that take advantage of newer FPGA family features.

Reconfigurable processors with custom instructions are an effective way of implementing reconfigurable logic systems. Reconfigurable processors offer a more flexible environment of development than conventional reconfigurable systems while offering similar high levels of performance.

References

[1] M. Gokhale, W. Holmes, A. Kosper, D. Kunze, D. Lopresti, S. Lucas, R. Minnich, and P. Olsen. SPLASH: a reconfigurable linear logic array. In *International Conference on Parallel Processing*, pages I-526-I-532, 1990.

[2] P. Bertin, D. Roncin, and J. Vuillemin. Programmable Active Memories: a Performance Assessment. *Research on Integrated Systems: proceedings of the 1993 symposium*, pp. 88-102, 1993.

[3] P. Athanas and H. Silverman. Processor reconfiguration through instruction-set metamorphosis. *IEEE Computer*, March 1993.

[4] M. Wazlowski, L. Agarwal, T. Lee, A. Smith, E. Lam, P. Athanas, H. Silverman, and S. Ghosh. PRISM-II Compiler and Architecture. *Proceedings: IEEE Workshop on FPGAs for Custom Computing Machines*, pp. 9-16, April 1993.

[5] Iseli, C. and E. Sanchez. Spyder: A Reconfigurable VLIW Processor using FPGAs. *Proceedings: IEEE Workshop on FPGAs for Custom Computing Machines*, pp. 17-24, April 1993.

[6] J. Davidson. FPGA Implementation of a Reconfigurable Microprocessor. *Proceedings of the IEEE 1993 Custom Integrated Circuits Conference*, pp 3.2.1 - 3.2.4, 1993.

[7] XILINX: *The Programmable Gate Array Data Book.* San Jose, CA, 1992.

DPGA-Coupled Microprocessors: Commodity ICs for the Early 21st Century

André DeHon
Artificial Intelligence Laboratory
Massachusetts Institute of Technology
Cambridge, MA, 02139

Abstract

During the past decade the microprocessor has become a key commodity component for building all kinds of computational systems. During this time frame large, reconfigurable logic arrays have exploited the same advances in IC fabrication technology to emerge as viable system building blocks. Looking at both the technology prospects and application requirements, there is compelling evidence that microprocessors with integrated reconfigurable logic arrays will be a primary building block for future computing systems. In this paper, we look at the role such components can play in building high-performance and economical systems, as well as the ripe technological outlook. We note how the tight integration of reconfigurable logic into the processor can overcome some of the major limitations of contemporary, attached reconfigurable compute engines. We specifically consider the use of integrated Dynamically Programmable Gate Array structures for the configurable logic and examine the advantages rapid reconfiguration provides in this application.

1 Introduction

Continuing advances in semiconductor processing have allowed the integration of increasing functionality into single-chip microprocessors. Today's high-performance microprocessors sport 2-3 million transistors and include multiple functional units and large on-chip memories. Microprocessors built for low-cost and embedded systems heavily integrate peripheral control to reduce the chip count for complete systems.

As technology continues to advance, room remains to enhance performance with additional, fixed functional units and reduce costs by integrating more of the computing system onto the microprocessor IC. Nonetheless, simply adding fixed functional capacity will not produce the highest performance on the broadest class of applications nor allow the construction of the broadest range of low-cost systems. Much of the economy in the use and production of microprocessors has come from their commoditization. Integration of fixed functional capacity risks overspecialization and reduced volume utilization per design investment.

For broader application, future microprocessors should dedicate a portion of their silicon real-estate to reconfigurable logic. The reconfigurable logic can be specialized in application-specific ways to provide application acceleration and in system-specific ways to serve as support logic implementing system-specific functions. A single reconfigurable microprocessor design can serve as the principal building block for a wide range of applications including personal computers, embedded systems, application-specific computers, and general- and special-purpose multiprocessors. The wide field of application for the reconfigurable microprocessor allow it to draw heavily on economies of scale and volume production.

In this paper, we look at the technology push (Section 2) and application pull (Section 3) which argue compellingly for the tight integration of reconfigurable logic into commodity microprocessors. We review contemporary efforts to accelerate application-specific computing tasks (Section 4) to emphasize the range of application where reconfigurable logic has already proven itself capable of acceleration and to review the typical shortcomings of contemporary systems. We review the Dynamically Programmable Gate Array Architecture (DPGA) (Section 5) in the context of microprocessor integrated reconfigurable logic and show that the DPGA architecture overcomes some of the limitations of contemporary reconfigurable logic systems. With this background in place, we take a broader look at the roles DPGA-coupled processors can play in future computing systems (Section 6). Finally, we look at the acceptance path for this technology (Section 7), take a reprise look at the costs and benefits relative to fixed functional units (Section 8), and look at the challenges ahead (Section 9) before concluding.

0-8186-5490-2/94 $03.00 © 1994 IEEE

2 Technology Trends

Semiconductor processing has continued to improve steadily, allowing the fabrication of smaller and smaller devices. This trend shows little signs of abating. Effective device densities and IC capacity improve at an exponential rate. We are all now quite familiar with the progress of microprocessors where operational performance increases by roughly 60% per year while the number of gates increases by 25% per year. With 3 million gates available for today's modern microprocessors, we can expect to have over 12 million gates available by the end of the century.

As gate densities have improved, more of the computing system has been integrated onto the microprocessor die and larger processors have been implemented. What started as minimal instruction stream control and a simple, 4-bit ALU, has grown with the available area to include multiple, 64-bit functional units including hardwired floating-point support. The basic microprocessor design has expanded to include large, on-chip memories to prevent off-chip i/o latency from significantly degrading performance. Today's high-performance microprocessors move towards higher execution rates using aggressive pipelining and superscalar execution utilizing multiple functional units. Caches increase with instruction throughput in an attempt to prevent off-chip i/o latency from limiting effective computational throughput. Today's cost-conscious microprocessors move to integrate common system and peripheral functions onto the IC die to reduce system cost and power consumption.

Just during the past 6-8 years, we have seen reconfigurable logic emerge as a commodity technology comparable to memories and microprocessors. Like memories, reconfigurable logic arrays rapidly adapt to new technology since the design consists of an array of simple structures. Also like memory, the regularity allows designers to focus their time on adapting the key logic structures to extract highest performance from the available technology. Each reconfigurable array can be designed and tested as a single IC design yet gains volume from the myriad of diverse applications to which the general-purpose array is applied.

Our growing microprocessors can continue their current trends by including more memory, more FPUs, more ALUs, and more system functionality, but it is not clear this will be the most judicious use of the silicon real-estate becoming available in the near future. Addition of fixed functional units will not bring about broad-based acceleration of applications *in proportion to the area these fixed units consume*. For a given application, the fixed functional units can be arranged to provide almost proportional improvements. However, each application class will require a different selection and arrangement of units to achieve such improvements. Any fixed collection of functional units, control, and data paths will necessarily be suboptimal for most applications.

Improvement in microprocessor performance and system cost can be achieved through specialization and integration. However, such specialization must be balanced against market size to maintain commodity economics. The danger is that overspecialization will reduce the market base and not allow the resulting microprocessors to benefit from commoditization.

The incorporation of reconfigurable array logic into our growing microprocessor provides an alternative growth path which allows application specialization while benefiting from the full effects of commoditization. Like modern reconfigurable logic arrays, a single microprocessor design can be employed in a wide variety of applications. Application acceleration and system adaptation can be achieved by specializing the reconfigurable logic in the target system or application.

3 Application Outlook

Despite ubiquitous use, contemporary microprocessor architectures are poorly matched to most of the applications they run. For almost any application, one can conjecture additions or modifications to prevalent microprocessor architectures which would significantly enhance the application's performance. However, the additions differ from application to application, and there is insufficient commonality among applications to merit inclusion of such additions in a microprocessor with a broad application base. The performance advantage gained by employing specialized coprocessors for high-performance graphics, video processing, signal processing, and networking further demonstrates the performance penalty which accompanies using a general-purpose microprocessor over processors specialized to handle more limited application domains.

Incorporating reconfigurable logic into the general-purpose microprocessor, allows applications to specialize the processing hardware to match the application requirements while allowing a single microprocessor design to maintain its appeal across a broad range of application bases. Special-purpose architectures have long been recognized as one path to higher performance, application-specific computing systems. As we will review in the following section, recent research in the area of customizable computing systems demonstrates that reconfigurable logic can be effectively employed to accelerate many computational tasks. By including reconfigurable logic in the microprocessor, we combine the application-oriented benefits of architecture specialization with the economic benefits of commoditization.

4 Contemporary Reconfigurable Computing

4.1 Reconfigurable Compute Engines

Several research groups have built reconfigurable compute engines to extract high application performance at low costs by specializing the computing engine to the computation task.

- Athanas and Silverman introduce the PRISM (Processor Reconfiguration through Instruction-Set Metamorphosis) architecture which couples a programmable element with a microprocessor [21]. From each application program, new processor "instructions" are synthesized in the reconfigurable element which are designed to accelerate the application. PRISM-I and PRISM-II prototypes have been built which couple common microprocessors with Xilinx FPGAs [23].

- Cuccaro and Reese at the Supercomputing Research Center augmented a CM-2 with reconfigurable logic units by using Xilinx FPGAs in place of the CM-2 floating point processors [9]. The reconfigurable logic can be configured to perform common operations which are ill-suited to the fine-grained SIMD processing elements in the CM-2.

- The Supercomputing Research Center has built a series of programmable systolic arrays known as SPLASH [18] [7]. Each SPLASH array attaches to a host workstations and is composed from a number of Xilinx FPGAs in an array fashion along with support memory. SPLASH has seen heavy use in genome sequence matching applications [16].

- DEC Paris's PAM (Programmable Active Memories) is an array of Xilinx FPGAs attached to a host workstation [5]. The DEC team has demonstrated significant performance improvements on many applications by appropriate specialization of the PAM accelerator.

- Algotronix's CH2x4 provides a 2×4 array of CAL 1024 FPGAs along with memory in an ISA, PC-compatible card form factor [2].

Numerous other reconfigurable computing engines have been and continue to be built due to their favorable cost/performance ratios.

4.2 Application Sampling

Reconfigurable computing engines such as these have been effectively employed in a wide-rage of applications, including:

1. **Binary operations** – Reconfigurable logic can perform binary operations very efficiently and with substantial parallelism. When applications require the evaluation of large, regular binary operations, reconfigurable compute engines can offer significant advantage over the fixed logic available in typical processors. The PRISM research project demonstrates the kinds of advantages provided by this class of specialization [22].

2. **Arithmetic** – When the arithmetic operations required by a computation do not exactly match those provided by the ALU/FPU in conventional microprocessors or when the arithmetic operations admit to substantial bit-level parallelism, there is ample room to specialize reconfigurable logic to provide higher performance [11] [20] [4] [9].

3. **Encryption/Decryption/Compression** – Encryption/decryption and compression applications require application of simple sequences of arithmetic and logic operations to large datasets. The operations required are often not native to typical microprocessors. Specialized computing engines can provide the appropriate operators and make use of the parallelism and regularity in the application to extract high performance [20] [4].

4. **Sequence and string matching** – By recognizing the application's natural structure and specializing a configurable compute engine to take advantage of the structure, researchers have managed to achieve very high performance at modest costs [14] [12] [16].

5. **Sorting** – Sorting tasks exhibit natural, fine-grained parallelism. By exploiting this parallelism, large sorting tasks can be performed efficiently with sorting networks built from configurable logic [17].

6. **Physical system simulation** – Simulating physical phenomena often require repeated evaluation of state-variables using very regular computations, often of limited precision. Compute engines specialized to evaluating particular systems of equations can achieve significant advantage over general-purpose processors [4].

7. **Video and image processing** – The fine-grained, bit-level parallelism available in most image processing applications make it highly amenable to acceleration using fine-grained processing arrays (*e.g.* [4] [11]).

A common theme in these applications is that application-specific specialization of a reconfigurable computing system provides orders of magnitude higher performance than general-purpose microprocessors or workstations. The costs of the reconfigurable logic are typically less than that of the base processor/workstations being augmented. We often see "supercomputer" level performance from systems which cost orders of magnitude less to assemble. For several applications, the specialized, reconfigurable compute engine demonstrates the best performance reported on any machine.

The applications reviewed here were reported on a widely varying collection of reconfigurable architectures of various sizes. We cannot, fairly, conclude that a single reconfigurable architecture will necessarily exhibit directly comparable performance gains. Nonetheless, the ensemble demonstrates a clear potential for application acceleration via specialized reconfigurable logic across a large range of application.

4.3 Some Common Themes

One theme we see exploited in many of these application is the advantage of exploiting bit-level parallel computation. The reconfigurable array can manipulate a large number of bits in parallel, whereas conventional processor technology focusses on fixed, word-wide data manipulation using word sizes of at most 64 bits in today's microprocessors.

When ALUs are implemented in reconfigurable logic, they can be specialized to perform exactly the function required by the application. This specialization allows the use of more economical functional units both in terms of area and operational speed. This economy can enable the reconfigurable logic to support numerous functional units simultaneously to extract high performance through parallelism.

Another recurring theme is application-specific data flow between functional elements. In a conventional processor it is necessary to spend computational cycles moving data around to match the fixed functional resources and data paths provided. This weakness is often aggravated by limited data-transfer bandwidth within the processing system. In a reconfigurable compute engine, it is possible to customize the data paths between compute elements, as well as the compute elements themselves, to match the application. Rather than juggling intermediate results in and out of registers and memory, the compute engine can be customized so data flows directly from producer to consumer. The specialized data movement is often localized between portions of reconfigurable logic avoiding bandwidth bottlenecks on shared data paths.

4.4 Limitations of Current Systems

Despite the high performance contemporary reconfigurable computing systems provide, they do exhibit a couple of common limitations:

1. **Low Bandwidth and High Latency Interface** – Since contemporary reconfigurable compute engines are attached to host processors as peripherals, they are generally attached to a peripheral bus with limited bandwidth and high latency to the processor. The high overhead of communicating with the the attached reconfigurable engine limits the kinds of acceleration possible and prevents close cooperation between the fixed and reconfigurable logic units. The low bandwidth similarly makes communication expensive and limits the throughput achievable with the reconfigurable compute engine.

2. **High Reconfiguration Overhead** – Since the reconfiguration costs are high in almost all contemporary reconfigurable logic technologies, the reconfiguration time must be amortized over a large amount of processing to justify reconfiguring the compute engine. Often, this means that a single configuration must be maintained throughout an application even when different portions of the application might be accelerated with different kinds of specialized logic. This high-reconfiguration costs also makes it impossible to employ contemporary reconfigurable compute engines productively in multitasking or time-shared systems.

Tight integration of the reconfigurable logic into the base microprocessor can significantly decrease communication latency between the fixed functional units and the reconfigurable logic. Similarly, when the processor and reconfigurable logic share the same die, higher bandwidth is easily available for high throughput processing employing reconfigurable logic. By reducing the communication overhead between the base microprocessor and the reconfigurable logic, we can greatly increase the kinds of application-specific specialization which provide significant acceleration.

5 Dynamically Programmed Gate Arrays

The Dynamically Programmable Gate Array (DPGA) architecture [6] is particularly well-suited for reconfigurable computing. Unlike normal Field-Programmable Gate Arrays (FPGAs) where the function of each array element is fixed between relatively slow reconfiguration sequences, the DPGA array elements may switch rapidly among several, pre-programmed configurations. This rapid

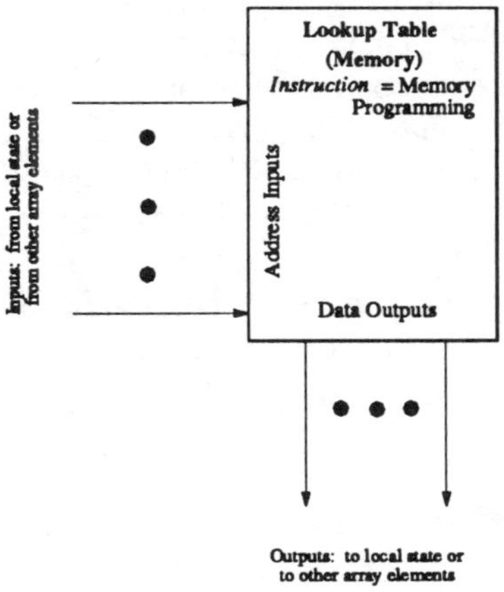

Figure 1: Computational Unit for FPGA AE

reconfiguration allows DPGA array elements to be reused in time without significant overhead. Applications can preload multiple, specialized array personalities and switch among configurations rapidly.

Like FPGAs, DPGAs are composed of a tesselation of simple computational array elements. Each array element can perform a simple logical function on several input bits producing one or more output bits. Many modern FPGAs are best modelled as programmable lookup tables. The lookup table programming constitutes the configuration of each array-element (See Figure 1). Between array elements programmable interconnect allows the array elements to be linked up as required by the application. The interconnect in FPGAs is typically configured by programming pass gates and multiplexors. Each DPGA array-element uses a second lookup table to map a broadcast configuration selection into a local configuration (See Figure 2). The broadcast configuration behaves like the broadcast instruction in a SIMD array, telling each array-element which function to perform on the next clock cycle. Unlike a SIMD array, the indirection through a pre-programmed, context lookup table allows each DPGA array element to perform a different function in response to the broadcast configuration identifier. In a similar manner, the configurable interconnect in a DPGA array has a table of loaded configurations and selects between configurations based on the current array context identifier.

At the cost of somewhat larger array elements and interconnect, the DPGA serves as a multiple-context FPGA. Within the space of preloaded contexts the DPGA can switch personalities completely from one clock cycle to the next. The DPGA configuration lookup table effectively serves as a cache of array element configurations. By giving each array element a small configuration cache, we

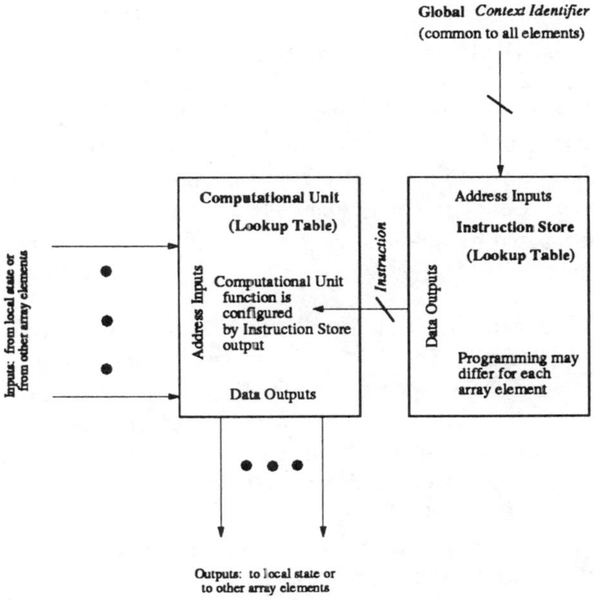

Figure 2: DPGA Array Element

effectively get very high reconfiguration bandwidth by performing lookups locally at all array elements in parallel. By pipelining the context lookup, DPGA cells need run no slower than comparable complexity FPGA or SIMD logic units.

The multiple loaded context now allow us to utilize the array elements more efficiently. In the most straightforward application, this rapid reconfiguration allows a single DPGA array to be loaded simultaneously with multiple configurations. The DPGA can switch between configurations to accelerate different portions of an application. If the configurable array is too small to hold an entire acceleration logic block, the block can be partitioned across multiple context and evaluated in stages. An application can also make use of the DPGA's capacity to perform computations where the processing elements vary both spatial and temporally. This allows computational functions to be placed where intermediate data resides in the reconfigurable array, taking further advantage of application-specific locality and data flow.

Finally, DPGAs are naturally suited to conventional multitasking or fine-grained multithreading (*e.g.* April [1], *T [19]). In these applications, each thread or context may require a different array personality. By partitioning the DPGA contexts and assigning a different context, or sets of contexts, to each thread or task, array reconfiguration will not complicate sharing the processor between tasks or threads.

6 DPGA-Coupled Processor Applications

The DPGA-coupled processor can be efficiently and economically employed as the key computational building block in almost all kinds of computing systems. The computational power and flexibility this component provides will allow it to subsume the role of more traditional microprocessors as well as many processors which have been specialized for application-specific domains. Following is a sampling of DPGA-coupled microprocessor applications:

- **General-Purpose Workstations and Personal Computers** – The DPGA logic can be employed for application-specific acceleration. Each application program can configure the reconfigurable array in the manner most beneficial to the application. The operating system and applications can also specialize the DPGA logic to serve in coprocessing roles for compute-intensive functions such as compression, encryption, signal processing, or protocol processing. For many of these compute-intensive tasks, high performance is desirable in bursts, but not continually. Configuring DPGA logic to perform these tasks as needed is much more economical than employing dedicated, application-specific coprocessors. The reconfigurable logic can also be employed for minimally intrusive profiling or statistics collection. Information on the dynamics of program execution and resource utilization is becoming increasingly important for high-quality program optimization.

- **Special-Purpose Computing Machines** – The attached DPGA logic can be specialized to configure the microprocessor to the special-purpose application. The designer building the special purpose computer provides added value by specializing both the configured architecture and the application software. In this scenario, the designer can use all the techniques developed to accelerate applications in general-purpose computing setting. Further, knowing that his application is dedicated to a particular application, he can often realize greater specialization.

- **Embedded Systems** – For embedded systems, the DPGA-coupled processor can provide intelligent, integrated control with no external components for interfacing. Part of the reconfigurable logic can be employed as system-specific glue logic.

- **Multiprocessor Systems** – DPGA-coupled processors can be employed in a variety of ways to produce high-performance multiprocessors. Part of the DPGA logic array could be used to build a tightly-integrated network interface (*e.g.* [10] [19]) to adapt the microprocessor for multiprocessing. Part of the DPGA logic could be used to construct application-specific synchronization primitives or communication networks. Each node may employ the DPGA logic for task acceleration in the same manner as single processor special- and general-purpose computers. The fine-grained, bit-level parallelism provided by the DPGAs can compliment the coarse-grained parallelism which is easiest to extract from microprocessor-based multiprocessors.

7 Acceptance Path

Integration can evolve smoothly from today's research-oriented, reconfigurable compute engines to commoditized, DPGA-coupled microprocessors. Contemporary, reconfigurable compute engines (Section 4) are attached as peripherals to host workstations and personal computers and serve as a first step in the direction of processor integrated, reconfigurable logic. The next step will be to provide reconfigurable logic coprocessors which can be more tightly integrated with the fixed-logic processor in general-purpose computing systems. With minor design effort, the reconfigurable logic can be integrated onto the same die as a core processor. ASIC vendors (*e.g.* LSI Logic, VLSI Technology Inc., Texas Instruments), which provide core-processors and compiled memories could provide first-generation, FPGA- or DPGA-coupled microprocessors in the current or upcoming ASIC technologies with minor up-front design overhead. Native integration of DPGA arrays into microprocessor designs will require the processor to be designed with the attached reconfigurable logic in mind. This may entail additional processor instructions for computational cooperation between the fixed and reconfigurable logic as well as some rethink of which portions of the processor should be implemented as hardwired functional resources.

Similarly, the "programming" necessary to efficiently employ these machines can evolve towards native integration with conventional compiler technology. The earliest reconfigurable compute engines were configured through explicit, human-crafted gate-designs. Increasingly, the behavior for these reconfigurable computing engines is described at a behavioral level in hardware description languages (*e.g.* VHDL, Verilog). In contemporary cases, experts familiar with the reconfigurable architecture develop the configurations for accelerating each application. PRISM [21] and dbC [13] demonstrate that conventional programming languages can be restricted or extended to allow programmers more comfortable with programming languages to express computations in a way which can be readily compiled for implementation on reconfigurable logic. For the near future, experts and more sophisticated users can write subroutines for the reconfigurable logic and provide them as library routines. General programmers can make use of the provided library routines for program acceleration simply by accessing them like any other library routine from their high-level programming language. If we make a large library of parameterizable, hardware subroutines known to a profiling compiler, we can employ the compiler to profile applications and select the hardware configurations and library routines which best accelerate each application. The compiler can treat the replacement of sequences of instructions on the processor's fixed logic with known, hardware subroutines as a potential optimization transform and evaluate the relative merits in a manner similar to conventional compiler transforms. Eventually, hardware synthesis technology and conventional compiler technology will converge and the compiler will manage both the reconfigurable and fixed resources on the microprocessor.

8 Costs and Benefits of Reconfiguration

For fixed functionality, we will always be able to achieve higher performance or produce smaller IC dies by "fixing" the logic functionality rather than customizing a reconfigurable array. However, when we specialize a design for fixed logic functionality, we limit the range of application. The reduced market volume of the specialized die may offset any savings due to decreased die size. Further, for each advance in processing technology, design and engineering effort are required for the specialized design to track processing technology. Just as it is often more prudent to ride the commodity microprocessor technology wave and take advantage of the regular advances in process technology, it will often be more beneficial to stay with programmed, reconfigurable logic and track process technology by moving to the newest DPGA-coupled microprocessors.

We may also see the emergence of hybrid solutions like the Xilinx HardWire Gate Arrays [24]. In systems where the configured logic is employed in a fixed manner, stable designs can migrate from the reconfigurable microprocessor to a microprocessor with an equivalent gate array which can be programmed at the mask level. This provides some of the advantages of fixed, specialized logic by reducing die size while retaining many commodity advantages. The tooling cost is low since few masks are required to personalize the generic design. Further, the specialized logic can follow the hard-wired array through processing advances.

When designing native microprocessors with integrated, configurable logic, we have the opportunity to migrate functionality which has traditionally been implemented as processor fixed logic into reconfigurable logic. In particular, we can consider moving some of the more complicated control structures, especially those dealing with exception handling, into reconfigurable logic. This migration can provide considerable flexibility and a number of practical advantages, including:

- Feature interaction, particularly with exception and error conditions, have a history of being one of the hardest parts of a processor design to get correct (*e.g.* [8] [15]). Careful relocation of this interaction logic into the reconfigurable logic allows later binding and post-fabrication modification of interaction behavior.
- The fault, interrupt, and system call behavior of many, modern microprocessors is often quite mismatched with the needs of the operating system [3]. Migrating some critical control over the management of fixed resources in situation such as these into reconfigurable logic will allow the operating-system designer the freedom to specialize the control handling to better match operating-system requirements.

9 Challenges

Designing efficient and widely applicable DPGA-coupled microprocessors will provide several engineering and architectural challenges. The space of design options is large and a number of tradeoffs will be necessary to extract a balanced design allowing efficient acceleration and adaptation across a large range of applications. The key tradeoffs which must be considered when designing a DPGA-coupled microprocessor include:

- **Processor↔reconfigurable logic interfacing** – The interface between the fixed and reconfigurable logic will be one of the most important aspects of the composite architecture. The interface will determine the kinds of functions to which the reconfigurable logic can be efficiently employed. This interface will have a critical effect on the communication overhead between fixed and reconfigurable logic.
- **Grain-size** – There is no consensus among the contemporary FPGA community as to the appropriate grain-size for primitive reconfigurable elements. To a large extent, optimal array-element grain size depends on available silicon implementation technology and reconfiguration implementation techniques. Grain-size will remain an important parameter to re-evaluate with advances in processing technology, array architecture, and array application.
- **Area and pin allocation** – Microprocessor designers must partition available silicon real-estate among on-

chip memories (*e.g.* caches), fixed-functional units (*e.g.* ALUs, FPUs), fixed control, and reconfigurable logic. In addition to any dedicated, microprocessor bus-interface pins, some pins should be dedicated to the reconfigurable logic for use in system-specific interfacing, reconfigurable array expansion, and specialized control and communications.

- **Multitasking and state interaction** – The reconfigurable array introduces a large amount of state associated with each computation in progress. Both the array configuration and the intermediate data values within the array are necessary to describe the computation at any point in time. In general-purpose computing systems which must share computational resources (*e.g.* time-shared or multitasking workstations, personal-computers, or multiprocessors), it is generally necessary to snapshot and restore computational state so that tasks can be interleaved in time on the same computational hardware. As noted in Section 4.4, the overhead necessary to reconfigure contemporary reconfigurable engines is quite large making such time-sharing impractical.

  The DPGA architecture can mitigate this drawback by providing on-chip, context caches for array configurations and memory for computed intermediate values. However, the number of on-chip contexts each DPGA instance provides is fixed. Sharing reconfigurable resources among a larger number of users or tasks will require provisions for offloading and restoring computations. To further mitigate the expense of unloading and reloading a context, reconfigurable-array savvy compilers can explicitly identify points in the computation where the state inside the reconfigurable array is minimal. By specializing context loading and unloading code to store and retrieve only the necessary state and reconfiguration, the compiler can produce lower overhead code for context swapping.

10 Conclusion

Microprocessors with tightly-integrated, rapidly reconfigurable logic promise to be a prime commodity building block for computing systems during the early part of the next century. We have seen that we can achieve high application performance by specializing the computational resources to the application. A microprocessor with integrated reconfigurable logic allows us to take advantage of application-specific specialization for extracting high performance while maintaining broad-based, high-volume appeal to reap the benefits commoditization. Tightly coupled DPGA processing arrays overcome the primary limitations of contemporary reconfigurable compute engines by significantly reducing the overheads associated with both processor↔array communications and array reconfiguration.

Acknowledgements

This work was supported in part under ARPA contracts N00014-91-J-1698 and DABT63-92-C-0039. Thomas Knight, Jr., Michael Bolotski, and Ian Eslick provided valuable input to the development and presentation of these ideas.

References

[1] Anant Agarwal, Beng-Hong Lim, David Kranz, and John Kubiatowicz. APRIL: A Processor Architecture for Multiprocessing. In *Proceedings of the 17th International Symposium on Computer Architecture*, pages 104–114. IEEE, May 1990.

[2] Algotronix Ltd., Edinburgh, UK. *The Configurable Logic Data Book*, 1990.

[3] Thomas Anderson, Henry Levy, Brian Bershad, and Edward Lazowska. The Interaction of Architectures and Operating System Design. In *Fourth International Conference on Architectural Support for Programming Languages*, pages 108–120. ACM, April 1991.

[4] P. Bertin, D. Roncin, and J. Vuillemin. Programmable Active Memories: A Performance Assessment. Prl report, DEC Paris Reserch Laboratory, 85, Av. Victor Hugo, 92563 Rueil-Malmaison Cedex, France, June 1992.

[5] Patrice Bertin, Didier Roncin, and Jean Vuillemin. Introduction to Programmable Active Memories. PRL Report 3, DEC Paris Reserch Laboratory, 85, Av. Victor Hugo, 92563 Rueil-Malmaison Cedex, France, June 1989.

[6] Michael Bolotski, André DeHon, and Thomas F. Knight Jr. Unifying FPGAs and SIMD Arrays. Transit Note 95, MIT Artificial Intelligence Laboratory, September 1993.

[7] D. A. Buell. A Splash 2 Tutorial. Technical Report SRC-TR-92-087, Supercomputing Research Center, Bowie, Maryland, December 1992.

[8] Robert P. Colwell. Latent Design Faults in the Development of Multiflow's TRACE/200. In *Proceedings*

of The Twenty-Second International Symposium on Fault Tolerant Computing Systems, pages 468–474. IEEE Computer Society, July 1992.

[9] Steven A. Cuccaro and Craig F. Reese. The CM-2X: A Hybrid CM-2/Xilinx Prototype. In Duncan A. Buell and Kenneth L. Pocek, editors, *Proceedings of the IEEE Workshop on FPGAs for Custom Computing Machines*, pages 121–130, Los Alamitos, California, April 1993. IEEE Computer Society, IEEE Computer Society Press.

[10] William J. Dally et al. The Message-Driven Processor: A Multicomputer Processing Node with Efficient Mechanisms. *IEEE Micro*, pages 23–39, April 1992.

[11] Frederick Furtek. Arithmetic Benchmarks for the CLi6000. In Duncan A. Buell and Kenneth L. Pocek, editors, *Proceedings of the IEEE Workshop on FPGAs for Custom Computing Machines*, Los Alamitos, California, April 1993. IEEE Computer Society, IEEE Computer Society Press. Paper does not appear in printed proceedings; contact author `fred@clogic.com`.

[12] Maya Gokhale, William Holmes, Andrew Kopser, Sara Lucas, Ronald Minnich, Douglas Sweely, and Daniel Lopresti. Building and Using a Highly Programmable Logic Array. *IEEE Computer*, 24(1):81–89, January 1991.

[13] Maya Gokhale and Ron Minnich. FPGA Computing in a Data Parallel C. In Duncan A. Buell and Kenneth L. Pocek, editors, *Proceedings of the IEEE Workshop on FPGAs for Custom Computing Machines*, pages 94–101, Los Alamitos, California, April 1993. IEEE Computer Society, IEEE Computer Society Press.

[14] Dzung T. Hoang. Searching Genetic Databases on Splash 2. In Duncan A. Buell and Kenneth L. Pocek, editors, *Proceedings of the IEEE Workshop on FPGAs for Custom Computing Machines*, pages 185–191, Los Alamitos, California, April 1993. IEEE Computer Society, IEEE Computer Society Press.

[15] Intel Corporation. *A90960CA16,S V594 A-4 Stepping, Errors and Exceptions*, rev. 2 edition, April 1990.

[16] Daniel Lopresti. Rapid Implementation of a Genetic Sequence Comparator Using Field-Programmable Logic Arrays. In Carlo H. Séquin, editor, *Advanced Research in VLSI*, pages 138–152, Cambridge, MA, April 1991. MIT Press.

[17] Wayne Luk, Vincent Lok, and Ian Page. Hardware Acceleration of Divide-and-Conquer Paradigms: a Case Study. In Duncan A. Buell and Kenneth L. Pocek, editors, *Proceedings of the IEEE Workshop on FPGAs for Custom Computing Machines*, pages 192–1201, Los Alamitos, California, April 1993. IEEE Computer Society, IEEE Computer Society Press.

[18] et. al. M. Gokhale. SPLASH: A Reconfigurable Linear Logic Array. In *Proceedings of the International Conference on Parallel Processing*, pages 526–532, August 1990.

[19] Rishiyur S. Nikhil, Gregory M. Papadopoulous, and Arvind. *T: A Multithreaded Massively Parallel Architecture. In *Proceedings of the 19th International Symposium on Computer Architecture*. ACM, May 1992.

[20] M. Shand and J. Vuillemin. Fast Implementations of RSA Cryptography. In Earl Swartzlander Jr., Mary Jane Irwin, and Graham Julien, editors, *Proceedings of the 11th Symposium on Computer Arithmetic*, pages 252–259, Los Alamitos, California, June 1993. IEEE Computer Society, IEEE Computer Society Press.

[21] Harvey F. Silverman. Processor Reconfiguration Through Instruction-Set Metamorphosis. *IEEE Computer*, 26(3):11–18, March 1993.

[22] M. Wazlowski, L. Agarwal, T. Lee, A. Smith, E. Lam, P. Athanas, H. SIlverman, and S. Ghosh. PRISM-II Compiler and Architecture. In Duncan A. Buell and Kenneth L. Pocek, editors, *Proceedings of the IEEE Workshop on FPGAs for Custom Computing Machines*, pages 9–16, Los Alamitos, California, April 1993. IEEE Computer Society, IEEE Computer Society Press.

[23] Xilinx, Inc., 2100 Logic Drive, San Jose, CA 95124. *The Programmable Gate Array Databook*, 1989.

[24] Xilinx, Inc., 2100 Logic Drive, San Jose, CA 95124. *Product Description and Selection Guide*, April 1993.

Field Programmable Gate Array Based Reconfigurable Preprocessor

Brian Box

Lockheed Sanders
NCA01-2244 CS 868
Nashua, N.H. 03060

Abstract:

Preprocessing has typically been an application area where programmable solutions have been unable to meet the required performance. Custom hardware implementations of preprocessors, however, are seldom reusable, flexible enough to allow algorithm exploration or quickly realized. The Configurable Hardware Algorithm Mappable Preprocessor (CHAMP) technology is a solution to these problems.

Recent developments in Field Programmable Gate Array (FPGA) hardware and software have made a reconfigurable preprocessor with custom hardware performance but generic hardware flexibility possible. The key advancements are larger, faster RAM and Electrically Erasable devices, routers with deadline timers, and synthesis tools which can work with user definable macros. Ongoing work in the areas of partitioning, synthesis, placement, packaging and compilation will make reconfigurable preprocessors more powerful.

The present CHAMP implementation is based on Xilinx FPGAs. Its architecture consists of multiple reconfigurable processing elements connected through both a ring network and a global crossbar network. It is packaged as a VME 6Ux160 slave board with two high speed reconfigurable parallel interfaces. In order to allow development at the algorithm level while retaining preprocessor performance, off-the-shelf development tools have been integrated with a custom library of macros (the firm macro library) as part of the CHAMP design process.

As a verification of the CHAMP technology, an advanced IRMW application was mapped onto the CHAMP architecture achieving greater than 1 BOPS of real time throughput while utilizing 75% of the CHAMP board's processing resources. The current CHAMP design process will be evolved into a more automated process by taking advantage of new tools as they become available which will further enhance the value of this technology.

1.0 Introduction

A reconfigurable board which provides custom hardware performance would have a wide range applications. A board which can do everything is still, however, beyond the current capability of technology but a reconfigurable board targeted toward preprocessing algorithm implementations is now possible. The Configurable Hardware Algorithm Mappable Preprocessor (CHAMP) technology, which is being developed by Wright Labs AAAT and Lockheed Sanders, is reconfigurable hardware targeted towards the implementation of preprocessor algorithms.

This paper will introduce IRMW preprocessors, FPGAs, and then the goal of the CHAMP technology. The second section concentrates on the decisions that were made in terms of implementing technology, architecture and design process. The final section discusses some results and future plans.

1.1 Nature of IRMW Preprocessors

The processing of images such as for Infrared Missile Warning (IRMW) requires highly parallel processing to deal with the large amount of real-time data. The initial processing of this data which is typically performed with customized hardware is preprocessing. The customized hardware performs data independent real-time processing functions which are not feasible with general purpose processors. Current state-of-the-art sensors can sample at 1000 frames per second and for a 128 X 128 image that results in 16M pixels per second [1]. Many IRMW algorithms require more than 70 operations per pixel which translates to a throughput of more than 1 Billion Operations Per Second (BOPS) which is beyond

---

This research was supported in part by U.S. Air Force contract No. F33615-92-c-1093

0-8186-5490-2/94 $03.00 © 1994 IEEE

any practical implementation using general purpose processors.

A generic IRMW algorithm is shown in Figure 1.

Figure 1: Generic IRMW Preprocessor Algorithm

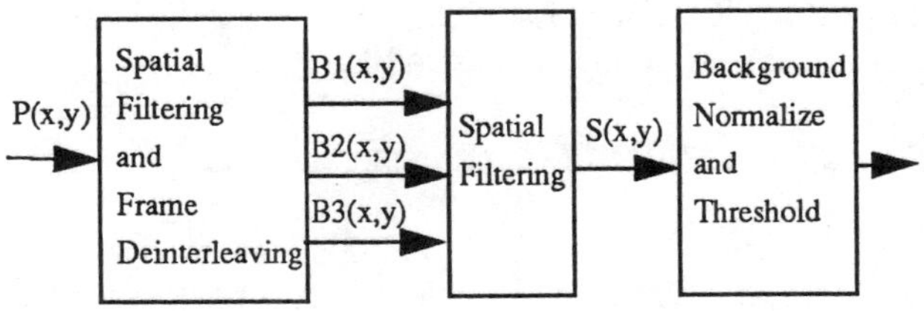

This algorithm and most IRMW preprocessor algorithms are data independent and so perform the same function on each pixel regardless of the values of the pixel data. The key elements are spatial filtering, spectral filtering and background normalization. Each element can take on one of several different filter types. For example, the spatial filter could be a Laplacian, median or morphological filter and could work on windows of 3 X 3, 5 X 5 or 7 X 7 pixels. In the past, changing between these configurations, for performing algorithm investigation or demonstration, involved the development of new custom hardware.

1.2 Introduction to FPGAs

Field Programmable Gate Arrays (FPGAs) offer hardware programmability with custom hardware performance. FPGA devices, available today, have capacities up to 20K gates and which can be configured to perform application specific functions. FPGAs are made of smaller logic blocks each of which is (depending on the technology and how it is utilized) between 1 and 160 gates. FPGAs have, for more than 8 years, been providing custom hardware performance on the single device level.

To apply FPGAs to a problem like preprocessing, a number of FPGAs have to work together and the design tools for applications requiring multiple FPGA designs are not yet sufficiently effective. Many designs using multiple FPGA have been done but most are manually partitioned by the designer. In fact, to date, most of the high level FPGA design work (synthesis, partitioning, mapping) has been done without using automated tools.

Recently, advances in the areas of FPGA synthesis, layout, partitioning, routing and FPGA densities have made a reconfigurable preprocessing board possible. Synthesis tools are now available which will allow the designer to specify a custom set of macros to be used by the tool (i.e. Synopsys's Designware Developer). Significant work on FPGA partitioners are beginning to yield results (i.e. University of Cincinnati, North Carolina State University). Deadline timers which are routing tools which place and route the FPGA based on the desired clock rate are available (i.e. Xilinx and Neocad). Tools which will then optimize a design by moving logic from one side of a flip-flop to the other are also available (i.e. Actel's Acsel). Most importantly is the advent of significantly larger FPGAs offering densities in excess of 13,000 gates and with plans in 1994 for devices in excess of 20,000 gates.

1.3 Goal of CHAMP

Simply put, the goal of the CHAMP program is to create a reconfigurable preprocessor which is directly mappable from algorithms. The preprocessor should be reconfigurable, in system, in a fraction of a second so that it can be reconfigured even during a mission. The mapping should be done, ultimately, with fully automated tools.

The requirements for the implementing technology, board architecture and design process were derived through the examination of several preprocessor algorithms. The minimum processing requirement was 1 BOPS. The minimum input data rate required was 25 MHz and the minimum data processing rate was 16 MHz. The minimum input data width was 16 bits and the internal precision requirements varied, with some as high as 64 bits. The types of operations included additions, subtractions, multiplications, divisions, comparisons and multiplexing as parts of filters operating on 3 X 3, 5 X 5 and 7 X 7 windows of data.

2.0 CHAMP Implementation Technology Selection

The implementing technology selection drove both the architecture and design process selection and so needed to be first.The choices for implementing logic technology were discrete digital circuitry (SSI and MSI), Programmable Logic Devices (PLDs), microprocessors, and Application Specific Integrated Circuits (ASICs). The Architectures these would be used with were (at a high level) either a sea of logic resources which would be combined dynamically to form the necessary functions; a set of completed functions which the data would be fed to in a programmable sequence; a group of processors each of which could perform many different functions and could be programmed as needed; or some combination of the three architectures.

A PLD implementation would be the best solution for a dynamically programmable sea of logic resources because PLDs have both logic and interconnect resources which can be configured for a variety of applications and there are many tools to support both single and multiple device designs. An ASIC implementation would be the best solution for a set of fixed functions because an ASIC can efficiently implement many fixed functions of adder, multiplier or divider complexity. An implementation based on microprocessors would be the best solution for the large processor type architecture because microprocessors are efficient implementations of powerful general purpose, software programmable solutions. The discrete logic implementation was not the best solution for any of the architectures and so was eliminated from consideration.

The selection of the implementing technology was then combined with the selection of the high level architecture. The criteria for the decision came from the examination of the preprocessor algorithms and the CHAMP goals. The criteria was: expandability, utilization, ability to perform the functions, ability to meet the necessary performance, existence of tools to map algorithms to the board or devices, complexity of the necessary process for mapping algorithms to the board, ability to deal with surprises (exceedances of the minimum requirements), and reconfigurability. All the solutions were believed to be able to meet the criteria. The selection was based on how well each of them met the criteria. The evaluation of how each measured against the evaluating criteria was based on experience with each technology and estimations of how it would perform in the high level architectures. Table 1 indicates the relative strengths of each approach versus the criteria.

Table 1: Implementation Technology Selection

Criteria	ASIC	Micro-processor	PLD	Discrete
Expandability		+	+	-
Utilization		-		-
Funtions	+	+		+
Performance	+			+
Tools for algo-rithm mapping	=	+		
Complexity of Process			-	
Surprises	-	-	+	-
Reconfigur-ability		+	+	-

The decision was made to use PLDs based on their flexibility in dealing with new functions, the existence of design tools and processes, their reconfigurability and their ability to meet the performance requirements. The decision of homogeneous versus heterogeneous was decided in favor of homogeneous because it would result in a more straightforward design process and would reduce the risk of inefficiencies due to having inappropriate resources for a function. Other types of processing, it was decided, could be accomplished with other boards or through the use of daughter cards

2.1 CHAMP PLD Technology Selection

The choices for which type of PLD to use included RAM based FPGAs, One Time Programmable (OTP) fuse or anti-fuse based FPGAs and PLDs, Electrically Erasable (EE) FPGAs, and Ultra Violet (UV) erasable PLDs. The criteria for selecting the PLD technology were ease of reconfigurability, available devices at high densities, effectiveness of the design processes, and effectiveness at performing the required functions. The evaluation was based on experience with PLDs of each type. Table 2 indicates the relative strengths of each approach versus the criteria. The decision to go with RAM based FPGAs was an obvious one. EE devices did not exist at high enough densities and removing the OTP and UV erasable from the board for reconfiguration was not a serious consideration.

Table 2: PLD Technoloy Selection

Criteria	RAM	UV Eraseable	Elecrically Eraseable	One Time Program-mable
Density	+		-	+
Funtions	+			+
Effectiveness of Process	-	+		
Reprogram-mability	+	-	+	-

The next decision was which RAM based FPGA technology to use. The candidates were Xilinx 2000 series, Xilinx 3000 series, Xilinx 4000 series, Atmel AT6000 series, AT&T ORCA, and Altera Flex 8000. The criteria for this decision were the effectiveness of the design process, available devices at high densities, third party tool support, effectiveness at implementing the functions and effectiveness at pipelining. The evaluation was based on experience with each FPGA type or through discussions with FPGA designers who had experience with the devices. Table 3 indicates the relative strengths of each technology versus the criteria.

The decision to use Xilinx 4000 series FPGAs was based on the available devices, the efficiency of implementing pipelines with the Configurable Logic Blocks (CLBs) used as RAM, and the ability to perform the necessary functions. The device and package were then easily selected. The XC4013 (a device rated at 13,000 gates with 576 CLBs) was the largest Xilinx 4000 series device available and, since the board needed to be double sided in order to meet the processing density, the MQ208 (a 208 pin metal quad flat pack) was selected.

Table 3: RAM Based FPGA Technoloy Selection

Criteria	Xilinx 2K	Xilinx 3K	Xilinx 4K	Atmel AT6000	AT&T ORCA	Altera Flex 8K
Density	-		+			+
Third Party Tools		+	+			
Effective-ness of Process	-	-				+
Functions	-		+		+	+
Pipelining			++	+	++	

2.2 CHAMP Architecture Selection

Once the sea of logic resources architecture was selected, it was necessary to decide what basic structure would connect the resources. One possibility was to connect the XC4013s in a fixed pattern such as a ring or hypercube. The other end of the spectrum was to employ global crossbar and be able to select any pattern of communication. The key advantage of the fixed interconnect pattern was efficiency because the resource could be used for interconnection or processing as needed. The disadvantages included the possibility that data would have to be pipelined through several devices to reach its destination consuming large amounts of the precious Input Output Blocks (IOBs) on each device and that performing a poor job on the enormous partitioning task could lead to insurmountable inefficiencies. The key advantages of the crossbar interconnection are the efficient use of the IOBs since the data can travel, using the crossbar, directly to its destination, and the reduction in the complexity of the required partitioner since it wouldn't care which function a device performs relative to its neighbors only that the IOB and CLB resources are not exceeded by the functional requirements. The main disadvantage is the amount of resources being dedicated to interconnection and not processing.

Based on the algorithms that were examined, a compromise between the fixed and crossbar interconnect schemes was selected. The compromise traded some processing resources for purely interconnect resources but also required that the processing resources perform some of the interconnection. The key disadvantage remained the complexity of the partitioning task. The algorithms that were examined indicated that most were made of sections which communicated to each other with 32 bits or less of data and that the implementing of these sections typically required between 250 and 1000 CLBs. Internal to the sections, the data could become very wide (as much as 64 bits). It was determined that a goal of the architecture should be to contain these sections in processing elements and then use the fixed and crossbar interconnects for interconnecting the processing elements.

Some of the sections of the algorithms required frame to frame interaction. As a frame of data (as large as 16K words) is too large to be stored in an XC4013, external RAM was needed to support the processing logic. Since the algorithms were data independent, a RAM with 2 independent ports was the perfect solution. The amount of data storage that was needed relative to the number of processing resources was roughly 1 frame of data for every 1000 CLBs. So a dual port RAM of size 16K by 32 bits was associated with each processing element containing 2 XC4013s. The CHAMP Processing Element (PE) is shown in Figure 2.

Figure 2: CHAMP Processing Element

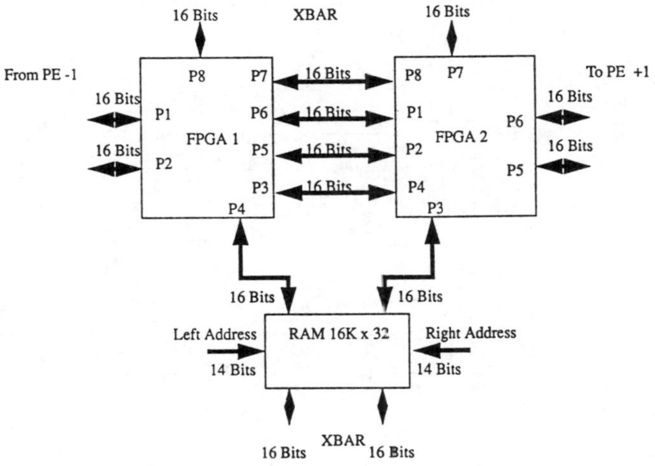

The driving factor in the control scheme was the dataflow nature of the algorithms which allowed the separation of the control and the data. The control which performs the addressing of the dual port RAMs and the starting and stopping of sections of the algorithm was placed in FPGAs external to the processing and interconnect devices. The control scheme includes counters for each address for the dual port RAMs, control for I/O with external boards and sensors and a 32 bit counter for starting "events" relative to a single start signal. The control strategy is shown in Figure 3. The separating of the processing and interconnect from the control reduces (slightly) the complexity of the partitioning task.

The options for implementing a RAM based crossbar included the Aptix technology, the Icube technology or FPGAs. The Aptix was very dense but not available in surface mount. The Icube was less dense but was available in surface mount. The winner, however, was the FPGA implementation because the others did not have internal flip-flops for clocking the data before connecting to the dual port RAMs. The FPGA technology was the least applicable to the interconnect task but because the access time of the dual port RAMs was the driving factor in the system performance (20 MHz even with no skew through the crossbar), the FPGA implementation was the best solution.

The present CHAMP implementation (shown in Figure 4) is a 6U VME board with 8 CHAMP PEs. It includes a large 3-port RAM (256K by 16) for the storage of multiple frames of data, a 16-bit high speed input interface, a high speed 16-bit output interface, a VME interface, and 4 32-bit sensor interfaces. There is, also, logic for the downloading of all the FPGAs using the VME interface (depending on VME performance, reconfiguration time is less than 50 msec.) except for the VME interface FPGA which is loaded from a serial prom.

2.3 CHAMP Design Process Selection

The design process has an input of the algorithm and an output of the programming necessary to make the board perform the algorithm at the required speed. CHAMP needed a design process that could be automated and could perform the task reliably. The steps in the design process were algorithm verification, synthesis, mapping, PE FPGA design, Control FPGA design, Interconnect FPGA design, and Board Verification.

The key element in the design process was the actual FPGA design process. The routing of the XC4013s could be accomplished by hand using Neocad's EPIC or Xilinx's XACT, or with the Neocad or Xilinx automated routing tools. Since hand routing can not be automated, it was eliminated. Essential to the automated routers meeting the performance requirements is a deadline timer. The Neocad router's deadline timer could not handle alternate edges of the clock (although it either does now or will soon) and so the Xilinx autorouter, PPR (Partition Place and Route), was the only option.

In order for the XC4013 to perform the necessary functions at the required speed, an internal feature known as fast carry logic needed to be used. The fast carry logic allows the high speed rippling (1.5 ns for 2 bits) of carries for adders, subtractors, counters etc.[2] The only methods of using fast carries and PPR together are through an XNF

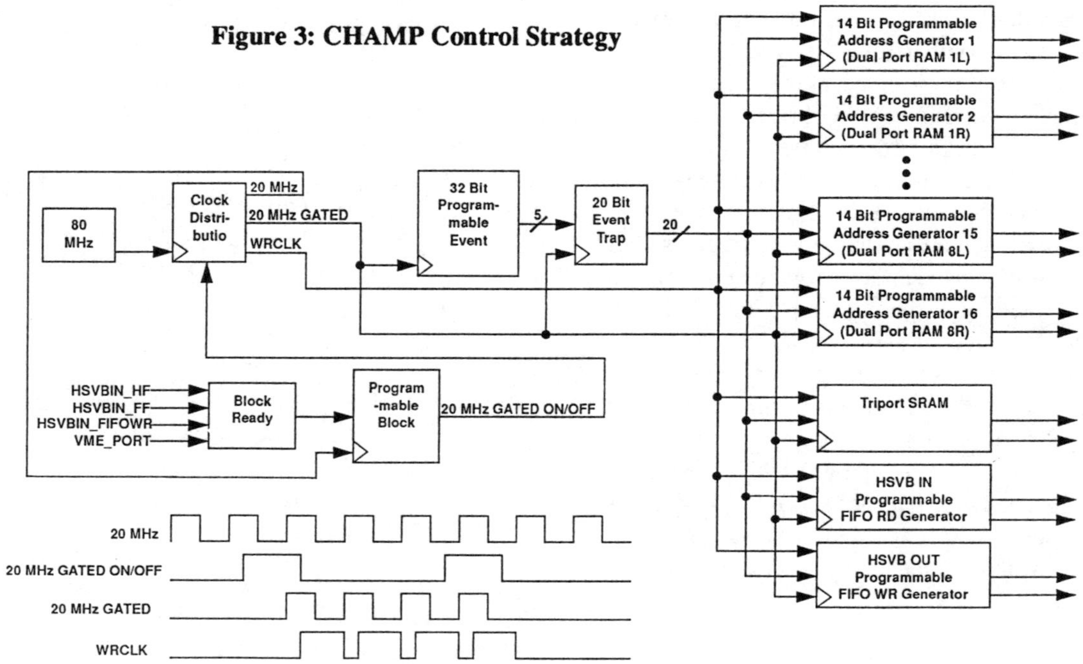

Figure 3: CHAMP Control Strategy

Figure 4: CHAMP Architecture

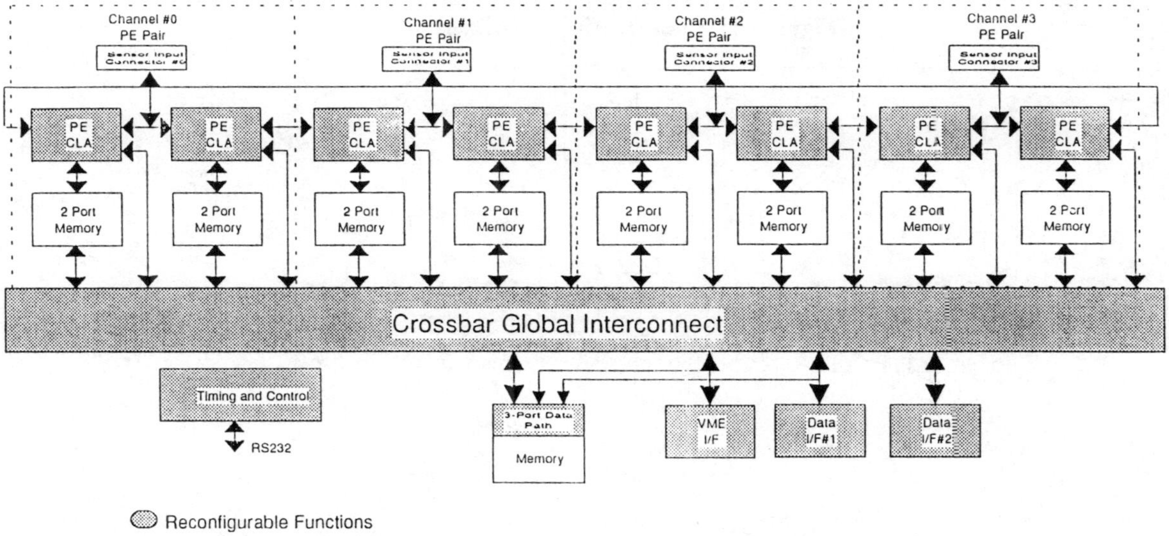

(Xilinx Netlist File) file created by either Xilinx's HMGEN, Xilinx's XBLOX or using Xilinx's hard macros. Since the functions necessary were not entirely supported by XBLOX or hard macros, HMGEN offered the only complete solution. Inefficiencies in the placement performed by the PPR tool were sufficient to prevent the necessary utilization of the XC4013s and so the placement of the CLBs had to be locked down before using PPR.

The HMGEN tool could perform this task but its input was an LCA file which would have to be generated in the XACT tool. The only way to automate the generation of an LCA file in XACT was by executing a batch file. We were forced to develop our own design process, which we called Firm Macros, for creating these executable batch files (EXC files). This process allows us to reuse a library of macros that we create which can range in size from 1 CLB to an entire XC4013. The EXC files are in ASCII and can be easily manipulated and created by an automated program (unlike a schematic). The present Firm Macro Library (FML) contains over 100 macros.

The front end of the design process (synthesis and mapping) has yet to be automated but there are tools available now which can be integrated to the FML and will lead to a seamless fully automated process. The top level CHAMP design process is shown in Figure 5.

Figure 5: CHAMP Design Process

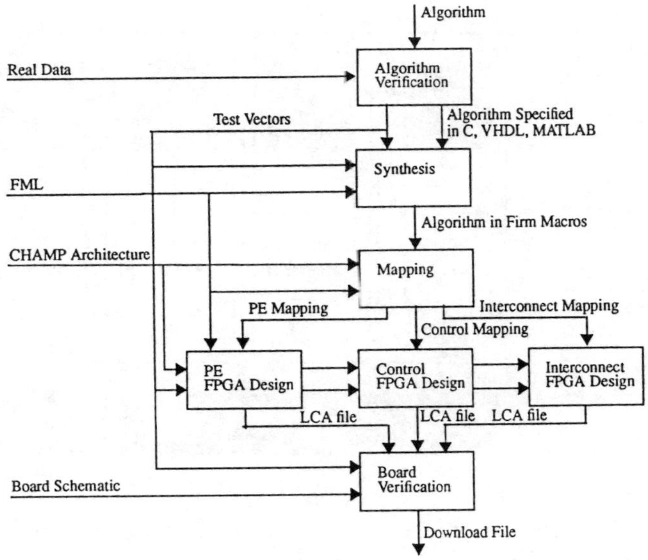

3.0 Mapping of a Sample Algorithm

The CHAMP architecture and preliminary design process were validated by the mapping of a challenging IRMW algorithm. The algorithm (shown in Figure 6) includes a high pass, spectral and median filters, a background normalizer and threshold detection. The IRMW algorithm was developed by Naval Research Laboratory. The IRMW data and algorithm analysis were provided by Wright Laboratory, Avionics Division. The high level functions include 3 X 3, 5 X 5 and 7 X 7 window operators, multipliers and a divider. The algorithm (shown in Figure 7) required 75% of the CHAMP processing CLBs when mapped onto the CHAMP architecture. The duplication of the front end of the algorithm is due to the need to process 2 separate input streams until they are combined in the spectral filter.

The mapping involved running the executable C code implementation of the algorithm to produce outputs which corresponded with the input data that was provided.

Figure 6: Demonstration IRMW Algorithm

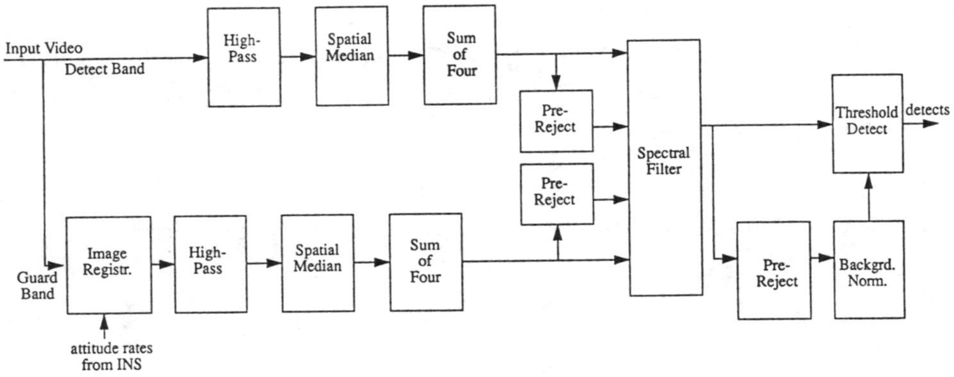

Figure 7: Algorithm Mapped on CHAMP

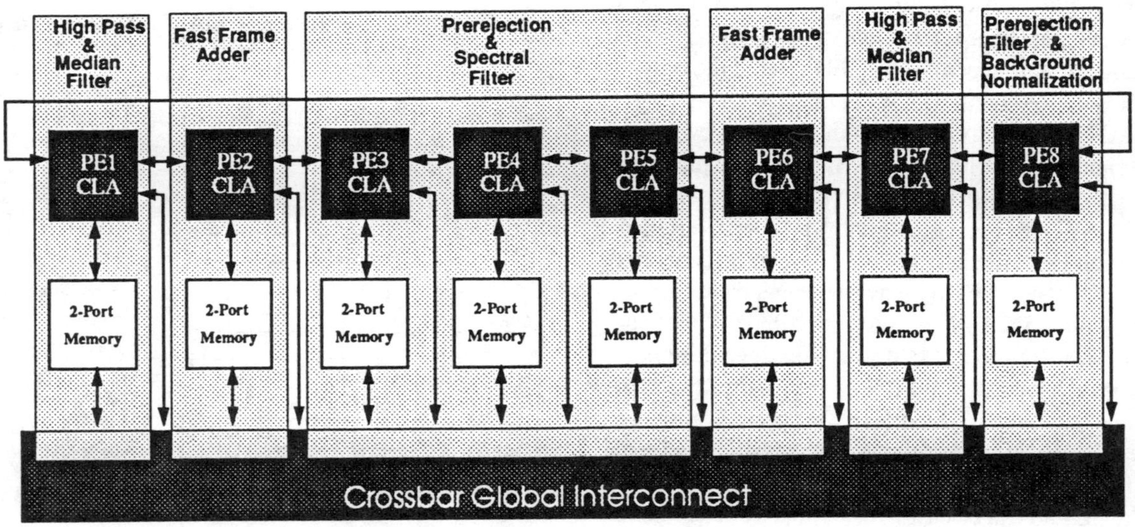

The algorithm was then rewritten in MATLAB so that the necessary internal precisions could be calculated and their effects on the output could be observed. The MATLAB simulations also created test vectors at internal points of the algorithm for verifying the individual FPGAs.

Then the algorithm was separated into sections (i.e. spectral filter, median filter, background normalizer) and each section was sized by adding the sizes of its component parts. The details of the mapping process are better illustrated by focusing on a single element of the algorithm.

3.1 Mapping Results for the Spatial Median Filter

The median filter works on the pixel (P(i,j)) and its 8 nearest neighbors. The nearest neighbor pixels are sorted from lowest to highest as (x(1), x(2), ...,x(8)), then the result D(i,j) is:

$$D(i,j) = P(i,j) - (x(4)+x(5))/2.$$

An efficient implementation of this [3] is shown in Figure 8. Pipelining for aligning data is accomplished by using the delay macro. Due to timing and routing

Figure 8: Spatial Median Filter

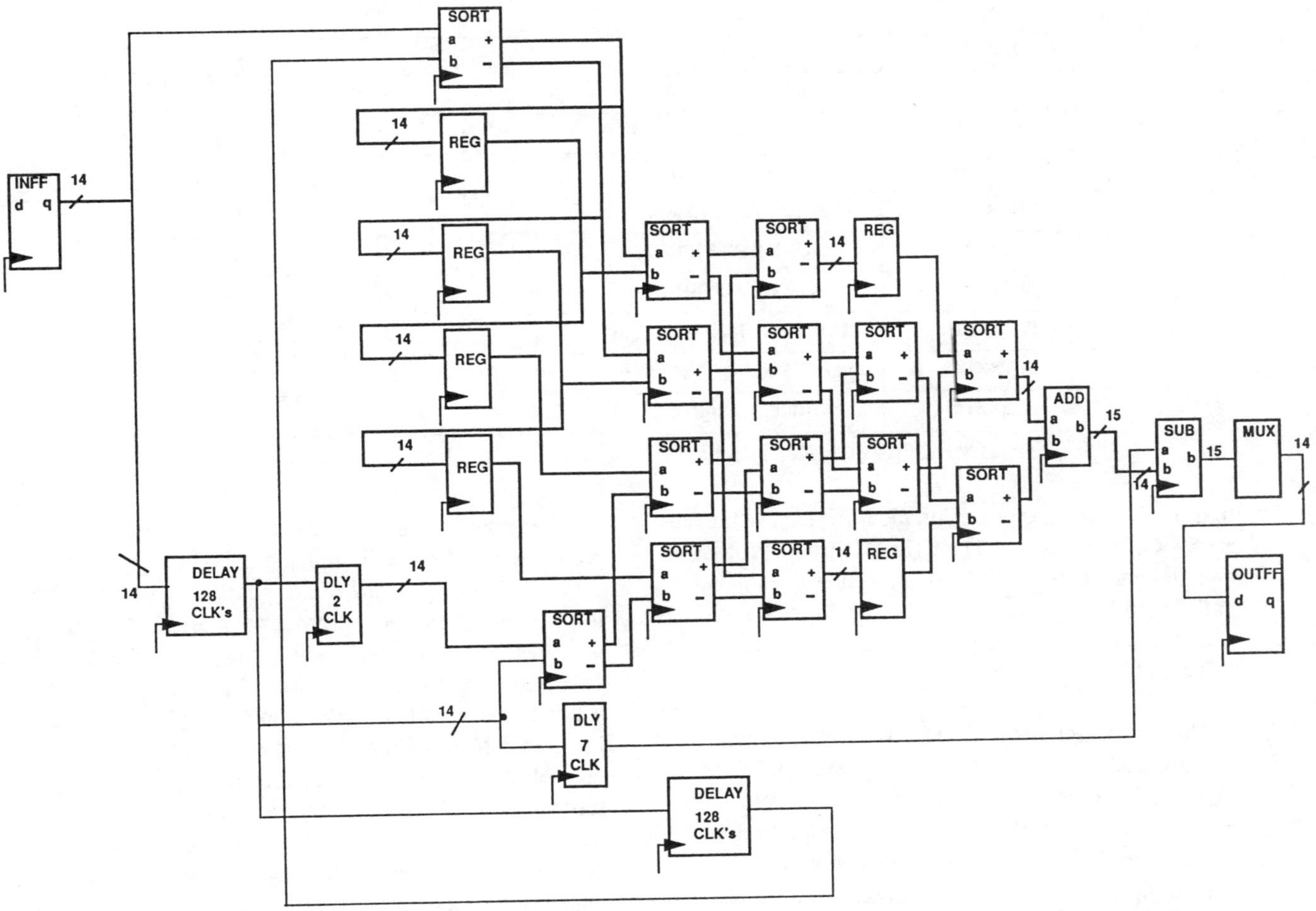

conciderations, the maximum delay macro is 32 clocks, and larger delays are made of several of these smaller macros. For reasons of implementation efficiency, a comparator and multiplexer which work together to form a sort function are combined in the same group of CLBs and are 1 macro known as a sort macro. There are 3 types of sort macros: sort out high (output is the highest of the input busses), sort out low (output is the lowest of the input busses), and sort out both (both higher and lower outputs are available). The macros used by the spatial median filter and their CLB sizes are shown in Table 4. This function performs 960 MOPS running at 20 MHz [1], requires 387 CLBs, and is roughly 24,920 gates. It requires 387 of the 1152 processing CLBs of 1 PE or about 4.2% of the processing resources on the CHAMP board.

Once the size of the function is determined, with the present design process, the placement of the macros in the FPGA is done by hand, meaning that the locations of the macros are calculated by a designer. This task takes about 45 minutes for a very experienced FPGA designer.

Assuming the macros being used exist, the creating of the EXC file by using a text editor to merge the appropriate macro text files takes another 45 minutes. The rest of the process (executing the EXC file, running HMGEN, and PPR) is automated and requires 2 more hours on a 486DX266 PC. It is worth noting that before running HMGEN on an XC4013, a simple translation program must be run to make the LCA file compatible.

3.2 CHAMP Status

As of January of 1994, the design of the CHAMP board is completed and it is in the fabrication process. The CHAMP concept will be first demonstrated in March 1994 with a configuration that implements the IRMW algorithm. The application of the CHAMP technology to a wide range of other algorithms is being explored. The FML has over 100 macros to date and is actively being used by several Lockheed Sanders programs. More macros are being added by these and other programs on a

Table 4: Spatial Median Filter CLB Count

MACRO NAME	DESCRIPTION	NUMBER OF MACROS	NUMBER OF CLB'S/ MACRO	TOTAL
ADDXXT1	14 BIT, ADDER	1	8	8
DLYXXT4	14 BIT 02-CLK DELAY	1	9	9
DLYXXT5	14 BIT 07-CLK DELAY	1	9	9
DLYXXT6	14 BIT 32-CLK DELAY	8	17	136
MUXXXT9	14 BIT, 2:1 RAILING MUX	1	7	7
REGXXT3	14 BIT, REGISTER	6	7	42
SRTXXT2	14 BIT, SORT-OUT-HIGH	3	8	24
SRTXXT3	14 BIT, SORT-OUT-LOW	3	8	24
SRTXXT4	14 BIT, SORT-OUT-BOTH	8	15	120
SUBXXT1	14 BIT, SUBTRACTOR	1	8	8

TOTAL CLB COUNT FOR THIS FUNCTION IS..387

regular basis. Some designs using the FML have achieved over 96% CLB utilization. The CHAMP design process is being automated through the use of a synthesis tool and potential partitioning tools are under consideration.

3.3 CHAMP Future

The application scope of the CHAMP technology will continue to grow. New PEs can be developed for the CHAMP architecture which will increase the application potential of the CHAMP technology. A second PE type with increased RAM and data dependent control is being planned to optimize other signal processing functions, such as histogramming, typically required for electronic warfare applications. The development of daughter cards which would provide the CHAMP card with direct interfaces to standard high speed busses like Turbo Channel and Mercury Computer's RACEway is being considered. The CHAMP technology can be put on an MCM to increase the processing density and reduce system cost. The efforts to complete the automation of the CHAMP design process will continue. More tools and FPGAs will be incorporated as better ones become available.

3.4 Conclusion

FPGA technology has advanced to the point of making reconfigurable boards for real-time preprocessing possible. The CHAMP technology has taken advantage of the technological advances and combined an optimal architecture with a design process allowing superior results to make a reconfigurable preprocessor not just a possible solution but a preferred solution to many preprocessor algorithm implementations.

CHAMP offers the rapid prototyping of algorithms for proposals, demonstrations, and experiments and provides many obvious benefits in terms of reduced design schedules, design costs, and risk. One less obvious benefit, is the benefit to software development of having hardware to aid in debugging far earlier in the design cycle. Another possible advantage of CHAMP technology, is having the same CHAMP hardware perform a different function for each phase of a mission thus dramatically reducing cost, size, weight and power while increasing the flexibility, upgradabilty, functionality, reliability and maintainability of the system. As the tool, FPGA, packaging, and RAM technologies improve the CHAMP technology will offer a solution to an even wider range of problems.

Bibliography

1. Lazarus, R.B. and Meyer, F.M., "Realization of a Dynamically Reconfigurable Preprocessor," Proc. of IEEE National Aerospace and Electronics Conference, May 1993.

2. The Programmable Logic Data Book, Xilinx Inc., 1993.

3. Knuth, D.E., "Sorting and Searching," Volume 3 of The Art of Computer Programming, Addison-Wesley, 1973.

Virtual Hardware for Graphics Applications Using FPGAs

Satnam Singh

Dept. Computing Science
The University of Glasgow
Glasgow G12 8QQ
United Kingdom
Email: satnam@dcs.glasgow.ac.uk

Pierre Bellec

R&D (FPGA Group)
Compass Design Automation
Sophia Antipolis
France
Email: bellec@compass.fr

Abstract

The suitability of FPGA devices for implementing graphics algorithms is analysed by a series of experiments. The performance of simple and complicated graphics algorithms on two kinds of FPGAs are compared with the performance of existing custom graphics chips and against general purpose processors with specialised instruction sets. Various architectures for incorporating FPGA based systems into graphics workstations are discussed. Finally, a new design method (based on virtual memory) is presented that exploits the dynamically reconfigurable nature of FPGAs.

1 Introduction

Are FPGAs a suitable technology for realising graphics algorithms in hardware? A preliminary attempt to answer this question is the subject of this report. Existing graphics hardware falls broadly into two categories. The trade-offs between the two techniques are characterised by speed and flexibility considerations. Some graphics chips are designed specifically to perform a limited number of graphics operations very quickly, e.g. the IBM 8514/A. At the other end of the spectrum are general purpose processors with instruction sets specialised for graphics operations, e.g. the Texas TMS34020. Custom designed graphics chips execute faster than general purpose graphics processors, but lack their flexibility.

The primary advantage of using FPGAs in many applications is their ease of reconfiguration. To be viable in the graphics devices market, FPGA based graphics hardware has to execute faster than general purpose graphics processors, which offer a higher degree of flexibility. FPGA solutions cannot hope to match the performance of custom VLSI graphics chips, but FPGAs can offer superior flexibility. Is there a sufficient gap between the existing graphics hardware technologies to accommodate FPGA based graphics systems?

This report presents the results of using Xilinx and Altera FPGAs to realise typical graphics operations like circle drawing. This provides data for comparison with custom graphics chips. We have also implemented algorithms for rendering shaded images of solid spheres. Such complex graphics algorithms permit performance comparisons with general purpose graphics processors. Our findings are very encouraging, showing that FPGAs have sufficient density to absorb complicated graphics algorithms yet still provide real time rendering of shaded solids on large colour displays.

We also report on our experience of using a commercial CAD system for the design entry, place and route, simulation and testing of graphics algorithms. We discuss the problems of trying to achieve device independence and present some of the drawbacks of existing FPGA software with an ASIC heritage. The automatic layout is examined with a view to better exploiting the resources available on FPGA devices.

Multi-media applications now require high performance from microcomputers for the processing of animation and sound. Related multi-media support services like real-time data compression and decompression are also required. All of these operations can be performed in software if the processor (and the rest of the system) are fast enough. Designing a specific set of chips to support these operations would result in much higher performance but this approach is expensive. If a new data compression technique is to be used, then this change is difficult to accommodate. What is required is easily modified on reconfigurable hardware which is flexible enough to implement a variety of tasks. In recent years special purpose processing of this nature has been the realm of ASIC devices. A case in point is the new Atari Jaguar system that uses ASIC technology for its graphics chips. FPGAs may be able to penetrate this part of the ASIC market, providing cheaper and more flexible solutions.

Having performed the empirical analysis of specific graphics algorithms on FPGAs, we then propose a variety of architectures for incorporating FPGA based graphics systems into graphics workstations. An FPGA based graphics system could provide a rich collection of graphics commands that extend the instruction set of the host processor. To cope with the idea of implementing very large and complex circuits that perform a disparate set of operations, we introduce the notion of *virtual hardware*. This is a methodology for structuring large designs so that they can execute on a shared and limited physical resource. This methodology has become viable only because of the dynamically reconfigurable nature of FPGA devices and promises exciting and unusual execution models for this kind of hardware. We show how this approach can be applied to the design of a very large graphics circuit which can execute on a small number of FPGAs.

2 Graphics hardware

A typical architecture for a colour graphics workstation consists of a bus shared by a general purpose processor (e.g. a SPARC CPU), the primary memory (a dozen or so megabytes, e.g. 24MB) and input/output peripherals. One important output device is the video controller chip (e.g. the Hitachi 6845) which translates an area of memory designated as the *framestore* into a sequence of RGB and synchronisation signals which are in turn sent to a colour monitor. Graphics applications 'draw' by modifying the framestore, which can be viewed logically as a 2D array of pixel colours.

Graphics operations require a very large number of memory accesses to the framestore to deliver an acceptable level of performance. The video controller reads through the entire framestore and computes RGB signals for one frame every 0.013 seconds for a 75Hz display. Often the processor and video controller are attempting concurrent access to the framestore over the shared system bus, with degraded performance. Bus arbitration usually favours the video controller since it has a real-time deadline to meet. Dual-ported video memory chips (VRAMs) (e.g. Texas TMS34082) allow independent access for the processor and video controller, thus reducing bus acquisition clashes.

Graphics operations can also be computationally intensive. Drawing a line typically takes two or three additions and one test and two jumps for each pixel. Drawing a filled circle of radius r pixels will require $2r$ lines to be drawn with approximately πr^2 pixel write operations. To relieve the main processor from the burden of performing these calculations and making these frequent memory accesses, this work can be off-loaded to a graphics co-processor chip. Graphics processors usually provide support for basic 2D operations like line drawing and filling polygons. The framestore can be connected to the graphics processor on a separate bus from the main processor. An example of a graphics processor is the IBM 8514/A graphics processor [1]. This completely relieves the host system from performing time-consuming memory-address calculations.

The Texas Instruments' TMS34020 Peripheral Display Processor is an example of a fully programmable 32-bit processor with an instruction set specialised for graphics operations. Coupled with a Texas TMS34082 this system can rapidly perform 3D geometric transformations and clipping required for 3D graphics. The TMS34020 can use VRAM for the framestore and DRAM for program and code storage. Both memory subsystems are accessed over the same bus. The chip also on provides timers to produce video scanout and DRAM refresh signals.

The TMS34020 provides an elegant method for accessing pixmaps by their (x, y) coordinates, the translation to the framestore address being performed automatically. The chip can copy 8-bit pixels, automatically performing aligning, masking and clipping of rows of pixels. The transfer rate of the device approaches the bandwidth of the system's full memory (18 million pixels per second). A draw and advance instruction (DRAV) draws a pixel and advances the (x, y) coordinate in parallel. Used for the inner loop of the midpoint circle algorithm this device can draw 2 million pixels per second.

3 Graphics algorithms on FPGAs

The implementation of several graphics algorithms is described. The algorithms are chosen to invite comparison with custom graphics chips and with general purpose processors that have specialised graphics instruction sets.

The algorithms were developed using a version of the Ruby algebraic hardware description language [2]. This language describes behaviour *and* topology using basic but powerful features of relational calculus. Circuits are composed with combinators that specify not only the behaviour of the composite component but also its layout. This language has been successfully used to develop many designs for the Algotronix range of CAL1024 FPGA devices by Wayne Luk [3]. A system called NSI [4] allows circuit layouts to be automatically extracted from a subset of Ruby behavioural descriptions [5].

Our variant of the Ruby language is implemented in the purely functional lazy programming language Haskell. This general purpose language provides a powerful type system that allows very generic circuits to be specified and a class system which can be used to conveniently structure large circuits. We have written translators from our Ruby representation into various VHDL [6] subsets. First, the designs were translated into a subset acceptable by the Alliance V1.9 VHDL compiler and simulator tools. After preliminary tests, the translator was retargeted to produce a subset acceptable by the Compass VHDL compiler. This description is then processed by the Compass design tools to produce netlists; perform placement and routing; programming and then testing.

We have chosen three graphics operations of varying computational intensity. The first algorithm is the standard midpoint circle algorithm [7] which draws the outline of a circle. This algorithm is representative of many other kinds of graphics operations like line drawing. The 'C' code for this algorithm is shown below. The circle outline is given by successive (*x*,*y*) coordinates and *r* is the radius.

```
d = 3 - 2*r ;
while (x < y)
{ if (d < 0) d += 4*x +6 ;
  else { d += 4*(x-y) +10; y--; }
  x++ ; }
```

The second algorithm we consider is drawing a solid circle. This is again based on the midpoint circle algorithm but involves filling a region. Finally, we analyse the performance of the fast spheres algorithm for rendering shaded spheres [8]. We have implemented and analysed the optimised version of this algorithm. Tests are still under way on the generalised fast spheres algorithm. A head on view of a shaded sphere (in greyscale) is shown in Figure 1. This algorithm represents a much more complex class of algorithms that are rarely found in hardware, although fast spheres [9] has been implemented on the Pixel-Planes system [10]. Pixel-Planes can draw about 1,300 spheres at 11 frames per second (where each sphere is roughly 30 pixels in diameter).

The implementations perform as many calculations as possible in parallel and do not attempt to share expensive resources like arithmetic units. The fast spheres algorithm calculates shade colour indices based on the unit vector towards the light source ($\boldsymbol{L} = (lx, ly, lz)/\sqrt{(lx, ly, lz)}$) and the unit normal $\boldsymbol{N}$ (whose most problematic term is $-\sqrt{(r^2-x^2-y^2)}$). The algorithm uses differences and approximations to avoid expensive operations. With reference to [8], we use an approximation value of p=8 which gives excellent accuracy on a 256 colour Sun IPX and on a 16-bit colour Macintosh computer. The fast spheres algorithm approximates the difficult sphere equation:

$$z - z_0 = -\sqrt{r^2 - x^2 - y^2}$$

with the simpler expression:

$$z - z_0 = \frac{r^2 - x^2 - y^2}{r}$$

The fast spheres graphics hardware that we have implemented performs only integer calculations involving addition and shifting and comparison. For each sphere, the host system has to perform one real-valued calculation.

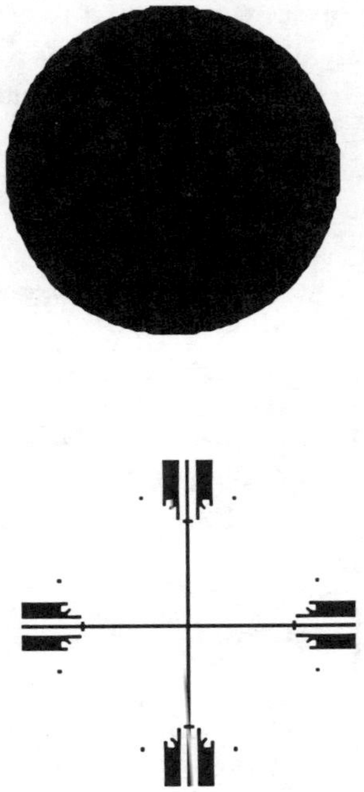

Figure 1: Top: Head on view of a fast sphere (dithered). Bottom: Rendered at 20MHz

For the optimised algorithm one pixel value is produced per clock tick by performing calculations of the form:

$$f(x+1, y) = f(x, y) + N_C(x, y)$$
$$N_c(x+1, y) = N_c(x, y) + K_c$$
$$L_c = E_c + F_c$$

At the end of each scan line, three additions, two assignments, one increment and one comparison is performed.

4 FPGA architectures

We have found that RAM based FPGA architectures like the Xilinx xc4000 or the Altera flex8000 are very suitable for graphics algorithms. Devices can be actively or passively reprogrammed an infinite number of times and thus constantly re-programmed for different functions. A small FPGA device can thus become a large and efficient device for supporting graphics applications. In order to test our graphics program, we have selected the cmos RAM-based Xilinx xc4000 architecture. The resources available are sketched in Figure 2.

The basic logic element of the xc4000 architecture is the CLB (Configuration Logic Block). Each CLB includes two look-up tables that can configure any logic function of a limited number of inputs and two flip-flops. The look-up tables can also be configured as a RAM element. CLB flip-flops have a dedicated clock-enable pin which controls the muxing of input and internal data. For arithmetic functions involving additions some dedicated resource in the CLB should be used to propagate efficiently the carry logic.

The basic element interfacing the internal logic with the outside world is the IOB (Input Output Block). Each IOB includes simple input and output buffers, tri-state capability for bi-directional pads or device isolation and storage elements. IOB registers can be used to latch or synchronise input and output signals or to store internal logic when no more flip-flops are available in the core of the device.

Routing resources include highly buffered global networks and internal tristate functions for bus structures.

An efficient gobal feature controls the state of each register and each tri-state output function of the device. The periphery of the device includes edge decoders implementing decode logic more efficiently than the internal CLBs. The independence of the resources remaining available when others are being used and the numerous possible configurations of each element make this architecture very powerful but also very complex.

5 Compass FPGA solution

Compass Design Automation has been providing solution for FPGA designers for one year. It currently supports Xilinx, Actel and Altera architectures with various entry points such as VHDL or Verilog Language, state machine or datapath descriptions in textual or graphics format, automatic technology migration from any ASIC or FPGA library to the target FPGA library, and schematic entry.

On ASIC technologies, the area occupancy and the intrinsic performance are cell-specific. The occupancy is known in advance since the area cost is a simple addition of the cost of each component instantiated in the design. Only the wiring capacitance values need to be backannotated to complete the knowledge of the designer with the performance of the chip and provide her or him with the possibility to do re-optimisation. On FPGA technologies it is difficult to predict the area cost and

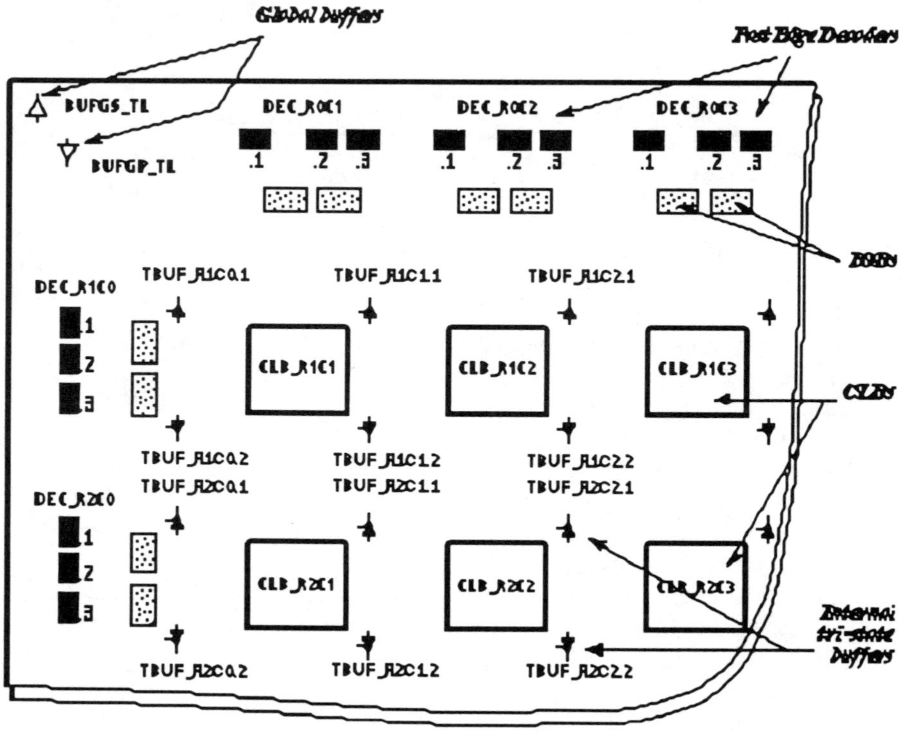

Figure 2: XC4000 Resources

impossible to know the exact performance of a design made of gates before it is actually placed and routed. The cell level is no longer the physical level of the resources and is too high a level to do the same work as on ASIC designs.

Because of the limited density and performance of FPGAs, an efficient exploitation of the layout resources can be seen as the main priority of CAD Tools. Compass which was created from VLSI Technology has a strong experience in ASIC design methodologies and it was its challenge to provide a complete and efficient solution to FPGA designers. The decision was made to integrate in the flow an optimizer with expertise in FPGA architectures thus performing collapsing, minimisation, factorisation and technology mapping in regard of the target device. The optimized output netlist in the vendor-supported input format maps directly to basic elements like Xilinx CLBs and IOBs, Actel Logic and IO Modules or Altera LEs/Macrocells and IOEs/IO Control Blocks instead of the input *high level* gates.. This module knows how to implement gates into the look-up tables of the Xilinx CLBs; it knows that Xilinx IOBs include registers to synchronise or latch input and output signals or to implement internal registers for better area usage. This FPGA optimizer interfaces smartly with the place and route software allowing the FPGA library to be handled like any ASIC library in the Compass Tools. As a result designers benefit from a complete and fully-integrated design environment still providing an efficient device utilization which results in low occupancy and high performance of the final design.

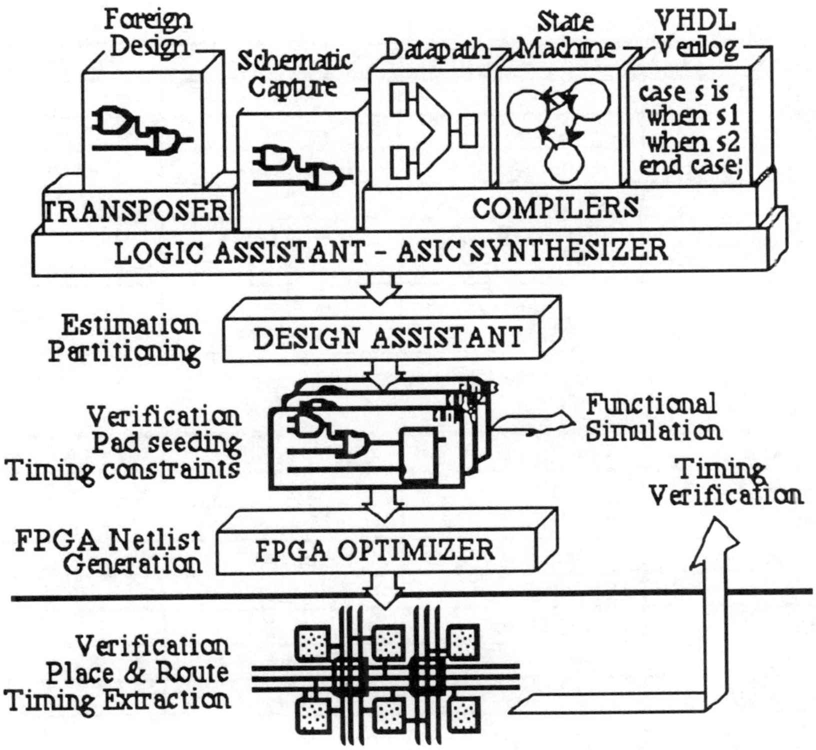

Figure 3: Design Flow in the Compass Tools

6 Implementation results

The effort required to design, place, route and simulate the graphics algorithms described above is now detailed. We describe the performance of our implementations with a view to establishing the possibility of offering real time animation.

In the case of our graphics designs we used purely behavioral VHDL code. The internal logic was directly mapped into the CLB look-up tables and CLB flip-flops while the IOB flip-flops were used as storage elements for the pixels coordinates. We used the fast carry logic when implementing operations involving additions and substractions and the global buffers for the clock and control signals. In our circle example described below, 20 IO registers are used to latch the two 10-bit output busses providing the pixels coordinates. Table 1 presents the statistics for the Xilinx xc4000 implementation of the circle and sphere circuits. "P" denotes "packed CLBs" and "O" denotes "occupied CLBs".

For an FPGA solution to be viable, it must deliver a significantly superior performance than general purpose display processors. The straight forward implementation of our circle circuit can draw 12 million pixels per second, comfortably outperforming the Texas TMS34020 which can calculate 2 million pixels per second for the same algorithm (midpoint circle). The programmed chips perform correctly at their maximum frequencies based on their critical paths. A degenerate solid circle produced by clocking the circuit at 20MHz is shown in Figure 1.

Xilinx XC4000	Circle (Outline)	Circle (Solid)	Fast Sphere
Synthesis	30s	50s	22mn
Optimisation	7mn	15mn	20mn
Place and route	4ms 35s	10mn 24s	30mn
Device	4003APC84	4004APC84	4010CB196
CLB Utilisation	61/100 (P) 78/100 (O)	88/144 (P) 107/144 (O)	347/400 (P) 379/400 (O)
Critical Path	84.0ns	92.3ns	135.10ns
Time to draw,r=100	47.518ms	2.89ms	4.23ms

Table 1: Results for the Xilinx XC4000 implementation

Altera Flex8000	Circle (Outline)	Circle (Solid)	Fast Sphere
Synthesis	30s	30s	n/a
Optimisation	7mn	15mn	n/a
Place and route	4ms 35s	10mn 24s	n/a
Device	EPF828LC84	EPF828LC84	n/a
Utilisation	134/204 64%	185/208 89%	n/a
Critical Path	92.4ns	85.4ns	n/a
Time to draw, r=100	52.3ms	2.64ms	n/a

Table 2: Results for the Altera Flex8000 implementation

Other important timing constraints are memory speeds. Static memory is expensive and rarely used for framestores. A framestore based 15ns static memory might offer little advantage if used in FPGA applications that have a minimum critical path of 84ns. An 80ns DRAM framestore offers a much cheaper alternative without severe performance degradation. However, as we improve our results by better utilising the resources on FPGAs, we expect our timings might fall low enough to merit the use of static memory.

The Xilinx implementation can render a sphere of radius 30 in 3.81e-4 seconds, i.e. 2627 spheres in a second. The Pixel-Planes system uses custom graphics to render 1,300 spheres at 11 frames per second i.e. 14,300 spheres per second. By optimising the arithmetic in our design we hope to close this gap a little, but current FPGA technology is still not good enough to compete with custom VLSI graphics systems. The Altera Flex8000 results are shown in Table 2. Note that the Compass optimiser was not used. An implementation of the fast spheres algorithm also exists on a 2 by 3 array of Algotronix CAL1024 devices, but performance data for this circuit was not available.

These results can be improved further by tuning the the Compass ASIC Synthesizer and by using the timing driven feature of the place and route software. However for our naive implementation, we very quickly achieved encouraging results.

We expect our results will still compare favourably with the new Atari Jaguar system, which includes 64-bit RISC graphics processor with 4K of zero wait-state internal static memory and delivers 26.6MIPS. An independent 64-bit blitter processor (on the same chip) provides high speed logical operations and hardware for *z*-buffering and Goudraud shading. The display is 720x526 with 16.7 million colours.

7 Design automation for FPGAs

Providing a complete *design automation.* on an FPGA architecture with an optimal resource utilization is not an easy task, especially on a rich architecture like the Xilinx xc4000. Using the fast carry logic currently requires the instantiation of hard macros; mapping to the edge decoders can be done only by the attachement of an attribute on a dedicated cell and require specific rules; configuring a look-up table as a RAM element is done by the use of an independant Xilinx program; global buffers drive certain pins of the CLBs and some are not accessible when others are already in use; controling globally the registers requires the attachement of attributes when registers are to be initialized with the value '1'; etc ... Many examples show that an efficient resource exploitation requires a very expert knowledge of the architecture. With the availability of new FPGA devices this becomes a problem for CAD tools and thus FPGA designers.

A first approach consists in having CAD developers aquire the expertise of each FPGA architecture and develop for each resource a specific mapping. This is a time-consuming short-term investment with high engineering-cost. The work is not *portable* to new architectures and results in a high delay between silicon and software availability. This approach is the one that has been adopted until now and is due to limitations or complexity of the place and route software.

Since FPGA founders have the expertise of the silicon, it makes sense that they do the mapping themselves. To do so they need to get the function to implement at a high level. If an adder is expanded into gates during synthesis, the placer will not recognise it as an adder and won't use the carry logic resource. This approach gives more work to the founder but all the CAD tools don't need to acquire the expertise of each new architecture. The efficiency is constrained by the founder software and the amount of information that CAD tools can pass to it. It is a longer term investment if the founder guarantees the portability on each new architecture. In that case, the software and hardware can be available simultaneously. This approach is currently adopted by Xilinx and Compass with their XBLOX and X-SYN products.

An even more generic approach consists in having a standard over all the FPGA founders. The LPM library (Library of Parameterized Modules) defined by Electronic Industries Associates is a library of high level modules and parameters. Its goal is similar to the Xilinx XBLOX library described above. However LPM includes internal tri-state buffers which are not available on Altera and Actel devices or registers with both set and clear control pins while Xilinx registers have only one control pin. In other words this standard is not fully compatible with most FPGA architectures. What will "LPM compatible" mean ? If CAD tools need to customize the library for each architecture it is no more a standard. The support by FPGA vendors of each LPM component resulting in unefficient implementations is not acceptable. Is this new standard for FPGA design software actually viable without a standardization of the FPGA hardware ? If not, the success of LPM might depend on whether or not FPGA founders are ready to implement new functions on the silicon in order to standardize their software ...

8 FPGAs as graphics co-processors

A straight forward approach to using FPGA devices to implement graphics operations is to simply replace the graphics co-processor with an FPGA network. Many interconnection variations are possible, and we only show one below. Notice that the framestore is only directly connected to the FPGA network and the video controller. The only way the processor can draw anything is by sending graphics commands to the FPGA network. This avoids the need for a shared bus with acquisition conflicts from the main processor, the FPGA network and possibly a graphics co-processor. An FPGA network arranged in this network should provide at least a command to set a pixel with coordinate (x,y) to a given colour. Writing text characters could be rather slow if this is the only general purpose graphics operation available.

Applications that require a large number of pixel write operations where the pixel values can not be computed algorithmically (e.g. moving pixel-map images around the display or writing lots of text) would suffer unduly by having the pixel write operations filter though the FPGA network without any advantage. Such applications would benefit from a bus shared by the main processor (or some DMA device) and the FPGA network with the framestore, where the FPGA network is used only when its offers some performance advantage. Even for pixel map copying, FPGAs have their application. Pixel maps could be cached in RAM local to the FPGA network and written to the framestore without the intervention of the main processor and without conflicts with its system bus.

9 Virtual Hardware

Modern operating systems extend the memory space available to applications by the provision of *virtual memory*. The virtual and physical address spaces are divided into fixed size *pages* e.g. 4K. A page can be either currently in the physical memory of the system ("swapped in" RAM) or it may be resident on a fast secondary storage medium ("swapped out" to disk). Pages with addresses in use are automatically swapped in by special memory management hardware. Pages in the physical memory that have not been accessed for a while are automatically swapped out to make room for more active pages. A table is maintained to keep track of the mapping between physical memory pages and virtual pages. The localised nature of memory accesses of many software packages results in an acceptable level performance of degradation (memory accesses are *very* slow when a page has to be swapped in). Virtual memory allows computer systems to provide much more memory for applications than the physically available memory.

We propose that the same technique can be applied in a limited manner to virtualise hardware. Our analogy of physical memory (the primary storage medium) is an array of FPGA devices. The secondary storage medium can be a local ROM-based system which stores a large number of FPGA configurations. Alternatively, the FPGA devices can be connected to a host processor over a fast bus, allowing programming from the physical memory of the system. The latter solution affords a higher degree of flexibility since the configuration information can be changed very quickly or even generated in real time.

Such an organisation opens up a new methodology for designing hardware. Instead of designing a library of independent graphics circuits we propose the design of a huge virtual graphics circuit that performs a large number of graphics operations. The virtual circuit would be impossible to fabricate with existing VLSI technologies. Instead, the FPGA configuration information for the virtual circuit would reside in the primary memory of a host processor connected via a fast bus. The Sun SS10 system bus shifts over 80MB per second.

Assume the virtual device can perform the circle and sphere algorithms described earlier. When a circle needs to be drawn, the part of the virtual circuit that draws a circle is automatically fetched over the fast bus and swapped into some free space in the FPGA network. The calculation about exactly where the circuit is swapped in can be done easily in real time by the host processor. Software performing this function is in effect a run time system for the virtual hardware.

For even a modest size of FPGA network, a circle drawing algorithm will take up very little space. Another operation can occur in parallel with the circle circuit. For example, a line could be drawn by swapping a line drawing circuit into a free area of the FPGA network. Both circuits can now produce pixel values to be written to the framestore. This raises the issue of concurrent access to the framestore which requires arbitration and possibly an unacceptable level of performance degradation. Indeed, if these circuits produce (x,y) coordinates at roughly the same rate, then the parallel execution of these circuits might be almost as slow as their sequential execution.

Many techniques exist to ease the problem of concurrent access to a shared memory. Several switch networks can be readily applied for the connection of the FPGA network to the framestore memory subsystem [11]. The situation is eased by the fact that framestores are usually made up of many independent memory devices that can of course be accessed in parallel with a suitable switch matrix. By attempting to schedule graphics operations on different parts of the screen concurrently, memory access conflicts can be minimised. Another interesting observation is that the switch matrices themselves can be implemented using FPGAs! Hypercube structures have already been neatly accommodated onto Algotronix CAL1024 devices.

A major overhead with this approach is the speed with which new circuit configurations can be loaded into FPGA devices. The configuration information can be sent over a very fast bus, so the transmission of this data is assumed not to be a bottleneck. The dominant speed factor for loading a new circuit is the configuration speed of FPGA devices. Fortunately the Xilinx devices can be programmed in real time with each cell being 'randomly' accessible like a conventional memory location. Other FPGAs, like the Algotronix CAL1024 devices, also offer impressively fast programming speeds.

The reconfiguration cost is quickly recouped in graphics animation applications that clock a circuit hundreds or thousands of times. Reconfiguration of the next circuit to be executed can occur in parallel with the execution of the current circuits if the target FPGA chips for the current circuits are not in use. This approach might constrain too tightly the algorithm for placing a new circuit onto the FPGA, but as we will see later this method is very applicable to certain organisations of FPGA arrays.

Virtual memory is divided into pages to facilitate the swapping process. The method above uses 'pages' whose granularity is the size of circuit to be swapped in. This greatly complicates the process of swapping the virtual resource into some available physical resource. Another advantage of virtual memory is that different programs which have common read-only data can share a physical page. A hardware analogy is easily found when one realises that the sphere drawing circuit has as a subcircuit most of the circle drawing circuit. If a circle drawing circuit has already been swapped in, then this circuit could be replicated on the FPGA network. This avoids the transmission of the circle drawing subcircuit of the sphere circuit.

To accelerate the process of replicating circuits that are currently realised on the FPGA network (or have recently been realised) subcircuits could be cached in RAM local to the FPGA network. This avoids the retransmission of subcircuits that have been cached. Designs constructed in a modular and hierarchical style based on cell libraries should be particularly amenable to this kind of optimisation.

Another important consideration is the physical topology of the FPGA network with respect to the framestore. Numerous organisations are possible, so we discuss only a few and no doubt preclude many other good topologies. We consider graphics circuits that produce as their output (x,y) coordinates and a pixel value to be written to the corresponding framestore location. The translation from Cartesian coordinates to a memory address can typically be accomplished by a simple fixed size circuit which could be automatically placed for each drawing circuit in the FPGA network. For the moment, assume 2D arrays of FPGAs. Also assume that the framestore is accessible through all four edges of a rectangular array of FPGAs. The framestore may be dual ported to allow access by the host processor or some other graphics chip. Virtual sub-circuits should be placed in the FPGA network so that their output sections are as close as possible to the periphery of the network.

Circuits cramped in the middle section of a network which have long wires running to a peripheral location might suffer unacceptable delays. Placing such circuits in real-time is computationally expensive. The FPGAs could be partitioned into zones of different size and shapes. Zones would be chosen to have good access to the periphery of the network. Now the run time system need only match a virtual subcircuit with a zone (which is much quicker) and this results in a better mapping from virtual hardware to physical resource. We consider virtual pages to be subcircuits and physical pages to be zones on FPGA networks. Virtual memory and physical memory pages are the same size, so our analogy is not exact. An advantage of the zone scheme is that it is easier to reconfigure zones while other zones on different chips are executing.

10 Conclusions

We have shown that FPGAs can implement simple and complex algorithms with a performance level that places them comfortably in between custom graphics chips and general processors with specialised graphics instruction sets. The key advantage of using FPGAs in graphics applications is their flexibility. Devices can be reconfigured quickly to implement various graphics algorithms. New graphics algorithms are easily incorporated.

The preliminary implementation of the fast spheres algorithm can be run in real time with a 1000 by 1000 display using around 10 frames per second. As we refine our design, we expect this rate to rise to 20 frames per second. A good application for fast spheres is the rendering of clouds (by rendering thousands of small spheres). This would be particularly useful in an aircraft flight simulator, but these displays are typically much larger. Once the arithmetic has been optimised on the Xilinx FPGA devices we hope to demonstrate real time performance for such large displays.

Having demonstrated the viability of implementing graphics algorithms on FPGA devices we have proposed several architectures for actually deploying these devices as graphics co-processors. We then extend the potential of FPGA devices for representing very large circuits by introducing the concept of virtual hardware, fashioned after virtual memory.

In the near future we expect to realise clipping and z-buffering operations on FPGAs, thus increasing the real time performance of our graphics algorithms even further. When z-buffering is added we can easily modify our circuits to produce (x,y,z) coordinates and then conditionally update the corresponding framestore pixel depending on the z values.

The ability to swap in subcircuits from a virtual circuit into a physical resource raises many of the same issues as those encountered in the use of virtual memory. Fortunately, many of the problems have the same solution. Hardware virtualisation also opens up the possibility of developing circuits using a new methodology. The concept simply involves designing a large circuit without regard to the physical resource. The mapping of virtual hardware to a physical resource is performed by the virtual hardware run time system. Clearly this approach does not work well for all large circuits, but we believe there are enough suitable applications.

Once FPGAs become more sophisticated, other exciting possibilities open up. In particular, the idea of the FPGA hardware reconfiguring itself rather than simply receiving programming information externally is rather appealing. Self modifying hardware: is it hardware anymore or just software with an identity crisis?

Acknowledgements

We would like to thank John Patterson and Rob Sutherland of the Glasgow Interactive Systems Team at the Department of Computing Science at the University of Glasgow. Both provided valuable feedback about the feasibility of adapting graphics techniques for execution on FPGA technology. Jacques-Oliver PiedNoir at Compass reviewed early versions of the paper. Compass

Design Automation provided the facilities and software for the programming and testing of the FPGA devices used. Franck Chiniard and Nathalie Anglada have also provided valuable support at Compass. John Gray of Algotronix listened with patience to our ideas and Wayne Luk at Oxford University shared his experience of using formal hardware description languages for FPGA circuits. Will Partain of the GRASP team at Glasgow provided vital support for the Glasgow Haskell compiler.

References

[1] Ben Cahill. *Drawing on the 8514/A*. Byte Magazine. March, 1990.

[2] Mary Sheeran and Geraint Jones. *Circuit Design in Ruby. Formal Mehtods for VLSI Design*. J. Staunstrup (editor). North-Holland, 1990.

[3] Wayne Luk and I. Page. Parametrising Designs for FPGAs. In FPGAs, W. Moore and W. Luk (editors). Abingdon EE&CS Books. 1991.

[4] Satnam Singh. *Analysis of Hardware Description Languages* PhD Thesis. The University of Glasgow, Scotland, UK. 1991.

[5] Satnam Singh. *Behavioural Synthesis form Algebraic Descriptions*. SASIMI'93. Nara, Japan, 1993.

[6] IEEE Std. 1076-1987. IEEE Standard VHDL Reference Manual. 1987.

[7] J.E. Bresenham . *A Linear Algorithm for Incremental Digital Display of Circular Arcs*. Communications of the ACM, 20(2), February 1977.

[8] John Patterson. *Fast Spheres*. EuroGraphics '85.

[9] H.J. Fuchs, J.P. Hultquist, S. Spach, J.D. Austin, F.P. Brooks, J.G. Eyles and J. Pulton. *Fast Spheres, Shadows, Textures, Transparencies, and Image Enchancements in Pixel-Planes*. Computer Graphics 19(3), 1985.

[10] John Eyles, John Austin, Henry Fuchs, Trey Greer, John Poulton. *Pixel-Planes 4: A Summary*. Advances in Computer Graphics Hardware II. Eurographics Seminars, Springer-Verlag. 1988.

[11] R. J. Sutherland. *A Multiprocessor Architecture for High-Qulity Interactive Displays*. Eurographics '86. Lisbon, 1986.

A Reconfigurable Monte-Carlo Clustering Processor (MCCP).

C.P. Cowen and S. Monaghan
Neural and VLSI Systems Group
Department of Electronic Systems Engineering
University of Essex
Colchester, CO4 3SQ England

Abstract

A generic Monte-Carlo problem architecture, implemented earlier in a dedicated FPGA computer, is extended to incorporate a wider range of more complex Monte-Carlo and percolation problems. The new algorithms, which are implemented in the same computer architecture, execute an order of magnitude faster than on comparable DSP hardware, as with the earlier and simpler algorithms.

Introduction

This paper is one of a series [1, 2, 3] concerned with the design and implementation of an inexpensive PC-AT hosted FPGA-based computer (henceforth to be called the processor) which can be configured to implement in hardware a range of Monte Carlo (MC) algorithms currently used in statistical physics. MC simulations offer a good 'laboratory' for investigating the potential of FPGA-based computing machines for several reasons:

1. They are simple enough to be implemented in FPGAs [1].
2. There are a wide range of Monte-Carlo algorithms to exploit the reconfigurability of these machines.
3. MC simulations often require the computational resources of dedicated hardware [4, 5].
4. MC methods are increasingly used in areas other than statistical physics.

In addition, parts of an MC simulation resemble low-level multi-dimensional image processing tasks [2].

The range of MC problems previously implemented in the reconfigurable hardware include (using image processing terminology to describe the character of the MC simulation) : single-bit pixels with local windows with a fixed processing element [1], single-bit pixels with local windows with a pixel dependent processing function [2] and multi-bit pixels with a fixed processing element [3].

In all cases the processing element was based on the classical MC methods [6].

The motivation for this work was to extend the capability of the processor by implementing a class of MC algorithms [7] which are extensively cited in the physics literature and which to our knowledge have not previously been implemented in hardware. As a by-product, the processor can also be used to study the important problem of percolation, which arises in many engineering contexts.

Monte-Carlo Clustering Techniques

Overview

Monte-Carlo (MC) simulations are typically carried out on systems comprising a large number, N, of microscopic particles which interact with their neighbouring particles. For further details see [2, 3] and references therein.

The idea of a Monte-Carlo simulation is to sample the distribution of microscopic states occupied by these N particles to obtain the system's average or macroscopic properties. A good MC simulation uses importance sampling to generate significant and independent samples rapidly [6]. In this respect, the classical MC methods fail for the simulation of some systems under certain conditions, e.g. the simulation of a ferro-magnet at its critical temperature, T_c [8]. Here, the time required to generate statistically independent samples grows in a power-like fashion (critical slowing down) with the size of the system under simulation. This restricts the maximum system size that can be simulated. In recent years, a new class of algorithms have been developed, known as cluster

0-8186-5490-2/94 $03.00

algorithms [7], which to a large extent resolve this difficulty for certain important systems.

This paper will consider only the two-dimensional *Ising Model* [8], where each of the N particles are represented by 1-bit quantities, known as *spins*, and arranged in an $M \times M$ square lattice.

Swendsen-Wang Clustering

The Swendsen-Wang algorithm for the Ising Model [7] was one of the first clustering algorithms to appear. The algorithm consists of the repeated application of two stages, the first of which is the formation of clusters. Figure 1 shows a small example lattice of spins of arbitrary values. During the first stage of the algorithm, the value of each spin in the lattice and those of its nearest neighbouring spins are examined in turn.

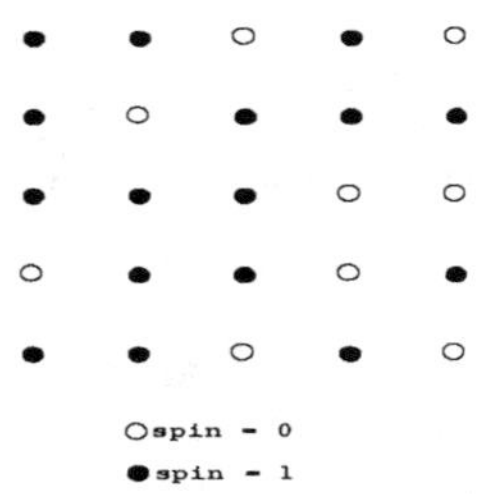

Figure 1: Spin system

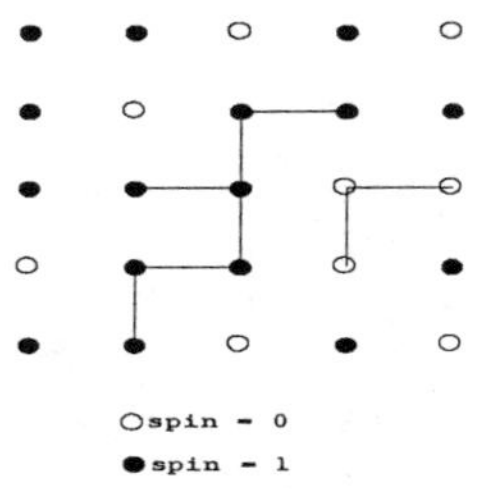

Figure 2: Spin system with clusters

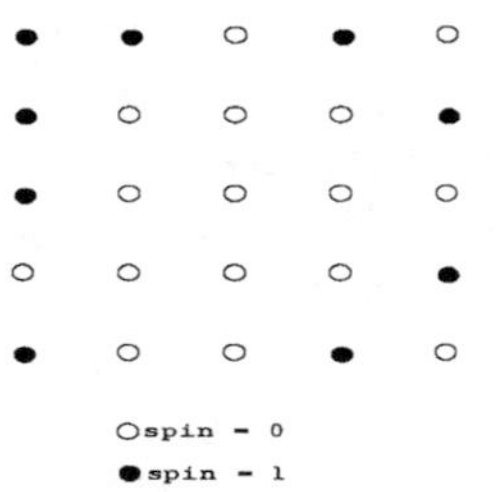

Figure 3: Spin system after clustering

Whenever two neighbouring spins are found to have the same value, a bond (or link) is established between them [7] according to the probability:

$$p = 1 - \exp(-\Delta K) \tag{1}$$

$$\Delta K = \frac{1}{k_B T} \tag{2}$$

where k_B is Boltzmann's constant and T is the system temperature. This construction is related to the well known bond percolation problem.

At the end of this first stage, the lattice will consist of a number of spins bonded together in clusters. In figure 2, two clusters are shown: one consisting of seven spins, the other of three. Any unconnected spins can be considered as clusters with just one spin. The largest possible cluster size contains all the spins in the lattice.

During the second stage of the algorithm, clusters with two or more spins are located and all the spins in the cluster are assigned a common value. Whenever a spin with a bond to another is found, the other spins in this cluster can be found by following all bonds until the cluster has been exhausted. The new value assigned to each of the spins in the cluster is decided with equal probability. Figure 3 shows the state of the lattice after one update. In this example, the larger cluster has been changed, but the spins in the smaller have remained the same. Whether or not the values of the constituent spins of a cluster have changed, the bonds that join them are removed, and the image is ready to be processed again.

For a 64×64 Ising lattice, independent samples can be generated about 25 times [7] faster than with the use of the 'classical' algorithms. For larger systems, the improvement is even greater. Indeed in the problem which originally motivated this research, the lattice size is required to be 1024×1024. This size of lattice is currently used in certain difficult problems associated with Ising Model.

Processor Architecture

The Monte-Carlo Clustering Processor (MCCP) architecture used to implement the Swendsen-Wang algorithm is shown in figure 4. There are two main parts to the processor corresponding to the two stages of the clustering algorithm.

Forming Clusters

The image memory (fig. 4) stores the lattice of spins and the link information. In the two dimensional

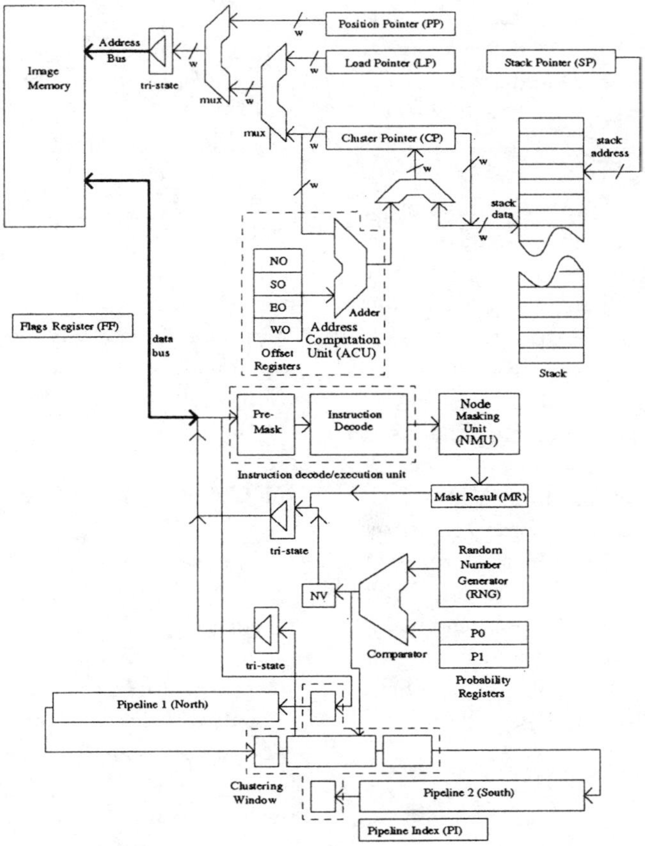

Figure 4: MCCP Architecture

Ising Model, there are four nearest neighbours, north, south, east and west, so the dataword stored for each lattice site looks like figure 5.

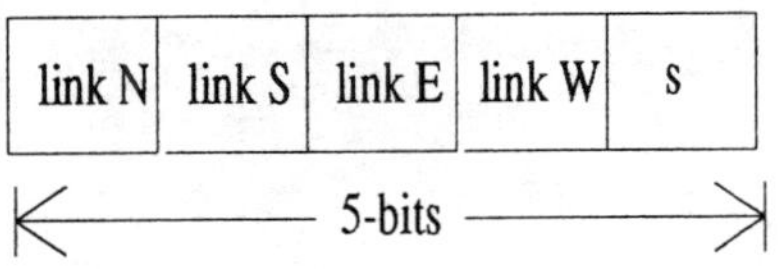

Figure 5: MCCP data representation for 2-dimensional Ising Model.

The first stage of the algorithm is performed sequentially, by passing the entire lattice through a pipeline. This pipelined arrangement and the associated address generators are very similar to that of the processors described in [2, 3]. Two address registers are used in this operation. The Load Pointer fetches the next spin into the pipeline and the Position Pointer writes the processed dataword with link information back to the memory. The clustering window contains a register where the five-bit dataword is formed. During the clustering process, if two neighbouring spins have equal value, a random number is generated and compared with the probability in register *P0*. This register contains the value p given in equation 1. Only north and east links of a given spin need be generated. When the whole image has been processed, a flag instructs the processor to go into the second stage of the algorithm.

Processing the Clusters

The second section of the processor examines the lattice and looks for clusters of spins. Whenever a cluster of spins is found, the cluster is explored by following the links to neighbouring spins. This is a highly recursive process. Since there are four possible links in two dimensions, a stack is provided to store addresses of any spin with links to more than one other spin. *The Cluster Pointer* (CP) is used to address the cluster and can be post-modified by the appropriate amount to allow it to follow the links in any of the four directions as well as being loadable from the stack.

At the core of the MCCP there is a finite-state machine that operates on node (link) information, moving around clusters and masking out the links as it does so. In accordance with the Swendsen-Wang Algorithm, a new value for the spins in each cluster is assigned with a probability of a half, stored in register *P1*. When the end of a cluster is found the processor returns to the point in the lattice where it found this cluster and searches for any others. Thus each cluster is processed in turn by being unlinked and having its spins set to a new value. When all clusters have been processed, the appropriate flag is adjusted and the clustering stage can begin again.

Instruction Set

There are several operations that the finite state machine must carry out, modifying the CP register, masking out links information, setting flags etc. To simplify the design process, these operations have each been given DSP-style instruction mnemonics and these are summarized in table 1. Unlike conventional instruction sets, the MCCP instruction op-codes are formed from a combination of the node information and the machine status, which is governed by the previous instruction and stored in the flags register.

Architectural Parameters

The basic MCCP architecture depicted in figure 4 is scalable to a variety of problem types and sizes. The main factors that influence the actual parameters such as bus and register sizes are the following:

1. The number of spins, N, in the lattice. The width of the lattice will be denoted by M (in the case of the square lattice $N = M^2$)

2. The number of bits representing each spin, B_{bits}. (In the case of the Ising Model the $B_{bits} = 1$).

3. The number of dimensions in the system, d. (In this paper $d = 2$).

4. The number of bits used to represent the generated pseudo-random numbers, R_{bits}.

Table 2 lists the parts of the MCCP architecture and how they are affected by these factors. Note that in figure 4, the internal bus width is denoted by w, where $w = \log_2 N$. It is worth pointing out that the intent is to simulate the relatively large lattice sizes of upto $N = 1024^2$, but in order to test the processor's operation a small, 'toy' 8x8 system was implemented and its parameter values are included in the rightmost column of table 2. The table gives a maximum value for the stack, but in most cases less will be required.

FPGA Implementation

This section considers the arrangement and interconnection of FPGAs and associated memories into which the generic MCCP architecture will be placed. One of the main influencing factors will be pinout cost. As the problem size increases, the bus sizes increase logarithmically (see table 2). The Monte-Carlo processor described in [3] uses the arrangement shown in figure 6, but this is not fully suitable for the 1024^2 problem. An extra memory is required to incorporate the stack if the processor is to operate at its most efficient. Referring to figure 4, it can be seen that the addressing and data processing parts may be separated by placing all the address registers, the address computation unit and the stack controller into one FPGA and the instruction decode, RNGs, comparators, cluster pipeline window and the state machine that provides the clock signals into another. The resulting architecture is shown in figure 7. Bus widths etc are given in table 2.

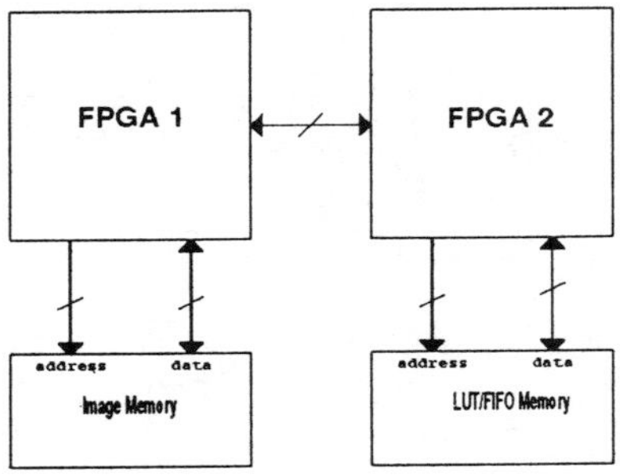

Figure 6: FPGA/memory architecture 1

The highest pin-out cost is for FPGA 1. For the $N = 1024^2$ problem, 60 pins are required to address

FLAGS			Node Data				Instruction Set
CM	DM	SE	N	S	E	W	Instruction Nmemonic
Zero Node Group							
0	1	1	0	0	0	0	CLR DM; (or DM = 0;)
0	1	0	0	0	0	0	POP CP;
Single Node Group							
0	1	X	0	0	0	1	MR = EMASK(CP+EO),(CP) = MR;
0	1	X	0	0	1	0	MR = WMASK(CP+WO),(CP) = MR;
0	1	X	0	1	0	0	MR = NMASK(CP+NO),(CP) = MR;
0	1	X	1	0	0	0	MR = SMASK(CP+SO),(CP) = MR;
Multi-Node Group							
0	1	X	0	0	1	1	PUSH CP,MR = EMASK(CP+WO),(CP) = MR;
0	1	X	0	1	0	1	PUSH CP,MR = SMASK(CP+WO),(CP) = MR;
0	1	X	0	1	1	0	PUSH CP,MR = EMASK(CP+SO),(CP) = MR;
0	1	X	0	1	1	1	PUSH CP,MR = EMASK(CP+WO),(CP) = MR;
0	1	X	1	0	0	1	PUSH CP,MR = NMASK(CP+NO),(CP) = MR;
0	1	X	1	0	1	0	PUSH CP,MR = NMASK(CP+NO),(CP) = MR;
0	1	X	1	0	1	1	PUSH CP,MR = NMASK(CP+NO),(CP) = MR;
0	1	X	1	1	0	0	PUSH CP,MR = NMASK(CP+NO),(CP) = MR;
0	1	X	1	1	0	1	PUSH CP,MR = NMASK(CP+NO),(CP) = MR;
0	1	X	1	1	1	0	PUSH CP,MR = NMASK(CP+NO),(CP) = MR;
0	1	X	1	1	1	1	PUSH CP,MR = NMASK(CP+NO),(CP) = MR;
Cluster Search Mode Group							
0	0	X	0	0	0	0	NV = RNG CMP P1;
0	0	X	X	X	X	1	SET DM; (or DM = 1;)
0	0	X	X	X	1	X	SET DM; (or DM = 1;)
0	0	X	X	1	X	X	SET DM; (or DM = 1;)
0	0	X	1	X	X	X	SET DM; (or DM = 1;)

Table 1: MCCP Instruction Set Summary

Parameter	Value	8x8 example
Register sizes (bits)		
Address Registers (PP, LP, CP)	$\log_2 N$	6
Stack Pointer (SP)	$\log_2 N$	6
Offset Registers	$\log_2 N$	6
Pipeline Index (PI)	$(M-2)$	N/A
Cluster Register (CR)	$2d + B_{bits}$	5
Mask Result Register (MR)	$2d$	4
New Value Register (NV)	B_{bits}	1
Probability Registers (P0, P1)	R_{bits}	8
Bus widths (bits)		
Image Memory Address	$\log_2 N$	6
Image Memory Data	$2d + B_{bits}$	5
Stack Address	$\log_2 N$	6
Stack Data	$\log_2 N$	6
Internal address buses	$\log_2 N$	6
Miscellaneous		
Comparator size (bits)	R_{bits}	8
Stack max. size	$N - 2(M-1)$	6
Pipeline length (total)	$2(M+d+1)$	22
Ram FIFO sections (size)	$(M-2)$	N/A
Image memory capacity	N	64

Table 2: MCCP architecture scaling parameters.

the stack and the image memory and provide the stack data bus.

The toy problem

An implementation of a 'toy' $N = 8^2$ problem is possible on the board used for previous Monte-Carlo processors, which has the architecture shown in figure 6.

FPGA	CLBs
FPGA1	49
FPGA2	43

Table 3: CLB counts for $N = 8^2$ lattice problem.

Because the pipeline is short enough to be contained entirely within one of the FPGAs, no FIFO memory is needed. SRAM2 can then be used to implement the stack memory and the stack controller placed in FPGA2. The CLB counts for each of these two Xilinx 3030 FPGAs are shown in table 3.

The bus sizes are given in table 2. In addition there are a number of connections between the two FPGAs which include clock signals and control signals from the instruction decoder/sequencer.

Performance

Processor performance for the classical MC algorithms is easy to quantify and is invariably given in terms of million-updates per second. A clustering algorithm is not as straightforward to quantify and although figures can be given in terms of millions-updates per second, a more meaningful quantity is the amount of time taken to process an image of given size and at given temperature.

The first part of the algorithm is a sequential operation and the time taken is given by:

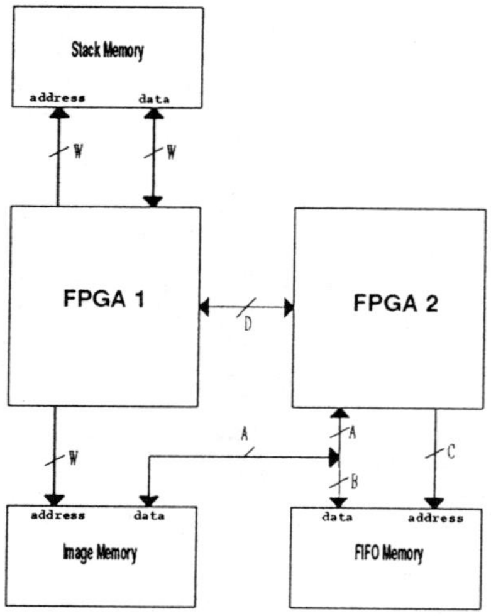

Figure 7: FPGA/memory architecture 2

$$T_{clus} = t_c \, C_{clus} \, N \tag{3}$$

where t_c is the processor's clock period, C_{clus} is the number of clock cycles required to process each spin, and N is the number of spins in the lattice.

The average number of processing steps, $F(\Delta K)$, required by the declustering part of the algorithm is shown for a 40×40 system in figure 8.

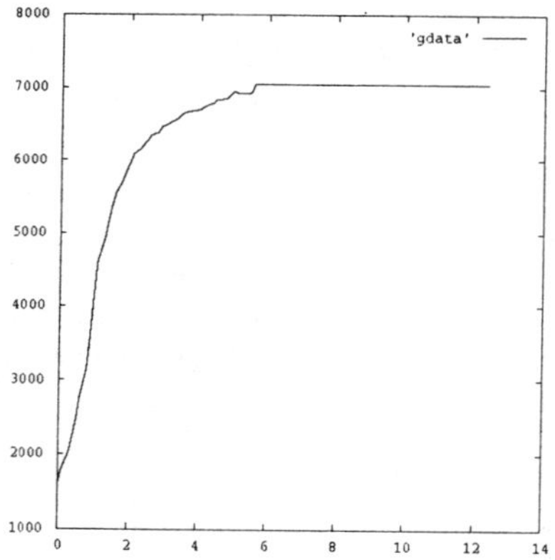

Figure 8: Processing steps, $F(\Delta K)$ vs. Temp for a 40x40 lattice

The asymptotic region of the graph corresponds to a fully linked lattice, where all the spins are linked into one big cluster. Fortunately, values of $\Delta K > 2$ are of little interest since $\Delta K \approx 0.44$ at the point at which the classical Monte-Carlo methods exhibit critical slowing down. At this point, the MCCP is operating at approximately a third of the maximum value of $F(\Delta K)$.

The time taken to decluster and update is therefore given by:

$$T_{declus} = t_c C_{declus} \alpha N F(\Delta K) \tag{4}$$

Total sweep time then is:

$$T_{sweep} = T_{clus} + T_{declus} \tag{5}$$

MCCP versus DSP implementation

To obtain an idea of the MCCP's efficiency, the algorithm was coded in assembly language on a popular Digital Signal Processor (DSP) [9] to do similar tasks.

Processor	N	Temp	$T_{clus}(\mu s)$	$T_{declus}(\mu s)$	$T_{sweep}(\mu s)$
DSP	8^2	$T \to 0$	245.0	721.0	966.0
MCCP	8^2	$T \to 0$	16.9	68.4	85.3
DSP	8^2	$T \approx T_c$	190.0	312.0	502.0
MCCP	8^2	$T \approx T_c$	16.9	39.9	56.8

Table 4: MCCP vs. DSP performance - 8×8 Ising model

Processor	N	Temp	$T_{clus}(s)$	$T_{declus}(s)$	$T_{sweep}(s)$
DSP	1024^2	$T \approx T_c$	1.88	3.36	6.30
MCCP	1024^2	$T \approx T_c$	0.28	0.37	0.65

Table 5: MCCP vs. DSP performance - 1024^2 Ising model

The current implementation of the processor has $C_{clus} = C_{declus} = 4$, and runs from a 15MHz clock giving $t_c \approx 66ns$. The DSP has an instruction cycle time of $80ns$. Table 4 gives a summary of the results obtained for the 8×8 model.

Percolation

In implementing the Swendsen-Wang algorithm, we have also gained the capability to study percolation problems. The declustering part of the MCCP can be used to study the properties of clusters formed, for example to determine if a cluster extends across the entire lattice (percolation). This opens up a number of possible applications of the processor.

Conclusions

It has been shown that the reconfigurable Monte-Carlo processor, described in earlier papers, can accommodate a new class of Monte-Carlo algorithm if the MCCP problem architecture described here is used. This is a necessary step towards developing a general-purpose Monte-Carlo processor which offers the performance of dedicated hardware to a wide range of Monte-Carlo problems.

It can be seen from the performance analysis that the same order of magnitude performance gain offered by previous MC processors over software is obtained by the clustering processor.

By developing the MC problem architecture (Fig.4) to perform clustering algorithms, the range of applications to which the processor can be put is increased. In particular, it also possible to study percolation problems. In this case, the basic algorithm was implemented in two Xilinx 3000 series FPGAs and three memories, on the Monte-Carlo processor described in this paper. This conclusion should also be true for large FPGA custom computing machines [10, 11].

References

[1] S. Monaghan, T. O'Brien, and P. Noakes. *FPGAs*, page 363. Abingdon CS Books, 1991. Edited by W. Moore and W. Luk.

[2] S. Monaghan. Gate level reconfigurable Monte Carlo processor. *JVSP*, 6:139 – 153, 1993.

[3] S. Monaghan and C.P. Cowen. Multi-bit reconfigurable processor for DSP applications in Statistical Physics. *Proc. FPGA for Custom Computing Machines FCCM'93*, 1993. sponsored by IEEE Computer Society.

[4] R. Pearson, J.L. Richardson, and D Toussaint. A fast processor for monte-carlo simulation. *Journal of Computational Physics*, 51:241–249, 1984.

[5] J. H. Condon and T. Ogielski. Fast special purpose computer for Monte-Carlo simulations in statistical physics. *Rev. Sci. Instrum*, 56(9), 1985.

[6] K. Binder, editor. *Applications of the Monte-Carlo Methods in Statistical Physics.* Springer-Verlag, 1984.

[7] Robert H. Swendsen and Jian-Sheng Wang. Nonuniversal Critical Dynamics in Monte Carlo Simulations. *Physical Review Letters*, 58(2), January 1987.

[8] L.D. Landau and E.M. Lifshitz. *Statistical Physics. Part 1.* Oxford: Pergamon Press, 1980.

[9] Analog Devices. *ADSP-2101 Data Sheet*, 1990.

[10] J.M.Arnold, D.A Buell, and E.G. Davis. Splash 2. *In Proc. 4th Annual ACM Symp. on Parallel Algorithms and Architectures*, pages 316 – 322, 1992.

[11] P. Bertin, D. Roncin, and J Vuillemin. Introduction to Programmable Active Memories. June 1989. Technical Report No3, DEC Paris Research Laboratory.

CAFCA :
(Compact Accelerator for Cellular Automata) the Metamorphosable Machine

Pierre Marchal[1], Eduardo Sanchez[2]

[1] Centre Suisse d'Electronique et de Microtechnique SA, Maladière 71, CH-2007 Neuchâtel

[2] Logic System Laboratory, Swiss Federal Institute of Technology, CH-1015 Lausanne

Abstract:

Partial differential equations have conventionally formed a basis for mathematical models of continuous systems. Cellular automata provides an alternative approach. The large scope of applications of cellular automata (in biology, physics, operational research, sociology, computer science and so on) will surely increase the need of such a tool. The basic constitutive cells are discrete and ideally suited to simulation by digital computers. Their property of only interacting in a local environment naturally leads to a new idea of processing : cellular processing. In fact, the simulation of cellular automata with mainframe computers, even with parallel multiprocessors is always slowed down by the bottleneck of inputs/outputs. This paper describes the architecture of a compact accelerator for cellular automata. This multi-expandable machine is based on a pipeline architecture which concurrently performs computations and displays results. The underlying principle is to spy on the display bus by grabbing the data flow pouring out to the display device and simultaneously to evaluate the state of each automaton in the network. The performance of the machine reaches the video rate : it computes and displays the state of the 1,024 by 1,024 16-bit automata 24 times per second. FPGAs play a key role in the architecture of the system.

Keywords and phrases:

Cellular automaton, parallel computing, pipelined architecture, accelerator, FPGAs.

1• Introduction

The idea of sequential computing machines, i.e., a sequential program and its data loaded inside the memory of the machine, is credited to John von Neumann and it dates from the 1940s [1]. Until recently, Computer Science as a whole has been developed on this concept. Because their realisation is now technically possible, massively parallel systems, i.e., very large scale multiprocessors concurrently working and exchanging data, are gradually revolutionising the computing market.

Ironically, this brilliant up-to-date principle of a parallel machine is also credited to John von Neumann in his research of self-reproducing automata that can overcome the problem of device reliability [2]. In this paper we describe the hardware implementation of a SIMD machine embedding one million 16-bit automata locally exchanging data. The system is characterised by an architectural structure in which simultaneously pipelining, systolic and fully parallel templates are intimately interleaved.

Section 2 introduces the field of discrete iterations in mathematics explaining the reasons why cellular automata are becoming widely used. The large scope of CA is briefly described. Section 3 explores the possible and efficient CA implementations. For each solution, advantages as well as drawbacks are exhibited. Section 4 describes the investigation of an FPGA based architecture leading to a compact cellular automata accelerator. The principle of display bus spying is presented as well as the custom VLSI chip that has been realised. Section 5 reviews the performance of the machine before the concluding remarks of Section 6.

2• Cellular Automata Paradigm

Discrete dynamical systems are time evolving systems in which space, time and cells themselves are basically discrete. One of the key fields of discrete dynamical systems is the one that investigates the evolution of automaton networks. An automaton network may be defined as a (large) set of cells (finite automata) locally interconnected, which evolve in discrete time steps through mutual interactions. Throughout this paper, we will focus on the simplest sub-class formed by Cellular Automata (CA) [3], [4]. A CA is an automata network in which :

- the interconnections are restricted to be local and regular,
- the transition function is restricted to be identical for each automaton.

The paradigm of these CA is the emergence of a coherent global behaviour for the overall system only issued from local interactions [5]. This very simple but powerful model covers a very large scope of possible behaviours : starting with **very simple local evolution rules** given from the state of the neighbouring cells, it is possible to produce (model) **extremely complex global behaviour** for the overall system. For instance, the "Game of Life" proposed by J. H. Conway, is a very well known CA in which the state of a cell (dead or alive) is governed by the state of its neighbouring cells. Birth and survival are guided by 2 simple rules in an 8-neighbours surrounding : 3 living cells lead to a birth, 2 or 3 living cells allow a cell to survive, in all other cases the cell is or remains dead. This simple CA has been extensively studied [6],[7] and, despite its simplicity, it exhibits universal computation ability [8].

Numerous CA models, have been proposed in various branches of Science:

- Biology (genetic nets, crystal growth, plant growth),
- Physics (magnetism, fluids dynamics, particles interaction),
- Chemistry (combustion, chemical reaction, diffusion reaction),
- Mathematics (automata theory, biomathematics, population evolution),
- Computer science (image processing, computer graphics, processor arrays).

From a mathematical point of view, all these discrete dynamical systems appear as interesting and even revolutionary alternatives to the very classical and traditional models using continuous dynamical systems, that is, usually differential or partial differential equations.

3• Efficient CA Implementation

Choosing an efficient CA implementation is difficult since there is a plethora of competing approaches which have very different characteristics and are, therefore, likely to be effective in varying degrees [9]. Three solutions will be considered here :

- massively parallel super computers,
- VLSI implementations,
- customised boards based on FPGAs,

Although massively parallel super computer machines are efficient enough to process the calculations, they present two main drawbacks. First, the processing part is either much too complicated (32-bit floating point units) or too simple (bit-serial processor). Secondly, these efficient processing machines are not as powerful in providing output results as in computation processing. These solutions are hence quite unsuitable : either the real-time display slows down the processing speed or post-processing requires too much space for storing intermediate results.

Almost any VLSI implementation that takes advantage of pipelining or systolic architectural templates is much more efficient than any conventional solution. Customising a VLSI chip implies fixing the level of generality of each cell : either a general purpose version or a dedicated one. In addition, generality and connectivity are conflicting criteria. Even if such investigations have already been realised [10], no silicon has been obtained due to the development prices. In the close field of Neural Networks (another sub-class of automata networks partially included in CA), the VLSI chips that have been designed provide good examples of components strictly dedicated to their respective applications. Their use anywhere else cannot be envisioned.

Although less comfortable than dedicated VLSI chips, accelerator boards provide an intermediate solution which is still interesting. As mentioned above, from a user point of view, generality is a must. In the last decade, two accelerator boards have been developed : the CAM-6 and the RAP-1 machines. The CAM-6 is a high performance machine designed at MIT [11]. Its speed is about one thousand times greater than that of a general purpose computer programmed to do the same task. Two boards implement the 65,536 8-bit sites that are evolving and displayed at 60 frames per second. The RAP-1 machine has been designed and built at Ecole Normale Supérieure de Paris [12]. It has been developed to investigate cellular fluid mechanics. It takes advantage of chip hardware characteristics. In the current version, ten full boards are necessary to simulate and display 130,000 sites, with 16 bits per site, at the speed of 50 frames per second.

The main limitations of these accelerators were their relative level of generality and their limited expandability. Fortunately, the rapid development observed, in the recent years, in the field of programmable devices and particularly FPGAs dissolves these limitations. With respect to these considerations, we have investigated an FPGA based architecture for an efficient and compact CA accelerator board.

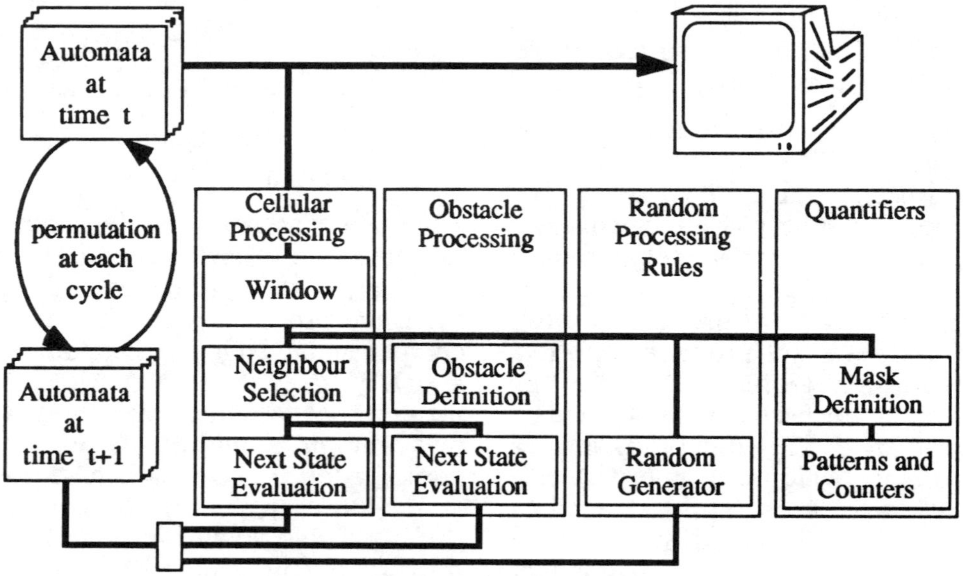

Figure 1.- Functional block diagram of the system.

4• Metamorphosable Hardware

Single Instruction Stream on Multiple Data Stream (SIMD) systems represent a convenient tool for CA's implementation since they satisfy exactly the definition criteria. As mentioned above, the system should display the state of each automaton at the video rate and it should perform the processing phase without slowing down the display.

Figure 1 depicts the functional block diagram of the system. Two memory blocks are necessary in order to perform synchronous update of the network. The memory block located on the top is used to store the configuration at time t and to pour out both the display device and the processing part. The memory block located on the bottom is used to store the configuration flowing out of the processing part at time t+1. At each cycle, the roles played by each memory block are exchanged. The underlying principle can be clearly seen : the CA calculation, realised in the processing part, is performed by spying on the display bus and grabbing its data flow.

The processing part is divided into four blocks:

• Cellular processing : In this block, the data flow is shaped into an active window in which the intervening neighbours are selected in order to evaluate the next state of the automaton. A pipelined architecture is used to process these calculations.

• Obstacle processing : This block defines the particular transition rules for a given set of points. Being mostly used in fluid dynamics in order to specialise the rule concerning the obstacles, it takes its name for this reason. This processing is performed concurrently with the conventional cellular processing.

• Random Processing Rules : In order to achieve probabilistic automata simulations, each automaton keeps the value of the previous state or evolves, according to the evaluations performed in the previous blocks (cellular processing and obstacle processing), depending on the value given by the random generator.

• Quantifiers : As the results given by a cellular automata are rather qualitative, this block provides some quantitative results. The user provides a pattern to be counted and an area to be observed. This block returns at each cycle how many times the given pattern has been found in the observed area. This computation is realised according to a systolic template.

The accelerator architecture includes some expandable features. The basic feature available is a cellular space (memory) of 1,024 by 1,024 cells each of which contains an embedded a 16-bit automaton. For a larger cellular space, one board may be added to double the size (1,024 by 2,048 cells) or three boards to quadruple the size of the cellular space (2,048 by 2,048 cells). In the same way, it is also possible to increase the automaton size by adding a board in the same manner (providing up to 32 bits). Due to the real parallelism, it is to be noted that these upgrades do not influence the processing speed. For instance, if four boards are used, the full cellular space (2,048 by 2,048 cells) is still updated 24 times per second.

The accelerator is exclusively composed of 3 types of components :

• memories : 5.5 MBytes of video-RAM are located in the cellular planes (2 * 2 MB), in the mask plane (1 MB) and in the obstacle plane (512 kB), and nearly 3 MBytes of fast static RAM are devoted to the transition Look-Up Table (2 MB), to the colour LUT (64 kB) and to the obstacle LUT (16 kB),

• programmable devices : 4 Xilinx FPGAs have been necessary plus a few couples of PALs for local control, 2 XC 3090 are used in the quantifiers' block, 2 XC 3064 are used for the obstacle processing, random generator as well as the parallel and serial control,

• glue logic : some tens of drivers and multiplexers.

In the days of the first investigations [13], no sufficiently large and fast FPGAs were available on the market to realise the cellular processing block. A full-custom VLSI chip with a bit-slice architecture was chosen for this block. As exemplified in figure 2, the single

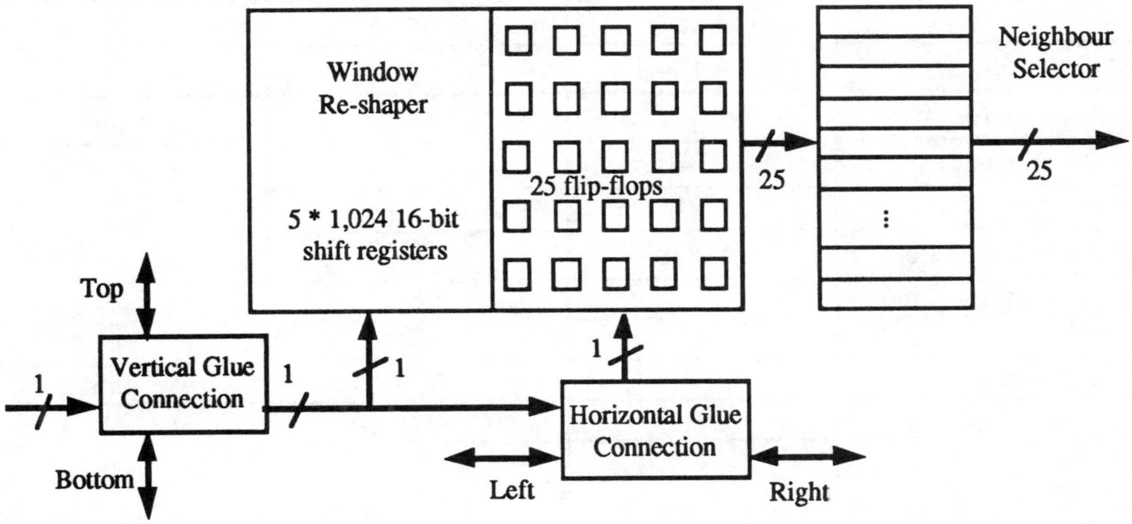

Figure 2.- Functional block diagram of the bit-slice VLSI chip.

bit-slice was composed of 5 * 1,024-bit shift registers and 25 selectable flip-flops, the selection of which was under the control of the particular automaton to be implemented. The 25 outputs of each bit-slice are or-wired in the present system so the basic architecture selects between the corresponding 400 bits, the 25 bits that would be used for the transition function.

The implementation of the next state evaluation block has been realised by a simple look-up table (LUT). If necessary, a systolic chip may be added before the LUT for more complex simulation needing some pre-processing. For advanced simulation, the solution can be much more complex. The only absolute constraint is that the solution should be performed with constant time operation (all calculations in the same amount of time).

Currently, with the recent advances in the field of programmable devices [14], the implementation of the accelerator benefit greatly from the new families of FPGAs available on the market. This benefit will come from several sources:

- lower development price and lower development time,
- lower chip cost at the prototype level,
- ease of implementation and modification,
- lower correction and modification time,
- intrinsic flexibility (re-progammability).

Realising the cellular processing part, using FPGAs, has lead us to a considerable improvement. The amount of logic available in new FPGAs is large enough to perform the explicit computation of the transition function and therefore to suppress the transition LUT (4 MBytes of fast static RAM). Furthermore, having the full cellular processing in a single chip (window re-shape, neighbours selection and transition evaluation) makes it possible to increase the distance of intervening neighbours, while keeping their number constant. This alternative is currently under investigation. The final choice between 2 XC 4020 from Xilinx and 4 A 1280 from Actel has not been decided. But re-programmability is a key parameter, so the Actel or any antifuse solution cannot be considered. SRAM solution like Xilinx, although implying more components, provides better opportunities.

5• Performance Comparison

Customised boards, while still much slower than truly parallel implementations, place a stepping stone across a gap that is perhaps too wide to bridge in one step, and can show in minutes what a parallel array would do in seconds and a more conventional simulation would take months to achieve.

The performance of the CAFCA system as compared to the performance of the CAM-6 and the RAP-1 machines are summarised in Table I.

	CAM-6	RAP-1	CAFCA
cellular space (cell)	256 * 256(1)	256 * 512(1)	1,024 * 1,024(1)
automata size (bits)	8	8	16(1)
internal state number	256	65,536	65,536(1)
window size	3 * 3	3 * 3	5 * 5
number of single rules	$> 10^{19,000}$	$> 10^{430,000}$	$> 10^{10,000,000}$
random generator (bits)	8	8	32
quantifiers	-	-	8
displayed colour	256	256	256
simulation rate (frame/sec)	60	50	24
computing power (MUpdates/second)	4	8	26

(1) expandable

Table I.- Performance comparison between accelerator boards.

As this system implies effective parallelism, an important remark is that doubling the board, doubles the system power (number of updates per second). A 4-board version runs at a rate of more than 100 MUpdates/second, for instance. This is the average simulation rate on a CRAY 2-XMP. It is clear that for an equivalent processing rate, the system price, even with a 4-board configuration, is some orders of magnitude less than the price of a CRAY 2-XMP. It is obvious than a CRAY is a general purpose machine, and the CAFCA is not so. But, on the other hand, learning how to use the CAFCA machine is much more simple than the same task on a CRAY.

6• Conclusion

Customised CA boards provide an efficient and interesting tool for people in search of fast CA prototyping, who cannot afford both to buy a CRAY or Connection Machine and to appoint the corresponding staff necessary to run and program these super computing machines. In addition, the new hardware technology provided by FPGAs boots the efficiency of the accelerator board approach. Future developments are oriented along two axes:

- realising an extension board for small workstations,
- implementing various algorithms on it (physics, chemistry, image processing and so on...), to provide users with detailed benchmarks.

Acknowledgement:

The authors want to acknowledge Prof. F. Robert (TIMA/INPG - France) for sharing his knowledge and love for CAs.

References

[1] H.H. Goldstine, *The computer from Pascal to von Neumann*, Princeton University Press, 1972.

[2] J. von Neumann, *Theory of self-reproducing automata*, (A.W. Burks Ed.), University of Illinois Press, 1966.

[3] D. Farmer, T. Toffoli, S. Wolfram, *Cellular Automata*, Proc. of the Interdisciplinary Workshop Los Alamos, Elsevier Science Publishers, North-Holland, 1984.

[4] H. Gutowitz, *Cellular Automata - Theory and Experiment*, MIT/North-Holland, 1991.

[5] S. Forrest, *Emergent Computation*, Proc. of the Interdisciplinary Workshop Los Alamos, MIT/North-Holland, 1991.

[6] M. Gardner, "On cellular automata, self-reproduction, the Garden of Eden and the Game of Life", Scie. Amer., 224 (2), pp. 112-117, 1971.

[7] M. Gardner, *Wheels, Life, and other Mathematical Amusements*, Freeman, 1983.

[8] E.R. Berlekampf, J.H. Conway, R.K. Guy, *Winning ways for your mathematical play*, Vol. II, chap. 25, Academic Press, 1982.

[9] K. Hwang, "Advanced Parallel Processing with Super computer Architecture", Proc. of the IEEE, Vol 75, n° 10, Oct. 1987.

[10] P. Marchal, "Cellular Processing : Alternative Approach to Massive Parallelism", Proc. of the Economical Parallel Processing Conference, Zürich, May-June, 1988.

[11] T. Toffoli, N. Margolus, *Cellular Automata Machines - A New Environment for Modeling*, MIT Press, 1987.

[12] A. Clouqueur, "RAP-1, a Cellular Automaton Machine for Fluid Dynamics, in *Lattice Gas Methods for Partial Differential Equations*, (G.D. Doolen Ed.), Addison-Wesley Publishing Comp., pp 251-266, 1990.

[13] P. Marchal, "Display Spying Process Machine: Massively Parallel Concurrent Computation & Display", Proc. of the European Workshop on Massively Parallel Computing, COST 229 - W.G. 4, Leysin, March 1992.

[14] A. El Gamal, "Field-Programmable Integrated Circuits - Overview and Future Trends", Keynote Address of the IEEE International Conference on Computer Design : VLSI in Computers & Processors, ICCD'92, Cambridge, Ma Oct. 1992.

Global control synthesis for an MIMD/FPGA machine

Philippe Dhaussy, Jean-Marie Filloque, Bernard Pottier, Stéphane Rubini
Laboratoire d'Informatique de Brest
Université de Bretagne Occidentale et Télécom Bretagne, BP 809, 29285 Brest
e-mail : <name>@univ-brest.fr

Abstract

Embedding a FPGA *circular array into* MIMD *architectures allows to synthesize fine grain circuits for global computation support. These circuits operate concurrently with the distributed applications. They provide specific speed-up or additional services such as communication protocols or global controllers. This article describes an architectural model for such controllers with practical examples implemented on ArMen FPGA/multiprocessor. A multi-assignment language deriving from* UNITY *formalism is proposed to implement the controllers with a high degree of parallelism. Their hardware synthesis principles are given.*

Key-words: FPGA, ArMen, communication, control.

Introduction

Parallel architectures and computation models are used in a large variety of situations such as regular intensive computations with pipelines or systolic arrays, massive data parallel applications, irregular distributed applications for simulation, industrial control or modeling. Controlling parallel programs is achieved using operations such as synchronization, process termination detection, evaluation of predicate or global scores on distributed values,... Control depends largely on the irregularity of the application. It ranges from implicit coordinations based on a global clock or local asynchronous protocols, to situations where the program must share its time between computation of global states and productive tasks.

Examples of hardware supports for control are low level local communication handshakes, cache coordination, bus arbiters, specific control networks or higher level functions such as Ultracomputer *fetch-and-op* primitive [8] and global virtual time services for distributed simulation. Ultra-computer is a MIMD machine having a built-in synchronization primitive that enables one-cycle memory-access for all processors. A more general solution is used in Thinking Corporation CM5 with a control network having one ALU in each node. It can be noticed that global control operations remain specific and are executed one at a time.

The design of a new parallel architecture embedding a linear network of FPGAs has been an opportunity for re-evaluation of hardware control. The *ArMen* machine allows to reprogram the global resource swiftly and thus, releases the constraints on both generality of hardware and singularity of control-flow. ArMen FPGA resource can be used as local or global accelerators, as a specific communication channel, and finally as a specific and independent support for parallel program control. Implemented circuits include synchronization barriers, mutual exclusions, control for *all-to-one* and *systolic* communications, synchronizer for the dining philosophers problem.

There are no immediate solutions available for the specification of such control programs. Control can be seen as a set of concurrent evaluations applied to arrays of distributed values. Global controller architectures can be defined using regular structures made of arrays of automata and linear networks of operators. A programming model based on concurrent *multiple assignments* is suitable to describe concurrent transfers on arrays as well as parallel operations. This is the aim of the *UCA* language, a derivative from the UNITY formalism [5].

This paper is organized as follows. The first

section presents the ArMen architecture. The second section introduces the global controllers principles, and gives some implementation details and performances from several realizations. A hardware synchronizer will be used as an illustration for the third part of the paper which describes UCA programs and implementation methods.

1 ArMen : a parallel FPGA-based architecture

ArMen [12] is a modular distributed memory architecture where processors are tightly connected to an FPGA ring, so-called *logic layer*. Each ArMen node (fig.1) has a processor connected to a bank of memory and a large FPGA. Current hardware uses TRANSPUTERS and Xilinx LCA3090 on 6U format cards and a 20MHz local clock. The processor loads configuration data into the FPGA in a 100 ms delay using memory-mapped registers. The FPGA pinout is divided among four 36-bit ports. Its north port is connected to the local address/data multiplexed system bus. West and east ports are externally accessible on front edge connectors. Ribbon cables plugged into these connectors allow nodes to be assembled into a ring. South ports are available to implement input/output, to access additional hardware such as DSP subsystems, or to connect to another ArMen node.

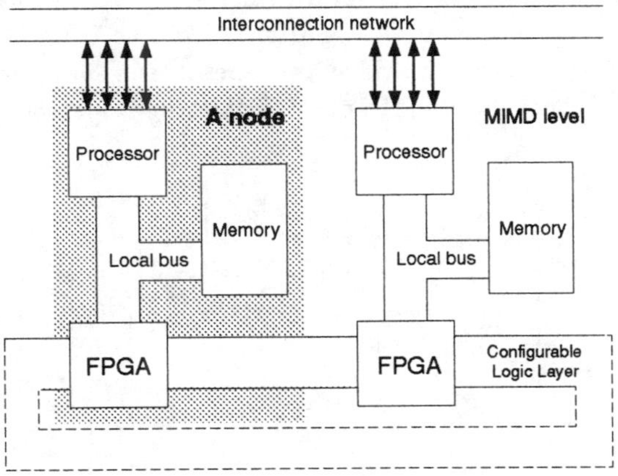

Figure 1: Two node ring architecture

The ArMen machine is a set of such nodes interfaced to a workstation hosting a transputer board. The machine executes the Trollius operating system [2] to ease the application developments. Trollius provides remote input/output, routing facilities and supports the loading and monitoring of processes on the nodes.

The *logic layer* is fully available to provide application speeds-ups or additional services. A simple taxonomy of FPGA-based circuits can be deduced from main data communication streams: (1) local accelerators with exchanges between node processor and FPGA, (2) *shared operators* with intensive processor array-FPGA ring exchanges, (3) *global processors* with intensive FPGA-FPGA exchanges.

Local FPGA-based accelerators can be fed and controlled using the MIMD framework. *Shared operators* provide micro-grain parallelism usable on large data arrays and overcome inter-node data dependency problems at the FPGA interface level. Furthermore, due to the ring topology and the presence of an additional node, it has been shown that too large data spaces can be folded on smaller machines. Shared operators are sporadically used in an SPMD mode by the application. They can be generated from a high level specification based on the cellular automata model. More explanations on this subject can be found in [1] or [4].

Global controllers fall in the third category. They can be associated to communication data paths for systolic communication as described in [10]. The following sections focus on global support for the control of distributed algorithms.

2 Global controllers

Following a paradigm proposed by Chandy and Misra, a parallel execution can be described as two superposed concurrent programs for *application* and *control*. Although neither application nor control are restricted to run on processors or FPGAs, this paradigm helps to explain the behavior of the FPGA network for control operations as well as the interaction with the MIMD "application layer".

2.1 Processors-controller coordination

ArMen hardware provides several mechanisms for data exchanges at the node level. The generic FPGA interface handles memory wait and interrupt signals from the processor. This enables a controller to block a processor or call an interrupt server process. Additionally, FPGA controllers are free to implement FIFO registers or double buffers providing asynchrony with the MIMD layer.

As a result there are several local communication strategies:

1. **tight coupling** where the processor memory interface is blocked by the FPGA until a ready condition is obtained from adjacent nodes. SPMD execution is achieved by high priority processes running a non-preemptive part of the program. Communications can proceed at the link level, but no process switching is allowed. Practical examples are found in systolic communication[10] and shared operators[4].

2. **loose coupling** with double register directional interfaces. This is a kind of shared variables where a processor can write local states, or read global values. Polling an FPGA-based status bit appears to be an alternative to tight coupling.

3. **asynchronous control from the FPGA** where interrupt lines allow the controller to call a process on the node or a process array on the machine.

Switching MIMD and SPMD modes is an interesting illustration for these mechanisms. During an MIMD phase, the controller computes concurrently one or several synchronization barriers. This computation consists of a global inspection of a vector of status bits into the node interfaces (**loose coupling**). When a barrier is reached, an interrupt wave is propagated into a pipeline to call a particular set of processes (**asynchronous control from the FPGA**). These processes gain the control of the whole machine in the same way a system task acts on a sequential machine with disabled interrupts. Then, the machine is used in a synchronous way. As there is no global clock, processor synchronism is deduced locally from the states of adjacent nodes (**tight coupling**). An SPMD phase ends with a global suspension of the task array.

2.2 Controller implementation

The global controllers can be built by composing the elements of the FPGA circular array. Each FPGA configuration is an assembly of standard components which are finite state machines, operator pipelines, local registers and interfaces as it is shown on figure 2. This is a general structure for global controllers.

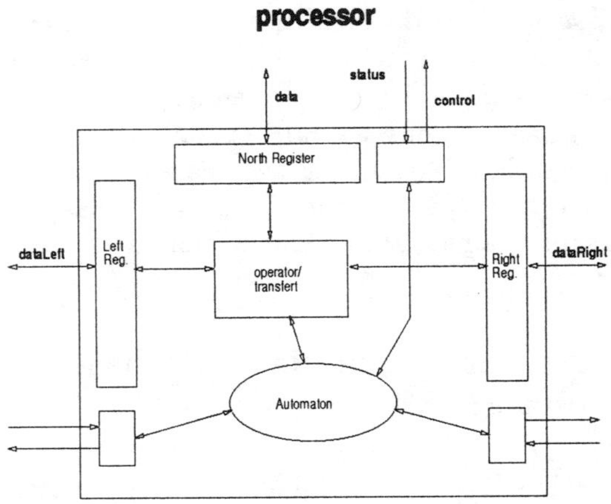

Figure 2: One node controller structure.

- Interfaces from adjacent FPGAs and local processor are structured into a data part and a control part. Data part from the processor is simply connected to the system data bus. Control lines can be either readable status lines or writeable control lines. Status lines from the processor can be loaded from the system address bus (multiplexed on ArMen).

- Operative parts have their input and output connected to the interface data parts. The composition of the operative parts are pipelines for global computations.

- Local automata are sequenced from a local clock. A current version of ArMen uses a 20Mhz signal produced by the processor. They fetch test information from status lines on east and west ports, as well as from the processor interface and operators. They produce values into control parts and operators.

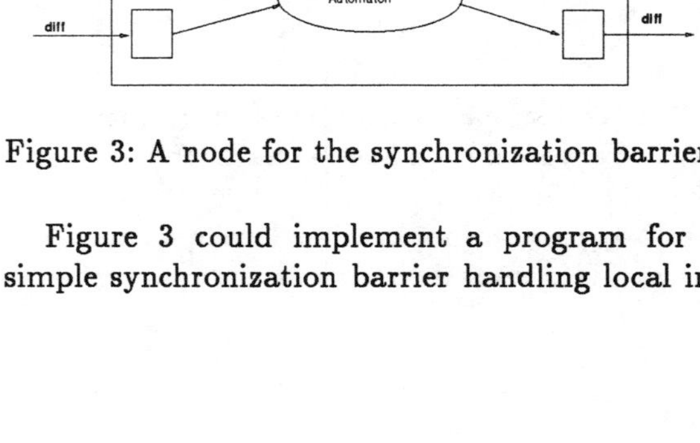

Figure 3: A node for the synchronization barrier.

Figure 3 could implement a program for a simple synchronization barrier handling local interrupts. Each processor writes a barrier request into its north register.

The operative part computes an *AND* condition on the array of the north ports. The automaton is in charge of an interrupt wave propagation. Values are passed across left and right ports.

The time complexity for *logic layer* computation is in the order of $\Theta(n)$ but local automata usually require very few clock cycles to proceed and it must be noticed that the controller acts *concurrently* with the MIMD machine.

2.3 Controller examples

This section summarizes some FPGA global controllers with their implementation scheme. The first three examples have pipelines carrying tokens which encapsulate integer values. Data transfer between two neighbor FPGAs is implemented with an asynchronous handshake. The three last examples are strictly control problems.

All-to-one communication : this circuit has been developed to extract execution traces from the parallel machine without disturbing communications and process scheduling. Tokens permanently circulate into the ring. They carry a value and a marker for full and empty conditions (fig. 4). Writing processors are blocked until an empty token is available. The collector node reads token values and passes their contents to the host computer. The measured data rate on the collector node is about 500 Kbytes/s.

Shared variable : a token holding a value circulates on the ring. Processes watch for the token, and retain it in order to change atomically its value. A distributed resource allocator has been built with this service.

Extremum function approximation : snapshot algorithms are fundamental paradigms of distributed computing. Applications are algorithms for the detection of stable properties such as termination of a distributed computation [11] or deadlock of a distributed system. Those algorithms can be used to compute monotonic functions of global states. For example, in the *Global Virtual Time* computation, a lower bound of all the local logic clocks in the network is evaluated. Timestamps are passed to a global circuit in the *logic layer* that computes the minimum value.

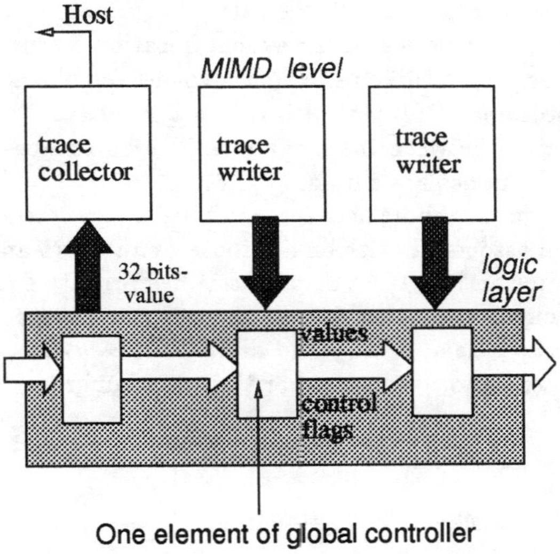

Figure 4: All-to-one communication : Tokens carry values and control flags.

For the termination detection problem, the current state of processes (*active, idle*) defines the set of values. Specific attention must be paid to computations on local non-monotonic values. Simple solutions are provided to resolve this problem [6].

Synchronizer for the mutual exclusion : the distributed control allows an exclusive resource to be shared. A wave distributes the privilege on the node ring (fig. 5). Arbitration is resolved in 75 *ns* average time per node with zero cost for the processor.

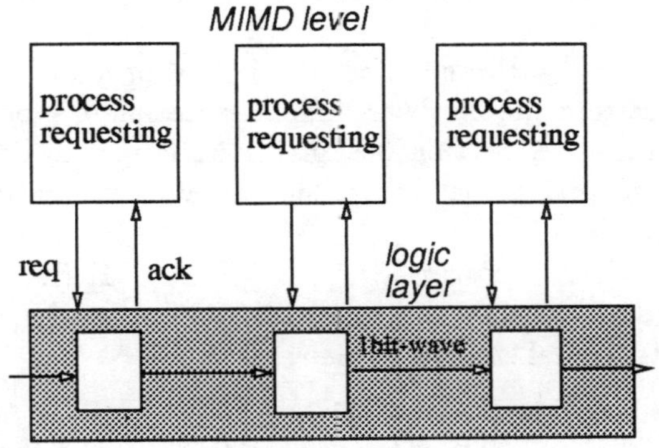

Figure 5: Mutual exclusion controller : a Boolean wave distributes the privilege.

Synchronizer for the dining logicians' problem : this is a classic synchronization problem proposed by Dijkstra, which involves neighboring conditions. The control involves a local synchronization between the neighbors. The automata of all the nodes are similar (fig. 6).

Two neighbors share two variables : an integer *fork* associated with an attribute *clean/dirty* and a Boolean *reqfork* . A process i has priority over a neighbor j if and only if the fork they share is at i and clean or at j and dirty. With *reqfork*, a process informs a neighbor that it is hungry.

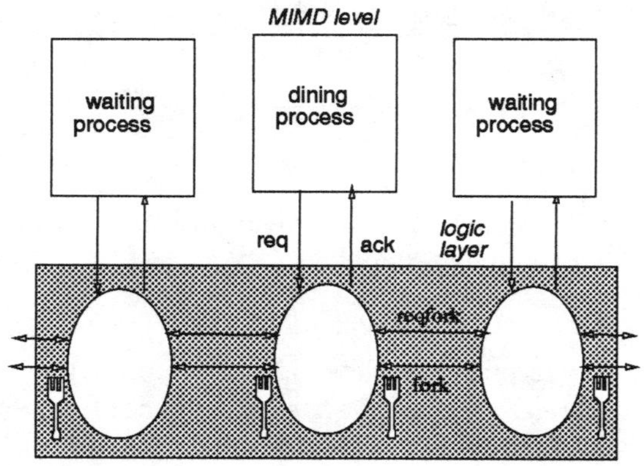

Figure 6: Dining logicians' controller with local synchronization.

Global synchronization : this circuit is frequently used to implement synchronization barriers on the machine and it is described in the next section.

2.4 A simple synchronization barrier

The synchronization barrier is proposed to illustrate the hardware implementation of global controllers. Section 3 explains a method to describe this global controller and its compilation scheme.

When a process $P_i, i \in [0 \,..\, N-1]$ (for N nodes), reaches the condition for the barrier, it sets a local state variable req_i.

When the global condition $\bigwedge_{\forall i \in [0 \,..\, N-1]} req\ [i]$ is set, an acknowledge wave (*ack*) is sent to the processes waiting for the barrier.

The implementation consists of two pipelines broadcasting the waves *wreq* and *diff* managed by the automata in node 0 (fig. 8) and node i, $\forall i \in [1 \,..\, N-1]$. (fig. 9).

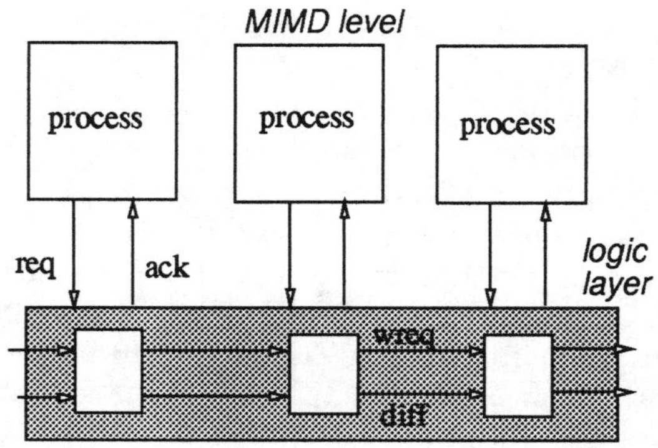

Figure 7: A service for synchronization barrier.

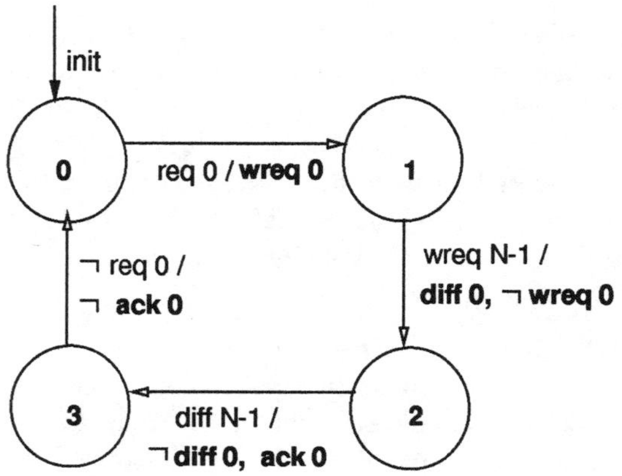

Figure 8: The node 0 automaton.

In these figures, the performed actions during a transition are noted with bold print.

2.5 Performances

For the synchronization barrier example given above, the wave propagation time between two logic circuits in the programmable logic layer is bounded by 2 clock ticks. The delay between the occurrence of the last *req* and the diffusion of this information to the last node is bounded by $3\ N \times T_e$, where T_e is the delay for one FPGA/FPGA transfer.

The processor network uses the control circuit with a simple read-write access to one memory address. Alternately, interrupt waves may be used to signal conditions on the network. Also, the synchronization barrier control does not involve overhead on the computation and communication resources of the processors. Several barriers can work concurrently.

Table 1 shows a summary of hardware resources used in previous examples. They do not depend on

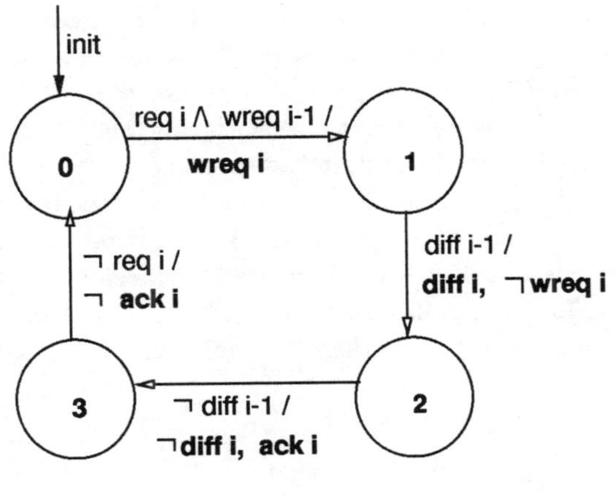

Figure 9: The node i automaton.

the number of nodes. The time required for one global condition computation, *i.e.* the delay between a condition becoming true and the last node learning it, is in the order of $\Theta(n)$. So, the pipeline models can give good performances up to some hundred nodes. Taking current integration density into account, they offer the best cost/performance ratio.

circuits	number of CLB's	number of IOB's
all-to-one-comm. (32 bits)	68	132
shared variable (8 bits)	44	29
mutual exclusion	14	4
dining logicians	43	10
strong synchronizer	7	6

Table 1: Complexity of different circuits

3 A programming model for global controllers

UCA is a language based on the concurrent *multiple assignments* model, close to the UNITY formalism [5] which provides a general programming paradigm.

It is used to describe the behavior of the control circuits which are implemented in the ArMen *logic layer*. The *multiple assignments* are quite similar to *Synchronized Transitions* [9] whose goal was to propose a hardware language to describe both synchronous and asynchronous circuits and to systematically transform them into efficient VLSI layouts.

A *UCA* program describes an execution as a set of guarded assignment statements which run concurrently. The execution of the *multiple assignments* is atomic and each one appears to be executed indivisibly. There is no hypothesis about the assignment execution order. Non-deterministic selection is only constrained by the following rule: *Every assignment statement is selected infinitely often* (fairness assumption).

The concurrent multiple assignments, the absence of control flow and use of program states can provide a level of detail that is adequate to represent hardware for initial logic design.

3.1 Multiple assignments

The general form of *multiple assignments* is

$$v1,\ v2,\ldots := e1,\ e2,\ldots \textbf{if}\ g$$

where v_i are variables, e_i, expressions and g is a Boolean expression generating the statement. A *UCA* program is run by repeatedly choosing a statement whose guard is true and executing it. All the variables are assigned simultaneously in a *multiple assignment*.

It is possible to generate a list of assignment statements by providing their common pattern. This feature has the form :

$$\langle\ \|\, ind\ :\ range\ ::\ statements\ \rangle$$

where *ind* is a list of indexes, *range* is a predicate on those indexes, and *statements* is a list of statements that mentions indexed variables. The above expression generates an instance of *statements* for each value of the dummy variables that satisfies *range*.

Multiple assignments and state variables model combinational functions and state registers. The communication is modeling by the sharing of the variables.

In *multiple assignments*, the simultaneity is represented by the operator "," and is implemented in a synchronous way in one FPGA. The ‖ operator allows assignments to be asynchronously composed. *Multiple assignments*, separated by ‖ operator, execute independently, each one in turn, whenever their precondition becomes satisfied. They are implemented either in a single node, or in several nodes. The parallelism is achieved through a non-deterministic interleaving of the *multiple assignment* together with synchronous internal assignments.

Implementation conditions ensure that the atomicity of *multiple assignments* is preserved by hardware implementation. The *UCA* compiler verifies these conditions.

3.2 *UCA* program structure

An algorithm is described by both these parts: one is compiled for the processor network (the *assign operative* section) and another implemented for the *logic layer* (the *assign control* section). This union construction allows both kind of executions with a single syntactic entity (*program*). In our work, the program which describes the behavior of the processors simulates an environment using the global controller functions implemented in the *logic layer*. The *declare* section names the variables used in the program and their types. The *initially* section is used to define initial values of some variables. The *assign* sections contain a set of guarded, multiple assignment statements, with the ‖ operator used as statement separator. During a program execution, the variables are initialized, and then statements are selected arbitrarily. In an infinite execution of the program, each statement is executed infinitely often.

In the current implementation, the *UCA* compiler produces C code (from section assign operative) and Boolean equations files (from section assign control). The *UCA* compiler verifies implementation conditions (section 3.4) which ensure that the semantics is preserved by hardware implementation. The C code describes the behavior of the communicating processes on the processors and interfaces with the Trollius communication layer. The Boolean equations correspond to the assignment statements of the variables in the *logic layer*. The XILINX tools transform the Boolean equations into a configuration file for each FPGA. This file is loaded locally during program execution.

3.3 Data distribution

The compilation principles of *UCA* programs for ArMen are based on the *data-driven parallelization* technique [3]. The data of a program is distributed on the node network of the machine. A program can be compiled for the ArMen machine if the compiler can allocate statically each variable on a single node (the owner of this variable) which is authorized to modify it. The programmer must specify where he wishes each variable to be with annotations to make the compilation phase easier. The programmer indicates, in the *declare* section of the *UCA* program, the type of desired allocation with the keywords *distribute* for the arrays and *locate* for the simple variable,

Each variable can be located either in the node memory or in the *logic layer*. The keyword *logic* specifies a variable implemented in the logic circuit. The compiler detects those read by the processor and allocates them in the interface of the logic circuit.

3.4 Conditions required by compilation

Some conditions are needed for the compilation and static checks are performed by the compiler. These conditions concern the locality of variable access.

To respect the semantics of the *UCA* programs, the updates of all the left hand-side variables of a *multiple assignment* must be simultaneous. So they must be owned by the same node and are to be allocated either all to the processor or all to the logic circuit. The part of the program compiled into logic circuits holds only assignments which have right and left side variables according to the neighboring locality principle.

Other conditions concern the allowable inter-chips connection complexity. The size of data transferred must be compatible with the connection resources of the architecture, *i.e.* FPGA/FPGA and FPGA/TRANSPUTER connections.

3.5 Program transformations

Program transformations are essential to guarantee the correct realization of logic circuits.

One transformation is carried out by the compiler and implements asynchronous handshaking to guarantee correct inter-FPGA data transfers of integers.

In a circuit, several assignments or read/write operations (Bernstein's conditions) can be enabled simultaneously on the same variable. This is a violation the atomicity principle. It can be the case for two assignments which share variables (Bernstein's conditions). An other transformation is carried out to guarantee a deterministic behavior of the program and is user-conducted. The compiler has to ensure that the guards of the assignments of a variable are exclusive. With a state graph built from the program, he detects and indicates to the user the dependent *multiple assignments* with non-exclusive guards with a state graph built from the program. Then, the user has to transform the guard of these assignments. Ongoing investigation involves the systematic introduction of a assignment-scheduling mecanism to resolve this problem.

3.6 Synchronization barrier program

With the *multiple assignments* formalism, the pipelines can be described with local variables. Fragments of a *UCA* program are presented below.

```
Program sync
declare
  N    : constant 8  --- number of nodes
       ...
  req  : array [N] of boolean  distribute 1
  ack, wreq, diff :
       array [N] of boolean  distribute 1 logic
initially
       ...
assign operative
  --  requests synchronization
       ...
  [] --  global condition ack
       ...
assign control
  - start of wreq wave on node 0
    wreq [0] := true
       if ( req [0] ∧ ¬ ack [0] ∧ ¬ diff [0])

  [] - start of diff  wave  on node 0
    diff [0], wreq [0] := true, false
    if ( wreq [N − 1] ∧ ¬ diff [0] ∧ wreq [0])

  [] - wreq wave on node i
    ⟨ [] i : 0 < i < N ::  wreq [i] := true
    if ( req [i] ∧ wreq [i − 1] ∧
       ¬ ack [i] ∧ ¬ diff [i]) ⟩

  [] - diff wave on node i
    ⟨ [] i : 0 < i < N ::
    diff [i], wreq [i] := true, false
       if ( diff [i − 1] ∧ wreq [i] ) ⟩
[]     ...
end
```

The complete program is shown in appendix.

3.7 Simulation and verification

Direct development on FPGAs leads to two kinds of difficulties. Firstly, the compilation cycle remains too large to allow comfortable debugging. Secondly, observation of parallel FPGA-based programs is clearly inaccessible with common software tools.

Sequential simulation helps to have confidence in algorithms by test and analysis. A compiler option allows a simulation program to be generated. In each step of this simulation a list of possible transitions is produced. The simulator can take transitions randomly or under user control. This tool is used to reach particular global states and observe progresses in a deterministic way.

Verification is a heavier but more accurate assistant tool for development. In the *UCA* programs, the parallelism is achieved through a non-determinism interleaving ($[\!]$) of the assign statements. The semantics of the programs is that of transition systems. The programs may be modeled as transition systems which describe all possible atomic transitions. This means that execution of a program containing transitions which are to be executed in parallel is represented by a non-deterministic interleaving of the atomic transitions. It has been shown that the finite transition systems are well-adapted to formal verification [13]. So, the principle is to produce a state graph for the program and then to verify expected properties for each vertex of the graph.

Some safety properties can be described to verify the correction of a program. The langage is extended to formulate invariants in an *assert* section. An example of assertion verified on the transition system is presented below :

```
assert
⟨  ∧  i : 0  <=  i  <  N ::
   (step [i] ==  P ∨ step [i] ==
               (P − 1  +  N) mod N) ⟩
```

The *step* variable records the advancement of the processes. P is an auxiliary variable and is only used to verify the assertion.

Other safety and liveness properties are more difficult to formulate. This point motivates experimentations with standard formal technique based on the *model checking*. This is achieved by a comparison of the problem specification and the transition graph deduced from the *UCA* programs. Currently, the *UCA* compiler is associated with a program verifier with an explicit specification of expected properties. A limitation of the *model checking* approach is due to the combinatory complexity. In some experimented algorithms, the stored behavior graph can contain as many as ten thousand states. However, this problem can be overcome by restricting attention to a class of algorithms where the variables are essentially Boolean and small integers. It is the case of the global controller algorithms.

Conclusion

UCA has been found to be useful for synthesis of global controllers. These circuits operate concurrently with the MIMD machine. They provide synchronization services, clocks, they ease the implementation of specific communication schemes. Propagation of synchronization information is in the order of 100 ns per node with no cost for the MIMD machine. Application fields are expected to be general purpose parallel architectures as well as small industrial processing systems.

Many problems are not currently solved by the language and its compiler. A global computation delay is far beyond the cycle time at the processor node level. So, global evaluations remain in the scope of distributed algorithms[7]. More work has to be done to allow automatic distribution of control computations between the processor and the FPGA arrays.

ArMen is used as an experimental machine to investigate the use of FPGA arrays inside parallel architectures. Global control is only one aspect of these investigations that include global operative parts, specific communications and local accelerators.

Acknowledgments

Acknowledgments are due to the French PRC-GDR [1] *Architectures Nouvelles de Machines and C^3*. Thanks are also due to Region Bretagne, ANVAR, and the Brest municipality for their support. Special thanks are given to the *Doctoral Network for System and Machine Architecture of the DRED*, french Ministry of National Education.

[1] Research programs funded by the Ministry for Research and CNRS

References

[1] K. Bouazza, J. Champeau, P. Ng, B. Pottier, and S. Rubini. Implementing Cellular Automata on the ArMen Machine. In P. Quinton and Y. Robert, editor, *Proceedings of the Workshop on Algorithms and Parallel VLSI Achitectures II*, pages 317–322, Bonas, France, June 1991. Elsevier Science Publishers B.V.

[2] Greg Burns, Vidha Radiya, Raja Daoud, and Raghu Machiraju. All About TROLLIUS. *Occam User Group Newsletter*, pages 55–70, July 1990.

[3] David Callahan and Ken Kennedy. Compiling programs for distributed-memory multiprocessors. *The journal of supercomputing*, 2:151–169, 1988.

[4] J. Champeau and al. Flexible Parallel FPGA-Based Architectures with ArMen. In *Proc. of HICSS'94 (to be published)*, Hawai, January 1994.

[5] K. Chandy and J. Misra. *Parallel Program Design, a Foundation.* Addison-Wesley, 1988.

[6] J. M. Filloque. *Synchronisation répartie sur une machine parallèle à couche logique reconfigurable.* PhD thesis, Université de Rennes I, France, November 1992.

[7] J.M. Filloque, E. Gautrin, and B. Pottier. Efficient Global Computation on a Processor Network with Programmable Logic. In *Proceedings of PARLE'91*, number 505 in LNCS, pages 55–63, Eindhoven, NL, June 1991. Springer-Verlag.

[8] A. Gottlieb and Alt. The NYU Ultracomputer– Designing a MIMD Shared Memory Parallel Machine. In *Proceedings of 9th Annual Symposium on Computer Architecture*, pages 27–41, Austin, Texas, USA, April 1982.

[9] M.Greenstreet J.Staunstrup. From high-level descriptions to vlsi circuits. *BIT*, 28(3):620–638, 1988.

[10] D. Lavenier, F.Raimbault, B. Pottier, and S. Rubini. Fine grain parallelism on an MIMD machine using FPGAs. In *FPGAs*

for Custom Computing Machines, Napa, CA, April 1993. IEEE.

[11] Friedemann Mattern. Algorithms for distributed termination detection. *Distributed Computing*, (2):161–175, 1987.

[12] B. Pottier. *ArMen, une machine parallèle intégrant un réseau de circuits logiques reconfigurables.* PhD thesis, Université de Rennes I, France, June 1991.

[13] J. P. Queille and J . Sifakis. Specification and verification of concurrent systems in cesar. In *lecture Notes in Computer Science*, volume 137. International Symposium on programming, Springer Verlag, Berlin, 1982.

A UCA program for a synchronization barrier

```
Program sync
declare
  N    : constant 8   --- number of nodes
  P    : integer 3
  step : array [N] of integer 3 distribute 1
  req  : array [N] of boolean  distribute 1
  ack, wreq, diff :
         array [N] of boolean  distribute 1 logic

initially
  ⟨ ▯ i : 0 ≤ i < N ::
    req [i], ack [i], wreq [i], diff [i], step [i] =
    false, false, false, false, 0 ⟩
  ▯ P = 0

assign operative
  -- requests synchronization
  ⟨ ▯ i : 0 ≤ i < N ::
    req [i] := true   if ( ¬ req [i] ∧ ¬ ack [i] ⟩

  ▯ -- global condition ack
   ⟨ ▯ i : 0 ≤ i < N ::
    req [i], step[i] := false, (step[i] + 1) mod N
       if (req [i] ∧ ack [i]) ⟩

assign control
  -- start of wreq wave
    wreq [0] := true
       if ( req [0] ∧ ¬ ack [0] ∧ ¬ diff [0])

  ▯ -- start of diff wave
    diff [0], wreq [0] := true, false
       if ( wreq [N − 1] ∧ ¬ diff [0] ∧ wreq [0] )

  ▯ -- start of ack wave
   diff [0], ack [0], P := false, true, (P + 1) mod N
       if (diff [0] ∧ diff [N − 1])

  ▯ -- wreq wave
   ⟨ ▯ i : 0 < i < N :: wreq [i] := true
   if ( req [i] ∧ wreq [i − 1] ∧
       ¬ ack [i] ∧ ¬ diff [i]) ⟩

  ▯ -- diff wave
   ⟨ ▯ i : 0 < i < N ::
   diff [i], wreq [i] := true, false
      if ( diff [i − 1] ∧ wreq [i] ) ⟩

  ▯ -- ack wave
   ⟨ ▯ i : 0 < i < N ::
   diff [i], ack [i] := false, true
      if ( diff [i] ∧ ¬ diff [i − 1] ) ⟩

  ▯ -- end of protocol
   ⟨ ▯ i : 0 ≤ i < N ::
   ack [i] := false   if ( ack [i] ∧ ¬ req [i] ) ⟩

assert
   ⟨ ∧ i : 0 ≤ i < N :: (step [i] == P ∨
               step [i] == (P − 1 + N) mod N) ⟩

end
```

Hardware-Software Codesign of Multidimensional Programs

Wayne Luk, Teddy Wu and Ian Page
Programming Research Group,
Oxford University Computing Laboratory,
11 Keble Road, Oxford, England OX1 3QD

Abstract

We present a method for parametrised partitioning of multidimensional programs for acceleration using a hardware coprocessor. The method involves a divide-and-conquer structure, with the "divide" and "merge" phases carried out by a general-purpose processor while the "conquer" phase is handled by application-specific hardware. The partitioning strategy has been captured in a simple functional language, and we have automated the production of partitioned programs in this language. Our approach has been tested on an FPGA-based system using a number of computer vision algorithms, including the Canny edge detector, and the performance is compared against executing the programs on the PC host.

1 Introduction

The objective of our research on hardware-software codesign is to develop systems containing both hardware and software components with higher quality, in shorter time, and at lower cost than existing ones. Recent advances in programmable logic, particularly Field-Programmable Gate Arrays (FPGAs), offer a rapid route for building reconfigurable hardware accelerators. It is clear that a cost-effective implementation can be obtained by combining fast but expensive hardware with slow but cheap microprocessors; in particular, methods for appropriate partitioning of computations for coordinated execution in hardware and in software are essential.

This paper describes a strategy for partitioning programs operating on multidimensional arrays of data. The aim is to convert such programs by correctness-preserving transformations into parametrised descriptions, which can then be used to generate efficient implementations with a variety of hardware-software trade-offs. Our method may be applied to overcome physical limitations – such as having an insufficient amount of memory – in hardware accelerators. It partitions an program into three steps: "divide", "conquer" and "merge". A general-purpose processor, usually proficient in executing relatively complex, data-dependent and variable size operations, can be used for dividing the input data into smaller pieces and for merging the results of processing the pieces. Purpose-built hardware is used for processing the partitioned data, often in a systolic mode [7].

Many algorithms can be expressed clearly and concisely in a functional language; functional programs are often used as executable specifications and in rapid prototyping. Moreover, simple equational transformations can be used to reason about functional programs. Our partitioning strategy has been captured in a functional notation adopted by Bird and Wadler [2]. In this notation, applying g to an argument x – which can itself be a function – will be denoted by $g\ x$; function application is left associative, so $g\ x\ y\ z = ((g\ x)\ y)\ z$. The infix operator $\cdot$ denotes function composition: $(f \cdot g)\ x = f\ (g\ x)$. It is the least binding among binary operators, so $f \cdot g\ x = f \cdot (g\ x)$.

It is straightforward to state the correctness requirement for a partitioning strategy in a functional notation. Let f be the program to be partitioned. Our partitioning strategy, given by $partition\ f$, is a composition of three functions $divide$, $conquer$ and $merge$,

$$partition\ f \quad = \quad merge \cdot conquer\ f \cdot divide$$

Later on we shall show that under certain conditions, this definition of $partition$ satisfies the correctness requirement that

$$partition\ f \quad = \quad f$$

In other words, the partitioning strategy does not affect the behaviour of f.

Our partitioning strategy has been implemented in a functional programming environment known as Gofer [5], which can be obtained by anonymous ftp from `nebula.cs.yale.edu` in directory `pub/haskell/gofer`. The Gofer language is very similar to the notation that we use, although there are minor syntactic differences. It should not be difficult to implement our method in other functional languages such as Orwell, Miranda or SML.

0-8186-5490-2/94 $03.00 © 1994 IEEE

A number of partitioned programs, including sorting and computer vision routines, have been tested on an FPGA-based hardware accelerator known as CHS2x4 [1]. The CHS2x4 is a full-length IBM AT card which communicates with the host computer through the AT bus. The board consists of three subsystems: the Computation Subsystem which holds eight CAL 1024 chips [6] arranged in a two by four array, the Memory Subsystem which contains 256 kilobytes of SRAM, and the Interface and Control Subsystem which deals with the communication between the board and its host machine. At present data transfer between the CAL chips and the on-board memory is restricted to sequential input and output over a byte-wide channel, controlled by invoking C-library routines provided by the manufacturer. Each CAL chip is an FPGA consisting of 32 by 32 cells. Each cell has a one-bit input port and a one-bit output port on each of its four sides. An input port can be programmed to connect to one or more output ports, or to a function unit which can be programmed to behave either as a two-input combinational logic gate or as a latch.

In the following sections we present the partitioning strategy, and show how it can be adopted in developing multidimensional programs that can be speeded up by the CHS2x4.

2 Partitioning Strategy

As explained above, a simple approach has been adopted for partitioning programs: a slow engine is used for arranging data into fixed-size blocks that can be handled by a fast but resource-limited engine. Usually the former corresponds to a general-purpose processor, while the latter is implemented by application-specific hardware. Possible applications of this paradigm include computer vision and medical image processing, where the amount of data is often too large for the hardware coprocessor to handle at once.

Although the "divide" and "merge" phases for some computations involve simply partitioning the input data for the dedicated hardware and concatenating the results, this may not always be the case. For instance, in convolution-based algorithms it is usually necessary to replicate the pixels around the partition boundary in neighbouring blocks. This is taken into account by our partitioning method.

Let f be the function to be partitioned; f is required to satisfy certain conditions to be described later in this paper. To capture hardware constraints for implementing an n-dimensional program, we use n constants, $maxp_i$ with $1 \leq i \leq n$, to denote for each dimension the maximum number of elements in a partition. The function *partition* takes f as argument and returns the partitioned operation. It is defined in terms of three functions, *divide*, *conquer* and *merge*, each corresponding to one step in the partitioned program:

$$partition\ f \quad = \quad merge \cdot conquer\ f \cdot divide$$

Note that *divide*, *conquer*, *merge* and the conditions which f must satisfy are specific to the number of dimensions of the program, although the basic principle behind the partitioning strategy is the same for programs of any dimension. Let us begin with the simple case of one-dimensional programs, and later extend the strategy to programs for higher dimensions.

3 Partitioning One-Dimensional Programs

A one-dimensional array of data will be represented by a list, the elements of which will be enclosed by square brackets. $\#xs$ denotes the number of elements in list xs. List construction is signified by a colon, so

$$\begin{aligned} a:[b,c,d] &= [a,b,c,d] \\ &= a:(b:(c:(d:[]))) \end{aligned}$$

The (++) operator appends two lists, for example

$$[a,b] +\!\!+ [c,d,e] \quad = \quad [a,b,c,d,e]$$

Two functions *take* and *drop* will be used in describing our partitioning method. Each of them takes a non-negative integer n and a list xs as arguments. The value of $(take\ n\ xs)$ is the initial segment of xs of length n, and the value of $(drop\ n\ xs)$ is the list which remains when the first n elements are removed: so

$$\begin{aligned} take\ 3\ [a,b,c,d,e] &= [a,b,c] \\ drop\ 3\ [a,b,c,d,e] &= [d,e] \end{aligned}$$

Clearly for $0 \leq i \leq \#xs$,

$$take\ i\ xs +\!\!+ drop\ i\ xs \quad = \quad xs$$

During the initial "divide" step, a list of data will be partitioned into a list of shorter lists of equal length, except possibly the last one. For some algorithms such as convolution, it is necessary to replicate the boundary elements; in other words, we need to include in each sub-array a number of elements in neighbouring sub-arrays. The number of replicated elements in successive partitions is given by the constant *margin*, and the maximum number of elements in each partition will be denoted by *maxp*; for n-dimensional programs these constants will become $margin_i$ and $maxp_i$

for $1 \leq i \leq n$. Let $maxp' = maxp - margin$: then $divide$ is implemented by the function $divide_1$ in one dimension,

$$\begin{aligned} & divide_1\ xs \\ & \quad = take\ maxp\ xs : (divide_1 \cdot drop\ maxp')\ xs, \\ & \qquad \text{if } \#xs > maxp \\ & \quad = [xs], \quad \text{otherwise} \end{aligned}$$

This recursive definition indicates that provided that $\#xs > maxp > margin$, the first $maxp$ elements of xs will form the first sublist of the partitioned list, and the remaining sublists can be obtained by applying $divide_1$ again to a version of xs shortened by dropping the first $maxp'$ elements. For instance, given $maxp = 3$ and $margin = 1$, $divide_1\ [0, 1, 2, 3, 4, 5] = [[0, 1, 2], [2, 3, 4], [4, 5]]$.

To process each sublist in the list produced by $divide_1$, $conquer$ is given by

$$conquer \quad = \quad map$$

where map applies the function g to each element of a list: $map\ g\ [x_0, x_1, x_2] = [g\ x_0, g\ x_1, g\ x_2]$.

Merging the list of results from $conquer$ is performed by the function $merge_1$ which is defined in terms of a binary operator $\odot$:

$$merge_1 \quad = \quad foldr1\ (\odot)$$

where $foldr1$ is given by

$$\begin{aligned} & foldr1\ (\odot)\ [x_0, x_1, \ldots, x_n] \\ & \quad = x_0 \odot (x_1 \odot \cdots (x_{n-1} \odot x_n) \cdots) \end{aligned}$$

We can now specify what it means for a partitioning strategy to be correct: the same result would be obtained whether or not partitioning is involved. Given the above definitions, it can be shown by induction that

$$f\ xs \quad = \quad partition_1\ f\ xs \tag{1}$$

provided that $\odot$ satisfies

$$\begin{aligned} f\ xs \quad = \quad & (f\ (take\ maxp\ xs)) \\ & \odot (f\ (drop\ maxp'\ xs)) \end{aligned} \tag{2}$$

Since $maxp' = maxp - margin$, Equation 2 shows that if we divide a list into two with $margin$ elements duplicated at the point of division, combining the results using $\odot$ should give the same value as that obtained without partitioning. Different $\odot$'s correspond to different ways of combining the partial results.

A simple example which satisfies Equation 2 is $f = id$, $\odot = +\!\!+$ and $margin = 0$, where id is the identity function given by $id\ x = x$. Another example is $f = sort$, $\odot = mergelist$ and $margin = 0$, where $sort$ sorts a list of elements into ascending order, and $mergelist$ merges two sorted lists to form a sorted list. This method for partitioning sorters has been implemented on the CHS2x4 system [9]. A more complicated example will be considered next.

4 One-Dimensional Convolution

Consider first the function $zipWith$, which takes a binary operator $\oplus$ and applies it to corresponding elements of two lists which may have different number of elements:

$$\begin{aligned} & zipWith\ \oplus\ [x_0, x_1, x_2]\ [y_0, y_1, y_2, y_3, y_4] \\ & \quad = [x_0 \oplus y_0,\ x_1 \oplus y_1,\ x_2 \oplus y_2] \end{aligned}$$

The length of the result is the same as the length of the shorter of the two arguments. Some readers may recognise that this definition of $zipWith$ is the same as that in Gofer, and is slightly different from $zipwith$ in [2].

One-dimensional convolution can be described by

$$convolve_1\ ws\ xs \quad = \quad map\ g\ [0..(\#xs - \#ws)] \tag{3}$$

where

$$g\ i \quad = \quad (foldr1\ (\oplus)\ .\ zipWith\ (\otimes))\ ws\ (drop\ i\ xs)$$

Note that $[0..m]$ corresponds to the list $[0, 1, \ldots, m]$. An experienced functional programmer may recast $convolve_1$ into a more succinct form using list comprehension [2], but we shall not go into the details here.

The correctness of the definition given by Equation 3 can be demonstrated using symbolic execution. Let us define

$$\begin{aligned} x \oplus y \quad &= \quad \text{“(”} +\!\!+ x +\!\!+ \text{“+”} +\!\!+ y +\!\!+ \text{“)”} \\ x \otimes y \quad &= \quad \text{“(”} +\!\!+ x +\!\!+ \text{“×”} +\!\!+ y +\!\!+ \text{“)”} \end{aligned}$$

and

$$\begin{aligned} ws \quad &= \quad [\text{“}w0\text{”}, \text{“}w1\text{”}, \text{“}w2\text{”}], \\ xs \quad &= \quad [\text{“}x0\text{”}, \text{“}x1\text{”}, \text{“}x2\text{”}, \text{“}x3\text{”}, \text{“}x4\text{”}, \text{“}x5\text{”}, \text{“}x6\text{”}, \text{“}x7\text{”}]. \end{aligned}$$

It can then be shown by hand or by the Gofer interpreter that

$$\begin{aligned} & convolve_1\ ws\ xs \\ & \quad = [\text{“}((w0 \times x0) + ((w1 \times x1) + (w2 \times x2)))\text{”}, \\ & \qquad \text{“}((w0 \times x1) + ((w1 \times x2) + (w2 \times x3)))\text{”}, \\ & \qquad \text{“}((w0 \times x2) + ((w1 \times x3) + (w2 \times x4)))\text{”}, \\ & \qquad \text{“}((w0 \times x3) + ((w1 \times x4) + (w2 \times x5)))\text{”}, \\ & \qquad \text{“}((w0 \times x4) + ((w1 \times x5) + (w2 \times x6)))\text{”}, \\ & \qquad \text{“}((w0 \times x5) + ((w1 \times x6) + (w2 \times x7)))\text{”}] \end{aligned}$$

The above is an example of symbolic simulation. The corresponding numerical evaluation can be obtained by replacing symbolic operations and symbolic data by numerical ones.

From the properties of functions such as *take*, *drop* and *zipWith*, it can be shown that $convolve_1\ ws$ satisfies Equation 2 with $\odot = +\!\!+$ and $margin = (\#ws) - 1$. In other words,

$$\begin{aligned} & convolve_1\ ws\ xs \\ & \quad = convolve_1\ ws\ (take\ maxp\ xs) \\ & \qquad +\!\!+\ convolve_1\ ws\ (drop\ maxp'\ xs) \end{aligned}$$

Hence by Equation 1,

$$convolve_1\ ws\ xs \quad = \quad partition_1\ (convolve_1\ ws)\ xs.$$

5 Partitioning Multidimensional Programs

An n-dimensional array will be represented by a list with n nested levels. Given that $g^0 = id$ and $g^i = g \cdot g \cdot \ldots \cdot g$ (i times) and $hd\ (x : xs) = x$, the definitions of *divide*, *conquer* and *merge* can be generalised to deal with nested lists:

$$\begin{aligned} & divide \\ & \quad = map^{n-1}\ divide_n \cdot \ldots \cdot map\ divide_2 \cdot divide_1 \end{aligned}$$

$$\begin{aligned} & conquer \\ & \quad = map^n \end{aligned}$$

$$\begin{aligned} & merge \\ & \quad = merge_1 \cdot map\ merge_2 \cdot \ldots \cdot map^{n-1}\ merge_n \end{aligned}$$

Also for $1 \le i \le n$, let $maxp'_i = maxp_i - margin_i$, and

$$\begin{aligned} & divide_i\ xs \\ & \quad = map^{i-1}\ (take\ maxp_i)\ xs \\ & \qquad : (divide_i \cdot map^{i-1}\ (drop\ maxp'_i))\ xs, \\ & \qquad\quad \text{if } \#(hd^{i-1}\ xs) > maxp_i \\ & \quad = [xs], \text{ otherwise} \end{aligned}$$

and there exist n binary operators $\odot_1, \odot_2, .., \odot_n$ such that for $1 \le i \le n$,

$$\begin{aligned} & merge_i \\ & \quad = foldr1\ \underbrace{(zipWith\ (zipWith \ldots (zipWith\ (\odot_i)) \ldots))}_{i-1\ terms} \end{aligned}$$

Given that f is the program to be partitioned, then these binary operators should satisfy

$$\begin{aligned} f\ xs \quad = \quad & \underbrace{(zipWith\ (zipWith \ldots (zipWith\ (\odot_i)) \ldots))}_{i-1\ terms} \\ & (f\ (map^i\ (take\ maxp_i)\ xs)) \\ & (f\ (map^i\ (drop\ maxp'_i)\ xs)) \end{aligned} \tag{4}$$

for $1 \le i \le n$.

A Gofer program has been written which can generate the appropriate Gofer definitions of *divide*, *conquer* and *merge* for a given number of dimensions. For instance, the following definitions are produced for $n = 3$:

$$\begin{aligned} & divide \\ & \quad = (map \cdot map)\ divide_3 \cdot map\ divide_2 \cdot divide_1 \end{aligned}$$

$$\begin{aligned} & conquer \\ & \quad = map \cdot map \cdot map \end{aligned}$$

$$\begin{aligned} & merge \\ & \quad = merge_1 \cdot map\ merge_2 \cdot (map \cdot map)\ merge_3 \end{aligned}$$

The definitions of $divide_1$ and $merge_1$ have been given in a Section 3. The definitions of $divide_2$ and $merge_2$ are similar to those of $divide_3$ and $merge_3$, and will not be included below.

$$\begin{aligned} & divide_3\ xs \\ & \quad = (map \cdot map)\ (take\ maxp_3)\ xs \\ & \qquad : (divide_3 \cdot (map \cdot map)\ (drop\ maxp'_3))\ xs, \\ & \qquad\quad \text{if } \#((hd \cdot hd)\ xs) > maxp_3 \\ & \quad = [xs], \text{ otherwise} \end{aligned}$$

$$\begin{aligned} & merge_3 \\ & \quad = foldr1\ (zipWith\ (zipWith\ (\odot_3))) \end{aligned}$$

The next section outlines the application of our partitioning strategy to two-dimensional programs for processing images on computer.

6 Implementing Partitioned Programs

Many hardware accelerators have fast local memories, but sometimes these memories may not be large enough to hold all the data. For instance, the memory available on the basic CHS2x4 system restricts the image size to around 19600 pixels in our implementation of the Sobel edge detector (see Section 7). This limitation can be overcome by our partitioning strategy.

To obtain an efficient implementation and to be able to use the libraries provided by the manufacturer, the partitioning strategy for two-dimensional arrays is implemented in C. In order to assist converting a program in C to its partitioned version, a C function `partition` has been developed. The following fragments of an imperative program were produced by hand, and we are currently exploring automated methods for generating them from descriptions in the functional notation adopted in the preceding sections.

Since C allows global variables, in our implementation we pass the position of the top left corner and the size of the sub-images as parameters in function calls instead of passing sub-images as parameters. This method avoids copying sub-images and increases efficiency, since dividing an image into sub-images becomes calculations of the positions of the top left corner and the size of sub-images. It follows that the data structure for an image may include the following fields (Figure 1): `top` and `left`, the x and y co-ordinates of the top left-hand corner of the sub-image; `ht` and `wd`, the height and width of the sub-image; and `buf`, the memory location holding the first pixel of the image. Other fields that are required for a particular program and or for a specific image storage format, such as the number of pixels in an image, may also be included in the data structure.

```
typedef struct
{ int            top, left;
  int            ht, wd;
  pixel *_huge   *buf;
} image;
```

Figure 1 Data structure for storing images.

The function `partition` requires six parameters: `process`, the name of the function (corresponds to f in the preceding section) for processing the image; `im`, the image to be processed; `max_ht`, the maximum height of a sub-image; `max_wd`, the maximum width of a sub-image; and `margin_ht` and `margin_wd`, which correspond to $margin_1$ and $margin_2$ in the preceding section.

Calculating the positions of the top left corner, the width and the height of sub-images can be performed by a nested for-loop (Figure 2); although there are some optimisations, on the whole the code is written for clarity rather than for efficiency. Since the three stages of the partitioning strategy will be executed sequentially on the CHS2x4, it is more efficient to include the *conquer* step in the same nested loop as *divide*, so the line "`(*process) (&subim);`" corresponds to *conquer* f. This applies the function `process` to each sub-image. Merging is included in `process`, because different programs may require different ways of merging the results. If the merging is performed by $+\!\!+$, partial results can be written into the memory block specified by the top left corner, width and height of the sub-image.

To use `partition` properly, the following procedure is suggested. Starting from a C program that implements the function f to be partitioned as a C function `process`,

1. Find the appropriate values for the parameters `max_ht`, `max_wd`, `margin_ht` and `margin_wd`.

2. Modify the functions for processing an image to operate on the proper sub-images.

```
partition (void
  (*process) (image *),
  image *im, /* pointer to an image */
  int max_ht,     int max_wd,
  int margin_ht, int margin_wd)
{
  image subim;
  int   max_ht' = max_ht - margin_ht;
  int   max_wd' = max_wd - margin_wd;

  subim.buf = im->buf;
  for (subim.top = 0;
       subim.top + max_ht' < im->ht;
       subim.top += max_ht')
  {
    subim.ht = max_ht;
    /* insert code for      */
    /* the inner loop here */
  }
  subim.ht = im->ht - subim.top;
  /* insert code for the   */
  /* inner loop here again */
}
```

The code for the inner loop is given by

```
for (subim.left = 0;
     subim.left + max_wd' < im->wd;
     subim.left += max_wd')
{
  subim.wd   = max_wd;
  subim.size = subim.ht * subim.wd;
  (*process) (&subim);
}
subim.wd   = im->wd - subim.left;
subim.size = subim.ht * subim.wd;
(*process) (&subim);
```

Figure 2 An example of partitioning in C.

3. Look for a method for combining the results from sub-images. The eligibility of the method can be checked by finding a binary operator $\odot$ for merging the partitioned results in each dimension such that Equation 4 is satisfied.

4. Modify the program to perform the selected merging method.

5. Replace the function call to process the image by a call to `partition`.

To benefit from the use of the hardware coprocessor, the speed loss due to overhead in partitioning should be smaller than the speed gained by using the coprocessor. Moreover, the amount of overhead should not increase faster than the time required for processing the image as the image size increases. We can analyse the conditions for obtaining an efficient partitioning as follows.

Let N^2 be the number of pixels of an image. The processing time is at least $O(N^2)$. Overhead is introduced in each step of the partitioned process. The time for dividing the image is $O(N^2)$, as can be seen from the for-loops in `partition`.

The amount of overhead in merging the results depends on the merging operator $\odot$. It is obvious that this should be no worse than $O(N^2)$ for the partitioning strategy to be efficient. The total overhead will then be $O(N^2)$, which means that it is of the same order as, or shorter than, the time required for processing the image.

Further improvement in speed can be obtained if the divide and merge steps can be executed in parallel with the conquer step. This is not possible with the CHS2x4 system, but one can develop a hardware platform with several banks of local memories accessible by the general-purpose processor, such that the hardware can operate on data in one of the memory banks while the software is dividing the data and combining the results in other memory banks. The optimal partitioning can be obtained when the hardware and the software processes complete the execution in a similar length of time.

7 The Sobel Edge Detector

Using the strategy described in previous sections, we have partitioned two programs for detecting edges in images, one by Sobel [7] and the other by Canny [3]. The size of a partition is determined by the amount of memory available in our CHS2x4 system. The result of applying the Sobel edge detector will be given in the rest of this section, while the Canny edge detector will be discussed later.

The Sobel edge detector involves a two-dimensional convolution using the masks

$$[[-1,-2,-1],[0,0,0],[1,2,1]]$$

and

$$[[-1,0,1],[-2,0,2],[-1,0,1]]$$

to produce the image gradient in the horizontal and in the vertical direction. The squares of the two gradients are then summed together and compared against a threshold. Our implementation consists of adders, subtractors, registers, multiplexers, magnitude extractors and a multiplier.

Table 1 compares the Sobel edge detector in software on a 386-based PC against the FPGA-assisted version. The stages *put*, *pipe* and *get* respectively correspond to transferring the image data from disk to the local memory on the CHS2x4 board, piping the data through the FPGA circuitry, and getting the results from the board. Even with the slow software-controlled FPGA execution, a speedup of over 20 times can be obtained if data transfer overhead to and from disk is not included (software time/*pipe* time), while a speedup of a factor of two is observed if we include the data transfer overhead. Notice that the total time for the hardware-assisted version is not equal to the sum of the time required for *put*, *pipe* and *get*; the difference (given by *others*) accounts for the time spent on dividing the image into sub-images and combining the results, and on routines for timing the program. Since this length of time is around 5% of the total processing time, our partitioning strategy appears to incur a modest overhead for this system.

Image size (pixels)	Software	Hardware and software	
25600		*put*	0.45
(160x160)		*pipe*	0.16
		get	0.55
		others	0.06
Total time (seconds)	2.19		1.22
40960		*put*	0.71
(160x256)		*pipe*	0.21
		get	0.89
		others	0.11
Total time (seconds)	4.28		2.19
50176		*put*	0.88
(224x224)		*pipe*	0.28
		get	1.04
		others	0.10
Total time (seconds)	4.39		2.30
84956		*put*	1.55
(268x317)		*pipe*	0.39
		get	1.80
		others	0.21
Total time (seconds)	7.09		3.95

Table 1 Comparing performance of Sobel edge detection in software and in hardware/software.

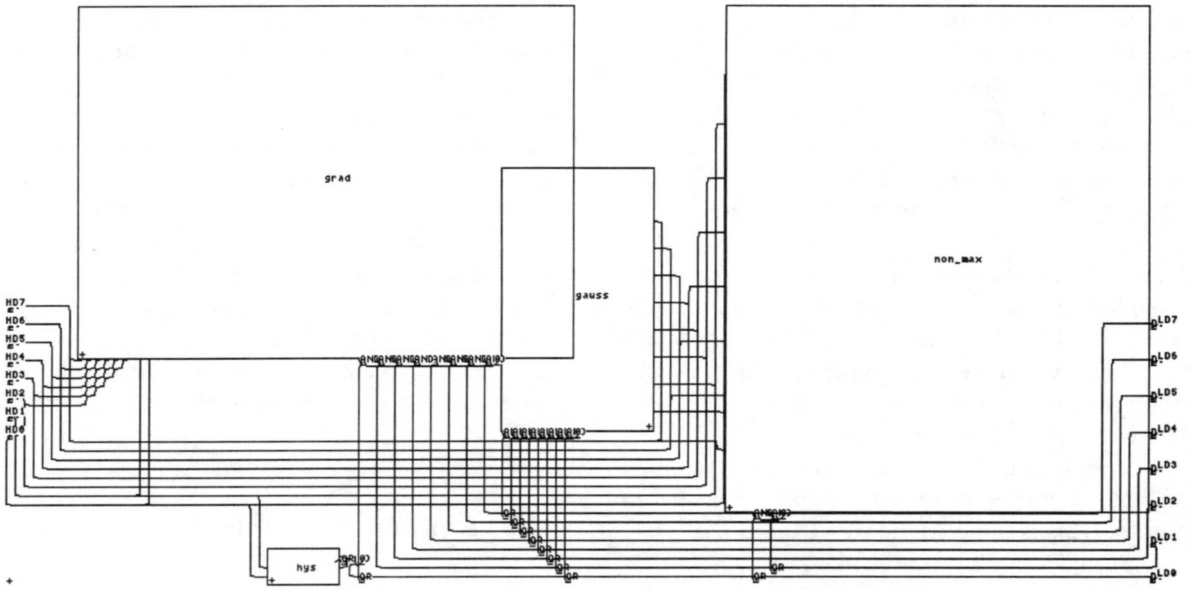

Figure 3 Hardware design for the Canny edge detector.

8 The Canny Edge Detector

The Canny algorithm [3] is a more elaborate edge detector than the Sobel algorithm. It consists of four stages: two-dimensional Gaussian smoothing for removing noise in the image, gradient calculations for extracting the potential edge points, suppression of non-maximum edge points for generating local maxima, and thresholding and hysteresis of the local maxima for recovering broken edges.

Our hardware design for the Canny edge detector is shown in Figure 3. It consists of four blocks, `gauss`, `grad`, `non_max` and `hys`, which are invoked one at a time by dynamically reconfiguring the control logic, such that their inputs are taken from the input port on the left and their outputs are multiplexed by or-gates (labelled "OR" in the diagram) to the output port on the right. The overlapped region reflects an optimisation in the use of FPGA cells; there are no connections between circuits belonging to different blocks. These blocks were developed by hand, although there are now various compilers that can be used to automate their production [8].

The block labelled `gauss` contains adders and shifters for implementing a Gaussian filter using the mask

$$[[1, 2, 1], [2, 4, 2], [1, 2, 1]].$$

The `grad` block computes the image gradient by calculating the difference in magnitude between a given pixel and its four neighbours; circuits for arithmetic and multiplexing are included. Non-maximum suppression and thresholding are performed by the `non_max` block, which is an array of registers, comparators, multiplexers and a multiplier. The `hys` block is responsible for hysteresis and is constructed from several gates and registers. Example input and output images are given in Figure 4.

The final stage of Canny's algorithm, hysteresis, complicates the merging of results from sub-images. For reasons that we shall not go into here, the pixels near the edges of the image and neighbouring sub-images must be combined using the logical "or" operation. This is an example where merging is performed by a binary operator other than $++$.

Our implementation involves several arrays, each of length equal to the maximum size of sub-images, to store intermediate results. To reduce memory usage even further, we only read in part of the image at any time instead of the whole image. Partial edge results are written to a file so that the array can be reused to store results of the next sub-image. This method permits an image of arbitrary size to be processed, although the program runs slower as there are more accesses to disk.

Figure 5 compares the processing time for a software Canny program against that for a hardware-assisted version for images of various sizes. The processing time by the software version is non-linear in the number of pixels of the images, since it increases with the number of edges in the image. In contrast, the processing time by the hardware-assisted version increases linearly with the num-

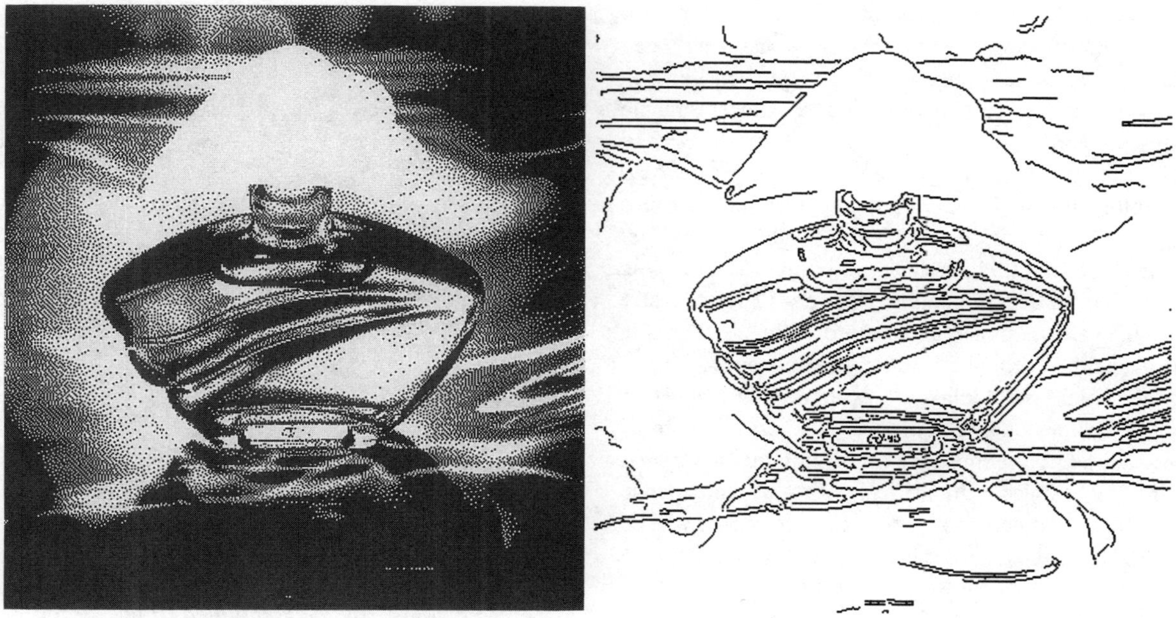

Figure 4 The image "Perfume" and the result of applying Canny's algorithm.

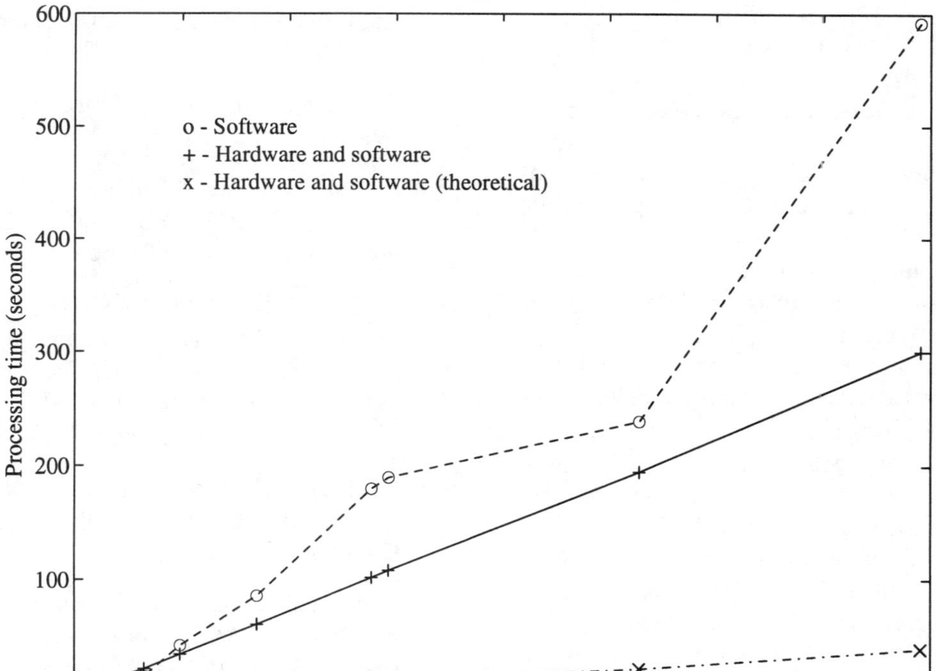

Figure 5 Comparing performance of our implementations of Canny's edge detector.

ber of pixels and is independent of the number of edges. This explains why the software version sometimes outperforms the hardware-assisted version: it happens when there are relatively few edges in the image. In general, the hardware-assisted version is around 39% faster than the software version.

Notice that around 88% of the measured time is devoted to communication with the PC; the corresponding times for the Sobel edge detector are given by the *put* and *get* figures in Table 1. If this overhead is not included, then the hardware-assisted design is approximately 13 times faster than the software version. Furthermore, if the input-output bottleneck can be eliminated so that the only speed limitation is the critical path delay, we estimate that a speedup of about 300 times can be achieved. The critical path of the hardware can be reduced by improving the layout and by adding latches along the critical path – at the expense of increasing power consumption and latency. This will be necessary if the edge detector is to operate at video rate.

9 Summary

A codesign strategy has been presented for developing flexible and efficient implementations for systems containing both hardware and software components. A framework based on functional programming has been used in describing and verifying the hardware-software partitioning strategy. This approach facilitates the production of parametrised realisations with a range of cost/performance trade-offs. Our experiments indicate that for a number of applications, the overhead associated with the partitioning strategy is acceptable.

Further work includes studying the use of other formalisms for multidimensional arrays (such as [10]) and other data structures, which may simplify program description and verification. The refinement from such high-level descriptions to a hardware notation – for instance Ruby (see [8],[9]) – would be investigated.

We are also exploring the theory and practice of generating the hardware, the software and their interface from high-level descriptions. Concurrency and synchronisation can be captured effectively in a framework based on CSP [4], and our HARP system [11], which contains a Xilinx FPGA, a transputer and other components, would be used in experimenting with different variations of our partitioning method.

Acknowledgements

The hardware Sobel edge detector was implemented by Steve Chiu. Thanks to Mark Jones, John O'Leary, Mike Spivey and Alan Wenban for comments and suggestions. The support of Oxford Parallel Applications Centre, Esprit OMI/HORN project, Scottish Enterprise and Xilinx Development Corporation is gratefully acknowledged.

References

[1] Algotronix Ltd, *CHS2x4 Custom Computer User Manual*, 1992.

[2] R. Bird and P. Wadler, *Introduction to Functional Programming,* Prentice-Hall International, 1988.

[3] J. Canny, "A computational approach to edge detection," *IEEE Transactions on Pattern Analysis and Machine Intelligence*, Vol. PAMI-8, No.6, pp. 679–698, November 1986.

[4] C.A.R. Hoare, *Communicating Sequential Processes*, Prentice Hall International, 1985.

[5] M.P. Jones, *An Introduction to Gofer*, Oxford University Programming Research Group, 1991.

[6] T. Kean and J. Gray, "Configurable hardware: two case studies of micro-grain computation," in *Systolic Array Processors,* J.V. McCanny, J. McWhirter and E.E. Swartzlander Jr. (eds.), Prentice Hall, 1989, pp. 310–319.

[7] S.Y. Kung, *VLSI Array Processors*, Prentice Hall, 1988.

[8] W. Luk and I. Page, "Parameterising designs for FPGAs," in *FPGAs*, W. Moore and W. Luk (eds.), Abingdon EE&CS Books, 1991, pp. 284–295.

[9] W. Luk, V. Lok and I. Page, "Hardware acceleration of divide-and-conquer paradigms: a case study," in *Proc. IEEE Workshop on FPGAs for Custom Computing Machines*, D.A. Buell and K.L. Pocek (eds.), IEEE Computer Society Press, 1993, pp. 192–201.

[10] R. Miller, *A Constructive Theory of Multidimensional Arrays*, Oxford University Programming Research Group, 1993.

[11] I. Page and W. Luk, "Compiling occam into FPGAs," in *FPGAs*, W. Moore and W. Luk (eds.), Abingdon EE&CS Books, 1991, pp. 271–283.

[12] A. Wenban, J. O'Leary and G.M. Brown, "Codesign of communication protocols," *IEEE Computer*, Vol. 26, No. 12, pp. 46–52, December 1993.

A Reconfigurable Compute Engine for Real-Time Vision Automata Prototyping

G.M. Quénot*, I.C. Kraljić, J. Sérot, B. Zavidovique

Laboratoire Système de Perception
DGA/Etablissement Technique Central de l'Armement
16 bis avenue Prieur de la Côte d'Or, 94114 ARCUEIL Cedex FRANCE
Email: ik@etca.fr

Abstract

This paper describes a Reconfigurable Compute Engine (the Data-Flow Functional Computer, or DFFC) developed at ETCA and dedicated to rapid prototyping of real-time vision automata. The Computer consists of a regular 3D array of very coarse grain application-specific FPGA called the Field-Programmable Operator Array (FPOA); each FPOA includes 2 Configurable Data-Paths (CDP) and 10 Input/Output Ports (IOP). Specific development tools allow an easy and efficient use of the Computer: a high-level description (in a functional language) is compiled into a DFFC configuration using an Operator Library. Several significant applications (connected component labeling, non-linear filtering, colored object tracking) have been implemented using our tools. An environment for automatic derivation of vision automata from a DFFC configuration is currently under development.

1 Introduction

Field-Programmable Gate Arrays have seen widespread use as reconfigurable computing elements in the past few years [2, 3, 4, 9]. The advantages are obvious: low cost, highly reconfigurable, short design time. Indeed, today's FPGAs can implement an extremely wide range of applications (glue logic functions, processors, co-processors...) due to their generic architecture: current FPGAs contain a large number of very simple basic cells. For example, Xilinx's FPGAs are composed of a large matrix (8×8 up to 24×24) of identical Configurable Logic Blocks (CLBs), each containing 1 or 2 flip-flops and a combinatorial function generator [10]. But this universality can be a drawback when a more specific range of applications is aimed at. Considering data-path-intensive image processing applications, "useful" modules (16-bit ALU, multiplier...) are rather inefficiently implemented (low operating frequency and integration). Another problem with FPGAs is their lack of simplicity if one wants to go deep into the actual FPGA implementation: the basic elements are simple gates and flip-flops.

A better approach is to have a few basic cells of a much higher complexity and adapted to the target applications. There has been attempts to develop FPGAs with more complex cells [5] but their complexity is still far too low. This paper presents a device that is suitably considered a very coarse grain application-specific FPGA for image processing. Let us call it the Field-Programmable Operator Array (FPOA). Its granularity is at the operator level instead of at the gate level. Where the FPGAs' basic blocks include a few gates, the FPOAs' basic blocks include a few 8-/16-bit data-flow operators; and where the FPGA's I/O blocks and switch matrices handle 1-bit signals, the FPOA's basic I/O ports and switch matrices handle 10-bit busses (9 bits data, 1 bit backward acknowledge).

The Field-Programmable Operator Array was designed to process digital video streams on the fly [1]: at every time step all the operations corresponding to one iteration of the algorithm for one pixel are executed in parallel (Multiple Instruction streams Single Data stream) instead of one operation executed for all the pixels (Single Instruction stream Multiple Data streams) [6]. The FPOA-based computer operates with the digital video pixel clock and each processor (FPOA basic block) executes exactly one in-

*G.M. Quénot is now with Hyperparallel Technologies, Ecole polytechnique, X-Pole, 91128 Palaiseau Cedex, FRANCE. Email: quenot@hyperparallel.polytechnique.fr struction per cycle (one instruction can involve several operations). The coarse grain approach, although it remains limited so far to the target applications, has several advantages in terms of speed, density and easy programming.

Section 2 presents the Field-Programmable Operator Array's architecture and its programming, while Section 3 describes the Data-Flow Functional Computer compute engine (DFFC) built around the FPOA. The DFFC's development tools for rapid vision automata prototyping and a few applications are presented in Section 4. Section 5 concludes the paper and discusses future work related to the DFFC compute engine.

2 The Field-Programmable Operator Array

The FPOA's basic cells are the following:

1. an operating cell called the Configurable Data-Path (CDP).
2. an I/O cell called the Input/Output Port (IOP).
3. a routing cell called Switch Matrix.

An Input/Output Port is a bidirectional 10-bit bus interface and can be configured either as a sending, a receiving or a feedback port. Two Switch Matrices allow a Configurable Data-Path to access 6 IOPs corresponding to the 6 directions North, South, West, East, Up, Down, allowing CDPs to be mesh-connected into 3D arrays (but other 6-connected topologies are possible). Switch Matrices route full 9-bit data busses with a 1-bit backward acknowledge. Thus a complete working Field-Programmable Operator Array basic block includes 1 Configurable Data-Path, 6 Input/Output Ports, 1 Input Switch Matrix and 1 Output Switch Matrix (Figure 1).

The Field-Programmable Operator Array developed at the Système de Perception laboratory contains 2 such basic blocks (Figure 2); however in this FPOA, the 2 Configurable Data-Paths are coupled 'vertically': the upper-one's Down port is internally connected to the lower-one's Up port (thus an $n \times n$ 2D matrix of FPOAs actually implements an $n \times n \times 2$ 3D array of CDPs). This means that contrary to fine grain FPGAs, the internal and external FPOA connections are identical: there is no "break" between the inside of the FPOA and its outside. The Field-Programmable Operator Array's main features are summarized in table 1. Using a 0.6 μm technology, one can expect to include as much as 8 similar basic blocks on a single chip, and achieve operating frequencies in the 50-100 MHz range.

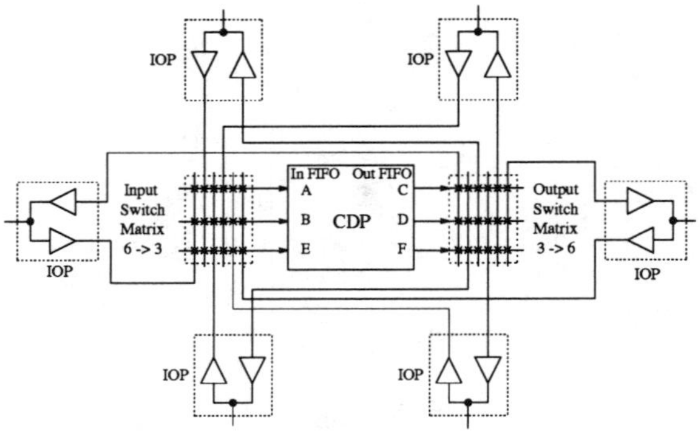

Figure 1: The Field-Programmable Operator Array basic block

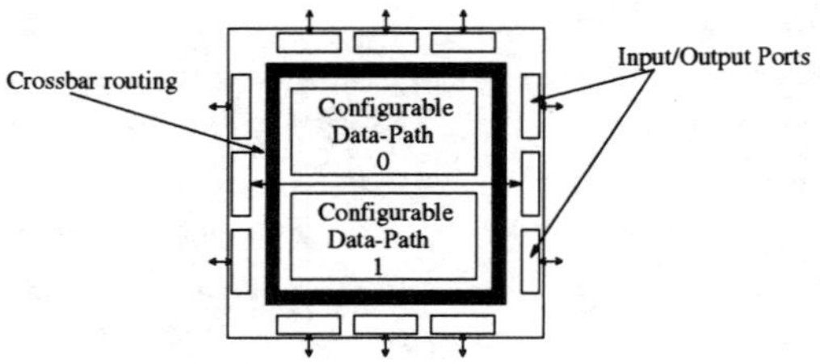

Figure 2: The Field-Programmable Operator Array

Package	144 pins PGA
Technology	1 μm CMOS
Die size	8.9 mm × 9.6 mm
Operating frequency	25 MHz
Configurable Data-Paths	2
External I/O Ports	10
Internal I/O Ports	2
Switch matrices	4
Programming technology	memory cells
Configuration bits	10,294
Logic gates	33,000
Internal memory	8.5 Kbits

Table 1: Characteristics of the Field-Programmable Operator Array

2.1 The Configurable Data-Path

The Configurable Data-Path (CDP) is the basic operating cell of the Field-Programmable Operator Array, its architecture has been designed to implement

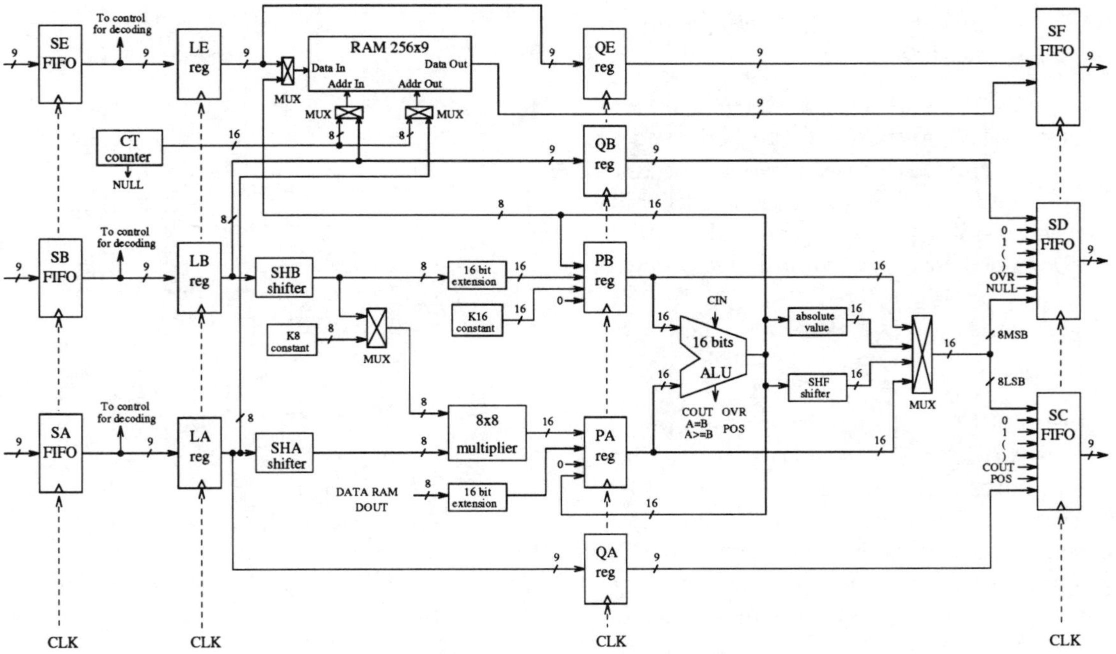

Figure 3: The Configurable Data-Path (controller not included)

efficiently a wide range of low-level image processing basic operators. Indeed, apart from arithmetic/logic operations (16-bit ALU, 8×8-bit multiplier), a single Configurable Data-Path can implement: an 8/16-bit histogrammer, an n-line/pixel delay, a line/column sum. Input to the CDP is 9-bit wide, allowing processing of 8-bit pixel numerical values (arithmetic/logic operations) as well as control values (beginning/end of frame/line; allowing line/pixel delays...).

The Configurable Data-Path is a programmable 3-stages pipelined data-path, it has 3 input stacks and 3 output stacks (Figure 3). These stacks are synchronous FIFOs with 8 9-bit words, their bandwidth is 25 MBytes/second. The FIFOs are necessary to avoid any dead-lock between CDPs. The data-path structure is the following: the first pipeline stage decodes the inputs and generates commands for the next stages, the second stage performs 8-bit operations (8×8-bit multiplication and 8-bit shifts), and the third stage performs 16-bit operations (2901-type ALU, absolute value, min/max and output shift). Other features are a 256×9 bits RAM which can be used as a FIFO, as a dual port RAM operator or as local RAM for specific purposes, and two 8-bit presetable counters cascadable into a 16-bit counter. The data-path can perform 50 million 8- or 16-bit operations/second.

The data-path is configured through a programmable state-machine (a 64×32 bits program is provided for its description). Each 32-bit word describes the type of data required on the data-path inputs, the operations to be performed, the data to be sent to the outputs and the next state. The execution of each state is validated only if the data required on the input FIFOs is present and if there is enough room on the output FIFOs. Each of the 6 FIFOs can be connected to one I/O Port through 2 Switch Matrices (Figure 1): an input FIFO is connected to the receiving part of the port, an output FIFO is connected to the sending part of the port. It must be underlined that the receiving part of one I/O Port can be connected to 1, 2 or all 3 input FIFOs and that one output FIFO can be connected to 1, 2..., or even all 6 sending parts of the IOPs. This feature allows the replication of data flows inside the CDP. Apart from operating functions, a CDP can simultaneously be used for routing purposes, i.e. the FIFOs/IOPs not used for the operating part can be configured as a routing channel.

2.2 Programming an FPOA

The function of a Configurable Data-Path is defined by:

1. A static programming register containing static definitions for the data-path (ALU operation, constants...).

2. A state-machine definition describing dynamic definitions for the data-path.

Programming its IOPs and Switch Matrices is done through a static configuration register independent from the CDP function, which specifies connections between FIFOs and IOPs. Thus both the functionality and the connections of a Field-Programmable Operator Array are defined by (re)programmable elements (actually memory cells) scattered through the Configurable Data-Paths, the I/O Ports and the Switch Matrices.

Practically, the FPOA is programmed (and tested) through a 1-bit scanpath, which internally splits into 6 different scanpaths. The whole programming (including scanpath selection) is done via 6 input lines: a clock, a reset, and a 4-bit command bus. All the FPOA's flip-flops (static programming and configuration registers, input/output FIFOs, counters, pipeline registers, data-path constants) are daisy-chained into scanpaths. Programming the program 64×32 RAM and the data 256×9 RAM is done by first programming the input FIFOs and then transfering their contents to the RAMs. A total of 5147 bits is needed to configure a Configurable Data-Path entirely (including data and state machine RAMs and FIFOs), and it takes about 15 ms per CDP to achieve the configuration.

3 The Data-Flow Functional Computer

The Data-Flow Functional Computer (DFFC) is a 3D $8 \times 8 \times 8$ array of FPOAs physically made of 8 boards containing each 8×8 FPOAs (see figures 4,5), thus implementing a 3D $8 \times 8 \times 16$ array of CDPs. The 1024 available data-paths allow large data-flow graphs to be implemented. Several different graphs can be simultaneously implemented and independently executed as long as they fit in the DFFC's 1024 Configurable Data-Paths. The highly regular structure of the Data-Flow Functional Computer allows only local connections (there are no "long lines" as in FPGAs). However long distance connections are possible through basic blocks configured as routing elements. An optimized place and route can yield a 30 to 50% CDP operating rate on a 3D array (this rate would be significantly lower on a 2D array). Among other possible topologies is a 2D array with 4-connectivity and longer connections using the 2 remaining I/O Ports.

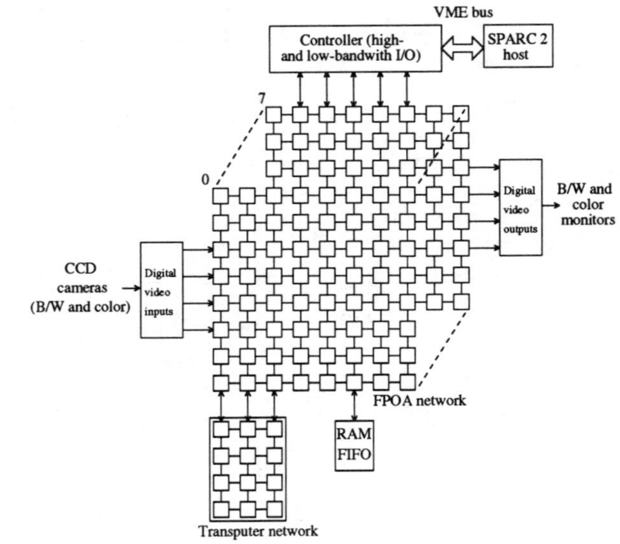

Figure 4: The Data-Flow Functional Computer's architecture

The DFFC's inputs/outputs are B/W and color cameras/monitors and low-bandwidth data-flow I/O ports. A SPARC 2 workstation is the host for the DFFC's programming environment. Current extensions include RAM boards configurable as Look-Up Tables or FIFOs; but any extension can be connected to the DFFC as long as it meets the IOP protocol (synchronous FIFO-like, 9 bits data, 1 bit acknowledge). The FPOAs' scanpaths are daisy-chained, thus the Computer is configured as easily as a single FPOA, through a scanpath and a few control signals. The presence of a T800 Transputer board allows to emulate also high-level image processing algorithms. The SPARC 2 host workstation runs the user-friendly graphical Development Tools implementing all the design flow layers: from high-level (design specification and input) to low-level (configuration and running of the DFFC) including the debugging phase. The Computer is synchronized with the digital video pixel clock (up to 25 MHz pixel; actually, the digital video I/Os are slave to the computer clock). A data flow requires 4 clock cycles to pass through a basic block: 3 internal CDP pipeline stages plus a cycle needed for the data to go from the output FIFO(s) to the neighbour's input FIFO(s). The 25 MHz maximum operating frequency is not a flip-flop toggle limit but the actual speed at which every part of the FPOA (data-path, state-machine, memory, FIFOs) can operate whatever the complexity of the operator assigned to a basic block. Unlike fine grain FPGA-based hardware emulators, the DFFC can operate at the actual speed

(a) (b)

Figure 5: The Data-Flow Functional Computer (a) and a 4×8×8 array of FPOAs (b)

of the emulated hardware since it is optimized at the operator level.

4 The DFFC Development Tools

The Functional Computer operates within a concept called **emulation-derivation** (Figure 6):

1. Emulation: an image processing algorithm is emulated in real-time on the Functional Computer. This phase **proves the existence of an architecture implementing the algorithm and validates its real-time behaviour on real-world scenes.**
2. Derivation: the validated Functional Computer configuration implementing the architecture is then automatically analyzed and **the actually used resources are optimized**. Two analysis levels are under investigation: the coarse one would produce a moderately optimized version using FPOAs and standard chips (FIFOs, RAMs), and the finer one would produce a fully optimized version using custom VLSI chips.

4.1 Emulation

The basic idea behind the implementation of an algorithm is to express it as a data-flow graph. The image processing algorithm to be emulated is expressed in a Functional-Programming language source file [8]. A compiler converts this source file into an operator Data-Flow Graph which is then translated into a Configurable Data-Path Graph. The compilation/translation phases use an Operator Library containing Data-Flow operators implementing the language primitives. Currently 2 libraries are available:

- A low-level library containing currently 150 single CDP operators (arithmetic and logic, comparators, constants, counters, 8-bit histogrammers, multiplexers...).
- A medium-level library containing 50 multiple-CDP macro-operators (convolvers, LUTs, 16- and 24-bit histogrammers...).

Whereas the low-level library is complete (it contains all the language basic primitives), the medium-level library can be extended easily with no need for intimate knowledge of the CDP's architecture.

The CDP Graph is mapped into an actual DFFC Network Configuration ready to be loaded. A complete 1024 FPOAs configuration is loaded in about 15 seconds. The algorithm is executed in real-time using the CCD cameras as input flows and sending the output flows to video monitors. Debugging is done by executing the algorithm step-by-step using the low-bandwidth interfaces and the possibility to access any

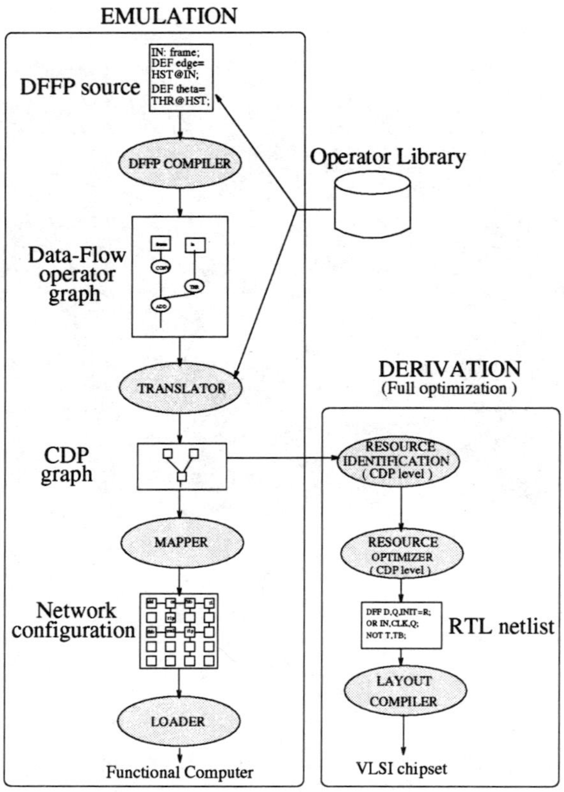

Figure 6: Design flow

FPOA register as well as the contents of the RAMs and FIFOs from the host. A Graph Compiler session is shown in Figure 7, while Figure 8 shows a typical Interactive Configuration Editor session. Both programs run on the SPARC 2 host.

We have developed some significant applications such as a non-linear Nagao-like filter, a connected component labeling and a colored object tracking (fully described in [7]). Table 2 shows a few examples of actual algorithms and their global resource utilization, i.e. the percentage of used ALUs, multipliers, Data RAMs... in each Configurable Data-Path. The CDP quotation in the table does not include CDPs used only for routing.

A Nagao-like filter is a non-linear "edge-preserving smoothing" filter, i.e. it removes high frequency spatial noise while preserving the edges of the original image. The functional programming language description of a Nagao-like filter emulated on the Functional Computer is shown in appendix A. Figure 9 shows results of our Nagao-like filter.

Connected component labeling consists in assigning a unique label to each connected region of a binary image. Appendix B describes the functional programming language source of the connected component labeling implemented on the DFFC computer. Results of a labeling are shown in figure 10.

4.2 Derivation

Our current research is the derivation of vision automata from emulation results. The actual DFFC configuration implementing the application is used as an input to the derivation software. A first approach is to replace the Configurable Data-Paths used only for routing by direct connections and the Configurable Data-Paths used as FIFOs by commercial FIFOs, and to keep other FPOAs (exactly as an algorithm emulated on a "classical" fine grain compute engine can be turned into a mix of FPGAs and standard LSI/MSI devices). This could result in an automaton implementable as a board or Multi-Chip Module (MCM). A second approach is based on a CDP-level 2-step analysis: identification of the effectively used CDP resources and optimization of these resources. The resulting automaton can be synthesized as a VLSI chipset (similar to the turn of an FPGA implementation into an ASIC). As indicated in table 2, a significant resource reduction can be expected at CDP level (local resource optimization). A global resource optimization phase will further reduce the chipset area; it will include resource sharing, controller collapsing.

5 Conclusion

We have presented a Data-Flow Functional Computer aimed at the rapid prototyping of vision automata. Algorithms are first emulated in real-time on the Computer, and our goal is to automatically derive the corresponding computer configurations into boards/MCM/VLSI chipsets, same behaviour and performance guaranteed but reduced resources. The Computer consists of a network of 512 Field-Programmable Operator Arrays. The FPOA is a custom-built very coarse grain FPGA whose architecture is adapted to implement efficiently low-level image-processing algorithms. A user-friendly graphical programming environment has been developed; it compiles a Functional Programming source file into a DFFC network configuration using an extensible Operator Library currently containing more than 200 low- to mid-level operators. Several significant applications have been successfully implemented on the Computer using our development tools. An environment for automatic derivation of vision automata from

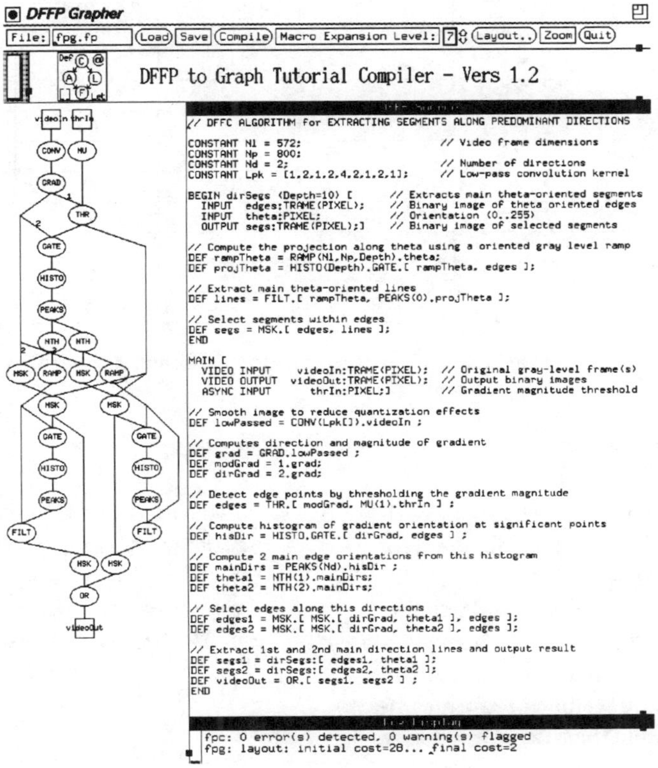

Figure 7: The Graph Compiler

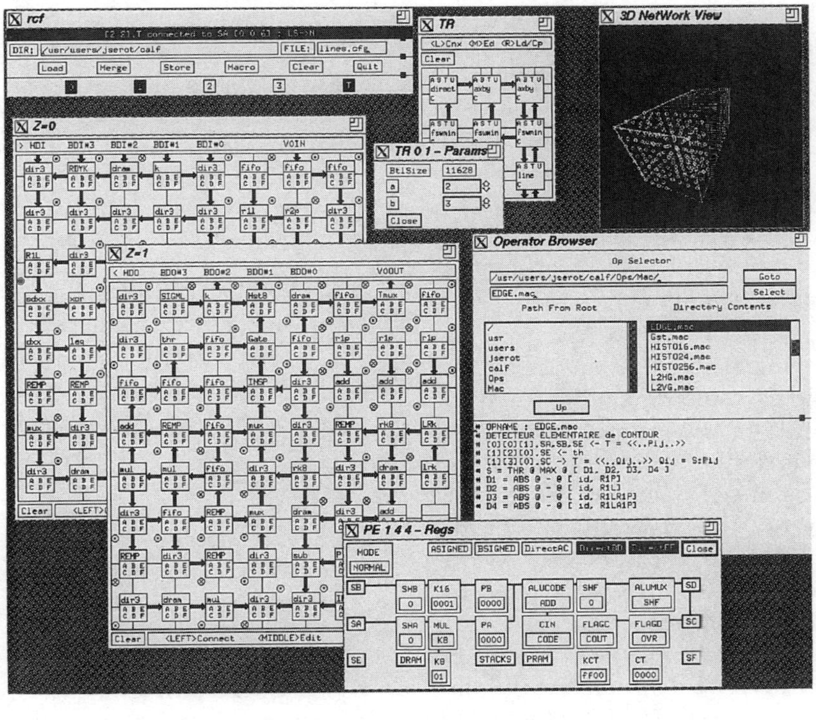

Figure 8: The DFFC's Interactive Configuration Editor

name	Edge detector	3×3 convolution	2048 word LUT	Nagao-like filter	Erosion
CDP number	13	22	25	86	110
I/O ports %	41	43	51	50	47
input FIFOs %	46	56	70	63	62
output FIFOs %	35	31	32	36	33
multiplier %	0	41	0	0	0
true ALU op %	23	36	0	37	43
Data RAM %	15	18	32	13	10
counters %	30	54	0	41	54
Prog RAM size%	3	8	0	9	10

Table 2: Global resource utilization for different algorithms

emulation results is under development.

The DFFC Compute Engine is dedicated to real-time image processing, and in this specific field of applications the advantages of a coarse grain Field-Programmable Operator Array over a standard fine grain FPGA are obvious. The operating frequency is application-independent, i.e. the real-time execution is guaranteed for any application. This is a major improvement over the unpredictable operating frequency of current FPGAs. The second important advantage is the easy programming and debugging of the Data-Flow Functional Computer. Indeed, the FPOA architecture allows the implementation of the functional data-flow paradigm to its fullest, thus permitting the programming of the Functional Computer from a high-level language with no involvement by the user in the translation process. But the application-specific architecture of the Field-Programmable Operator Array implies its unability to implement any kind of circuitry. This is actually the main drawback of the FPOA over a standard FPGA. We believe nonetheless that this lack of flexibility is largely compensated by the FPOA advantages cited above.

This Field-Programmable Operator Array is adapted for the on the fly computing of 8/16-bit integer values, and its field of applications is thus not restricted to real-time image processing. However applications outside of the image processing range have not been studied as yet. More generally, the Field-Programmable Operator Array concept (very coarse grain application-specific FPGA) can be adapted to other applications. New FPOAs should be developed to suit the application: for example, a 64-bit floating point basic operating cell would be adapted to the resolution of partial derivative equations by finite difference methods.

References

[1] E. Allart and B. Zavidovique. Functional Image Processing through Implementation of Regular Data-Flow Graphs. In *21st Annual Asilomar Conference on Signals, Systems on Computers, Pacific Grove, CA*, Nov 1987.

[2] J.M. Arnold, D.A. Buell, and E.G. Davis. Splash 2. In *Proc. of the 4th Annual ACM Symposium on Parallel Algorithms and Architectures*, pages 316–322, 1992.

[3] P. Bertin, D. Roncin, and J. Vuillemin. *Programmable Active Memories: a Performance Assessment (PRL Research Report 24)*. Digital Equipment Corporation, Paris Research Laboratory, March 1993.

[4] S. Casselman. Virtual Computing and The Virtual Computer. In *Proceedings of IEEE Workshop on FPGAs for Custom Computing Machines, Napa, CA*, pages 43–48, April 1993.

[5] D. Hill, B. Britton, B. Oswald, N-S. Woo, S. Singh, C-T. Chen, and B. Brambeck. ORCA: A New Architecture for High-Performance FPGAs. In *Proceedings of the Second International Workshop on Field-Programmable Logic and Applications, Vienna, Austria*, pages 52–60, September 1992.

[6] S.Y. Kung, S.C. Lo, S.N. Jean, and J.N. Hwang. Wavefront Array Processors: Concept to Implementation. *IEEE Computer 20(11)*, pages 18–33, July 1987.

[7] G. Quénot, C. Coutelle, J. Sérot, and B. Zavidovique. Implementing Image Processing Applications on a Real-time Architecture. In *Proceed-*

ings of Computer Architectures for Machine Perception, New Orleans, USA, pages 34–42, December 1993.

[8] J. Sérot, G.M. Quénot, and B. Zavidovique. Functional Programming on a Data-flow Architecture: Applications in Real-Time Image Processing. *International Journal of Machine Vision and Applications*, pages 44–56, May 1993.

[9] D. Van den Bout, J. Morris, D. Thomae, S. Labrozzi, S. Wingo, and D. Hallman. Anyboard: An FPGA-based, reconfigurable system. *IEEE Design & Test of Computers*, pages 21–30, September 1992.

[10] Xilinx. *The Programmable Logic Data Book.* 1993.

A Nagao-like filter functional programming source

All the undefined functions in the source files are standard library functions. These functions implement either a single Configurable Data-Path operator (e.g. `SUB`) or a multiple-CDP macro-operator (e.g. `CONV3`).

```
// Functional source implementing a Nagao-like non linear filter

// Line pixel number
CONSTANT Np=768;
// Normalized low-pass filter coef.
CONSTANT Lp=1, 2, 1, 2, 4, 2, 1, 2, 1, 16

// MAIN ----
BEGIN MAIN [
VIDEO INPUT In : FRAME(PIXEL);
VIDEO OUTPUT Out : FRAME(PIXEL); ]


// 3x3 neighborhood extraction (input: original frame)
DEF Vi = NEIG3 @ In;


// Disparity computation
DEF Ds = SUB @ [MAX Vi, MIN Vi];


// Low pass filtering (3x3 convolution using the Lp mask)
DEF Mn = CONV3(Lp) @ In;


// 3x3 neighborhood extraction (input: disparity frame)
DEF Vd = NEIG3 @ Ds;


// 3x3 neighborhood extraction (input: low pass filtered frame)
DEF Vm = NEIG3 @ Mn;


// Partial associative sorting

DEF Min1 = 1 @ Vd;
DEF Tmp1 = 1 @ Vm;
DEF Min2 = MIN @ [Min1, 2 @ Vd];
DEF Tmp2 = MUX @ [Tmp1, 2 @ Vm, EQU @ [Min2, 2 @ Vd]];
DEF Min3 = MIN @ [Min2, 3 @ Vd];
DEF Tmp3 = MUX @ [Tmp2, 3 @ Vm, EQU @ [Min3, 3 @ Vd]];
DEF Min4 = MIN @ [Min3, 4 @ Vd];
DEF Tmp4 = MUX @ [Tmp3, 4 @ Vm, EQU @ [Min4, 4 @ Vd]];
DEF Min5 = MIN @ [Min4, 5 @ Vd];
DEF Tmp5 = MUX @ [Tmp4, 5 @ Vm, EQU @ [Min5, 5 @ Vd]];
DEF Min6 = MIN @ [Min5, 6 @ Vd];
DEF Tmp6 = MUX @ [Tmp5, 6 @ Vm, EQU @ [Min6, 6 @ Vd]];
DEF Min7 = MIN @ [Min6, 7 @ Vd];
DEF Tmp7 = MUX @ [Tmp6, 7 @ Vm, EQU @ [Min7, 7 @ Vd]];
DEF Min8 = MIN @ [Min7, 8 @ Vd];
DEF Tmp8 = MUX @ [Tmp7, 8 @ Vm, EQU @ [Min8, 8 @ Vd]];
DEF Min9 = MIN @ [Min8, 9 @ Vd];
DEF Tmp9 = MUX @ [Tmp8, 9 @ Vm, EQU @ [Min9, 9 @ Vd]];


LET Out = Tmp9;

END
```

B Connected component labeling functional programming source

Note: one Transputer is involved in the equivalence-table compression (computing of a unique label for all the connected regions).

```
// Connected component labeling functional source


// Line pixel number
CONSTANT Np=768;

// MAIN ----
BEGIN MAIN [
VIDEO INPUT In: FRAME(PIXEL);
VIDEO OUTPUT Out : FRAME(PIXEL);
ASYNC INPUT Thr : PIXEL; ]


// Input 8-bit coded grey level image thresholding
DEF Bin= THRLD @ [In, $ @ Thr];


// Binary image horizontal labeling
DEF Lbh = HLABG @ Bin;


// Label propagation
DEF Lbv = VLABG @ [Lbh, Bin];


// Equivalent label detection
DEF Edl = EQDET @ [Bin, Lbv];


// Label equivalence resolution
DEF Ers = EQRES @ Lbv;


// Dynamic label look-up table loading and label image
transcoding
DEF Lbl = LABLUT @ [Lbv, Ers];


// Label image outputting
LET Out = Lbl;

END
```

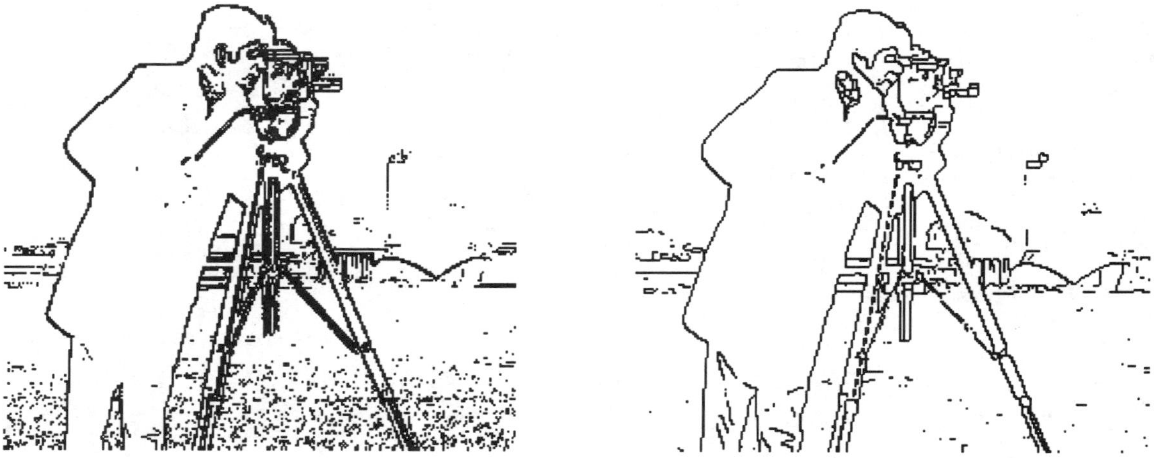

(a) Edge detection without preliminary Nagao-like filtering

(b) Edge detection with preliminary Nagao-like filtering

Figure 9: Nagao-like filtering

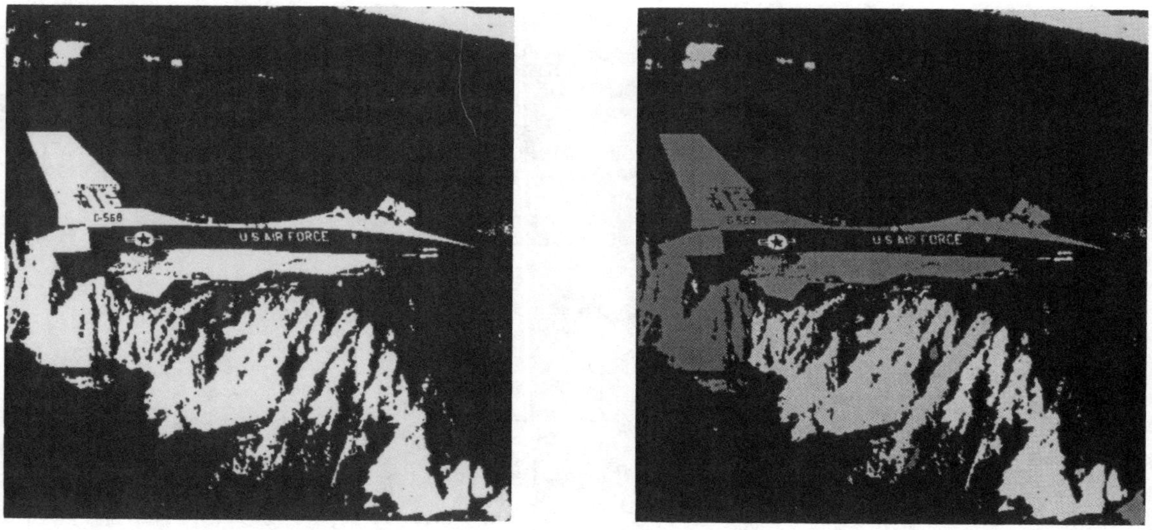

(a) Original binarized picture

(b) Resulting picture

Figure 10: Connected component labeling

An Asynchronous Approach to Efficient Execution of Programs on Adaptive Architectures Utilizing FPGAs

Lalit Agarwal, Mike Wazlowski, and Sumit Ghosh
Division of Engineering
Brown University, Providence RI 02912
{lka,mew,sg}@lems.brown.edu

Abstract

PRISM, a computer architecture consisting of a general-purpose core processor and a reconfigurable FPGA platform, was designed to bridge the gap between general-purpose and specialized computers. The proof-of-concept system, PRISM-I, suffers from several limitations, principal among them being: single bus-cycle restriction on the evaluation time of the function synthesized on an FPGA, inability to execute loops with dynamic loop-counts, and inefficient execution of control constructs such as "if-then-else". This paper presents a novel execution model in PRISM-II, that addresses the above limitations in a general manner. Also presented is a new framework for translating a C function into an FPGA-based custom architecture.

1. Introduction

Tradeoffs between economics and architectural flexibility have led to the design of general-purpose and special-purpose computers. While general-purpose computers cost relatively less and provide tolerable performance on a wide mix of application programs, special-purpose machines are expensive, yield excellent performance on a specific application or a class of applications, but perform poorly on other applications.

The literature records several efforts to integrate elements of special-purpose architectures, in order to improve performance on specific tasks, into a general-purpose framework. These efforts include the attachment of special hardware substructures, proposed by Estrin [1], enhancing processor instruction sets with specialized complex instructions [2] [3], dynamic microprogramming [4] [5], utilizing reconfigurable computing elements [6] [7] [8], and the use of coprocessors [9].

Unfortunately, all of the above efforts suffer from one or both of the following fundamental limitations: (i) The integration effort is determined at design time, is permanent throughout its life, and, therefore, incapable of addressing new application programs. (ii) The integration effort is neither automatic nor transparent to the programmer. and, therefore, requires the programmer to be knowledgeable in processor architecture and hardware design.

PRISM-I [10] has been the first system that attempts to address the above limitations and, demonstrate the feasibility of incorporating dynamic and automatic adaptation into a computer. In PRISM-I, the integration effort may be easily adapted to a large class of programs and is transparent to the programmer. The underlying philosophy of PRISM-I is to exploit the notion of "locality of reference [11]," which states an empirical finding that most programs spend 90% of their execution time in 10% of the code [12]. PRISM-I aims to expend effort and resources to increase performance of the smaller and frequently executed sections of the program, termed "critical sections," as opposed to the remainder of the less frequently executed sections.

In PRISM-I, reconfigurable hardware is used to augment the functionality of a general-purpose, core processor. A set of Field Programmable Gate Arrays (FPGAs) constitute the reconfigurable platform, and are dynamically configured to execute the critical sections of a program more efficiently. The less frequently accessed sections are executed on the core processor. The overall impact of PRISM-I is improved execution performance.

To achieve its goals, the synthesized hardware in PRISM must be faster in executing the critical sections, compared to a general-purpose processor. This requirement, in turn, translates into several low-level requirements for the synthesized hardware, namely, (i) simplicity, (ii) minimal communication overhead, and (iii) the exploitation of fine-grain, i.e. operator-level, parallelism. Requirements (i) and (ii) are particularly

0-8186-5490-2/94 $03.00

true for today's FPGAs, with lower gate counts and slower speeds. The need to exploit fine-grain parallelism is important because of frequently encountered small-sized critical sections.

A substantial amount of work in hardware synthesis has been reported in the literature. These efforts include Flamel [13] – a Pascal to hardware compiler, IBM's HIS system [14] which translates a VHDL behavioral description into a synchronous digital machine, and Cyber [15] which compiles programs in C and BDL into ASIC chips. In addition, Camposano [16] and Walker [17] report a survey of different high-level synthesis systems.

Most of the above approaches differ with regard to the high-level hardware description language, optimization and transformation techniques, and scheduling and allocation algorithms. However, they share a common underlying model of execution, namely, a synchronous digital machine comprising a datapath and a finite-state-machine-based central controller. Two key limitations of the synchronous approach, similar to those of Von Neumann's "stored program control," are: (i) A centralized controller imposes strict sequential execution of all instructions. This clearly results in the failure to exploit potential parallelism that may be inherent in the program [18]. (ii) Intermediate results or data are passed between successive instructions through the use of registers and storage units. This indirect mode of transfer not only slows down data communication among instructions, but may also cause side effects which may impose additional overhead.

In contrast, the data flow computational model is based on two fundamental principles [19]: (A.1) An operation can be executed as soon as all its required operands are available. (A.2) All operations are functions, i.e. there are no side effects arising from the intermediate results and data being stored in registers and storage units.

Although, the data flow model apparently promises higher performance, in reality, it suffers from several limitations. First, general-purpose data flow architectures, proposed in the literature [20] [21], are very complex. They require complex mechanisms for labeling tokens, storing data, and for communication between successive instructions. All of these impose high demand for silicon. Because of this, it is unrealistic to implement them on the current FPGAs that feature modest gate counts. Second, they also involve significant overhead in terms of execution time and require parallelism on the order of several hundred concurrently executable instructions in the programs [19], to outperform the conventional processors.

The limitations of both hardware-synthesis systems and general-purpose data flow architectures make them poor candidates for flexible, FPGA-based architectures that demand (i) inexpensive hardware platforms, (ii) maximum exploitation of parallelism inherent in critical sections, and (iii) minimal implementation overhead. While PRISM-I [10] aims to address a few of these limitations, it suffers from the following critical weaknesses: (i) The reconfigured hardware is constrained to evaluate functions within the a single bus-cycle of the core processor. As a result, critical sections whose critical-path delays exceed the core processor bus cycle, cannot be synthesized on the reconfigurable platform. (ii) The inefficient execution of critical sections that contain control constructs, e.g. "if-then-else". In general, control constructs may imply multiple, possible execution paths, each, possibly requiring a different execution time. The total time taken to execute the program depends on the actual path taken during an execution. In PRISM-I, the hardware design always chooses the execution time of the critical path which, while conservative, implies inefficiency. (iii) The inability to synthesize loops with dynamic loop-counts. This eliminates a large class of programs requiring iterative computations.

This paper introduces a new execution model in PRISM-II, that addresses the key limitations of PRISM-I. The execution model facilitates the exploitation of maximal fine-grain parallelism in the critical sections. It addresses critical sections that may require arbitrary execution times, contain control constructs such as "if-then-else," "switch-case", and loop constructs with static and dynamic loop counts. A new framework is also presented for translating a C function into custom hardware on the FPGA platform.

The remainder of the paper is organized as follows. Section 2 presents a brief overview of PRISM-II highlighting the configuration compiler and the hardware platform. Section 3 introduces a framework for the synthesis of custom architecture on the FPGA platform, the execution model the architecture is based upon, and its intermediate representation. Section 4 presents details on the algorithm for translating a C function into custom hardware on the FPGA platform. Section 5 presents the conclusions and plans for future work.

2. The PRISM-II System: Overview

The PRISM-II system consists of two principal components: a Configuration Compiler, that accepts a program in C, and translates it into executable code

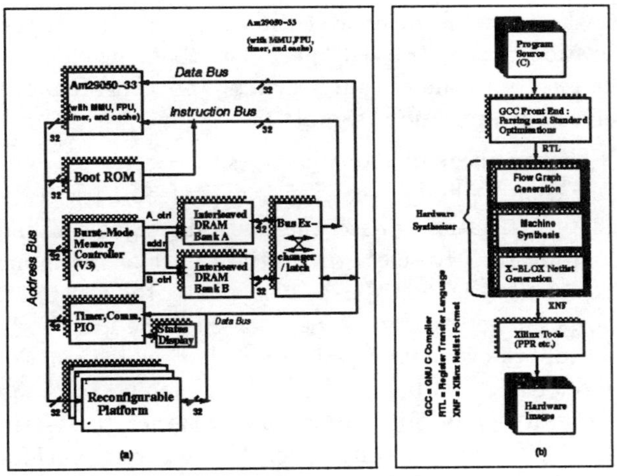

Figure 1: (a) PRISM-II Hardware Platform. (b) Structure of the Configuration Compiler.

for the hardware platform, and the hardware platform which ultimately executes the program.

2.1 Hardware Platform

The hardware platform, shown in Figure 1a, consists of (i) a core processor, namely the AMD AM29050 RISC processor [22], and (ii) a reconfigurable platform that consists of a set of FPGAs that are interconnected to the core processor through the latter's coprocessor interface. Details of the hardware platform can be found in [23].

2.2 The Configuration Compiler

The configuration compiler accepts a user program in C as input, and generates hardware and software images as output. The hardware image contains information that is necessary for synthesizing hardware corresponding to the critical sections, on the reconfigurable platform. The software image contains executable code that realizes the execution of the critical sections on the reconfigurable platform and the remainder of the program on the AM29050. Both hardware and software images are generated automatically without intervention from the user. A current underlying assumption in PRISM-II is that the critical section(s) of a program is identified a priori, by the programmer.

The configuration compiler consists of two principal components: (i) C parser and optimizer and (ii) a hardware synthesizer. The parser and optimizer constitute the front end while the hardware synthesizer forms the back end. To reduce development time, the parser and optimizer of the GNU C compiler **gcc** are utilized as the starting point and are modified to adapt to the needs of this research. The hardware synthesizer constitutes the core of the synthesis subtask and is being designed and developed in this investigation. Figure 1b presents the structure of the configuration compiler including its components and the flow of information, and is described in greater detail in the subsequent sections of the paper.

3. A Framework for Custom Hardware Synthesis in PRISM-II

This section presents a framework for custom hardware synthesis in PRISM-II. The critical section is first translated into an intermediate representation and then synthesized onto the FPGA platform. A novel execution model is proposed for developing the architecture of the synthesized hardware. The design of the intermediate representation and the architecture both utilize Control Flow Graph (CFG) and operator network of the critical section.

3.1 Flow Graphs

Control Flow Graph (CFG): The translation begins with a block-level CFG of the critical section. A CFG is a directed graph in which the nodes represent "basic blocks" [24] and the edges represent the flow of control.

Operator Network: In the next step of the translation, the "Flow Graph Generation" module shown in Figure 1b generates an Operator Network. It is a directed graph wherein the nodes represent the operators, and the edges represent the flow of values among them. A total of six different types of nodes are conceivable in such a network: constant, unary operator, binary operator, ternary operator, latches and input/output registers.

A constant node represents a constant value used in the program, the unary and binary operator nodes respectively represent unary and binary arithmetic and logical operators i.e. "NOT", "plus", "AND" etc. The only ternary operator that can be present is a multiplexor. A multiplexor selects one of two inputs, as dictated by a third select input. Two types of the multiplexor operators are supported – "merge-mux" and "loop-mux". The "merge-mux" selects one of two definitions of a variable arriving at a merge-node in a CFG. A merge-node is a node in a CFG corresponding to an "if-then-else" construct, where the two branches of the construct merge. The "loop-mux", present at the top of a loop, selects either the initial value of a variable or, its value fed back from a previous iteration. A "latch" stores the fed back value of a variable from a loop iteration, temporarily, and feeds it to the "loop-mux" in the next iteration. The "input/output" registers respectively store the inputs to and the output from an FPGA.

3.2 Model of Execution

PRISM-II's objectives include (i) exploitation of fine-grain parallelism, (ii) providing primitives for addressing iterative computations, (iii) efficient execution of control constructs, and (iv) an implementation on FPGAs that is efficient yet inexpensive. These objectives are encapsulated in the proposed execution model that provides the underlying basis for hardware synthesis on the FPGA platform.

The execution model consists of two principal components – (i) "Operator Network" and (ii) "Controller." The operator network is a specific organization of arithmetic and logic units intended to perform the actual computation. The controller, a finite state machine, controls the computation in the operator network, determines when the computation is complete, and generates the "end-of-computation" signal at the conclusion of the computation. The "end-of-computation" signal provides an asynchronous means of informing the core processor to fetch the results from the FPGA platform. Figure 2 presents a pictorial view of the execution model.

Prior to initiating execution, the input values are loaded into the input registers of the operator network and the controller is initialized. Operators execute as soon as their input operands are available and intermediate results and data are communicated from one operator to the next, directly through dedicated connections, thereby implying minimal communication overhead.

The controller plays the role of a timer that tracks the execution times of operators in the operator network. The controller stores information on the execution delays along all possible execution paths in the operator network and utilizes specific intermediate data values generated inside the network to track the actual execution path taken by the current instance of execution. The data values may include the predicates for the conditionals and predicates for loops. The presence of control constructs including "if-then-else" generates the possibility of multiple execution paths during the execution of a critical section. Where each of the possible execution paths may require a different execution time, it is important, for efficiency, that the controller track the actual path to precisely account for the time taken for execution. At the end of the duration of the "tracked" path, the controller latches the results in the output registers and generates the "end-of-computation" signal.

The execution of a loop involves three phases – "initialization," "body-execution," and "feed-back". In the "initialization" phase, the controller signals all the "loop-muxes," to select the initial values of the input variables to the loop. In the next phase, the controller allows the operator network to execute the loop-body in a data-flow manner, at the end of which, in the subsequent "feed-back" phase, the controller tests the loop exit condition to determine whether to iterate the loop further, or exit. When the controller decides to iterate the loop, it signals the latches to store the values of all feed-back variables and also signals the "loop-muxes," to select these values. After the "feed-back" phase, the loop-body may be executed again and the cycle continues until termination. To address the issue of nested-loops, an inner-loop is considered a part of the body of the outer-loop, and is executed in the outer-loop's "body-execution" phase.

In essence, the controller permits the operator network to execute, asynchronously, independently, and in a data-flow manner, while asserting minimal control over the latter's operations. Given that the data communication overhead among the operators is minimal – because of dedicated connections – the PRISM-II approach has the potential to exploit maximal fine-grain parallelism inherent in the critical section and result in higher performance relative to its sequential execution. The execution model is novel and unique in many respects. First, unlike PRISM-I[10], this execution model, permits evaluations of critical sections requiring arbitrary execution times, successfully addresses the issue of execution of loops with dynamic loop counts, and executes control constructs such as "if-then-else" and "switch-case", efficiently. Second, the model possesses some key advantages over existing models proposed in traditional high-level synthesis architectures [13], [14], and [15]. Traditional high-level synthesis architectures utilize centralized controllers that fail to exploit potential fine-grain parallelism. In contrast, such restrictions are absent in PRISM-II. In addition, unlike in the above architectures, the PRISM-II execution model permits direct and fast data communication among the operators.

Throughout the literature, data-flow architectures [20], [21] have always promised high performance for general-purpose computing but have failed to meet the expectations. Their complex mechanisms pose high demand for silicon and significant execution overhead.

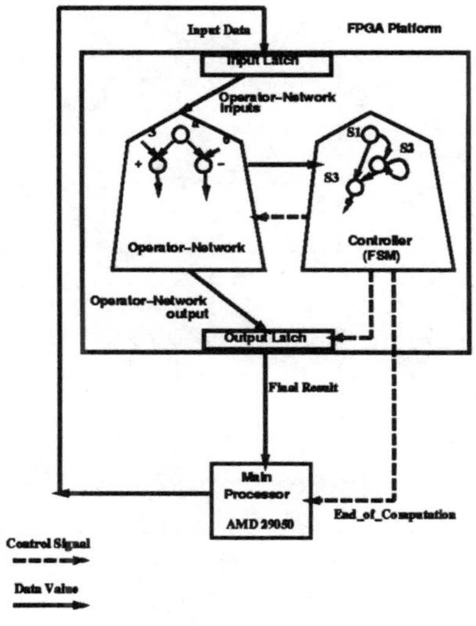

Figure 2: The PRISM-II Execution Model

As a result of the latter, to compete effectively with a conventional uniprocessor, a general-purpose data flow architecture requires programs with inherent parallelism in the hundreds [19]. The proposed execution model fully exploits data-flow concepts, namely A.1 and A.2 of section 1, and yet achieves high performance for critical sections of limited sizes.

3.3 Intermediate Representation

A critical section is expressed within the configuration compiler through an intermediate representation which is based on the execution model described above. The aim of this representation is to provide a technology-independent expression of the critical section, which once available, can be used to synthesize customized hardware using FPGA vendor tools.

The intermediate representation in PRISM-II is a "Machine Graph" that consists of the two components described above: an operator network and a Finite-State-Machine-based Controller, and the connections between them.

4. The Algorithm for Custom Architecture Synthesis

An algorithm is proposed for the synthesis of a custom architecture corresponding to a C function on the FPGA platform. The architecture is based on the execution model described above and consists of an Operator Network and a Controller. The algorithm is divided broadly into three modules: "Flow Graph Generation", "Machine Synthesis", and "X-BLOX Netlist Generation" as shown in Figure 1b. Pseudocode for the algorithm is shown in Figure 3. The algorithm accepts as input an RTL description – the internal representation of a program generated by the GNU C compiler **gcc** – of the function and ultimately generates a "hardware netlist" which describes the architecture corresponding to the function. The netlist, in turn, is utilized by the FPGA vendor tools to synthesize the target hardware on the FPGA platform.

```
build_architecture (RTL description)
{
   // creates operator network and CFG.
  createFlowGraphs();

  timeStampOperators();

  timeStampBlocks();

  createController();

  optimizeController();

  writeNetlist();
}
```

Figure 3: Pseudocode of algorithm for Custom Architecture Synthesis

1. **createFlowGraphs:** The operator network and the CFG for the function are constructed in this step using data flow analysis techniques [24].

2. **timeStampOperators:** Each operation in the operator network is assigned a time-stamp that indicates the earliest time it may complete execution. Through this assignment, a schedule is automatically created that also reveals the operations that may execute in parallel.

   A time-stamp is determined based on the premise that an operation may not execute until all of its input operands are present. Thus, it is computed as the maximum of the time-stamp values of all of the inputs plus the execution time of the operator node. The time-stamps of operations that have no inputs are set to zero, e.g, nodes representing constants. The time-stamps of operator nodes are computed utilizing a breadth-first search algorithm. Time-stamps serve as a useful mechanism to order data dependencies in a critical section.

3. **timeStampBlocks:** Time-stamps are computed for every basic block in the CFG utilizing the

time-stamps of the individual operations in the operator network. For each basic block, "starting time-stamp" and "ending time-stamp" values are computed. The "starting time-stamp" refers to the earliest time when all of the inputs to a block are available while the "ending time-stamp" is the latest time when all of the outputs from a block have been generated.

4. **createController:** The initial version of the controller (FSM) is a copy of the CFG, with its states corresponding directly to the basic blocks of the CFG. The states in this FSM are assigned the same "starting" and "ending" time-stamps as the basic blocks they are derived from.

5. **optimizeController:** The initial FSM, derived directly from the CFG, suffers from two key drawbacks. First, since the states are derived directly from the basic blocks in the CFG, the initial FSM fails to take advantage of any inter-block parallelism that may be present in the code. Second, for the same reason, it may contain more than the minimal number of states. In this two stage process, the initial FSM is first restructured to take advantage of the inter-block parallelism and then optimized to reduce its number of states.

   During the first stage, for every state in the FSM, "ending time-stamps" of its direct predecessor states are examined. Where the "starting time-stamp" of a state is less than the minimum of the "ending time-stamps" of its predecessor states, the "starting time-stamp" of the state is modified to that minimum value. As a result, the state may be initiated for execution earlier, thereby achieving concurrency. If, during this re-assignment of time-stamps, a state happens to bear the same "starting" and "ending" time-stamps, it is deleted. This restructuring of the FSM thus aims to exploit the inter-block parallelism. After this stage, durations are finally assigned to each state in the restructured FSM. The duration of a state is computed as the difference between its "ending" and "starting" time stamps.

   After durations have been assigned to the states, the FSM can be further optimized to reduce its number of states. In general, a state configuration in an FSM resembling the structure of an "if-then-else" construct, lends itself to optimization. As shown in Figure 4b, an unoptimized FSM derived directly from the CFG of an "if-then-else" construct which is shown in Figure 4a, contains 4 states and two paths between the "predicate" and the "join state". This FSM can be optimized to only two states as shown in Figure 4c. The rationale underlying the optimization is as follows. In Figure 4a, once the thread of execution reaches "BB0", it is certain that both "BB0" and "BB3", and one of "BB1" and "BB2" will be executed. Thus, "state0" in Figure 4c carries the sum of the durations of the "predicate-state", "join-state" and the smaller of the "then-state" and the "else-state". Duration of "state1" in Figure 4c is computed as the difference of durations between the "then-state" and the "else-state" in Figure 4b. The basic idea is extensible to nested "if-then-else" and other constructs such as loops and "switch-case". The details are not included here due to space limitations and can be found in [25].

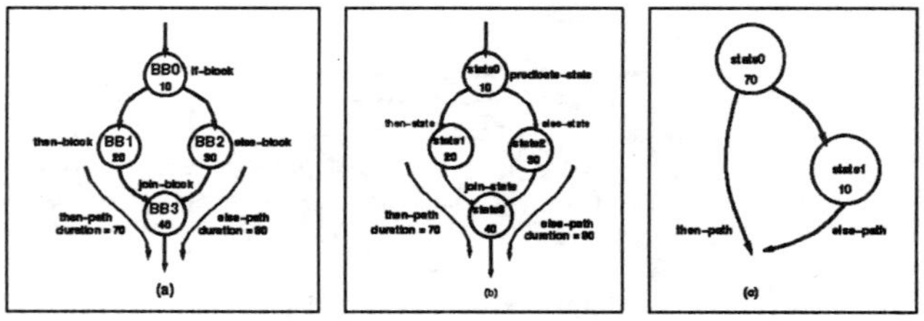

Figure 4: (a) CFG for an "if-then-else" construct (b) Corresponding Unoptimized FSM, (c) Optimized FSM

6. **writeNetlist:** The final FSM, representing the controller, and the operator network obtained in step 1 of the algorithm, are translated into the XBLOX [26] Xilinx Netlist Format (XNF) representation. Following the translation, **"xblox"** and **"ppr"** tools [27] are used to place and route the FPGA.

4.1 Limitations of PRISM-II

The limitations of PRISM-II, at the present time, include the following. (i) The execution model does not address memory references, pointers, data structures, including arrays and structs, and global and static variables that require accessing memory locations outside the FPGA. Global and static variables must be reimplemented in the form of explicit arguments of the critical section. (ii) Floating point types and operations are not supported because of their intense demand for silicon. (iii) The size of the data transfer is 64 bits for inputs and 32 bits for output.

4.2 An Example

To illustrate the principles of hardware synthesis in PRISM-II, a C function is shown in Figure 5.

```
int div(int d, int e)
{
 1.  int q = 0;                          | bb0
 2.  char samesign = 1;                  | bb0
 3.                                      | bb0
 4.  if (d < 0) {                        | bb0
 5.    d = -d;                           | bb1
 6.    samesign = ~samesign;             | bb1
 7.  }
 8.
 9.  if (e < 0) {                        | bb2
10.    e = -e;                           | bb3
11.    samesign = ~samesign;             | bb3
12.  }
13.
14.  loop:  d = d - e;                   | bb5
15.    if (d >= 0) {                     | bb5
16.
17.      q++;                            | bb6
18.      goto loop;                      | bb6
19.    }
20.
21.  if (samesign)                       | bb7
22.    return q;                         | bb9
23.  else
24.    return -q;                        | bb8
}
```

Figure 5: An example function to illustrate the synthesis of Operator Network and Controller.

The function aims to perform integer division and computes the quotient "q", given two integers "d" and "e". The purpose of this program is to illustrate the PRISM-II approach and the authors do not necessarily recommend its usage for integer division. It is selected mainly for the following reasons: (i) It contains a loop with a dynamic loop count. (ii) It contains "if-then-else" constructs.

First, the operator network and CFG are created for the code segment in Figure 5. The operator nodes corresponding to the basic-blocks of the code segment in Figure 5 are shown enclosed in dashed rectangular boxes in the operator network in Figure 6.

In Figure 6, the circular nodes represent constant values while the rectangular nodes represent unary or binary arithmetic or logical operators. The diamond nodes labeled "lt," "ne," and "ge" correspond to the boolean operators "less than," "not equal to," and "greater than" respectively. Multiplexors are expressed through rectangular-diamond nodes. Nodes labeled "mux_1," through "mux_5" represent "merge-muxes," that were introduced in section 3.1. For instance, the merge-mux, "mux_2," selects one of two definitions – "d" and "-d," of the variable "d" reaching line 7 in Figure 5. Nodes labeled "mux_6" and "mux_7" represent "loop-muxes" which were also introduced in section 3.1. For instance, "mux_7" selects either the initial value of the variable "q" which is "0" or the values fed back from subsequent iterations. The nodes labeled "latch" represent a latch that is utilized within a loop. The two initial input values to the operator network are stored in registers represented through shaded rectangular nodes labeled "d" and "e" at the top of Figure 6. The final result is stored in the register labeled "return" which appears at the bottom of Figure 6. Basic-blocks bb5 and bb6, correspond to the loop.

The CFG for the C function is presented in Figure 7a. Except for blocks bb4 and bb10, each of the blocks bb0 through bb10 in Figure 7a correspond to the basic blocks in Figure 5. The block bb4 in Figure 7a contains merge-muxes "mux_3" and "mux_4", whereas, block bb10 contains "mux_7". These blocks are created to house the muxes which are not present in the code.

Next, the operators in the operator network and the blocks in the CFG, are time-stamped. The time-stamps are shown adjacent to every operation in Figure 6. The starting and ending time-stamps are also shown adjacent to every block in Figure 7a.

In the subsequent step, an initial FSM controller is obtained as a copy of the CFG in Figure 7a, and is shown in Figure 7b. Next, the initial FSM is optimized by collapsing a few states onto other states and assigning them appropriate durations. In Figure 7b, states "ss0" and "ss1" have the same set of time-stamps. This implies the lack of data dependencies between "ss0" and "ss1" and hence, they may be executed concurrently. Thus, "ss1" is merged into "ss0," and the resulting FSM will show a direct link from the resulting state "ss0" (time-stamps 0 and 50) into "ss2" (time-stamps 50 and 65). Since the resulting state "ss0" and state "ss2" are now sequential, i.e, "ss0" directly followed by "ss2," they are merged into one state, "s'0," (time-stamps 0 and 65) which is shown in Figure 8a. States "s'1", "s'2", "s'3", and "s'4" in Figure 8a are derived directly from states "ss3", "ss4", "ss5", and "ss6" of Figure 7b respectively. State "ss9"

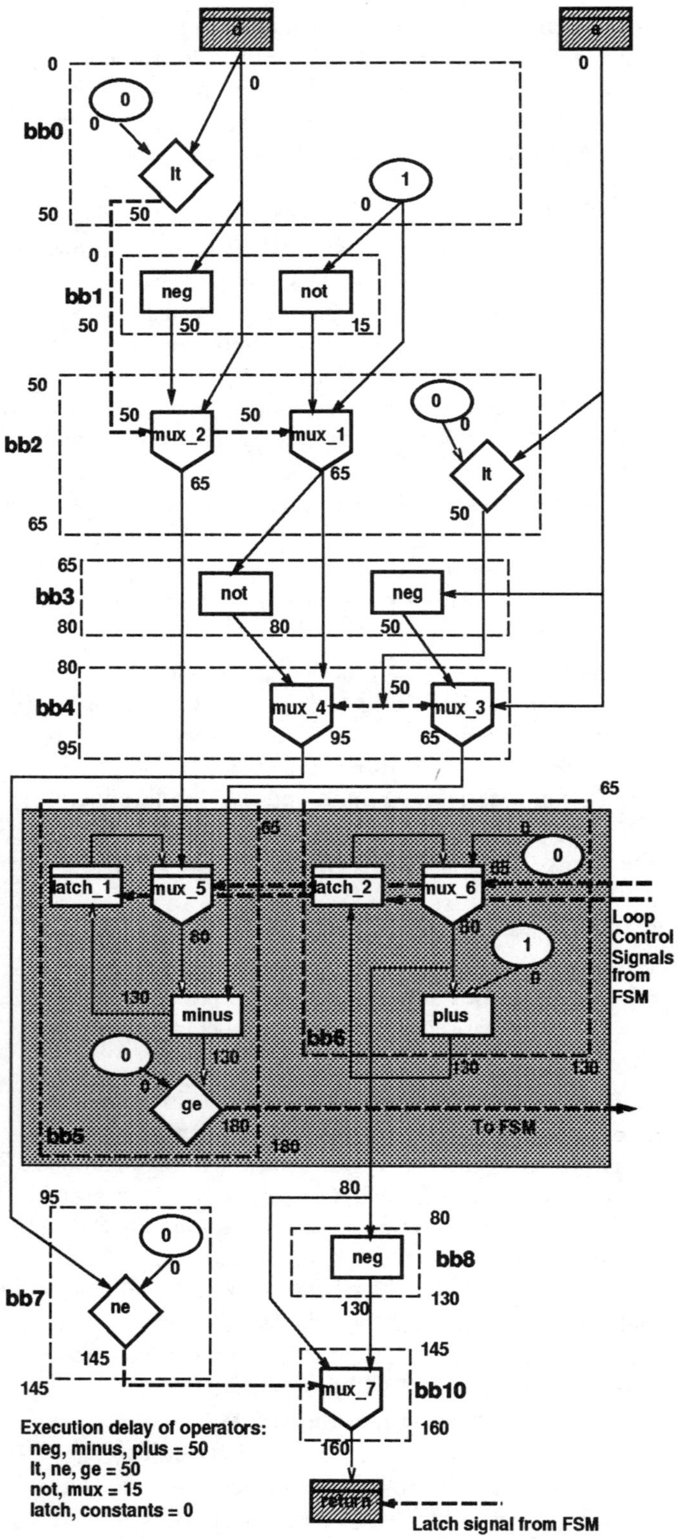

Figure 6: Operator Network for the C function in Figure 5.

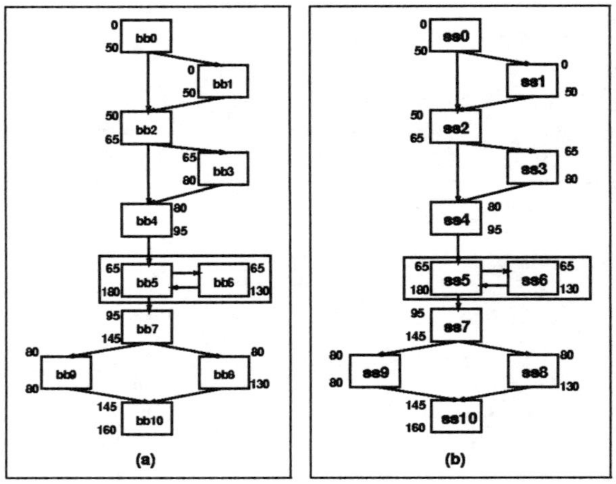

Figure 7: (a) CFG for the C function in Figure 5. (b) Corresponding Unoptimized FSM

in Figure 7b has the same starting and ending time-stamp values and is therefore deleted. In Figure 7b, state "ss8" is overlapped by state "ss7", and therefore, can be merged into the later. After this merger, state "ss7" and "ss10" in the same figure now become sequential, and hence, are merged into a single state "s'5" (time-stamps 95 and 160) as shown in Figure 8a.

The intermediate FSM obtained in Figure 8a is further optimized and the final FSM is shown in Figure 8b. The duration of state "s'3" in Figure 8a completely overlaps the starting and ending time-stamps of states "s'1", "s'2", and "s'5", and, therefore, the latter are merged into state "s'3". Furthermore, for the same reason, state "s'4" is merged into state "s'3." The resulting state is represented through state "s1" in Figure 8b.

Thus, the final FSM consists of only 2 states – "s0," and "s1". The duration of each state is computed as the difference between its "ending-time-stamp" and "starting-time-stamp". The duration for each state is shown within parentheses above its label in Figure 8b. The FSM controller in Figure 8b is in its simplest, irreducible form and therefore constitutes the final FSM.

Figure 9 presents the final "Machine-graph" consisting of the operator network and the optimized FSM (controller). Sets of operations in the operator network, that are executed within a particular state of the FSM, are shown enclosed by shaded rectangular blocks in the figure. The operations within "s0" complete execution at 65 time units, upon which state "s1" is initiated. State "s1" corresponds to a loop-state, i.e. the operations may be iterated more than once. First, the FSM signals the multiplexors, "mux_5" and

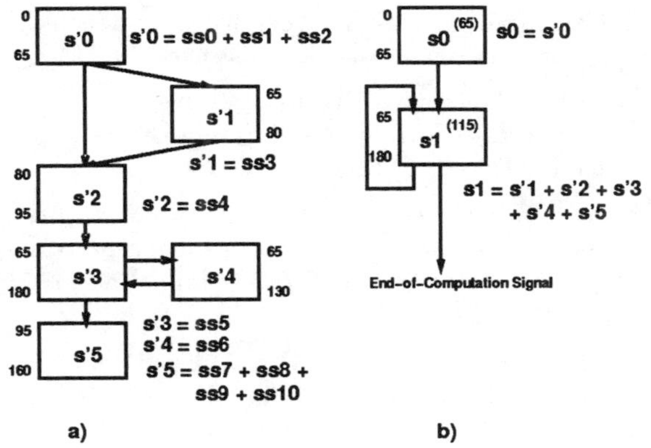

Figure 8: Optimized FSMs for the C function in Figure 5

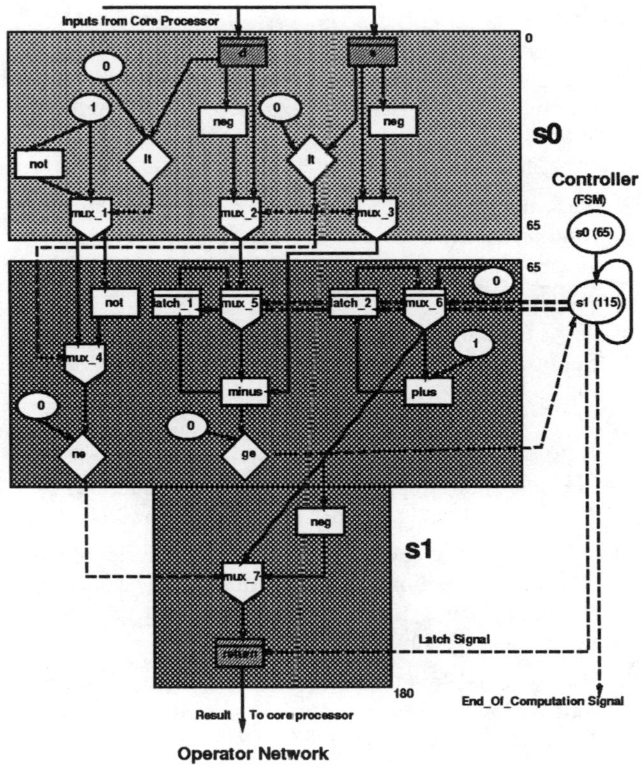

Figure 9: Machine Graph for the C function in Figure 5.

"mux_6," in the operator network to choose the initial values of variables "d" and "e" respectively. The first iteration of state "s1" completes at 180 time units. The FSM, then tests the boolean value generated by the operator "ge" in the Operator Network to determine whether to continue execution of the loop. This signal is represented by a dashed-line from node "ge" to state "s1" in the FSM. Where the loop continues to be executed, the FSM first instructs the two "latch" operators in the operator network to latch the feedback values of the two variables "d" and "q". When it returns to the state "s1," the FSM instructs the muxes – "mux_5" and "mux_6," to choose the values from their corresponding latches rather than select the initial values. Next, the operations within the loop are executed. Upon termination of the loop, the FSM latches the final result from the output of "mux_7" into the register labeled "return", and generates the "end-of-computation" signal which is propagated to the core processor, informing it of the availability of the final result.

The final machine is then instantiated with XBLOX library modules and a netlist file is generated to program the reconfigurable FPGA testbed.

5. Conclusions and Future Work

This paper has introduced a significant conceptual advancement to PRISM-II, a general purpose adaptive computing system. Its novel execution model and framework for translating a C function into an FPGA-based custom architecture were presented. In this system, specialized hardware is synthesized on an FPGA-based reconfigurable platform that efficiently executes the frequently executed sections of a program written in C. Speeding up the execution of the frequently executed section(s) greatly enhances the overall program performance. The reconfigurability of the hardware platform permits it to be reused for different applications. Thus, a general-purpose architecture is realized which, in addition, is tailored specifically for each application. The synthesis process is automatic and transparent, thereby allowing the user to concentrate on the application and not the architecture.

The authors are currently engaged in implementing PRISM-II, i.e. integrating the design of the reconfigurable FPGA testbed with the configuration compiler augmented by the new execution model. In addition, research into extending the execution model to include external memory accesses and pointers is under progress and will be reported in a future publication.

6. Acknowledgements

The authors gratefully acknowledge the support of the National Science Foundation through grant MIP-9021118. Gratitude is also expressed to Xilinx, Advanced Micro Devices, Viewlogic, Texas Instruments, AMP Inc., and V3 Corporation for their software and equipment support.

References

[1] G. Estrin. Organization of computer systems: The fixed-plus variable structure computer. In *Proceedings of the Western Joint Computer Conference*, pages 33–40, 1960.

[2] G. Radin. The 801 minicomputer. In *Proc. Symposium for Architectural Support for Programming Languages and Operating Systems*, Palo Alto, California, March 1982.

[3] R. A. Brunner. *VAX Architecture Reference Manual.* Digital Press, Bedford, Massachusetts, second edition, 1991.

[4] T. G. Rauscher and A. K. Agrawala. Dynamic problem-oriented redefinition of computer architecture via microprogramming. *IEEE Transactions on Computers*, C-27(11):1006–1014, November 1978.

[5] C. Papachristou and V. Immaneni. Vertical migration of software functions and algorithms using enhanced microsequencing. *IEEE Transactions on Computers*, 42(1), January 1993.

[6] Maya Gokhale et al. SPLASH: A reconfigurable linear logic array. In *International Conference on Parallel Processing*, pages I–526–I–532, 1990.

[7] Jeffrey M. Arnold, Duncan A. Buell, and Elaine G. Davis. SPLASH 2. In *ACM Symposium on Parallel Algorithms and Architectures*, 1992.

[8] P. Bertin, D. Roncin, and J. Vuillemin. Programmable active memories: A performance assessment. Research Report 24, Digital Paris Research Laboratory, March 1993.

[9] P. Callahan. Dynamic instruction set coprocessors. *MILCOM*, pages 19.1.1–19.1.6, 1988.

[10] P. Athanas and H. Silverman. Processor reconfiguration through instruction-set metamorphosis: Architecture and compiler. *IEEE Computer*, March 1993.

[11] J. Hennessy and D. Patterson. *Computer Architecture: A Quantitative Approach.* Morgan Kaufmann, San Mateo, California, 1990.

[12] Donald E. Knuth. An empirical study of FORTRAN programs. *Software-Practice and Experience*, 1:105–133, 1971.

[13] Howard Trickey. Flamel: A high-level hardware compiler. *IEEE Transactions on Computer-Aided Design*, CAD-6(2), March 1987.

[14] Camposano R., Bergamaschi R.A., Haynes C.E., Payer M., and Wu S.M. The IBM high-level synthesis system. In *High-Level VLSI Synthesis*, pages 79–104. Kluwer Academic Publishers, 1991.

[15] Wakabayashi K. Cyber: High level synthesis system from software into ASIC. In *High-Level VLSI Synthesis*, pages 127–151. Kluwer Academic Publishers, 1991.

[16] R. Camposano and Wolf W., editors. *High-Level VLSI Synthesis.* Kluwer Academic Publishers, 1991.

[17] Robert A. Walker and Raul Camposano, editors. *A Survey of High-Level Synthesis Systems.* Kluwer Academic Publishers, 1991.

[18] Richard Buehrer and Kattamuri Ekanadham. Incorporating data flow ideas into von neumann processors for parallel execution. *IEEE Transactions on Computers*, C-36(12), December 1987.

[19] D. D. Gajski, D. A. Padua, D. J. Kuck, and R. H. Kuhn. A second opinion on data flow machines and languages. *Computer*, February 1982.

[20] J. B. Dennis. Data flow supercomputers. *Computer*, 13(11):48–56, November 1980.

[21] Arvind and R. Nikhil. Executing a program on the MIT tagged-token dataflow architecture. In *Proceedings of the Conference on Parallel Architecture and Languages Europe*, volume II of *Lecture Notes in Computer Science*, pages 1–29, Eindhoven, 1987. Springer.

[22] Advanced Micro Devices, Inc. *AM29050 Microprocessor User's Manual*, 1991.

[23] M. Wazlowski, L. Agarwal, et al. PRISM II compiler and architecture. In *Proc. of the IEEE Workshop on FPGAs for Custom Computing Machines*, Napa, California, April 1993.

[24] A. V. Aho, R. Sethi, and J. D. Ullman. *Compilers. Principles, Techniques, and Tools.* Addison-Wesley, Reading, Massachusetts, 1986.

[25] Lalit K. Agarwal. Synthesis of Custom Architectures for C Functions utilizing FPGAs. Master's thesis, Brown University, Providence, RI, 1994.

[26] Xilinx Inc. San Jose, California. *X-BLOX Design Tool User Guide*, 1992.

[27] Xilinx Inc. San Jose, California. *XACT Reference Guide*, 1992.

A Case Study on Hardware/Software Partitioning

Axel Jantsch, Peeter Ellervee, Johnny Öberg, and Ahmed Hemani

Royal Institute of Technology
KTH-Electrum, ESDlab, Electrum 229, S-16440 Kista, Sweden
Email: axel@ele.kth.se

Abstract

We present an analysis of a fully automatic method to accelerate standard software in C or C++ by use of field programmable gate arrays. Traditional compiler techniques are applied to the hardware/software partitioning problem and a compiler is linked to state of the art hardware synthesis tools. Time critical regions are identified by means of profiling and are automatically implemented in user programmable logic with high level and logic synthesis design tools. The underlying architecture is an add-on board with user programmable logic connected to a Sparc based workstation via the system bus. We present an analysis and case study of this method. Eight programs are used as test cases and the data collected by applying this method to programs is used to discuss potentials and limitations of this and similar methods. We discuss architectural parameters, programming language properties, and analysis techniques.

1 Introduction

The microprocessor has established commonly accepted design paradigms for hardware and software design. The instruction set of the processor is the interface of the two worlds. The problem of processor design is to implement a given instruction set as fast as possible. Software engineers have to express their algorithms with a given instruction set. Because of the stability and similarity of most instruction sets programmers can use high level languages and compilers as a more convenient interface.

Field programmable Gate Arrays (FPGAs) begin to blur the line between hardware and software. They provide a flexibility in implementing a given algorithm that cannot be achieved by traditional microprocessors. However, microprocessors are highly optimized for general purpose programs, written in an imperative language and compiled by optimizing compilers. In general it can therefore not be expected to gain any performance improvement by switching from a micro processor based to an FPGA based implementation for a given program. Many special purpose and computational intensive algorithms, however, can be implemented in an FPGA more efficiently due to the greater flexibility in allocating exactly those hardware resources that needed. Many approaches which exploit this idea require that the partitioning is done by the designer and that the hardware parts have to be specified in a notation different from the software parts. In contrast we propose a uniform specification for both parts, namely C or C++, and we provide an algorithm that performs the partitioning. The hardware parts are implemented by means of high level and logic synthesis tools.

The architecture of the demonstrator system consists of a SparcStation IPX with a user configurable add-on board that is connected to the workstation via the system bus [8]. User configurable logic can be provided either as FPGA from Xilinx or as a logic emulator system with up to 100,000 gates from Quickturn [4].

Objectives of this research are (a) to define the class of programs that are well suited for acceleration with the proposed architecture and (b) to explore the relations between properties of the program and architectural parameters. Although we are concentrating on conventional programs we are convinced that our results are relevant for embedded system design and that our techniques can be easily adopted to this area, since similar approaches have been taken there ([5] [7] [2]).

Figure 1 shows the overall design flow. The source program is partitioned by an extended version of the GNU CC compiler [16] into hardware and software parts. Although we can process C++ programs in the same way as C programs we do not take special properties of C++ into account during the analysis. Therefore we have selected only C programs as test cases for this study. The hardware partition is derived from one or more source code regions and translated automatically into behavioral VHDL. VHDL is used to describe hardware at the structural and behavioural level. The behavior of a hardware component is described as an algorithm which is sufficiently similar to

0-8186-5490-2/94 $03.00 © 1994 IEEE

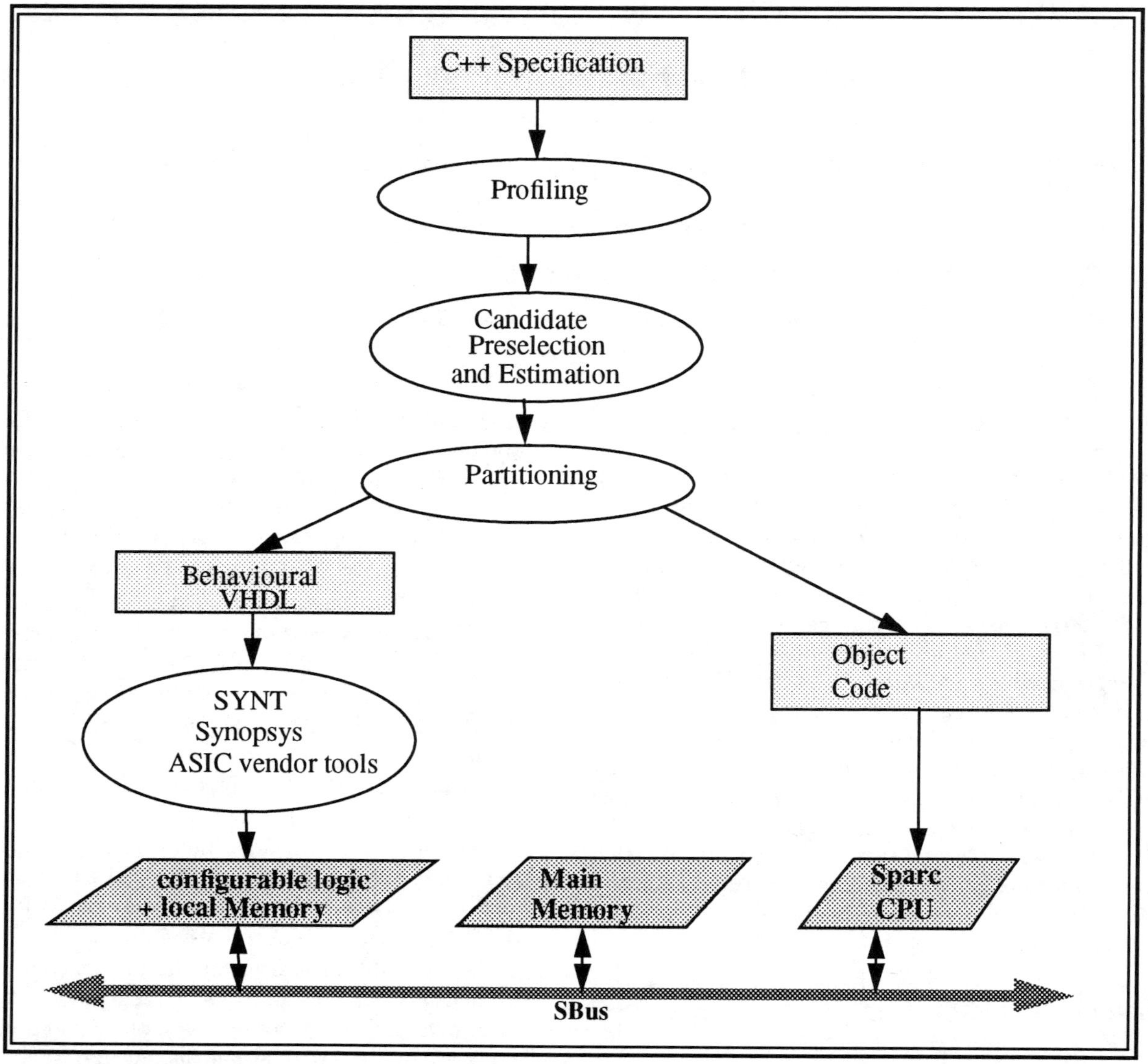

Figure 1. Design flow

imperative programming languages like C to make the translation process painless. The high level synthesis system SYNT [10] [9] translates the behavioural description into a structural VHDL description by allocating hardware units and scheduling operations in control steps. The logic synthesis system Synopsys and finally ASIC vendor specific place and route tools transform the design into configuration files for the field programmable logic. The software part will usually constitute the larger fragment and is compiled for the host workstation.

Figure 2 outlines the board architecture. The board is connected to the system bus and has access to main memory via the L64853 DVMA component which implements direct virtual memory access. The XC4003 FPGA handles the interface between the application design and the DVMA IC. It is configured at startup from a ROM. The XC4005 implements the application design. It has access to two banks of local memory which can be accessed concurrently to allow a fast local memory access. It can be replaced by a plug adapter from Quickturn logic emulator system, which allows to implement an application design as large as 100,000 Gates. From the point of view of the application software and design there is no difference between implementing the design in a single FPGA or in the logic emulator. Only the configuration process differs.

In the following sections we discuss related work, briefly describe the participating and present an analysis of the key factors for acceleration of C programs by means of field programmable hardware and automatic partitioning. Results of experiments are presented to support our arguments.

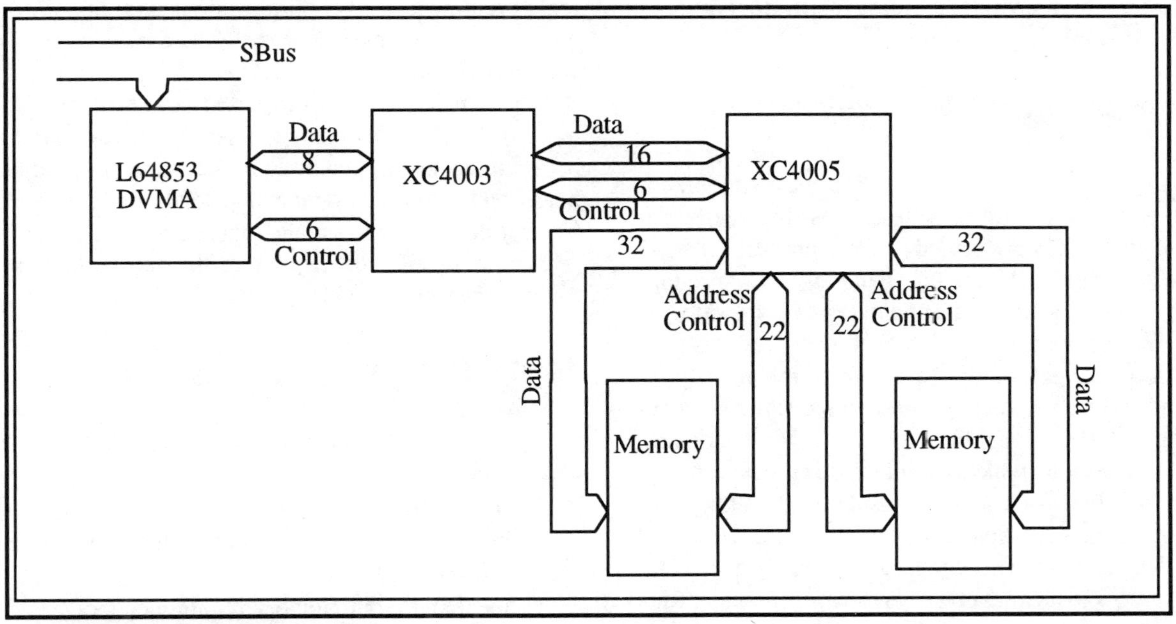

Figure 2. Board architecture

2 Related Work

Bertin, Roncin, and Vuillemin [3] report impressive speedups for ten algorithms by utilization of an array of FPGAs. They carefully choose and design the algorithms to optimally suit the given hardware. In some of their examples the performance gain originates by reformulating the algorithms. Their examples are small and special purpose applications as opposed to the large and general purpose programs we are investigating in this study.

Luk, Lok, and Page conducted a study [15], which shows how an application can benefit from available FPGAs by carefully partitioning the application and tailoring the hardware partition for the given architecture. However, the main benefit comes from carefully choosing or designing the algorithm with the available software and hardware architecture in mind. Unfortunately, this approach is not feasible for automatic partitioning of a given algorithm.

Athanas [1] ambition to automatically partition a C program in HW and SW parts and implement the HW parts in FPGAs is similar to ours but less general. He considers only pure combinational circuits without using high level synthesis techniques. He does not allow main memory access from the FPGA board and the partitioning process is guided by a human user.

Koch and Golze describe a coprocessor board [13] which is in design and purpose of use similar to our board. However, they focus on the board design and have not presented a method to partition and implement a given algorithm.

Ernst and Henkel [7] use an extension of C as specification language for embedded controller design. Their objective is to extract code segments for implementation in hardware when timing constraints are violated. Their partitioner is based on simulated annealing and considers every segment of C statements as a possible candidate, which is inefficient since most of the segments are not good candidates when the program includes loops. The profiling data is collected by a simulator which is much slower than the compilation and execution of a C program. This makes it hard to run long programs with extensive test data.

Martin Edwards [5] describes a system in C, collects profiling information by compiling and executing the program. He considers only functions as candidate regions and may miss more promising larger or smaller regions like inner loops. As in Athanas' work the regions are selected by a human user and no automatic partitioning is reported yet.

The work on the Mark-I architecture by Lewis et al. [14] has the goal to accelerate a class of programs by defining an application specific instruction set that is executed on an array of 16 Xilinx FPGAs. The definition of a special purpose instruction set for a given program is similar to the identification of candidate regions and their implementation in FPGAs. Lewis et. al. have not yet automated the partitioning, but focused on the development of the board architecture.

Our approach allows (a) efficient collection of profiling data due to usage of C and C++ as specification languages, (b) fast partitioning due to a candidate preselection scheme, and (c) high complexity of the hardware partition due to a logic emulation system.

3 Partitioning and Implementation

The partitioning is based on profiling information and cost and performance estimation of possible hardware implementations. It is performed in three phases: (1) candidate preselection, (2) memory mapping and speedup estimation, (3) allocation of candidates to hardware or software. In the first phase a set of code regions are selected as candidates for hardware implementation. These candidates are basically inner loops, leaf functions and loops and functions that include other candidate regions. Code regions which include floating point operations or library functions are not considered as candidates. The FPGA implementation has access to main memory via the DVMA component connected to the system bus. Thus, references to any data type can be implemented. But since main memory access is slow we use a three level memory hierarchy. The fastest access is possible if the data resides inside the FPGA which is feasible only for small data types. It is preferred for local and temporary variables. Local, on-board memory is slower but can be as large as 4 MB. The second phase of partitioning allocates all memory referenced by a candidate in one of these storage locations. Then it estimates cost and performance of the hardware implementation. Currently the estimation is straight forward and simple but we intend to employ a more sophisticated neural net based estimator [6]. The performance of the software implementation is measured during execution of the program. Finally an algorithm based on dynamic programming selects the candidates which will be implemented in the FPGA.

The preliminary mapping strategy of candidate regions onto user configurable logic, is only possible due to the progress in high level synthesis techniques and tools during the last ten years.

Each region that is selected for hardware implementation is translated into a VHDL process. This translation is straight forward since all simple data types and operators of C can be expressed in behavioural VHDL when the appropriate arithmetic packages are used. Access to complex data types are transformed into address calculations and primitive memory access operations. Pointers are regarded as memory addresses. For the main program the invocation of such a region is similar to a function call. Values that reside in registers at the time of the invocation and are used or updated inside the region are passed as parameters.

The generated VHDL code is processed by SYNT [9][10], a high level synthesis system which generates a dedicated datapath and a separate controller. Synopsys tools perform low level optimizations and the ASIC vendor specific tools place and route the design and generate configuration files.

The remaining software part of the program is augmented with code that performs the communication between the software and the regions implemented on the board and a startup routine that loads the configuration files for the user configurable logic down to the board.

A more detailed description of the partitioning process can be found in [11][12].

4 Key Parameters

The main factors which affect the overall program speedup are

- the *relative temporal size* of the candidates, i.e. the percentage of run time the program spends inside the candidate region;
- local and main memory requirements of the candidate;
- the potential to map main memory to local memory;
- local and main memory access time.

We have investigated eight C programs, namely filter and filter2, two small FIR filter examples, hamming, a small program that calculates the hamming distance of one million pairs of numbers, sed, a stream editor, grep and egrep, two pattern matchers, gzip, a file compression program, and ghostscript, a program that visualizes postscript files on the workstation screen. 2523 code regions were identified in these programs as potential candidates for hardware implementation. The program analysis and partitioning has been performed with two sets of architectural parameters. They differ mainly in the access time to local and main memory which is shown in table 1. The

Table 1. Memory access time

	main memory	local memory
A1	500 ns	100 ns
A2	20 ns	20 ns

values of A1 are close to what we expect for our prototype architecture. A2 resembles a coprocessor architecture where the FPGA has access to memory as fast as the CPU. In the following sections we discuss each of the key parameters in turn.

4.1 Candidate Size

The fraction of the run time a program spends inside a region is called the *temporal size* of the candidate and is given in percent of the total run time of the program. It limits the program speedup that can be gained by improving on the implementation of a particular candidate. For those candidates that have been adopted as solution by the partitioning algorithm table 2 shows the candidate's temporal sizes as measured by profiling the programs, and the maximum and estimated speedups compared with a pure software implementation on a SPARCstation IPX running at 20MHz. The theoretical maximum speedup is

$$\text{max speedup} = \frac{1}{1 - \left(\frac{\text{temporal size}}{100}\right)}$$

and is achieved when the execution time of the candidate is 0. filter, filter2 and hamming are small programs and have been chosen as test cases for this analysis. However, they have not been written with the purpose to suit a hardware implementation as best as possible. Only in filter2 it has been taken care that no library functions or floating point operations are used. It has been derived from filter by replacing a call to a library function with an equivalent piece of code. This has enlarged the hardware implementable code section considerably and led to a speedup improvement by a factor 4. For the other programs the temporal candidate sizes are the most severe limitations to higher speedup factors. 97.8% of the 3500 candidates we have examined have a relative temporal size of less than 1%, which results in an average temporal size of these candidates of 0.6%. The average of those candidates that have a temporal size greater than 1% is 27.6%. In all cases the candidate region could not be enlarged due to library function calls or floating point operations. Although the gate count numbers are only rough estimations they demonstrate that one XC4005 FPGA is certainly insufficient. The complexity of the hardware partitions is in no case high and probably well in reach of a larger FPGA. All candidates can definitely be implemented on the logic emulator system. Hence, the limit to enlarge the candidate regions comes from unimplementable program code rather than from size restrictions of the hardware. This is underlined by the fact that the average gate count of the 3500 candidates is 2017 gates. 50% of all candidates are smaller than 705 gates; 90% are smaller than 4000 gates.

4.2 Memory Requirements

Access to memory is the second main obstacle to achieve higher speedup factors as it can be observed by comparing the speedups gained for architectures A1 and A2 in table 2. The problem is that the memory access of the FPGA has to compete with fast and very efficient caches of the CPU, which maintain a hit rate close to 100% for small and frequently executed code regions. Figure 3 shows how the maximum speedup for individual candidates decreases when the memory access per time unit increases. Candidates of all programs are plotted. The "o" signs mark candidates of architecture A1, the 'x' signs candidates of architecture A2. It can be observed that the maximum speedup decreases linearly with the memory access per time unit for both architectures. In fact, we have approximated the upper bound of the speedup by $\text{speedup} = 1.3/(a \cdot m)$ where a is the memory access time of main memory in micro seconds and m is the number of memory accesses per micro second. Figure 4 shows how the speedup of candidates of grep increases when the computation of the candidate dominates its memory requirements. The other programs show the same behaviour.

4.3 Mapping to Local Memory

The partitioning process attempts to map as much of the main memory, that is accessed by a candidate, to local memory or onto the FPGA. Since memory access is one of the main bottlenecks, moving data from slower to faster

Table 2. Temporal size of candidates and program speedup

	filter	filter2	hamming	sed	grep	egrep	gzip	gs
temporal size (A1)	15%	81.1%	93.8%	0%	0%	0%	0%	0%
temporal size (A2)	15%	81.1%	93.8%	14.7%	17.0%	62.1%	82.0%	5.7%
max speedup (A1)	1.18	5.29	16.13	1	1	1	1	1
max speedup (A2)	1.18	5.29	16.13	1.17	1.2	2.6	5.6	1.06
speedup (A1)	1.08	4.11	14.4	1.0	1.0	1.0	1.0	1.0
speedup (A2)	1.17	5.01	14.4	1.15	1.12	1.45	2.93	1.03
gate count (A1)	5120	5920	12416	0	0	0	0	0
gate count (A2)	5120	5920	12416	1120	5504	5984	11712	960

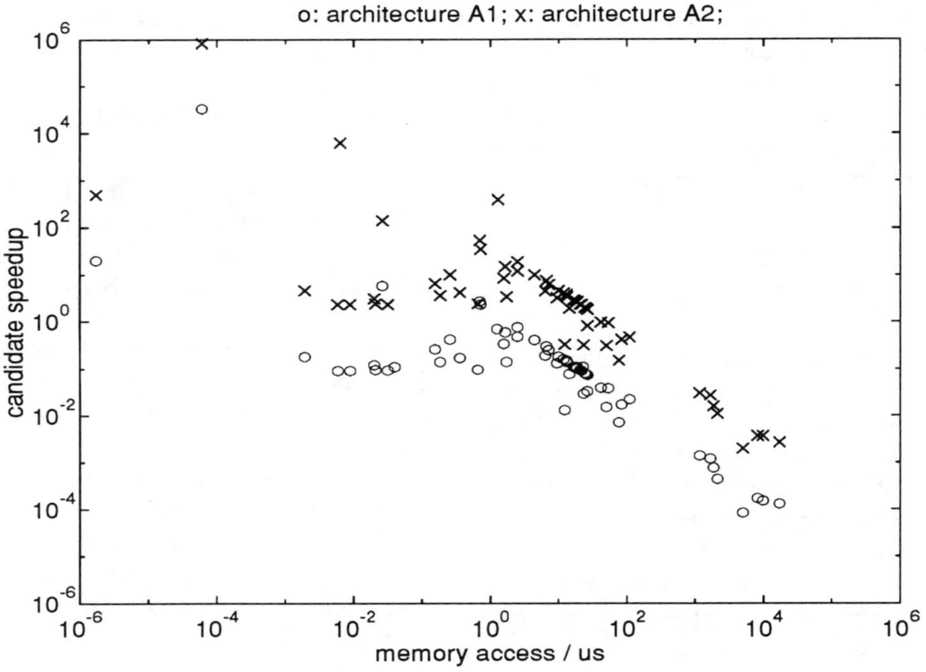

Figure 3. Speedup versus memory access

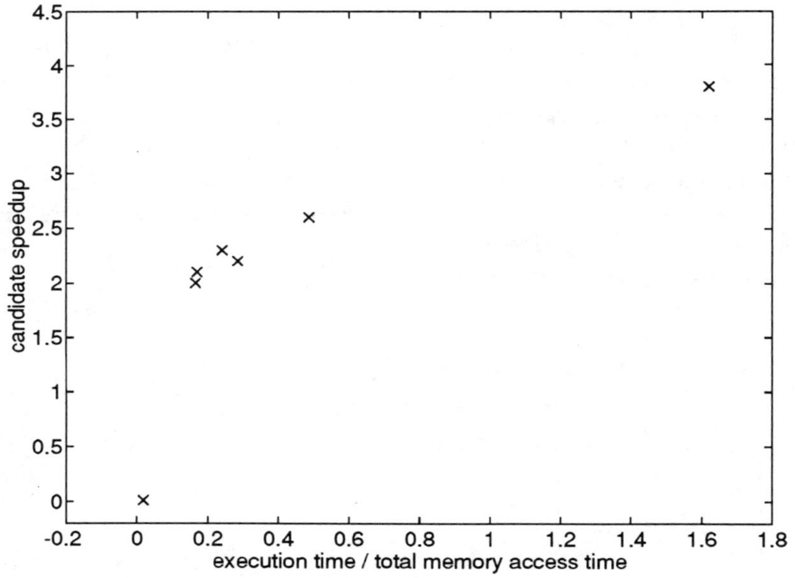

Figure 4. Speedup versus the ratio of execution time to memory access time

memory will improve performance. Table 3 shows the

Table 3. Improvements due to memory mapping

	a_L	a_R	s_L	s_R
A1	1.9	3.0	1.2	11.9
A2	1.0	3.0	1.0	4.3
average	1.4	3.0	1.1	8.3

reduction in memory access time and the improvements of speedup due to mapping of global memory to local memory and to registers on the FPGA. a_L and a_R are the average factors by which the memory access time could be reduced when mapping data to local memory or FPGA registers, respectively. s_L and s_R are the average factors by which the candidate speedup increased due to mapping of data to local memory or FPGA registers, respectively. The moving of data onto the FPGA has the most important affect whereas the local on-board memory is less successful. It does not have any affect for architecture A2 because the access time is equal for main and local memory. But even for architecture A1 with a difference of factor five in access time the speedup gain of 20% is not impressive. The reason is, that it is very hard to trace the usage of complex data types in C programs. The usage of simple data types is easier to trace but they are usually allocated on the FPGA. Arrays and records are frequently referenced via pointers, and the values of pointers are not known at compile time. We have not yet fully exploited the potential of moving data from main to local memory but since many special cases have to be considered each individual tactic will bring only small improvements and progress will therefore be slow.

The a_R factors in table 3 are not consistent with the s_R factors because they do not refer to the same candidates. Many candidates do not have main memory access because all their data is moved inside the FPGA. Since the memory access time is the divider in the a_R term, they are excluded in the calculation. These candidates contribute to the increase of speedup, reflected by the s_R values. Thus, the a_R factors underestimate the affect of moving data from main memory to the FPGA.

a_L and s_L are 1.0 for architecture A2 because local and main memory access time do not differ in A2. The a_R's of A1 and A2 are equal because the relative gain of moving data to the FPGA are the same for both architectures although the main memory access times differ. However, the relative gains in speedup are not the same since speedup is a comparison of hardware execution time to software execution time and for architecture A1 the memory execution time has a higher proportion in hardware execution time than for architecture A2, which makes it more beneficial to improve on memory access time in architecture A1.

Initial experiments with the utilization of the data locality in abstract data types of C++ indicate that the a_L factors come close to 5 and the s_L factors above 2 when complete objects can be implemented in hardware.

4.4 Memory Access Time

The access time to local and main memory is the most important architectural characteristic. The slower the access time is the more restricted is the class of programs that can be sped up. The yardstick to compare with is the effective memory access of the CPU which is close to one CPU clock cycle due to large and fast caches. Table 2 shows that the board we use as experimental architecture can only be used to speed up programs with minimal memory requirements.

5 Conclusions

The main obstacles to obtain higher speedup factors are (a) the relative small size of the candidate regions and (b) the frequency of memory access. Larger temporal candidate sizes can be achieved by applying the method to more specialized programs which by their nature spend almost all their run time in small areas. A second option is to rewrite programs like gzip or egrep to exploit available hardware better.

The memory access problem can be relaxed (a) by choosing a proper architecture, (b) by choosing proper programs, or (c) by choosing a proper programming language which allows for efficient analysis techniques. The ideal architecture would be an FPGA situated close to the CPU as a coprocessor and having the same conditions to memory access as the CPU. The slower the FPGAs memory access is compared to the CPUs the more restricted is the class of programs and code regions that can benefit from it. The programming language has an impact on how programs are written and what information is available about data items at compile time. C is not well suited for this purpose since its data abstraction mechanisms are poorly developed. We expect that an object oriented language would provide us with enough information about data items to allow almost optimal memory allocation and to minimize traffic between the FPGA on one hand and main memory and CPU on the other hand. So far we have mainly exploited the locality of control structures in loops and leaf functions. An object oriented language would allow us in addition to exploit the data locality.

6 Bibliography

[1] Peter M. Athanas, *An Adaptive Hardware Machine Architecture and Compiler for Dynamic Processor Reconfiguration,* PhD thesis, Division of Engineering, Brown University, Providence, Rhode Island, USA, September 1991.

[2] Th. Benner, J. Henkel, and R. Ernst, "Internal representation of Embedded Hardware-/Software Systems", *Second IFIP International Workshop on Hardware-Software Co-Design*, May 1993.

[3] P. Bertin and D. Roncin and J. Vuillemin, "Programmable Active Memories: Performance Measurement", *Proceedings of the First International Workshop on Field Programmable Gate Arrays*, February 1992, ACM SIGDA, pp. 57 - 59.

[4] M. Butts, J. Batcheller and J. Varghese, "An efficient logic emulation system", pp. 138 - 144, *Proc. IEEE Int. Conf. on Computer Design*, pp. 138 - 144, October 1992.

[5] Martin Edwards, "A Development System for Hardware/ Software Co-Synthesis using FPGAs", *Second IFIP International Workshop on Hardware-Software Co-Design,* May 1993.

[6] Peeter Ellervee, Axel Jantsch, Johnny Öberg and Ahmed Hemani, "Nestimator - A Neural Network Based Estimator", submitted to *EuroDAC 1994*.

[7] R. Ernst and J. Henkel, "Hardware-Software Codesign of Embedded Controllers Based on Hardware extraction", *Proceedings of the International Workshop on Hardware-Software Co-Design*, September 1992.

[8] Shousheng He and Mats Torkelson, "FPGA Application in a SBbus Based Rapid Prototyping System for ASDP", *ICCD* 1991.

[9] Ahmed Hemani and Adam Postula, "A Neural Net Based Self Organizing Scheduling Algorithm", *European Design Automation Conference*, pp 136 - 140, 1990.

[10] Ahmed Hemani, *High Level Synthesis of Synchronous Digital Systems using Self-Organization Algorithms for Scheduling and Allocation*, PhD thesis, Department of Applied Electronics, Royal Institute of Technology, Stockholm, Sweden, 1992.

[11] Axel Jantsch, Peeter Ellervee, Johnny Öberg, Ahmed Hemani, and Hannu Tenhunen, "A Software Oriented Approach to Hardware/Software Codesign", accepted for publication as poster at the *International Conference on Compiler Construction*, 1994, April.

[12] Axel Jantsch, Peeter Ellervee, Johnny Öberg, Ahmed Hemani, and Hannu Tenhunen, "Hardware-Software Partitioning and Minimizing Memory Interface Traffic"", submitted to *EURO-DAC '94*, 1994.

[13] Andreas Koch and Ulrich Golze, "An FPGA Based Co-Processor for SBus Workstations", 3rd International Workshop on Field-Programmable Logic and Applications ", 1993.

[14] David M. Lewis, Marcus H. van Ierssel, and Daniel H. Wong, "A Field Programmable Accelerator for Compiled Code Applications", *Proceedings of the IEEE Workshop on FPGAs for Custom Computing Machines,* April 1993.

[15] Wayne Luk, Vincent Lok, and Ian Page, "Hardware acceleration of Divide and Conquer Paradigms: A Case Study ", *Proceedings of the IEEE Workshop on FPGAs for Custom Computing Machines*, April 1993.

[16] Richard M. Stallman, *Using and Porting GNU CC,* Free Software Foundation, December1992, version 2.3.

From High Level Programming Model to FPGA Machines [1]

J.P. Banâtre, D. Lavenier, M. Vieillot
IRISA
Campus de Beaulieu
35042 Rennes Cedex, France

Abstract

This paper presents an approach for deriving a FPGA machine from a high level parallel programming model. The model is based on the chemical reaction metaphor : the data structure is a multiset and the computation can be seen as a succession of chemical reactions consuming and producing new elements according to specific rules.

Von Neuman architecture are not suited to this programming style; we show the utility of FPGAs for deriving adapted hardware architectures. Feasibility has been demonstrated on the DEC-PRL Perle-1 board with implementation of a representative algorithm.

1 Introduction

Writing a correct program is difficult. It is even more difficult when the target machine is a parallel machine and no parallel programming method is provided. A computational model which allows one to describe algorithms with as few sequentiality constraints as possible is then desirable. A model without any sequentiality, called Gamma (General Abstract Model for Multiset mAnipulation), has been proposed by J.P. Banâtre and D. Le Metayer [1]. The power of Gamma is the possibility of expressing algorithms in an abstract way, without any artificial sequentiality.

The basic structure in Gamma is the multiset and a computation proceeds by nondeterministic local rewriting on that multiset. Programs based on this model are a mis-mach for Von Neuman machine. This paper will show the relevance of FPGAs for deriving an adapted hardware architecture.

The main idea suited for the Gamma paradigm is the ability of a Gamma program to be decomposed into a restrictive set of primitive programs, called *tropes* [4]. From a hardware point of view, this is an interresting property since each primitive program is well defined and induces a specific architecture.

The paper present an investigation we have performed using the Perle-1 FPGA board [2] [3] developed by the DEC Paris Research Lab. In order to show the validity of our approach, we implement manually the prime factorization algorithm.

The paper is organized as follows: section 2 gives a short presentation of the Gamma formalism; section 3 introduces the set of primitive programs (***tropes***). Section 4 presents the implementation of the prime factorization problem on the Perle-1 board.

[1] this work is funded by a DECPerle-1 Research Initiative Contract

2 The Gamma Programming Paradigm

The Gamma model can be described as a multiset transformer: the computation is a succession of applications of rules which consume elements of the multiset and produce new elements. The computation ends when no rule can be applied. The application of rules is performed in a non-deterministic way.

The basic information structuring facility is the multiset. A multiset is similar to a set except that it may contain multiple occurrences of the same element. Atomic components of multisets may be of type real, character, integer or tuple of arbitrary type.

The main feature of the model is the Γ-operator, which can be defined in the following way:

Γ (R,A) (M) =
  if ∃ $x_1, ...x_n \in$ M such that R($x_1, ...x_n$)
    then Γ (R,A) ((M-$\{x_1, ...x_n\}$) ∪ A($x_1, ...x_n$))
    else M.

Operator R is called the "reaction condition"; it is a boolean function indicating under which conditions some elements of the multiset can react. The A function ("action") describes the result of this reaction. We point out that if the reaction condition holds for

0-8186-5490-2/94 $03.00

several subsets at the same time, the choice (which is made among them) is not deterministic; if these subsets are disjoint the reactions can even take place at the same time.

Let us take one example to illustrate the programming style entailed by the Gamma-model. The sieve of Eratosthenes can be written as follows:

sieve(n) = **Γ** (R,A) ({2, ... n}) **where**
R($x1, x2$) = multiple($x1, x2$)
A($x1, x2$) = $x2$

multiple ($x1, x2$) is true if and only if $x1$ is a multiple of $x2$.

The following figure describes the computation of **sieve(8)**. The lines between elements indicate reactions. Of course, this is one among the possible paths leading to the stable sate.

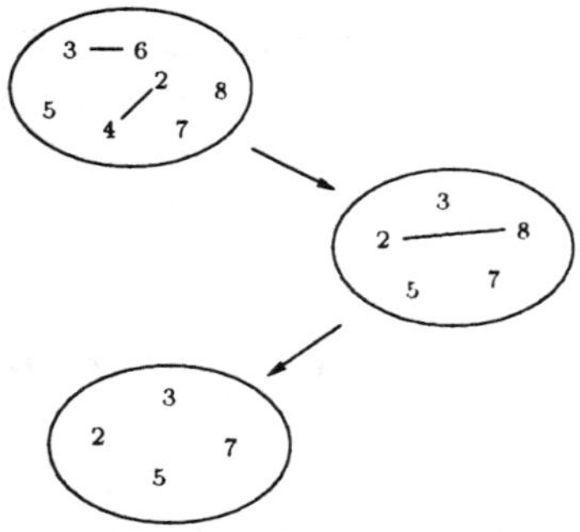

The Gamma-model presented above is not the most general definition; actually, the Γ operator can take any number of couples (Reaction,Action), each reaction condition indicating in which case the associated action can be applied. As an example, consider the *fibonacci* computation. It can be expressed as follows:

fib(n) = **Γ** (R3,A3) (Γ((R2,A2)(R1,A1)){n}) **where**
R1(x) = $x > 1$
A1(x) = $x - 1, x - 2$
R2(x) = $x = 0$
A2(x) = 1
R3($x1, x2$) = **true**
A3($x1, x2$) = $x1 + x2$

The initial number n is decomposed into a number of ones which are then summed-up to produce the result. The couples of Reaction/Action (R2,A2) and (R1,A1) work in parallel. Once the multiset is stable (i.e. no more reactions occur), the next Reaction/Action (R3,A3) is performed.

3 TROPES

3.1 Presentation

Tropes are a way of decomposing Gamma programs. They constitute a set of primitive program schemes, which together with just two basic combining forms provide an expressive parallel programming language. The *tropes* take the form of parametrized conditional rewrite rules in which computation proceeds in a non-deterministic local rewriting of a global multiset.

The following notation is used to denote multiset rewriting:

$$x_1, ..., x_n \rightarrow A(x_1, ..., x_n) \Leftarrow R(x_1, ..., x_n)$$

This rule can be interpreted informally as the replacement into the multiset of elements $x_1, ..., x_n$ satisfying the condition $R(x_1, ..., x_n)$ by the elements of $A(x_1, ..., x_n)$. Viewed as a single program, the result is obtained when no more rewrites can take place.

Two operators are used for combining programs: sequential composition $P_1 \circ P_2$; parallel combination $P_1 + P_2$. The intuition behind $P_1 \circ P_2$ is that the result of P_2 is passed as an argument to P_1. On the other hand, the result of $P_1 + P_2$ is obtained by performing the rewrites of P_1 and P_2 in parallel.

Five rewrite rules, called *tropes*, have been selected to provide a set of primitive programs:

- ⋆ $\mathcal{T}$ransmuter
- ⋆ $\mathcal{R}$educer
- ⋆ $\mathcal{OP}$timiser
- ⋆ $\mathcal{E}$xpander
- ⋆ $\mathcal{S}$elector

They are defined in terms of multiset rewrites. As an example, the *transmuter*, the *reducer* and the *expander* can be expressed in the following way:

transmuter	$\mathcal{T}(C, f)$	=	$x \rightarrow f(x) \Leftarrow C(x)$
reducer	$\mathcal{R}(C, f)$	=	$x, y \rightarrow f(x, y) \Leftarrow C(x, y)$
expander	$\mathcal{E}(c, f_1, f_2)$	=	$x \rightarrow f_1(x), f_2(x) \Leftarrow C(x)$

The *transmuter* applies the same operation to all the elements of the multiset until no element satisfies the condition C. The *reducer* decreases the size of the multiset by applying a function to pairs of elements satisfying the condition C. The *expander* decomposes the elements of the multiset into a collection of basic values. The interested reader can find a complete description of the *tropes* in [4].

The examples taken in the previous section can both be expressed as a combination of *tropes*. The sieve of Eratosthenes is simply a *reducer*:

$$\text{sieve}(n) = \mathcal{R}(multiple(x,y), y)\{2, ..., n\}$$

The Fibonacci computation is a combination of three *tropes* P_1, P_2 and P_3 :

$$\text{fib}(n) = P_3 \circ (P_2 + P_1)\{n\}$$

with

$P_1 = \mathcal{E}(x > 1, x-1, x-2)$	*expander*
$P_2 = \mathcal{T}(x = 0, 1)$	*transmuter*
$P_3 = \mathcal{R}(true, x + y)$	*reducer*

Note that this program can also be expressed using only the sequential combination operator :

$$\text{fib}(n) = P_3 \circ P_2 \circ P_1\{n\}$$

3.2 Synthesis

From an architectural point of view the decomposition into primitive programs provides an interesting way to simplify the synthesis of Gamma programs. As the *tropes* are well defined, a hardware skeleton may be associated with each of them.

The basic procedure for synthesizing a Gamma program is first to decompose it into *tropes*. This step is done manually. In other words, the programmer has to write a Gamma program using only a set of five primitives and two operators.

Once the *tropes* have been selected, the next step is to synthesize a corresponding architecture for each of them. Experiments have shown that the decomposition into *tropes* is not sufficient : depending on the types of the elements processed inside a *tropes*, the architecture could be rather different. An element can have the type singleton, pair, triplet, ..., etc and be composed of integer, character, etc. A pair of integers and a pair of characters have a different type. As an example, consider the *transmuter* :

$$\mathcal{T}(C, f) = x \rightarrow f(x) \Leftarrow C(x)$$

Remember that this *tropes* applies the same operation to all the elements of the multiset until no element satisfies the condition C. Two cases may be observed :

- the type of x is different from the type of $f(x)$,
- the types of x and $f(x)$ are identical.

In the first case ($\text{type}(x) \neq \text{type}(f(x))$), if an element x reacts, it will be transformed in $y = f(x)$. As the type of y is different of the type of x, we are sure that it will never react again. A possible skeleton architecture is :

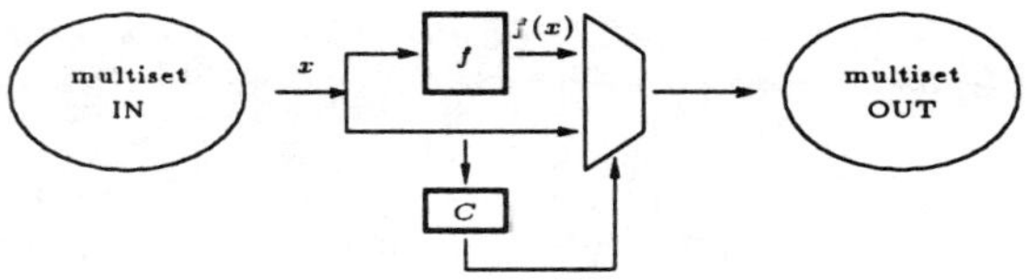

The boxes f and C stand respectively for the action and the reaction. The C box drives a multiplexer which, according to the condition computation, outputs x or $f(x)$.

In the second case ($\text{type}(x) = \text{type}(f(x))$), if an element x reacts, $f(x)$ must be tested since it may react again. A possible architecture is :

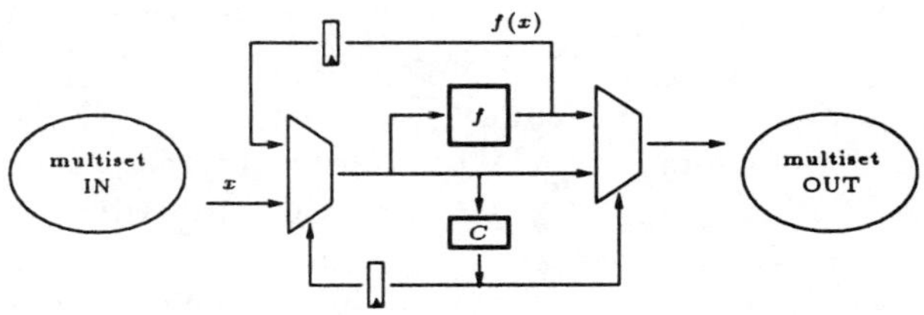

This second architecture is more complex and implies a more sophisticated control.

For each *tropes*, different skeleton architectures are provided depending on the difference of the input/output types. The choice of the right *tropes* can be done automatically by an analysis of the properties of the f function.

The idea behind the refinement of the decomposition in *tropes* is to simplify hardware mechanism. It will be faster and will save FPGA resources.

The final step is to assemble the *tropes*. The combination operators $\circ$ and $+$ tell us how this assembly must be done. Actually, we focus only on the $\circ$ operator, since many programs including the $+$ operator can be rewritten using only the $\circ$ operator. Furthermore, writing $P_1 \circ P_2$ leads naturally to considering the results of P_2 as being passed as an argument to P_1. Thus, the $P_1 \circ P_2$ combination corresponds to a pipeline of the *tropes* P_1 and P_2 as shown figure 1.

It must be pointed out that the parallel operator $(+)$ is more difficult to implement. Pipelining the *tropes* (using the $+$ operator) is then not possible. Data produced by a *tropes* must return to the input

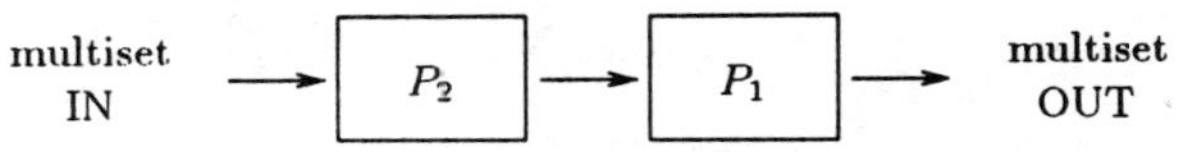

Figure 1: implementation of the sequential combination $P_1 \circ P_2$

multiset, in order to be computed by the other *tropes*. In a first approach we discard this possibility for two main reasons:

- most of the programs can be written using only the $\circ$ operator. The expressing capability of Gamma is thus restricted but is still an interesting computational model.
- one of the main objective of this work is to investigate the PAM synthesize pprocess. The restrictive model is easily sufficient for that purpose.

3.3 Implementation

The hardware platform we use is the PRL-DEC Perle-1 board [2]. It is based on the PAM (Programmable Active Memory) [3] concept : like RAM memory module, a PAM is attached to the system bus of a host computer. The processor can write into, and read from the PAM. Being an active hardware coprocessor however, the PAM processes data between write and read instructions. The specific processing is determined by the content of its *configuration memory*.

The Perle-1 board is built around a large array of bit-level configurable logic cells. This array is surrounded by local RAM banks used as a cache, a programmable clock generator and some additional logic to manage the host bus interface.

The central computational array consists of a 4×4 matrix of Xilinx XC3090 programmable gate arrays [5]. Four 32-bit wide RAM banks (1 MBytes) are provided on each side. The host bus interface is a TurboChannel interface delivering a 100 MBytes/s bandwith.

Programming Perle-1 consists of describing an architecture using an object oriented language (C++) and built-in primitive functions. More compact designs may be achieved by controlling the place and route process directly by software.

In order to manage efficiently a first implementation of *tropes* on Perle-1, we imposed some restrictions :

- only one *tropes* per FPGA,
- 16-bit datapath,
- use of the memory only if necessary.

As the matrix is a 4×4 matrix, a maximum of 16 *tropes* can be implemented. Actually, this is not really restrictive since the majority of Gamma programs can be written using very few *tropes*.

The next section presents an experiment we have performed in order to validate our approach.

4 Experiment

The goal of the experiment was twofold. First, we wanted to demonstrate that the Perle-1 board is a suitable platform to support the implementation of *tropes*. Second, we wanted to show that a machine derived from high level specifications, such as Gamma, may have performance as good as a Von Neuman machine executing a sequential program. As a validating example, we choose the prime factorization problem.

4.1 Prime Factorization Problem

A fundamental theorem of arithmetic states that every positive integer n can be written as a product of primes and that this decomposition in unique. This fact gives a one-to-one correspondence between positive integers and a multiset of prime numbers: for example, if $n = 120 = 2^3 * 3 * 5$ the corresponding multiset is {2,2,2,3,5}.

The prime factorization Gamma program can be expressed as a combination of 6 primitive programs :

$$\begin{array}{lcl} \text{factor(n)} & \equiv & (F6 \circ F5 \circ F4 \circ F3 \circ F2 \circ F1)\{(2,n)_1\} \\ \text{where} & & \\ F1 & \equiv & (a,b)_1 \rightarrow (a,b)_2, (a+1,b)_1 \Leftarrow a < b \\ F2 & \equiv & (a,b)_1 \rightarrow (a,b)_2 \Leftarrow a \geq b \\ F3 & \equiv & (a,b)_2 \rightarrow \Leftarrow \neg multiple(b,a) \\ F4 & \equiv & (a,b)_2, (c,d)_2 \rightarrow (c,d)_2 \Leftarrow multiple(a,c) \\ F5 & \equiv & (a,b)_2 \rightarrow (a,b/a)_2, a \Leftarrow multiple(b,a) \\ F6 & \equiv & F3 \end{array}$$

The initial multiset is composed of a pair, $(2,n)$. Three different types of elements are present : pairs of type 1, noted $(a,b)_1$, pairs of type 2, noted $(a,b)_2$ and singletons.

The sequence $(F2 \circ F1)$ $\{(2,n)_1\}$ produces a multiset of pairs $(i,n)_2$ where $2 \leq i \leq n$. $F3$ removes all pairs $(i,n)_2$ which does not satisfy the condition i *does not divide* n (noted $\neg multiple(i,n)$). After the execution of $F4$, the multiset contains the pairs $(i,n)_2$ where i is a prime and i divides n. $F5$ produces the prime factor and $F6$ removes the double pairs.

Each primitive program is then associated with a *tropes*. The correspondence between the primitive programs and the *tropes* is done by analyzing the input/output types. As an example, the primitive program $F1$ is a particular *expander* which takes one pair

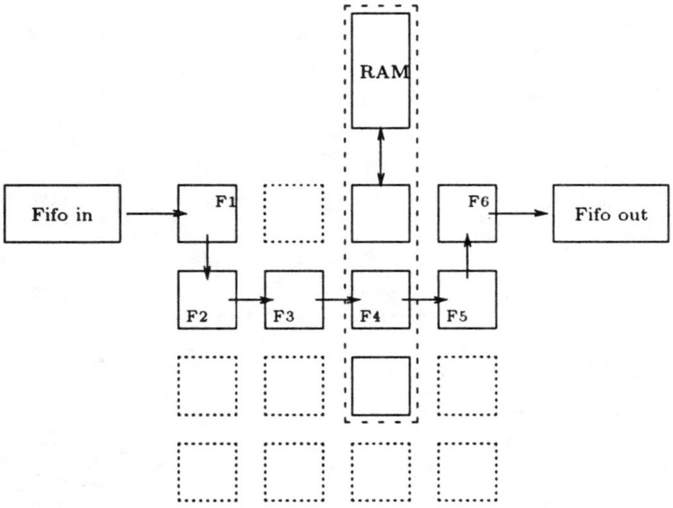

Figure 2: prime factorization implementation on Perle-1

of type $(a,b)_1$ and produces two pairs of different types $((a,b)_1$ and $(a,b)_2)$.

4.2 Perle-1 Implementation

The figure 4.2 shows the implementation done on the Perle-1 board. The *tropes* are pipelined from the input FIFO to the output FIFO. One FPGA contains one *tropes* except for the *tropes* corresponding to $F4$.

Actually, this *tropes* requires to make test on two elements (say a_1 and a_2). To be efficient, it was decided when defining the *tropes* skeleton architecture to implement concurrently two tests ($C(a_1, a_2)$ and $C(a_2, a_1)$) since both reactions have to be evaluated.

In the present case, the condition has to determine if a_1 is a multiple of a_2 which is not a low cost operator in terms of CLB resources. To minimize the size of this operator, it has been implemented using a divisor operator proceeding sequentially. The division step requires two operations, a shift and a subtraction (which are done in parallel).

Implementing this *tropes* in only one FPGA is nevertheless possible if one accept to decrease performances by providing only one reaction operator. The two conditions are then evaluated sequentially.

4.3 Performance Comparison

The implementation has been compared with a **similar** algorithm written in C and executed on two Sun workstations (Sparc-2 and Sparc-10). The algorithm, like the Gamma program, searches first for a prime number which divides n; then it produces the prime factors:

```
k = 0;
for(i=2; i<=n; i++){      /* F4 o F3 o F2 o F1 */
  if((n%i)==0){
    j = 1;
    while((j<=k) && ((i%tab[j]) !=0)){
      j++;
    }
    if(j > k){
      k++;
      tab[k] = i;
    }
  }
}
for (i=1; i<=k; i++){              /* F6 o F5 */
  v = n;
  while ((v%tab[i])==0){
    printf ("%d ",tab[i]);
    v=v/tab[i];
  }
}
```

The diagram below shows the execution time versus the number n. The performances of the Gamma machine are situated between the performances of the two Sun Sparc Stations. This implementation demonstrates that using suitable architecture for executing high level programming language, such as Gamma, may provide performance as good as a Von Neuman machine executing a sequential program.

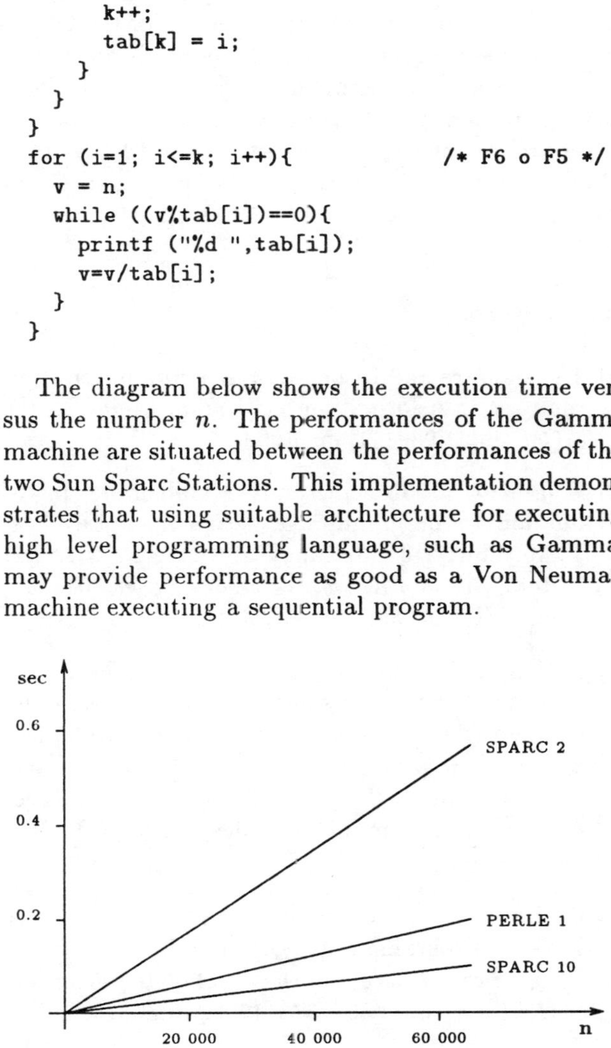

5 Future Work

Deriving a FPGA architecture from high level programming model using the composition of primitive programs (*tropes*) is a promising approach. Investigation for implementing the Gamma formalism on the Perle-1 FPGA platform has shown that it is realistic.

The next step is to automate this approach. Presently, specific skeleton architectures corresponding to a set of primitive Gamma programs have been defined. From these skeletons, the challenge is to synthesize efficient *tropes* and, given these *tropes*, to place them optimally on the FPGA matrix.

Software tools provided with the Perle-1 board allow direct synthesis in the same way as VLSI design. The tools support interactive placement of the CLBs, allowing the designer to control the hardware topology of the design. Experiments have shown that a *good* assignment of the CLBs with a few *judicious* routing directives may increase considerably the FPGAs possibilities: temporal performance is better and CLBs are economized.

References

[1] J.P. Banâtre and D. Le Métayer. Programming by multiset transformation. *communications ot the ACM*, 36(1):98–111, jan 1993.

[2] P. Bertin, D. Roncin, and J. Vuillemin. Introduction to programmable active memories. In J. McWhirter J. McCanny and E. Swartzlander, editors, *Systolic Array Processors*, pages 301–309, Pretice Hall, 1989.

[3] P. Bertin, D. Roncin, and J. Vuillemin. Programmable active memories : a performance assessment. In F. Meyer auf der Heide, B. Monien, and A.L. Rosenberg, editors, *Parallel Architectures and their efficient use*, pages 119–130, Lecture notes in Computer Science, Springer-Verlag, oct 1992.

[4] C. Hankin, D. Le Metayer, and D. Sands. A Parallel Programming Style and its Algebra of Programs. *Lecture Notes in Computer Science - PARLE 93*, (694):367–378, 1993. to appear.

[5] Xilinx. *The Programmable Gate Array Data Book*. 2100 Logic Drive, San Jose, CA 95124 USA, 1992.

Behavioral Synthesis for FPGA-based Computing

Herman Schmit, Lawrence Arnstein, Don Thomas, and Elizabeth Lagnese

Electrical and Computer Engineering Department
Carnegie Mellon University
Pittsburgh, PA 15213

Abstract

We describe how a behavioral synthesis system can be used to create designs for FPGA-based computing systems directly from a specification of the desired algorithm. This higher level of specification reduces design times and design errors. Our target hardware is called the Rasa Board and is composed of three Xilinx FPGAs interconnected with Aptix Field Programmable Interconnect Chips. We address two significant challenges in this research effort: the synthesis of multiple FPGA designs, and the improvement of the design through designer interaction.

1. Introduction

Future computing systems will likely consist of general-purpose processors interconnected with configurable hardware resources. Portions of the system behavior will be executed on the processors as software, while other portions will be executed on hardware configured specially for execution of that set of tasks. In [1], we discussed characteristics of tasks that influence their suitability to either hardware or software implementation, and criteria for selecting the implementation style for each task in order to maximize system performance in a cost efficient manner.

In order to build these mixed hardware/software systems, it will be necessary to configure the programmable hardware resources quickly and effectively. This paper discusses the configuration of such hardware resources from behavioral descriptions which are partitioned from a larger behavioral description of the whole system. We have constructed a prototype hardware/software system consisting of an FPGA-based hardware resource, called the Rasa board, and a 486-based PC. We have also constructed a set of design tools that creates designs for this hardware resource from specifications written in a behavioral subset of the Verilog language.

The keystone of this set of design tools is a behavioral synthesis system called SAM [2]. Like other behavioral synthesis systems, SAM accepts a behavioral specification and creates a design consisting of registers, state machines for control, functional units and interconnect to implement that behavior. The distinctions between SAM and logic synthesis tools such as the Synopsys Design Compiler are:

- SAM requires no explicit specification of time. If an operation doesn't have an execution cycle specified or implied, it will be scheduled by SAM based on the user-specified clock period and delay model.
- Lexical tokens in the behavior, such as values and operations, don't necessarily have a one-to-one correspondence with a hardware resource. For example, more than one add operation may be mapped to a particular adder and more than one value may be stored in a particular register. In choosing assignments of operations and values to data path components, SAM attempts to minimize the total size of the data path.

The structural description generated by SAM can be used as input to logic synthesis and module binding tools to create implementations in a variety of technologies. Systems similar to SAM have been used in industry to synthesize Viterbi decoder and FFT ICs [3]. These systems decrease design time, improve application portability, and reduce design errors.

In the development and initial experimentation with this system, we have encountered two significant challenges to effective synthesis of FPGA-based implementations. First, when a synthesized implementation cannot fit into a single FPGA we need to partition this implementation into smaller blocks that can fit into a set of interconnected FPGAs. We shall discuss our solutions to this problem, both in the architecture of our hardware resource and in the design process. Second, we have discovered that the human designer needs the ability to intervene in the synthesis process in order to correct or improve the design. We shall present a example that illustrates how the designer can interact with SAM in the design of a systolic array cell.

0-8186-5490-2/94 $03.00 © 1994 IEEE

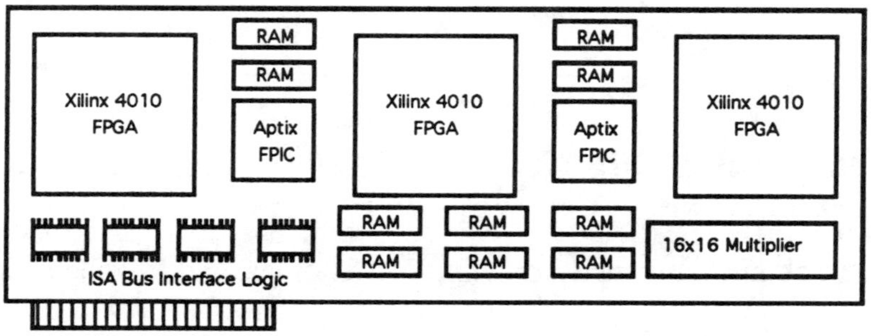

Figure 1. Rasa board

2. The Rasa board

The Rasa board architecture, shown in Figure 1, consists of three Xilinx 4010 FPGAs, ten 32K x 8 bit SRAMs, and a fixed-point multiplier chip all mounted on an Aptix Field Programmable Circuit Board (FPCB). The desired interconnection of board components is specified in a netlist, and the Aptix tools attempt to route all the interconnects through one or both Field Programmable Interconnect Chips (FPICs). The Aptix FPCB also provides an ISA bus interface board, which plugs into the backplane of the host PC.

Although not an unlimited resource, the Aptix FPCB provides extremely flexible interconnection between board components. This flexibility allows us to perform behavioral synthesis without being constrained to predefined interconnect structures.

Most other FPGA-based computing architectures, including SPLASH 2 [4] and AnyBoard [5], use fixed wires to interconnect FPGAs and other board resources. With a fixed interconnection scheme like these, a synthesis tool would have to either partition the algorithmic specification into the FPGA components prior to synthesis or fit the design into the interconnection scheme after synthesis [6]. Both of these alternatives can make it difficult or impossible to find a solution, depending on how well the algorithm fits into the interconnection scheme. Furthermore, both of these solutions require that the behavioral synthesis tool assign FPGA pins to particular signals in the implementation, which can lead to much lower internal utilization of the FPGAs [7].

3. Rasa design path

The Rasa Board design path, shown in Figure 2, consists of three major stages: behavioral synthesis using SAM; logic synthesis and module binding; and FPGA placement and routing. At all three of these stages we can estimate, with varying degrees of accuracy, how many FPGAs the implementation will require. If more than one FPGA is required, we need to determine how to partition this implementation. We begin the discussion of the design path by assuming that the implementation will fit into a single FPGA, and then we discuss partitioning a larger design into multiple FPGAs.

3.1 SAM

Synthesis of the behavioral description is performed by SAM. The Verilog behavioral description is first converted into a control and data flow graph (CDFG). SAM performs force-directed scheduling and allocation of this graph to create a structural description. In the scheduling and allocation stage, SAM attempts to minimize the size of the data path by sharing resources such as registers and functional units. The output structural description, also described in Verilog, consists of functional units (e.g. adders and comparators), multiplexors, inputs, outputs, and a controller.

SAM also has the ability to accept "assertions" that influence design decisions. These assertions are written in terms of objects in the behavioral specification, and they allow the designer to attack design weaknesses and make tradeoffs without giving up the algorithmic perspective. Section 4 will demonstrate how assertions may be used to improve the quality of a design.

3.2 Logic synthesis and module binding

Conversion of the structural specification to a gate-level specification takes place in the logic synthesis and module binding stage of the design path. We use an assortment of university tools to perform the functions of state-assignment and logic simplification for the controller, and module generation for the data path elements of the structural description. This gate-level description is then translated from Verilog into a set of XNF (Xilinx Netlist Format) files, which are the input to the Xilinx partition, place and route (PPR) tool. The pinouts to the FPGAs generated by PPR are used to create a board netlist, which is then input to the Aptix board routing tools. The resulting FPCB and FPGA configuration bitstreams can then be loaded to create a working Rasa board implementation.

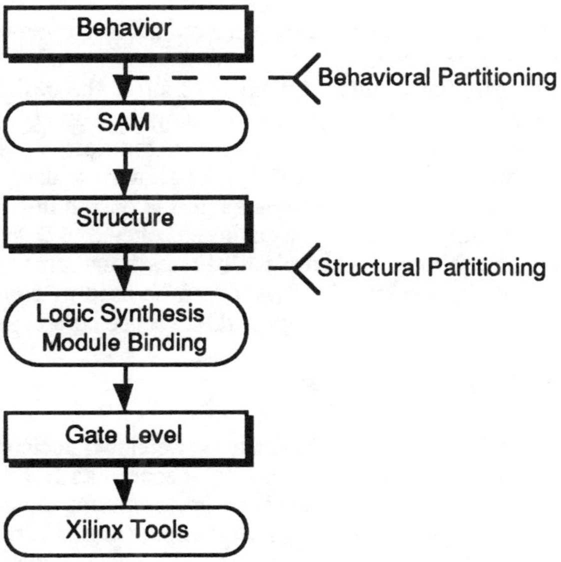

Figure 2. The Rasa Board Design Path

3.3 Partitioning

If an implementation exceeds the size of a single FPGA it will have to be partitioned. Partitioning can be performed at many points in the design path, but we have discovered that it is important to perform some form of partitioning at each stage of the design path. Our main partitioner works at the structural level, after behavioral synthesis and before logic synthesis and module generation. This structural partitioner first creates an initial placement of all the structural elements (e.g. adders, registers, controllers, and multiplexors) into the Rasa board's three FPGAs, and then attempts to optimize this partitioning using the technique of simulated annealing [8]. The objective of the annealing algorithm is to find a partition that meets the specified I/O and CLB capacities of each of the FPGAs. The number of CLBs on any FPGA is estimated using a cost model of the structural components.

Structural partitioning, while accurate and fast, cannot always create good, or even feasible designs. One reason is that SAM, in an attempt to better utilize functional units, can create such highly interconnected designs that even the best structural partitions require an unacceptably large numbers of IOs on each FPGA.

In order to address this problem, we have experimented with the APARTY behavioral partitioner [9]. APARTY detects operations and values that are related in the behavioral description and groups closely related operations and values into sets called behavioral partitions. Our behavioral synthesis tool can be run so that it is only allowed to share resources between operations and values in the same behavioral partition. The designs created using behavioral partitioning are less interconnected, which makes finding an acceptable structural partition easier.

In order to test this methodology we created a behavior consisting of a large set of equations using add and subtract operations. We performed behavioral synthesis of this specification without any behavioral partitioning and with behavioral partitioning enabled. Both designs were then partitioned at the structural level. The best structural partition found for each design is shown in Table 1.

	FPGA Partition	CLB Utilization	IOB Utilization
Without Behavioral Partitioning	FPGA #1	72%	78%
	FPGA #2	39%	67%
With Behavioral Partitioning	FPGA #1	63%	47%
	FPGA #2	43%	35%

Table 1. Behavioral Partitioning

Without behavioral partitioning, the structural partitioner could only find an unbalanced, highly interconnected design, requiring one of the FPGAs to utilize 72% of its available CLBs and 78% of its available IOs. Our experience is that such a highly utilized FPGA is difficult or impossible to place and route. Using behavioral partitioning, the structural partitioner found a more balanced, less interconnected design requiring only 47% of the available IOs and 63% of the available CLBs on the most crowded FPGA. This design is much more likely to place and route successfully.

It is interesting to note that when behavioral partitioning is used, the behavioral partitions don't always correspond to the best structural partitions. In this experiment, the functional units associated with the operations in one behavioral partition were all placed by the structural partitioner in one FPGA, but functional units associated with the other behavioral partition were placed in both FPGAs. If we moved all these functional units into the same FPGA so that the behavioral partition exactly corresponded to the structural partition, we obtained a design with more IOs on both FPGAs. This observation indicates that behavioral partitioning should not be used to replace but rather to assist structural partitioning.

Our structural partitioner presently requires that each structural component be placed in one and only one FPGA. This limitation can be costly because in many cases the IO count can be reduced by placing different logical parts of a single structural component in multiple FPGAs. As we shall show, this limitation is especially costly for controllers and multiplexors.

The controller created by SAM drives the control signals for the entire design. Requiring that the whole controller reside in one FPGA means every control signal to a structural component on a separate FPGA requires one or more IOs on both the source and destination FPGAs. A more efficient solution would be to have a set of intermediate signals, such as the current state of the controller, propagated to all FPGAs, and have the logic required to create the control for each FPGA generated from the intermediate signals on that FPGA.

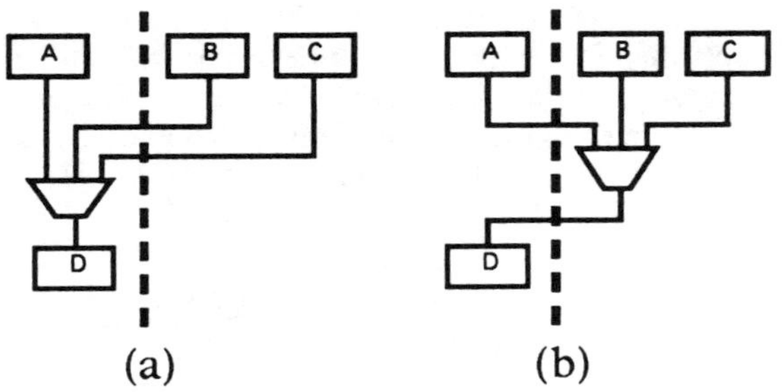

Figure 3. Structural partitioning of multiplexors

The problem with forcing whole multiplexors to reside on one FPGA is illustrated in Figure 3. In this example we assume that the generators (A,B,C) and consumer (D) of this data transfer cannot be moved across the FPGA partition implied by the dashed line. If the whole multiplexor is forced into one FPGA as shown in 3a and 3b, two sets of IOs are required on each FPGA. If on the other hand this multiplexor can be decomposed and split between the two FPGAs as shown in Figure 4, only one set of IOs are required.

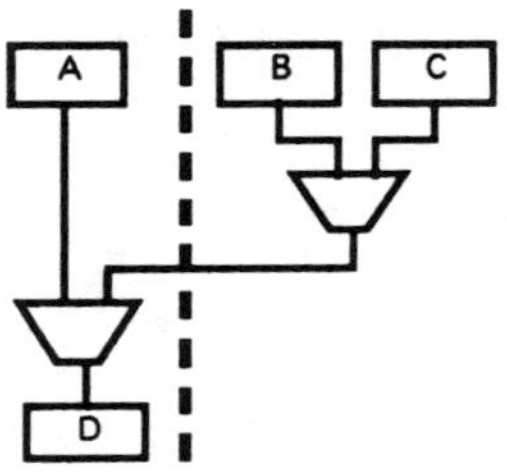

Figure 4. Partitioning Decomposed Multiplexor

There are two possible solutions to these problems. First, we could create a structural partitioner capable of performing multiplexor and controller decomposition. Second, if more accuracy is required, we could optimize the partition of the design after CLB mapping has been performed.

4. Improving the design through user interaction

Behavioral synthesis tools, by allowing the algorithmic specification of systems, free the user from determining most of the implementation details. This freedom from the implementation details is the key to accelerating design time, but it also separates a designer from the implementation so that it is difficult for the designer to determine what can be improved in the implementation and to force the synthesis tool to make the improvements when they are found.

The solution to this problem is to allow the designer to interact with the design process using the same behavioral terms that were used to specify the design. The Sylver design environment [10] [11] allows the designer to make queries and assertions about the design in terms of relationships between objects in the behavioral description. The following example illustrates how behavioral synthesis, in concert with Sylver, can be used to synthesize a cell from a systolic nucleotide sequence comparator.

4.1 Design example

The calculation of edit distance between two nucleotide sequences as described in [12] has become an informal standard application for FPGA-based computing devices. The goal of the algorithm is to compute the minimum cost of the transformations needed to convert one nucleotide sequence into another. Architecturally, we have chosen to implement the unidirectional systolic solution to this problem as described in [13]. Figure 5 shows the cell structure of the array.

There are two significant differences between our algorithm description and that given in [13]. First, we have decided not to use the modulo encoding of the edit distances. The use of modulo encoding would significantly reduce the size of our data paths, but we have omitted it for the sake of clarity of the description. Second, the costs of the various transformations are stored in an array that can be loaded from the host computer, rather than as a set of constants in the behavioral description. This difference results in our implementation having a small amount of additional control and data path logic.

Each cell is a small instruction set processor that allows the host computer to download different costs into the three arrays (R,I,D), shift in the target pattern, initialize the pipeline registers before a new computation is started and compute the minimum cost of transformation. The host computer synchronizes with the first cell of the array through the use of a four-way handshake protocol using the "Cin" and "Ack" signals. Cell-to-cell communication is completely synchronous, because the cells operate in lock-step.

A portion of the behavioral description of a cell is shown in Figure 6. This sample includes two of the seven instructions in the cell's behavior. The COMPUTE instruction causes the cell to compute the next value of Dij, and is the most complex of the instructions. The LOADR instruction loads the cost table for the Replace (R) array.

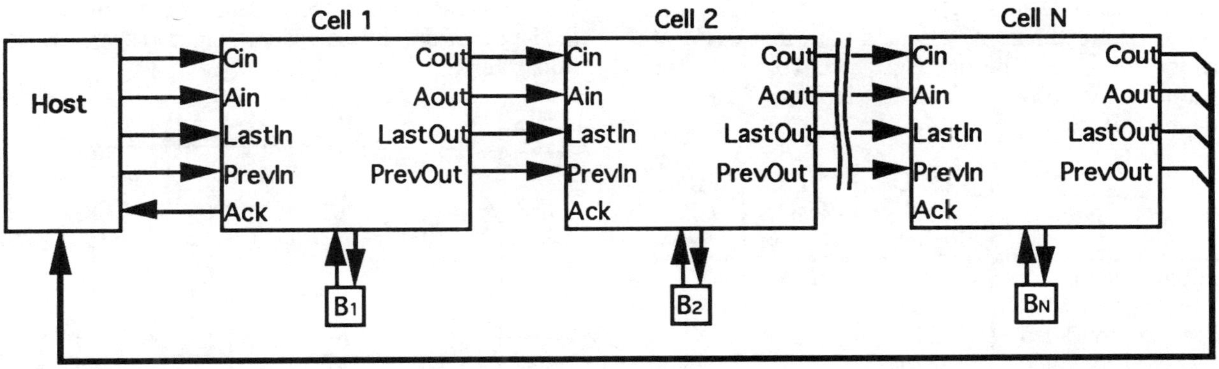

Figure 5. Nucleotide Comparator Cell Structure.

4.2 Insuring correct behavior

The behavior in Figure 6 is a complete specification of the internal behavior of an individual cell, but it is not sufficient to insure a correctly operating systolic array. Because cell-to-cell communication is done without any handshake, Cell N must not change the value on its "Cout", "Aout", "LastOut", and "PrevOut" output ports before they are read on the input ports "Cin", "Ain", "LastIn", and "PrevIn" of Cell N+1. We must therefore insure that the synthesis tool uses or saves the value on those input ports before it changes the value of the corresponding output port. We accomplish this by making assertions that tell SAM not to schedule an output port operation on any instruction before the corresponding input port operation is scheduled on every other instruction. For example, one of these assertions would state that the input operation represented by "Ain" on Line 6 of Figure 6 must occur before the output operation represented by "Aout" on Line 22. Creation of assertions is aided by a GUI that allows the user to simply highlight the tokens in the behavior and make assertions concerning them. The assertions are translated into forces that SAM uses to create an implementation that can successfully operate in lock-step with its neighbors. Assertions extend the user's ability to specify requirements that must be met in order to insure correct behavior.

Using this set of assertions, we created an initial design. We specified a clock period of 125ns because the Rasa board presently uses the 8MHz ISA bus clock. Because the delays in the actual FPGA design are dependent on placement and routing factors that are impossible to anticipate during behavioral synthesis, SAM uses a conservative delay model. SAM automatically schedules a behavior into the shortest schedule possible, according to its delay model and the clock period. In this case the shortest schedule is three clock cycles. A designer may vary the length of schedule, but in the sake of brevity we have decided not to explore designs with longer schedule lengths.

```
1.  always begin
2.     Cout = Cin;   // Command to next cell.
3.     case ({Ack, Cout})    // Select command.
4.     `COMPUTE: begin    // Compute Dij.
5.        Ack = 1;
6.        Aout = Ain;
7.        Dij1 = lastIn;
8.        Di1j1 = PrevIn;
9.        insert = Last + insertcost;
10.       delete = Dij1 + costD[Aout];
11.       replace = Di1j1 + costR[{Bj,Aout}];
12.       Dij = (insert < delete) ? insert : delete;
13.       Dij = (Dij < replace) ? Dij : replace;
14.       PrevOut = Last;
15.       Last = Dij;
16.       LastOut = Dij;
17.    end
18.    `LOADR: begin // Load Replace cost table
19.       Ack = 1;
20.       LastOut = LastIn;
21.       PrevOut = PrevIn;
22.       Aout = Ain;
23.       Bj = PrevOut;
24.       costR[{Bj,Aout}] = LastOut;
25.    end
26.    ...
27.    endcase
28. end
```

Figure 6. Behavioral Description

The initial design is called A, and its size and performance are shown in Table 2. The third column of this table shows the cost estimate of the data path that SAM attempts to minimize. The two right-hand columns show the results of the Xilinx PPR tool in terms of CLBs and minimum clock period.

	Description	SAM Data Path Estimate	PPR Results (CLBs)	Min. Clk (ns)
A	Initial Design	327	233	82
B	Small output MUX	320	221	92
C	Sharing Prohibited	318	200	71
D	MUXes Prohibited	316	177	73

Table 2. Design Results

4.3 Improving the design

We can use assertions not only to insure correct behavior, but also to enforce complex design explorations. For example, because it does not directly compare the estimated cost of multiplexors with other estimated costs, SAM has a tendency to create large, inefficient multiplexors. The largest multiplexor in design A is a 16 bit wide 6-to-1 multiplexor on the "LastOut" output port. This multiplexor is present because each of the instructions in our behavior generates a value for "LastOut". The COMPUTE instruction cannot generate its value for "LastOut" before the third step of the schedule, but all the other instructions can. Therefore if we use an assertion to force all the other instructions to store their value for "LastOut" in a temporary register in the first or second step of the schedule, we can use another assertion to reduce the number of the multiplexor inputs on "LastOut" to two. We have created an implementation, called design B, using these assertions. This assertion improves both the SAM data path estimate and the number of CLBs created by PPR. The degradation in minimum clock period is due to variability in PPR and is not inherent in the structural description synthesized by SAM.

Further improvements to this design center on the data path for the portion of the COMPUTE instruction that computes the three possible costs and selects the lowest one, shown in Lines 9-13 of Figure 6. This portion of the data path in design B is illustrated in Figure 7.[1] Even though there are two separate compare and select operations (Lines 12 and 13 in Figure 6), SAM has allocated only one comparator and one selector multiplexor, indicated by "<" and the "?" respectively. Two adders have been allocated, one to perform the addition on Line 9 and the other to perform the additions on Lines 10 and 11. SAM has attached a multiplexor to one of the inputs of the comparator and selector multiplexor, and to both of the inputs of the second adder in order to share these functional units.

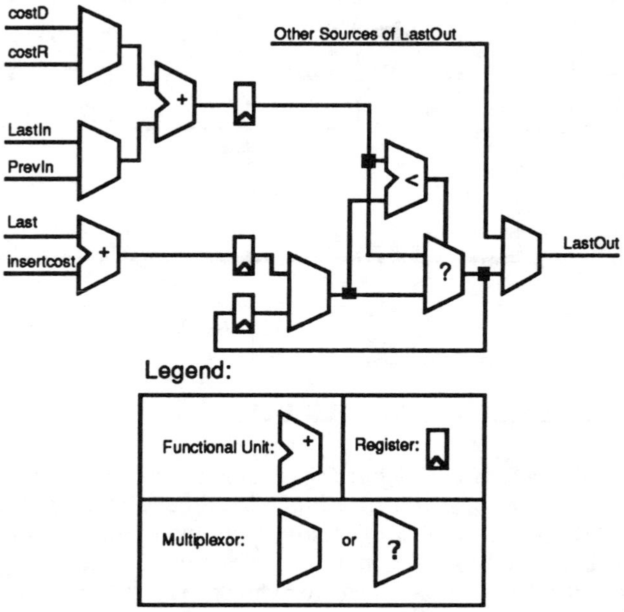

Figure 7. Design B Data Path

The multiplexors placed on the inputs of these functional units are as expensive in terms of CLBs as the functional units themselves, which suggests that maybe it would be better to allocate additional functional units. In our next design, we use assertions to prevent sharing between the addition and comparison operations in the behavior and thus eliminate the multiplexors on the adders or comparators. The data path for this design, called design C, is shown in Figure 8. SAM succeeded in eliminating the three unwanted multiplexors, but had to allocate an additional adder, comparator and multiplexor. Design C requires 21 fewer CLBs than design B. Although it is difficult to precisely determine where these CLBs are saved, we believe that the improvement is due to a reduction in required multiplexor control logic, and the merging of the two rightmost multiplexors.

---

[1] The Sylver design environment can be used to obtain all the information present in these data path diagrams using design queries. In this format, however, it is much more concise to show the diagram.

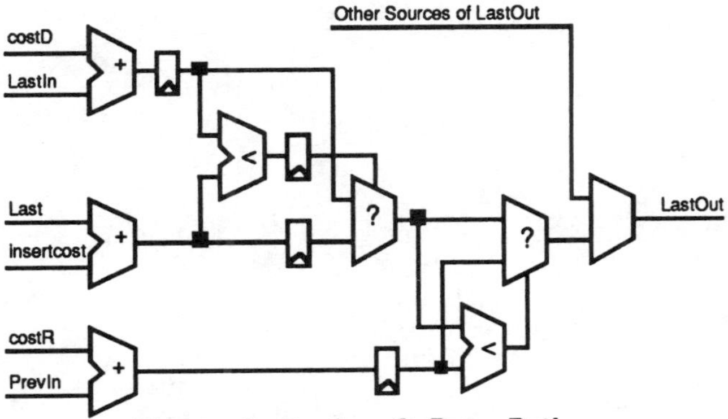

Figure 8. Design C Data Path

The assertions used to prevent resource sharing did eliminate the multiplexors on the adder and comparator, but maybe that was overkill. Instead of using assertions to prevent sharing between the functional units, we can use a different type of assertion to limit the size of multiplexors on the inputs of the functional units. Design D, shown in Figure 9, was obtained using this type of assertion to prevent the connection of any multiplexors to the inputs of the comparators or the adders. In this design SAM has found a way to reuse the single comparator and connected multiplexor for both selection operations, but it has done this by putting the multiplexors on the inputs of registers connected to the comparator, rather than the comparator itself. This design has 23 fewer CLBs than design C. We believe that this improvement is due a reduction in the total number of registers and the fact that the multiplexors and connected registers may be efficiently mapped to the same set of CLBs, using only intra-CLB interconnect.

As shown in this brief example, assertions allow the designer to easily vary and experiment with design alternatives. We have managed to improve the CLB count of the design by nearly 25%.

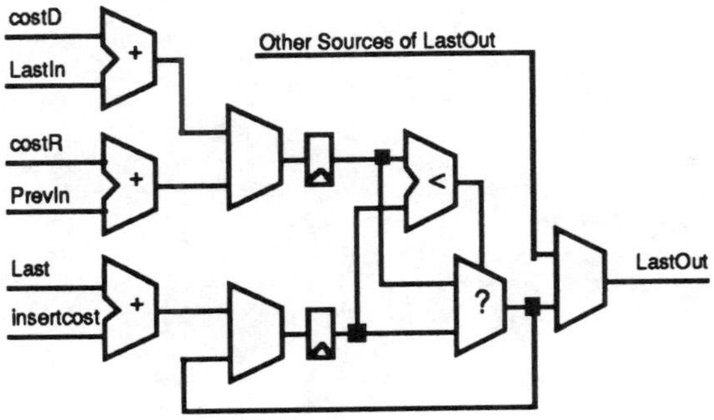

Figure 9. Design D Data Path

5. Conclusions

Behavioral synthesis systems such as SAM are suitable solutions to the problem of configuring of FPGA-based computing devices from a behavioral description. Using SAM, the designer is to some extent freed from understanding the details of both the design implementation and the target architecture. This freedom decreases design time and increases the portability of applications.

In order to create multiple FPGA designs from a single behavioral description, we have experimented with partitioning at the behavioral and structural levels. We have discovered that these different types of partitioning can work synergistically. Partitioning can be improved further if the structural partitioner is capable of decomposing multiplexors and controllers and placing portion of the logic on separate FPGAs where necessary.

The Sylver design environment allows the user to examine and improve the design through the use of queries and assertions, which are written in terms of the behavioral description. By interacting with the design process using Sylver, we have obtained a 25% improvement in the CLB count of our example design.

Acknowledgments

We acknowledge the Semiconductor Research Corporation (under contract 93-DC-068), the National Science Foundation (under contract MIP-9112930), General Motors Research, the Xilinx Corporation, and the Aptix Corporation for the funding of this project.

References

[1] D. Thomas, J. Adams, and H. Schmit. "A Model and Methodology for Hardware-Software Codesign." *IEEE Design and Test of Computers*, Vol. 10, No. 3, pp. 6-15, September 1993.

[2] R. Cloutier, and D. Thomas, "The Combination of Scheduling, Allocation, and Mapping in a Single Algorithm", *Proc. of the 27th DAC* . pp. 71-76, 1990.

[3] R. Goering, "Working Chips via Behavioral Synthesis", *EE Times*. Issue 771, p. 35, Nov. 8, 1993.

[4] J.M. Arnold, D.A. Buell, and E.G. Davis, "Splash 2", *Proc. 4th ACM Symposium on Parallel Algorithms and Architectures*, pp. 316-322, 1992.

[5] D. Van den Bout, et al. "AnyBoard: An FPGA-based Reconfigurable System." *IEEE Design and Test of Computers*, Vol. 9, No. 3, pp. 21-30, September 1992.

[6] Yung-Hua Hung, and A. Parker, "High-level Synthesis with Pin Constraints for Multiple-Chip Designs." *Proc. of the 29th DAC*. pp. 231-234, 1992.

[7] W. Höflich, "Increasing FPGA Speed and Density Using FPIC Devices", Application Note AN-2, *Aptix Data Book*, pp.93-99, 1993.

[8] S. Kirpatrick, C. D. Gelatt, Jr., and M.P. Vecchi. "Optimization by Simulated Annealing." *Science*, Vol. 220, Number 4598, May 13, 1983.

[9] E. D. Lagnese and D. E. Thomas. "Architectural Partitioning for System Level Design." *Proc. of the 26th DAC*. pp. 62-67, 1989.

[10] L.F. Arnstein and D.E. Thomas, "A General Consistency Technique for Increasing the Controllability of High Level Synthesis Tools." *Proc. of the ICCAD-93*, 1993.

[11] L.F. Arnstein and D.E Thomas, "The Attributed-Behavior Design Abstraction and Synthesis Tools," to appear in *Proc. of the IEEE/ACM High-Level Synthesis Workshop*, 1994.

[12] R.J. Lipton, and D. Lopresti, "A Systolic Array for Rapid String Comparison," *1985 Chapel Hill Conference on Very Large Scale Integration*, Henry Fuchs, ed., Rockville, MD: Computer Science Press, pp. 363-376, 1985.

[13] D. T. Hoang, "Searching Genetic Databases on Splash 2", *Proc. of the IEEE Workshop on FPGAs for Custom Computing Machines*, pp. 185-191, 1993.

PAM Programming Environments: Practice and Experience

Patrice Bertin
Hervé Touati
Digital Equipment Corporation
Paris Research Laboratory
85, avenue Victor Hugo
92500 Rueil-Malmaison, France

Abstract

Digital Equipment's Paris Research Laboratory started to investigate the use of FPGA-based reconfigurable hardware accelerators in 1988. We call them PAMs *for Programmable Active Memories. Over the past six years, we have designed and implemented four generations of PAM hardware and four generations of PAM programming environments. Several dozen people, ranging from inexperienced students to senior hardware designers, have used our systems [3]. A wide range of applications belonging to several important application domains have demonstrated the interest of these novel computing devices. In this paper we present the software lessons we draw from this collective experience.*

1 Introduction

In 1988, under the direction of Jean Vuillemin, Digital Equipment Corporation's Paris Research Laboratory (PRL) started to investigate the use of SRAM-based FPGAs for building reconfigurable hardware coprocessors. We call these coprocessors Programmable Active Memories or PAMs [2, 1]. PRL developed four generations of PAMs and four generations of PAM programming environments. We gathered the most experience with DECPeRLe-1, our third generation PAM board, and PerLe1DC, its programming environment.

24 DECPeRLe-1 boards were built, 7 of which have been installed in collaborating research sites around the world. The following data summarizes the most significant applications that were developed in 1993 for DECPeRLe-1 using the PerLe1DC programming environment[1]. Other work under way includes a large Viterbi decoder for deep-space probe data reception (Macquarie University, Sidney, Australia) and the second-level trigger of a deep-underwater neutrino telescope in the Aegean Sea (CERN, Geneva).

- A stereo vision system, used to compute *range maps* from simultaneous images obtained by two cameras. A software implementation of this system computes the correlation of a pair of images in 59 seconds on a SPARCstation II. A specialized board with four DSPs performs the same task in 9.6 seconds. The same task on DECPeRLe-1 runs in 0.28 seconds, over thirty times faster.
- A 3-D Heat Equation solver. Running at 25 MHz, it computes 40 billion operations (16 bit adds and shifts) per second.
- A digital audio 256-channel professional quality sound synthesizer, using additive synthesis and frequency modulation. An optimized DSP implementation of the same algorithm, running on a Motorola 56001 at 40 MHz, can only achieve 25 channels without the frequency modulation feature.
- For the second-level triggers of its planned Large Hadron Collider, CERN published several benchmarks algorithms. We studied and implemented on DECPeRLe-1 one of these benchmarks, the *hadron calorimeter* [4]. Besides being the most cost-effective, the solution provided by PAMs is today the *only* one that CERN could identify as meeting the bandwidth and latency requirements.

In this paper we present the lessons we draw from the development and use of PerLe1DC, our current generation PAM programming environment. Some of the ideas and algorithms presented here are well known. Our main goal is to show how a few simple ideas put together can lead to a design environment which is both low-cost and adequately productive.

The rest of the paper is organized as follows. In sections 2 and 3, we give a short presentation of DECPeRLe-1 and its requirements in terms of programming environments. In section 4, we discuss the main design decisions we made when developing PerLe1DC. In section 5, we present what worked well. In section 6, we present what did not work so well and what we would do differently today. In section 7 we present our future plans. Section 8 summarizes the main points of the paper.

[1] For performance comparisons, one should keep in mind that DECPeRLe-1 was built using 1991 state-of-the-art digital electronics technology.

0-8186-5490-2/94 $03.00 © 1994 IEEE

2 Background

2.1 PAMs

A PAM (Programmable Active Memory) is a reconfigurable hardware coprocessor tightly coupled to a host workstation. PAMs can have different shapes and sizes; our third generation board, DECPeRLe-1, is made out of 24 Xilinx XC3090 chips, 4 MB of static RAM, and a fast FIFO-based interface to the I/O bus of a workstation. For this we use Digital Equipment Corp. TURBOchannel bus protocol, which provides up to 100MB/s of bandwidth between an I/O device and the host's memory.

A PAM *program* comprises two interacting parts: *a sequential circuit description part*, which is compiled into FPGA configuration bitstreams; and *a software description part*, which is compiled into a piece of software to be run on the host workstation.

2.2 When to Use a PAM?

The main reason to go into the trouble of a PAM implementation of a given algorithm is to get performance unattainable in software. If the same performance can be obtained by executing a straightforward C program on a workstation, it makes little sense to use a PAM. To date, most of our applications have had a combination of the following characteristics:

- high computing power requirements (Heat equation solver, Viterbi decoder, sound synthesizer);
- high I/O bandwidth requirements (CERN calorimeter);
- real-time constraints (CERN calorimeter; stereoscopic vision system; sound synthesizer);
- data formats for which standard CPU hardware is not optimized (none of these applications use IEEE 64-bit floating-point computations);
- hardware interface capability (digital camera interface).

In all of these DECPeRLe-1 applications but the last, performance was critical, and heavy pipelining combined with careful low-level design optimization was the key to the solution.

3 Requirements

To obtain adequate performance with the available PAM hardware, the implementation has to be done with some minimum level of care. In a PAM program sloppiness bites twice: once in circuit density and device utilization (space) and once in circuit speed (time). As a consequence, one can easily get a factor of four or more slow down by a careless implementation of a good algorithm. Since performance is so critical to the economical viability of PAMs, high-level programming from behavioral descriptions is not going to be a practical approach; at least not until we reach the point where we can afford to throw away a factor of four in silicon resources (one has to keep in mind that we already pay a performance penalty by using SRAM-based FPGAs instead of raw silicon). Programmable interconnects are also slower and less dense than their hardwired counterparts. As a consequence, complex designs cannot be placed and routed automatically unless they do not attempt to reach high device utilization; even then, the resulting circuitry is significantly slower than what can be achieved with good hand-designed geometry.

Careful low-level circuit implementation has always been possible through a painful and laborious process: schematic capture. For PAM programming, schematic capture is not a viable alternative. Though it can provide the best performance, it is too labor intensive for large PAM designs.

Given these constraints, we have but one choice: a middle-ground approach where designs are described at the structural level and the structure can be annotated with geometric information to guide the physical design. More precisely, here is a set of properties that we think a PAM programming environmnent should have:

- The hardware description should be algorithmic. The size of the applications we develop precludes the use of schematic capture.
- It should be possible to compile the hardware description without any manual intervention at any intermediate stage of the compilation process. This requirement implies that the source program should contain mechanisms to annotate the hardware description with whatever placement or resource allocation directives needed to obtain the desired implementation quality.
- The level of abstraction provided by the programming environment should be the highest abstraction level that can be shared by most PAM applications, but not any higher. Our goal is to explore many different application domains; specialized high-level graphic entry systems are thus premature. General-purpose high-level graphic entry systems do not work.
- Mixed-mode (behavioral/gate-level) block level to system level simulation should be supported. Even though SRAM-based FPGA technology allows for development by trial and error, simulation remains a crucial development tool: mixed-mode simulation cannot be performed on FPGAs; gate-level simulation runs several orders of magnitude faster on FPGAs than in software, but compilation times are several orders of magnitude worse than for software. Thus both simulation techniques are needed: short simulation runs are better performed in software, long execution traces are better obtained from hardware.

4 Design Decisions

4.1 Choice of a Programming Language

Three choices are possible: a general-purpose programming language such as C++, a hardware description language such as Verilog or VHDL, or our own language. We have discarded so far the latter alternative, though we are still divided on the issue of whether the world has still room for a new hardware description language targeted at synchronous logic in general and FPGAs in particular. We are nevertheless continuing research in this direction.

The use of a complex hardware description language such as VHDL has several advantages: we can build on commercially available software packages; we can build upon the accumulated experience of hardware designers trained with the language. However there are several drawbacks with this approach for PAMs: we give away low-level control on circuit geometry, which is required for speed and density by most of our applications; we lose any chance to convert software engineers to PAM programming; there are much fewer VHDL programmers than C++ programmers.

The use of a general-purpose programming language does not suffer from these problems. First the solution is cheaper: we are tapping a much wider market in terms of training, documentation and programming tools. Though we need to develop a generic software library to handle netlists and simulation, the amount of work is limited (6 man-months). Moreover we keep full control on the generated result, and we can include circuit geometry information as desired. The training investment is limited, as most engineers, hardware and software alike, have had some exposure to C or C++.

4.2 Synchronous Circuit Entry

We decided on the use of C++ mainly because of its widespread use and its malleability. To describe synchronous circuits with C++ is straightforward: we just need to introduce a new type `Net`, overload the C++ Boolean operators to describe combinational logic, and add a primitive for the register initialized to zero. Using these simple constructs, a C++ program can be used to *generate* a netlist representing any synchronous circuit. This type of low-level description is made convenient by the use of basic programming constructs such as arrays and records, **for** loops and procedures, for which no special training is necessary.

The execution of such a program builds a netlist in memory; this netlist can then be analyzed and translated into an appropriate format (XNF or EDIF), or used for simulation. Linking a netlist description program with behavioral code (also written in C++) yields mixed-mode simulation with no special effort. To give an example of the ease of use of this description, here is the code representing a generic n-bit ripple carry adder:

```
template<int N>
RippleAdder: public Block {
  public:
    RippleAdder(): Block("RippleAdder"){}
    void logic(Net<N>& a, Net<N>& b, Net<N>& c,
               Net<N>& sum, Net& carry) {
      input(a);
      input(b);
      input(c);
      output(sum);
      output(carry);
      for (int i = 0; i < N; i++){
        sum[i] = a[i] ^ b[i] ^ c[i];
        carry[i] = (a[i] & b[i])
                 | (b[i] & c[i])
                 | (c[i] & a[i]);
      }
    }
};
```

4.3 Description of Geometry

At this level of description, we can easily annotate individual nets with placement or routing directives. For example to specify that our ripple-carry adder should be aligned vertically, with the corresponding carry and sum bits generated by the same logic block, we would simply add the following lines to the description of the adder:

```
void placement(Net<N>& sum, Net<N>& carry) {
  for (int i = 0; i < N; i++) {
    carry[i] <= sum[i];
    sum[i+1] <= sum[i] + OFFSET(0,1);
  }
}
```

Contrary to the silicon compilers of a decade ago [5], these placement annotations have no influence on the logic behavior of the generated netlist. They do not specify contacts; they only specify layout directives. More precisely, the placement annotations shown here play two roles:

- they specify the partitioning of logic into physical blocks;
- they specify absolute or relative placement of physical blocks on a discrete two-dimensional grid.

No assumption is made at this stage on the size of the physical blocks nor the size of the two-dimensional grid. PERLE1DC, the C++ software library that generates the annotated netlist, does not contain any information related to any particular FPGA family, and does not need to. Its only job is to perform consistency checks and solve placement constraints by propagation. Obviously, the programmer has to know some basic characteristics of the FPGA family being used. PERLE1DC is device-independent, the logic is device-independent, but the placement and logic partitioning annotations are not.

4.4 Mapping to FPGAs

The mapping of the logic and geometry is performed by a back-end tool which emulates the interface of a schematic capture software in order to guarantee that the placement and logic partitioning information is preserved by the FPGA vendor software. Logic that is not explicitly partitioned or placed by the user is passed unchanged to the FPGA vendor software for automatic partitioning and placement. In any case, the routing is left to the commercial tool.

4.5 When the Abstraction Breaks

In an ideal world, a PAM would be viewed as a large FPGA, and PAM programming would only involve describing the logic and annotating it with abstract geometric constraints, providing logic partitioning and placement both at the chip level and the logic block level.

Unfortunately, chip-to-chip interconnect is a scarce resource, and logically contiguous logic blocks on a PAM do not have the same interconnection delays when connected through a direct on-chip route or an inter-chip PCB trace, which sometimes makes it necessary to have precise control on which net gets connected to which I/O pin. Another concession to hardware reality was to provide direct support for bidirectional (tri-state) buses. These design decisions compromise the elegance and simplicity of the 2-D synchronous circuit programming model, but are absolute practical requirements.

4.6 System Level Tools

At the system level, the programming environment provides two main functions: a device driver interface, and full simulation support of that interface. The latter lets the designer simulate together the hardware and software parts of a PAM program. The former provides a few essential controls to the application program:

- the usual UNIX I/O interface, with open, close, read and write. Reads and writes can be either synchronous or asynchronous, and use programmed I/O or DMA transfers;

- download of the configuration bitstreams for the PAM FPGAs, and readback of their state (the values of all the flip-flops of all the chips);

- initialization and readback of the PAM memory banks;

- software control of the PAM board clock. Not only the speed of the clock can be set very precisely in software, but also its mode of operation: the clock can operate at full speed, in single step or in double step mode. In single or double step modes, readback can be activated to get an execution trace of the system. In double step mode, the clock runs at full speed every other cycle: this mode provides a very powerful way of isolating critical paths under real execution conditions.

4.7 Visualization Tools

Our emphasis on textual entry created the need for visualization tools. Fortunately, it is easier to display graphics than to make them editable, so we were able to develop several useful visualization tools with a moderate amount of effort. The simplest of these tools can read a netlist generated by PERLE1DC and display it in a hierarchical and simplified view of a PAM board. Net names and logic equations are displayed as they appear in the source program. This simple tool, developed using a public domain library for structured graphics, has been very helpful for finding errors in partitioning and placement directives.

Two visualisation tools can be used to browse through simulation or execution traces. The first of these tools, KRONO, developed at Digital Western Research Laboratory by Louis Monier and Joel Bartlett, is a simulation trace browser that operates at the level of the source hardware description, and understands the design hierarchy. The second of these tools, SHOWRB, developed by Mark Shand at PRL, operates on readback traces. It can display the state of every flip-flop in every FPGA of DECPERLE-1 at the rate of tens of frames per second. In conjunction with the double-step mode, it can be used to detect critical paths along execution traces.

4.8 Related Work

The idea of using a general-purpose programming language to describe circuits is not new [6]. Our placement constraints are strongly reminiscent of work done in module generators for custom VLSI [5]. The main difference here is that the behavior is entirely described by logic equations; placement directives have no influence on the logic.

5 What Worked

In this section, we present the features of our programming environment that we feel were successful. These features are sorted in decreasing order of importance.

- *Let users write module generators:* though difficult to write for custom VLSI, module generators are straightforward to write for the purely synchronous world of FPGAs, given the layout directives that our environment provides. Non-trivial module generators can be written by undergraduate students in a matter of a few days. This capability is the main reason why we could see untrained engineers or students develop complex applications spanning dozens of chips in a matter of a few months.

- *The attributed netlist abstraction:* it is the right way to handle the complexity of the underlying hardware and the need for user directives in a clean, uniform and extensible fashion. The logic behavior of the design is entirely contained in the netlist. Mapping the netlist to other technologies (e.g. ASIC) is therefore straightforward. Attributes need only be understood by certain back-end tools and can safely be ignored by all the others.

- *Simulation is useful:* mixed-mode simulation allows designers to certify datapath components before using them in complex designs. Full-system simulation eliminate the need for generating special input patterns to test the hardware part of the program. Full-system simulation also allows the simultaneous debugging of the application driver and the hardware description part.

- *Deterministic output is useful:* we went into extremes to make sure that the netlist generated by the design library was essentially insensitive to the ordering of equations in the source. That was beneficial in three ways: it helped making the compilation process more incremental, by helping detecting unnecessary runs of the place and route software; it made it possible to use simpler regression tests; it finally helped the routing process as it tended to lay out regular structures regularly.

The use of C++ as base programming language was also very handy to ensure upward compatibility, each time we had to change the application programmer's interface to the design library.

6 What Did Not Work

In this section we discuss design decisions that we feel now were inappropriate.

- The actual low-level partitioning of logic into FPGA cells under user directives should be done by FPGA vendor software without requiring the cumbersome interface of schematic capture tools.
- Simulation is never fast enough.
- The idea of using a generic intermediate format based on attributed netlists should have been pushed one step further. Not only should the intermediate format contain information passed to layout tools, such as physical placement or timing constraints, but it should also contain information relative to the source program, such as the file name and line number of the logical equation defining a net. Back-end debugging tools can use this information to point interactive editors to the incorrect statements in the source program.
- I/O blocks were handled in a device specific, ad hoc manner. They should be handled just like the rest of the logic: as a netlist with attributes to indicate physical placement.
- Tristate buffers should be handled as basic netlist primitives, even if that complicates the semantics of the netlist by creating two kinds of nets.
- The design hierarchy and net structures should be kept, as well as all net name aliases. Choosing among aliases the name with the largest visibility (the highest in the hierarchy) is a simple but acceptable alternative.

7 Future Work

In this section, we present areas where we think the most software work is needed.

To get high performance out of our designs, we frequently use an heavily pipelined design style. In some designs, the length of the pipeline exceeds 100 clock cycles. Controlling long and complex pipelines is difficult, and we do not have any tool to automate this task. We tried unsuccessfully to perform geometry-preserving, automatic retiming on Xilinx XC3090 devices [7]. For retiming to work, one must able to remove flip-flops from some of the outputs of a gate, but not all. With Xilinx XC3000 devices, this requires the use of the two logic block outputs, with the effect of reducing by up to a factor of two the density of the logic. The Xilinx XC4000 family does not suffer from this limitation, so automatic retiming could be made to work there.

Automatic logic partitioning among chips would also be useful. We do not believe in fully automatic tools being immediately usable for large boards; but for small homogeneous boards, or for large boards under some programmer assistance, better automation should be possible. Due to the delays incurred by going through inter-chip interconnect, logic partitioning should be able to insert retiming registers when required. Finally, any FPGA placement program should be able to handle floorplanning tasks, i.e. should accept relative placement constraints as imput. This capability is crucial to allow the development of module libraries.

8 Conclusion

We presented a set of simple, low cost tools with which we have demonstrated complex high performance PAM designs in a matter of a few months. We hope to see some of these ideas incorporated into products.

Acknowledgments

We would like to thank for their help Philippe Boucard, Didier Martineau, Harry Printz, Didier Roncin, Mark Shand, Peter Stubley and Jean Vuillemin of Digital Equipment Corporation's Paris Research Laboratory.

References

[1] Patrice Bertin. *Mémoires actives programmables: conception, réalisation et programmation.* PhD thesis, Université Paris 7, UFR d'Informatique, June 1993.

[2] Patrice Bertin, Didier Roncin, and Jean Vuillemin. Introduction to programmable active memories. In J. McWhirter J. McCanny and E. Swartzlander Jr., editors, *Systolic Array Processors*, pages 301–309. Prentice-Hall, 1989. Also available as PRL research report number 3.

[3] Patrice Bertin, Didier Roncin, and Jean Vuillemin. Programmable active memories: a performance assessment. In *Symposium on Integrated Systems*, Seattle, WA, USA, March 1993.

MIT Press. Also available as PRL research report 24.

[4] P. Boucard, J. Vuillemin, and M. Shand. Calorimeter Collision Detector on DECPeRLe-1. Technical Report 31, Paris Research Laboratory, Digital Equipement Corp., 85, ave. Victor Hugo, 92563 Rueil-Malmaison Cedex, France, 1993.

[5] D. D. Gajski, editor. *Silicon Compilation.* Addison-Wesley, 1988.

[6] Louis Monier and Jean Vuillemin. Using silicon assemblers. In E. Hörbst, editor, *Proceedings of the IFIP International Conference on VLSI*, pages 315–324, Tokyo, Japan, August 1985. Elsevier Science Publishers.

[7] H. Touati, N. Shenoy, and A. Sangiovanni-Vincentelli. Retiming for Table-Lookup Field-Programmable Gate Arrays. In *First Berkeley Workshop on FPGAs*, February 1992.

A Reconfigurable Data-Driven ALU for Xputers

Reiner W. Hartenstein, Rainer Kress, Helmut Reinig

University of Kaiserslautern
Erwin-Schrödinger-Straße, D-67663 Kaiserslautern, Germany
Fax: ++49 631 205 2640, email: abakus@informatik.uni-kl.de

Abstract

A reconfigurable data-driven datapath architecture for ALUs is presented which may be used for custom computing machines (CCMs), Xputers (a class of CCMs) and other adaptable computer systems as well as for rapid prototyping of high speed datapaths. Fine grained parallelism is achieved by using simple reconfigurable processing elements which are called datapath units (DPUs). The word-oriented datapath simplifies the mapping of applications onto the architecture. Pipelining is supported by the architecture. The programming environment allows automatic mapping of the operators from high level descriptions. Two implementations, one by FPGAs and one with standard cells are shown.

1. Introduction

For numerical computations with custom computing machines, word-oriented datapaths are necessary. A recent trend in FPGA architectures moves toward support of efficient implementation of datapath circuits. Xilinx XC4000 series [11] provides fast 2-bit addition at each logic cell by a special carry circuit. AT&T's ORCA [6] supports larger data manipulations. For example a 16 bit adder requires only four function blocks. Word-oriented datapaths are not directly supported by FPGAs currently available, since these circuits are evaluated for both random logic control and datapath applications. Word-oriented datapaths in reconfigurable circuits have the additional advantage of operators being mapped more efficiently. Thus they support programming environments for custom computing machines.

Hardware designers usually have no problem in using custom computing machines, since most of the programming models these machines provide are at hardware level. Algorithms have to be expressed by a hardware description language. Then they have to be synthesized to the dedicated hardware, or the application has to be edited via a schematic editor and mapped by an FPGA vendor tool [2], [1]. People coming from the software side are more used to program with a procedural high level language. To make custom computing machines more interesting to such people, a procedural model for high level programming is needed. Some custom computing machines, consisting of an accelerator board and a host, support function calls from high level languages to be executed on the accelerator board, but they are not able to configure the board from this level, e. g. [3]. Some researchers start to evaluate compilers for their boards to compile a high level input language directly. Gokhale and Minnich [4] for example present such a compiler to program an array of FPGA chips in a high level parallel C using a SIMD programming model. However still problems are the automatic mapping of loops, arithmetic and logic operators.

This paper introduces an Xputer [8] based methodology solving these problems which strongly supports arithmetic applications. The Xputer provides a hardware and a software environment for a reconfigurable ALU (rALU). The rALU has to compute a user defined compound operator only. A compiler for the Xputer supports the high level language C as input. The rALU programming environment has to compile arithmetic and logic expressions as well as conditions into the rALU. The machine paradigm of the Xputer is described in [7].

The reconfigurable data-driven ALU proposed here, consists of the rALU control and the reconfigurable datapath architecture (rDPA). The rDPA is a word-oriented scalable regular array of simple processing elements called datapath units (DPUs). The DPUs provide a higher granularity of the basic function units than usual FPGAs. This supports automatic mapping of arithmetic and logic operators to the rDPA. Using the Xputer with the data-driven rALU allows the programming from a high level language. The architecture does not only fit as a reconfigurable ALU for Xputers, it may also be used for any other

0-8186-5490-2/94 $03.00

kind of adaptable computer system as well as a universal accelerator coprocessor or for rapid prototyping of high speed datapaths.

First, this paper gives a short introduction to the hardware environment. Section 3 introduces the rDPA. An implementation with commercial FPGA chips and one with standard cells is shown and both are compared to each other. The usage as a rALU for Xputers is explained in section 4. The programming environment allows the mapping of operands and conditions to the rDPA automatically (section 5). The final sections present an example and conclude the paper.

2. Hardware environment

Many applications require the same data manipulations to be performed on a large amount of data, e. g. statement blocks in nested loops. Xputers are especially designed to reduce the von-Neumann bottleneck of repetitive decoding and interpreting address and data computations. High performance improvements have been achieved for the class of regular, scientific computations [7], [8].

An Xputer consists of three major parts: the data sequencer, the data memory and the rALU including multiple scan windows and operator subnets. Scan windows are a kind of window to the data memory. They contain all the data, which are accessed or modified within the body of a loop. The data manipulations are done by the rALU subnets, which have parallel access to the scan windows. The scan windows are updated by their corresponding generic address generators, which are the most essential part of the data sequencer. Each generic address generator can produce address sequences which correspond to up to three nested loops under hardware control. The term data sequencing derives from the fact that the sequence of data triggers the operations in the rALU, instead of a von-Neumann instruction sequence. Pipelining across loop boundaries is supported. Generally, for each nesting level of nested loops a separate rALU subnet is required to perform the computations associated with that nesting level. For most algorithms, only three nested loops are necessary for the computation, this means that in the worst case three rALU subnets are sufficient. The rALU subnets perform all computations on the data in the scan windows by applying a user-configured complex operator to that data. The subnets need not to be of the same type. Subnets can be configured for arithmetic or bit level operations. The data-driven reconfigurable datapath architecture proposed here is well suited for arithmetic, and in the FPGA version also for bit level operations.

The Xputer prototype, Map-oriented Machine 3 (MoM-3), has direct access to the host's main memory. The rALU subnets receive their data directly from a local memory or

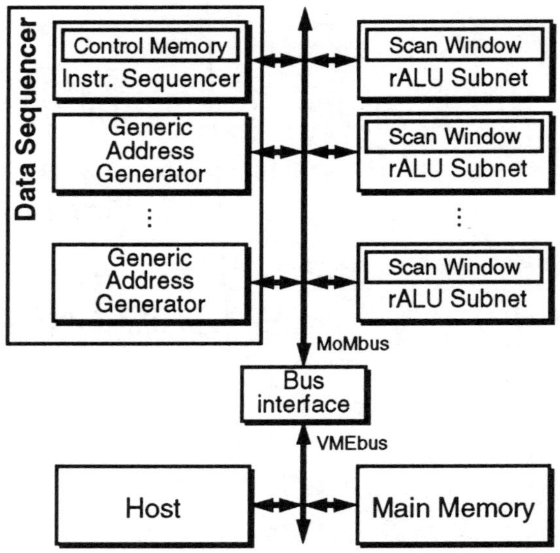

Figure 1. The Xputer prototype Map-oriented Machine 3 (MoM-3)

via the MoMbus from the main memory. The MoMbus has an asynchronous bus protocol. The datapath architecture is designed for the asynchronous bus protocol of the MoMbus, but it can also be used by a synchronous bus with minor modifications. Figure 1 shows our prototype MoM-3.

3. Reconfigurable datapath architecture

The benefit of using the reconfigurable datapath architecture (rDPA) within the Xputer paradigm stems from the development environment available. The programmer can benefit from the performance boost of custom operators to match the requirements of the application. He need not know much about hardware description languages or traditional input descriptions for FPGA synthesis tools. Instead the problem is formulated in a familiar procedural programming language and a compiler converts the loops of the application to GAG scan patterns. The statements consisting of expressions and conditions have to be mapped to the rALU only. Section 5 shows the automatic mapping onto the rDPA architecture.

The rDPA is the data manipulator of the data-driven rALU. The rDPA was designed to evaluate any arithmetic and logic expression from a high level description. Therefore the granularity of the basic operation is increased from the bitwise level to wordlevel with possible operations such as addition or multiplication. This greatly simplifies the automatic mapping onto the architecture. A regular structure like in systolic arrays is required for the scalability, also across chip boundaries. Systolic array structures combine intensive local communication and computation with decentralized parallelism in a compact package. The basic cell of the rDPA is called datapath unit (DPU), see figure 2a. Each DPU has two input and two output registers which may form some part of the scan window of the Xputer paradigm. The dataflow direction is only from west and/or north to east and/or south. The communication between the neighbouring DPUs is synchronized by a handshake. This avoids problems of clock skew and each DPU can have a different computation time for its operator. The operation in the DPU is data-driven, this means that the operation is evaluated when the required operands are available. After completion of the operation, the result in the output register of the DPU is declared to be valid. As soon as the input registers of the succeeding DPU are free, the data will be transferred and the next computation starts. In systolic architectures the high I/O requirements often make the integration into chips a problem. To reduce the number of input and output pins, a serial link is used for data transfer between neighbour DPUs (32 bits are converted into a series of 2 bit nibbles), as shown in figure 2b.

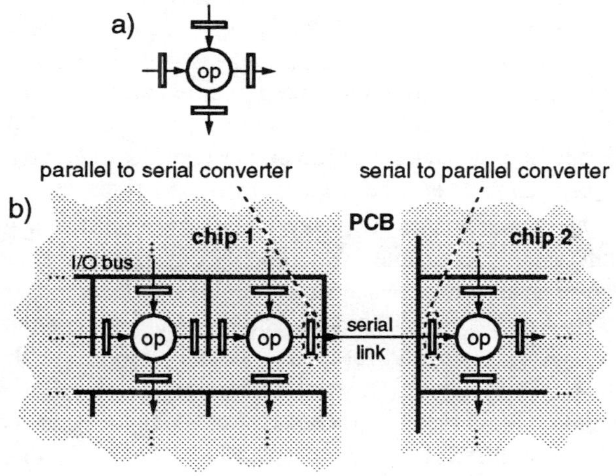

Figure 2. a) datapath unit (DPU), b) the scalable rDPA architecture between chip boundaries

A global I/O bus has been implemented into the rDPA permitting the DPUs to write from the output registers directly outside the array and to read directly from the outside. This means input data to expressions mapped into the rDPA do not need to be routed through the DPUs. Principally, the global I/O bus is used for reading and writing the scan window contents to the array. A single bus is sufficient for our Xputer prototype MoM-3 since the data from the main memory of the host is made available by the bus also. For other systems it may be better to have a dedicated input and output bus. The communication between the outside control unit and the DPUs is synchronized by a handshake like the internal communications.

Each DPU which has to communicate using the global I/O bus gets an address for its input and/or output register during configuration. The rDPA control unit can address a DPU register directly using the bus. The DPU where the address matches performs the handshake with the outside control unit and receives or sends the data. The propagation of interim results, which accounts for the largest bunch of communication, is handled through the internal communication paths, and therefore fully parallel.

An extensible set of operators for each DPU is provided by a library. The set includes the operators of the programming language C. Other operators such as the parallel prefix operator are provided. The parallel prefix operator [5] has an internal feedback. For example a queue of scan-max operators can be used for easy implementation of a hardware bubble sort [10]. The scan-max computes the maximum from the input variable and the internal feedback variable and gives the maximum as result and stores the other value internally. Operators can also be used for routing, even mixed with other operations, e. g. first multiply `a` with `b` and write the result to the south, then route variable `a` to the east.

Conditions are implemented in the rDPA in the following way. Each communication channel has an additional condition bit. If this bit is true, the operation is computed, otherwise not. In each case the condition bit is routed with the data using the same handshake. The condition operator sends to one neighbouring DPU a true condition bit, to the other one a false bit. The 'false' path is evaluated very quick, because the condition bit is routed only. With this technique also nested `if_then_else` statements can be evaluated. An example is shown in figure 3. The `then` and the `else` path can be merged at the end with a merge

a)
```
if (a < b)               (1)
   if (a > c)            (2)
      x = u + v * w;     (3)
   else                  (4)
      x = u - s * w;     (5)
else                     (6)
   x = w * t + v * z;    (7)
```

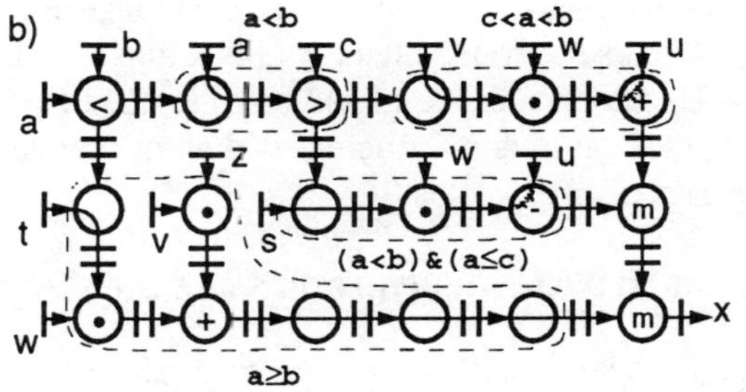

Figure 3. Example of a nested `if_then_else` **statement**

operator (m). This operator routes the value with the valid condition bit to its output.

With the proposed scalable model for the rDPA, the array can be expanded also across printed circuit board boundaries, e. g. with connectors and flexible cable. This makes it possible to connect the outputs of the east array boundary with the west one, to build a torus. The same is possible for the south and the north. With the data-driven concept, the user need not worry about synchronization.

For the implementation of the rDPA two possibilities are presented. The first is based on FPGAs and the second one is the based on standard cells.

3.1 FPGA implementation of the rDPA

The communication model of the DPU can be implemented into SRAM based FPGAs. A large reconfigurable datapath architecture can be implemented into multiple FPGA chips. The FPGA chips are arranged in an array with a single bus and configuration lines to each chip. All other wiring is local, therefore no field programmable interconnect component (FPIC) is required. On each FPGA, an array of DPUs is implemented depending on the size of the FPGA and the complexity of the operators. If a complex operator like a multiplication is implemented into an FPGA, the other DPUs can only be used for routing or simple operators in this chip. The rDPA programming environment, presented in section 5 takes this fact into consideration.

The implementation of the DPUs using FPGAs has the advantage that speed critical operators can be implemented fully or partly in parallel if necessary. Also the operations itself can be pipelined. The programming environment detects the critical path with the critical operations. Slow ripple carry adders can be substituted by conditional sum adders or other faster adders. A library of operators, which can be extended, is available in the rDPA programming environment. The communication channels are all the same for each DPU. The programmer has to put the macros for the operators and the communication together in a schematic editor. Then the DPUs are mapped with a vendor tool to the FPGA structure. This is done for each FPGA, no partitioning is necessary. Especially bit level operators are well suited for FPGA implementation. The DPUs are smaller, faster and a larger number can be implemented on a chip. Different widths of the datapath can be used also.

3.2 Standard cell implementation of the rDPA

The rDPA implemented with standard cells has a 32 bit datapath. The operators of the DPUs are configurable with a fixed ALU and a microprogrammed control. This means operators such as addition, subtraction or logical operators can be evaluated directly, whereas multiplication or division are implemented sequentially. A library of operators is available and new operators can be build with a microassembler. The standard cell implementation of the proposed model has a higher density of the arithmetic operations and the delay times are known for each operation. The time for synthesis of the rALU board is reduced because the operators in the DPUs are microprogrammed.

As mentioned before the array is scalable by using several chips of the same type. The DPU registers have no address before configuration. The only identification of the DPUs is their location in the rDPA array. Each DPU has an x- and a y-address like the elements in a matrix. A configuration word consists of a configuration bit which distinguish the configuration data from computational data. Further it consists of the x- and the y-address, the address of the DPU's configuration memory and the data for this memory.

Each time a configuration word is transferred to a DPU, the DPU checks the x- and the y-address. If the y-address is larger than zero, the address will be decreased by one and the configuration word will be transferred to the next DPU in y-direction. If the y-address is zero and the x-address is larger than zero, the x-address will be decreased by one and the configuration word will be transferred in x-direction. If both addresses are zero, the target DPU is reached and the address of the DPU's configuration memory shows the place where the data will be written.

One serial link at the array boundary is sufficient to configure the complete array, but multiple ports can be used to save time. The physical chip boundaries are completely transparent to the user. The communication structure allows dynamic in-circuit reconfiguration of the rDPA. This implies partial reconfigurability during runtime [9]. Filter coefficients, for example, can be changed during runtime to build adaptive filters. Further, the configuration technique allows to migrate designs from a smaller array to a larger array without modification. Even newer generation rDPA chips with more DPUs integrated do not need a recompilation of the configuration data.

4. Reconfigurable data-driven ALU

A subnet of the reconfigurable data-driven ALU consists of two main parts: the control for the rALU and the reconfigurable datapath architecture, as shown in figure 4. Subnets can run in parallel. Here the connection to the MoMbus is shown only.

The register file is necessary for optimizing memory cycles when the generic address generator runs with overlapping scan windows. This means that data of the actual scan window position is required in the consecutive posi-

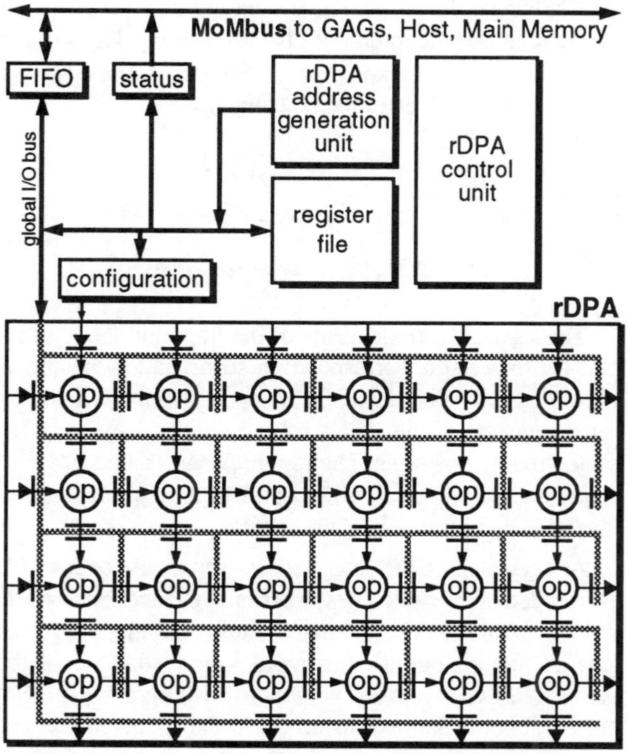

Figure 4. One subnet of the reconfigurable data-driven ALU

tion. This data can be stored in the register file and written back to main memory when its not needed any more. If there are flow dependencies between the variables in the scan window, the register file can also be used for storing the values. Additionally, the register file is used to store auxiliary variables. If a large statement has to be broken down because it does not fit into the current size of the rDPA, the auxiliary variable can be stored in the register file and read back over the global I/O bus, to the place where the computation of the statement is finished. The register file makes it possible to use each DPU in the rDPA for operations by using the bus for routing. If different expressions have a common subexpression, this subexpression has to be computed only once. If the rDPA does not provide the routing capacity for this reduction, e. g. if three or more subexpressions are in common, the interim result can be routed through the register file.

The address generation unit delivers the address for the DPU registers before each data is written into the rDPA over the bus. Normally the address is only increased by one, but it can also be loaded directly from the rDPA control unit.

The rDPA control unit holds a program to control the different units of the data driven rALU. The instruction set consists of instructions for loading data into the rDPA to a specific DPU from the MoMbus or the register file, for receiving data from a specific DPU, or branches on a special control signal from the generic address generators. The rDPA control supports context switches between three control programs which allows to use three independent virtual rALU subnets. The control program is loaded during configuration. The reconfigurable data-driven ALU allows also pipelined operation as shown in the example in section 6.

A status can be reported to the generic address generators (GAG) to inform on overflows or to force the GAGs to compute data dependent addresses. The input FIFO is currently only one word deep for each direction. This is sufficient because the data flow is regular to the main memory. Normally the rALU does not have to wait for data.

5. Programming environment

Statements which can be mapped to the rDPA array are arithmetic and logic expressions as well as conditions. loops are handled by the generic address generators. The input language for programming the rALU is the rALU programming language. The syntax of the statements follows the C programming language syntax (see also figure 3). In addition, the language provides the size of the used scan windows and the next handle position (relative to the actual position). The handle position is the lower left corner of the boundary of the scan window. By providing the handle position the rALU gets the necessary information for pipelining the complete statement block.

The rALU programming language file is parsed and a data structure like an abstract program tree is computed. Common subexpressions are taken into consideration. The operators of each statement are allocated with a straight forward algorithm. The number of DPUs used is optimized. Each allocated operator is then associated to a DPU in the rALU array. To recognize possible parallelization and to find data dependencies between the statements, a data dependency analysis is performed. Due to the global I/O bus of the rDPA array, the loading of the data and the storing are restricted to one operation per time. For best performance, an optimal sequence of these I/O operations has to be determined. Comparing an 'as soon as possible' (ASAP) with an 'as late as possible' (ALAP) schedule, the time critical path is detected. A priority function is developed from these schedules which gives the range of the I/O operations of the operands. With a list based scheduling method the optimal sequence of the I/O operations is found. Memory cycles can be optimized using the register file when the scan pattern of the GAGs works with overlapping scan windows.

The rDPA configuration file is computed from the mapping information of the DPUs and a library with the code

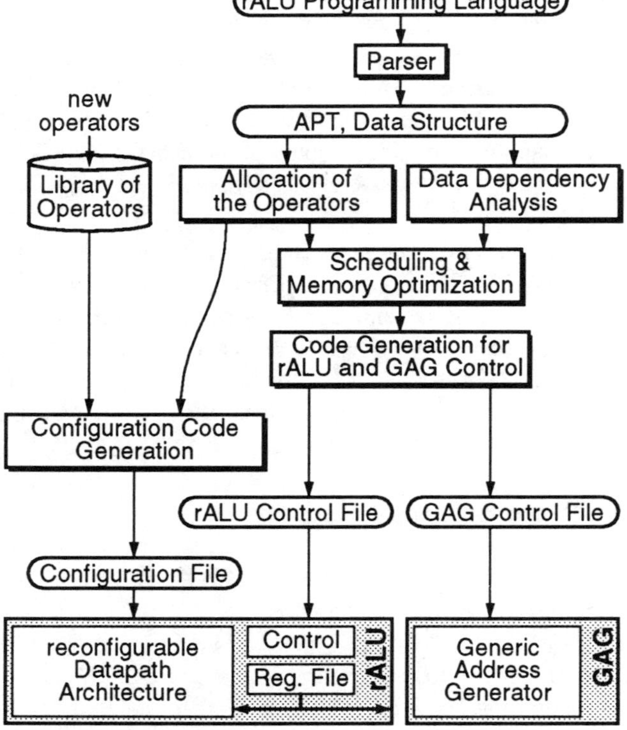

Figure 5. The rALU programming environment

of the operators. The configuration file for the rALU control unit and the configuration file for the GAGs is extracted from the final schedule of the I/O operators. For the FPGA implementation, the macros for the necessary operations are provided. The user has to put them together with a template of the communication in a schematic editor. The mapping is done by a vendor tool e. g. from Xilinx. Alternatively the environment provides a hardware description language file which has to be synthesized with a synthesis tool, e. g. Synopsys. The programming environment of the rALU is shown in figure 5.

6. Example: two dimensional FIR filter

The two dimensional FIR (finite impulse response) filter is one whose impulse response processes only a finite number of nonzero samples. The equation for a general two dimensional FIR filter is

$$y_{nm} = \sum_i \sum_j k_{ij} \cdot x_{n-i,m-j}. \qquad (1)$$

In this example a two dimensional filtering of second order is shown. Since the focus on this paper is only on the rALU for Xputers, the address generation for the data is not explained, please refer to [8]. Suppose the processed data is written into the same memory from which the data is read, one scan window is sufficient. It is of the size 3 by 3 as shown in figure 6c. All 9 scan window positions are for reading and the middle is also for writing. The window scans over the data map with a video scan, step width one. After each step it performs the equation:

$$\begin{aligned} w_{11new} = {} & w_{22}k_{22} + w_{12}k_{12} + w_{02}k_{02} \\ & + w_{21}k_{21} + w_{11}k_{11} + w_{01}k_{01} \\ & + w_{20}k_{20} + w_{10}k_{10} + w_{00}k_{00} \end{aligned} \qquad (2)$$

The k_{ij} are the coefficients of the filter and the w_{ij} contain the data at the corresponding scan window positions. Figure 6a shows equation (2) mapped into the rDPA. The input registers of the DPUs named with w_{ij} represent the scan window positions. The input registers named with k_{ij} represent the registers with coefficients of the FIR filter loaded at configuration.

At each step of the scan window three new data words are loaded, three old ones are removed and one output word is written back. Figure 6c shows the loading of the data. At the beginning, data word a_0 is loaded across the bus directly to w_{00}, b_0 to w_{01}, c_0 to w_{02}, a_1 to w_{10} and so on. As soon as data words arrive in the input registers of the DPUs the operation will be performed (data-driven). As shown in figure 6b the multiply-route operation evaluates the multiplication and routes the input data from west to the next DPU east. So the data required in the next step need not to be loaded again across the bus. The pipeline is filled by loading the first nine input data words over the bus, then the internal routing resources are used. Only the three new data words have to be routed by the bus. The execution is shown in figure 7. The first line shows the

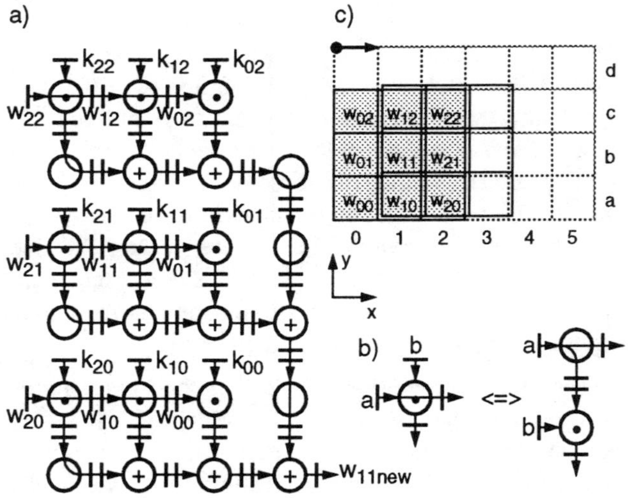

Figure 6. a) Two dimensional FIR filter mapped into the rDPA, b) equivalent operation of the multiply-route operation, c) the corresponding scan window

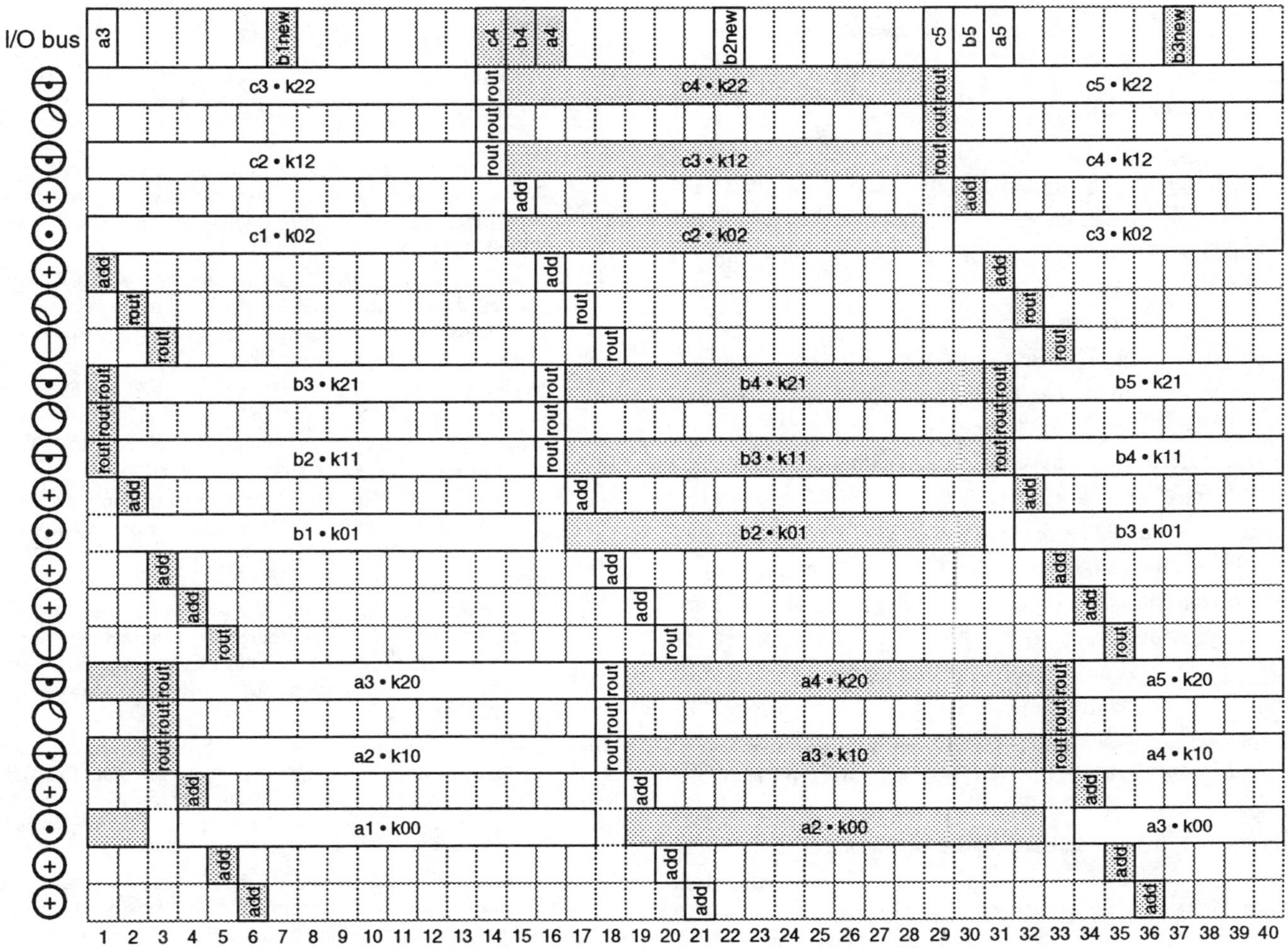

Figure 7. Pipelined execution of the two dimensional FIR filter

read and write operations using the global I/O bus of the rDPA. The following lines describe the operation of the multipliers, routing units and adders. Each column belongs to one time step. All boxes in one column are evaluated in parallel.

The prototype implementation of the rDPA works with 32 bit fixed-point and integer input words. Currently the host computer's memory is very slow. The clock frequency of the system is 25 MHz. In many applications the coefficients are set up in such a way that shift operations are sufficient and multiplications are not necessary. If high throughput is needed, DPUs can be linked together to implement a pipelined multiplier. Benchmark results are given in table 1. The performance figures are a worst case estimation of our prototype. The speed of the examples 2 to 5 depend not on the order of the filter as long as the necessary hardware (# of DPUs) is provided. The same is applies for example 6.

#	Algorithms	Operations	# of DPUs	Throughput (time steps)	Performance
1	1024 Fast Fourier Transformation	*, +, -	10	16 · 10240	50 Hz
2	FIR filter, n^{th} order	*, +	2(n+1)	15	0.6 MHz
3	FIR filter, n^{th} order	shift, +	2(n+1)	4	2 MHz
4	$n \times m$ two dim. FIR filter	*, +	2(n+1)(m+2)-1	15	0.6 MHz
5	$n \times m$ two dim. FIR filter	shift, +	2(n+1)(m+2)-1	4	2 MHz
6	Bubblesort, length n	scan-max	n-1	2	4.2 MHz

Table 1. Benchmark results

7. Conclusions

A programming model for an FPGA based hardware platform for a data-driven reconfigurable datapath architecture (rDPA) has been presented which strongly supports numerical applications. It may be used as a reconfigurable ALU (rALU) for custom computing machines (CCMs), Xputers (a class of CCMs) and other adaptable computer systems as well as for rapid prototyping of high speed datapaths. Together with the Xputer hardware and software environment a system has been implemented which is programmable in a high level language. The word-orientation of the datapath and the increase of the fine granularity of the basic operations greatly simplifies the automatic mapping onto the architecture. The scalable rDPA provides parallel and pipelined evaluation of the compound operators. An implementation with FPGA chips and one with standard cells is shown. The FPGA implementation supports variable width of datapaths, also for bit level operations. The standard cell version of the implementation of the rDPA is microprogrammable. It provides a higher density of the operators. The architecture is in-circuit dynamically reconfigurable, which implies also partial reconfigurability at runtime.

A prototype chip with standard cells has been completely specified in the hardware description Verilog and will be submitted for fabrication to the Eurochip[1] organization soon. It has 32 bit datapaths and provides arithmetic resources for integer and fixed-point numbers. The FPGA version is being implemented by using Xilinx software tools. The programming environment is specified and is being implemented on Sun SPARCstations.

1. Eurochip is a microelectronics project of the CEC.

References

[1] J. M. Arnold: The Splash 2 Software Environment; IEEE Workshop on FPGAs for Custom Computing Machines, FCCM'93, IEEE Computer Society Press, Napa, CA, pp. 88-93, April 1993

[2] S. Casselman: Virtual Computing and The Virtual Computer; IEEE Workshop on FPGAs for Custom Computing Machines, FCCM'93, IEEE Computer Society Press, Napa, CA, pp. 43-48, April 1993

[3] N. N.: Giga Ops: Technical Overview of C to Hardware Compilation and Development System for FPGA Computing; Pre-Release Documentation, Rev. 0.7, Giga Operations Corporation, Berkeley, 1993

[4] M. Gokhale, R. Minnich: FPGA Computing in Data Parallel C; IEEE Workshop on FPGAs for Custom Computing Machines, FCCM'93, IEEE Computer Society Press, Napa, CA, pp. 94-101, April 1993

[5] S. A. Guccione, M. J. Gonzalez: A Data-Parallel Programming Model for Reconfigurable Architectures; IEEE Workshop on FPGAs for Custom Computing Machines, FCCM'93, IEEE Computer Society Press, Napa, CA, pp. 79-87, April 1993

[6] D. Hill, B. Britton, B. Oswald, N.-S. Woo, S. Singh, C.-T. Chen, B. Krambeck: ORCA: A New Architecture for High-Performance FPGAs; in H. Grünbacher, R. W. Hartenstein (Eds.): Field-Programmable Gate Arrays, Lecture Notes in Computer Science, Springer-Verlag, Berlin, 1993

[7] R. W. Hartenstein, A. G. Hirschbiel, M. Riedmüller, K. Schmidt, M. Weber: A Novel ASIC Design Approach Based on a New Machine Paradigm; IEEE Journal of Solid-State Circuits, Vol. 26, No. 7, July 1991

[8] R. W. Hartenstein, A. G. Hirschbiel, K. Schmidt, M. Weber: A Novel Paradigm of Parallel Computation and its Use to Implement Simple High-Performance Hardware; Future Generation Systems 7 (1991/92), p. 181-198, Elsevier Science Publishers, North-Holland, 1992

[9] P. Lysaght, J. Dunlop: Dynamic Reconfiguration of Field-programmable Gate Arrays; Proceedings of the 3rd International Workshop on Field Programmable Logic and Applications, Oxford, Sept. 1993

[10] N. Petkov: Systolische Algorithmen und Arrays; Akademie-Verlag, Berlin 1989

[11] N. N.: The XC4000 Data Book; Xilinx, Inc., 1992

Compiling to the gate Level for a Reconfigurable Co-Processor

David Wo and Kevin Forward

Department of Electrical and Electronic Engineering,
The University of Melbourne, Victoria, Australia.

Abstract:

This paper describes a programmable coprocessor. A C-compiler has been written which compiles C code to the gate level relieving the programmer of the onerous task of programming the coprocessor. As not all of the code in most C programs will fit into the coprocessors FPGA, programs are first compiled using a standard C compiler. These programs are then profiled to determine which parts of the code make the most intense use of the processor. These parts are then compiled to the gate level and implemented in the coprocessor. Speedups in program execution time of about 20 are obtained by this method by comparison with an IPC Sparcstation.

1. Introduction

The ever increasing complexity of the tasks executed by computers has demanded higher performance from them. As a result, the evolution of computer architecture is strongly influenced by the quest for faster computers. The execution speed of a computer program is governed by three factors [1]:

- the number of instructions to be executed;
- the average number of clock cycles required to execute an instruction; and
- the clock frequency.

Over the years, many different methods and ideas have been used to achieve faster execution of computer programs based on these factors.

The most obvious way to increase the execution speed is to increase the clock frequency of the processor. However, integrated circuit technology and the laws of physics impose an upper limit to the clock frequency. The next avenue by which to achieve faster execution time is to change the computer architecture in order to decrease the average clock cycles per instruction.

Before the 1980s, most computers were using the traditional Von Neuman architecture where each instruction is carried out in four major sequences:

- fetches one instruction from the main memory,
- decodes it,
- executes it,
- writes the results back to the main memory if necessary.

If each stage takes one clock cycle to complete, then each instruction requires four clock cycles. In the 1980s, computer architects directed their attention towards the minimisation of the time required for the instruction cycle. Consequently reduced instruction set computers (RISCs) which employ pipelining and fast cache memory techniques were developed. RISCs utilise each clock cycle more efficiently. Other architectural motivations such as superscalar, superpipeline, and very long instruction word are now also used to reduce the average number of clock cycle per instruction.

Despite the speed improvements of these architectures, the performance of a single, serially executing processor is still being limited by the algorithmic barriers of many current applications such as simulation, real-time control, and digital signal processing. To achieve higher performance for these type of applications, multi-processors architecture is used to exploit the parallelism embedded in the algorithm. With two or more processors executing a single program, the average number clock cycle per instruction can be

0-8186-5490-2/94 $03.00

reduced by up to *n*, where *n* is the number of processors.

Multi-processors computers are very appealing to transaction processing systems, time-sharing systems and many scientific applications. The advantages of multi-processor computers is that they are expandable, and theoretically, the number of processors can be increased without limit. The drawbacks are that they are expensive to build, difficult to program and the speed up is restricted to the degree of parallelism of the software.

A cheaper but yet effective alternative to multi-processor computers is to add a dedicated application specific co-processor to a uni-processor computer. Implementing algorithms in hardware has resulted in coprocessors such as floating point co-processor or graphics co-processor which are employed in computers to speed up the computation of specific functions. Hardware implementation achieves its speed-up by three mechanism:

- hard-wired algorithm do not have to fetch instructions from memory;
- the exploitation of parallelism;
- asynchronous operation.

As an example of possibilities of hardware implementation; a speed up of greater than 10 times over a Cray 2 had been achieved by systolic arrays [2][3]. With the recent advances in field programmable gate array (FPGA) [4], it is possible to build a co-processor system which is reconfigurable [5]. Such co-processor systems comprise of one or more number of FPGAs connected to the computer system bus in such a way that it can be reprogrammed with a new algorithm for each application.

The major advantages of a reconfigurable co-processor system are:

- that it executes the algorithm in hardware, so only the necessary circuitry executes;
- it exploits the parallelism within the algorithm to decrease the average number of clock cycle per instruction; and
- unlike programmable logic array (PLA) where the device can be programmed once, the FPGA is very flexible and can be programmed with new algorithm as often as needed to suit the program.

Despite FPGAs advantages, programming FPGA at the gate level is very difficult and error-prone. Programmers find it easier to express their algorithms in higher level language. In this paper, example function is written in the C language, therefore translating the C function to gate level would require a C compiler whose target is a logic circuit. A gate array C compiler was developed with the intention to remove the burden of programming the FPGA at gate level.

Of course, it is nearly impossible to translate the entire C program to hardware since FPGA may not be able to fit the entire program. It is therefore useful to know where the speed bottleneck is for the given program. As a rule of thumb, 90% of the time is spent in 10% of the code. Hence, converting the functions that are frequently used to hardware will produce speed improvement. It is useful to have a profiling tool to analyse which function does the program is spending most of its time. From the profile information, the user can select the candidate function for hardware implementation.

This paper presents a co-processor system called RECON which will speed up the program execution by:

- selecting an appropriate candidate routine from a program;
- mapping the routine to hardware logic;
- configuring it into the FPGA; and
- providing data as well as control to the co-processor.

The operating system chosen for development is SunOS 4.1.x, which is a variant of BSD 4.3 Unix, and a subset of C programming language will be used to program the co-processor.

Section 2 describes the architecture and hardware of the RECON co-processor system. Programming of RECON system and the gate array C compiler are presented in section 3. Section 4 discusses the results obtained from running the co-processor system on an example function. The summary and conclusion in section 5 terminates this paper.

2. RECON Architecture

The RECON system consists of a Sun SparcStation host and a reconfigurable co-processor board. The hardware layout of the reconfigurable co-processor board is shown in Figure 1.

The board contains a LSI L68453A DMA SBus controller chip which handles the protocol

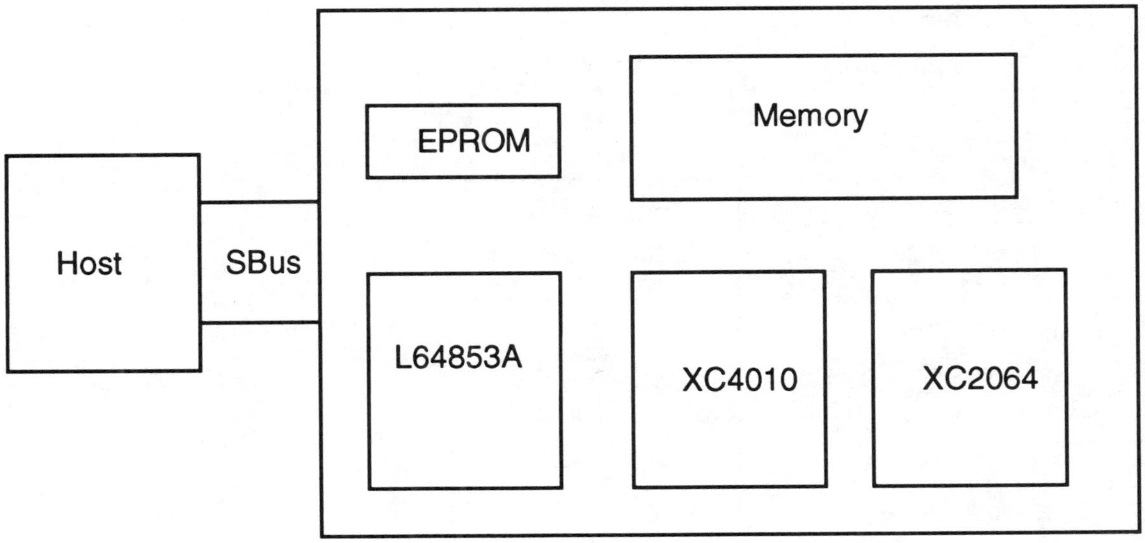

Figure 1. The architecture of RECON

to input and output data onto the host's SBus [6][13]. The board also contains two Xilinx FPGAs [4], a XC2064 FPGA as the co-processor controller and a XC4010 FPGA as the reconfigurable processor unit. The controller

- manages the incoming and outgoing data streams;
- configures the co-processor with the given algorithm; and
- signals the host when co-processor requires attention.

The host and the controller communicates via a status register in the controller. The reconfigurable processor unit is the core of the co-processor board. It has a 32 bit wide data path to the coprocessor's memory, and its address path is 16 bit wide. The size of the coprocessor's memory is 32K byte, directly addressable by the host. The memory stores the configuration information of the reconfigurable processor unit as well as the data to be processed by the reconfigurable processor unit. A 16K byte EPROM is used to configure the controller as the co-processor board is powered up. Finally, the coprocessor's system clock is a 25 MHz oscillator circuit.

The SparcStation host is responsible for downloading the configuration information to the coprocessor's memory and triggers the configuration process. It is also responsible for reading and writing data to the coprocessor's memory and starts the reconfigurable processor unit to execute the configured algorithm. The host may communicate with the co-processor system with both synchronous and asynchronous mechanisms. The host may receive an interrupt from the coprocessor's controller and reads the controller's status register to determine what action to take next.

Initially, the reconfigurable processor unit is an amorphous array of gates, therefore there is no fixed architecture. An appropriate target architecture is required to execute the algorithm in hardware. Currently, the co-processor system uses algorithmic state machines (ASMs) as the target architecture [7]. The advantages of using ASMs are:

- many algorithms require the type of sequential operation exhibited by ASMs;
- an ASM can lead to minimal circuit design; and
- well developed procedures for the design of sequential circuits already exists.

Each operation within the algorithm has an ASM state associated with it. The inputs to each state are the source variables, and the outputs

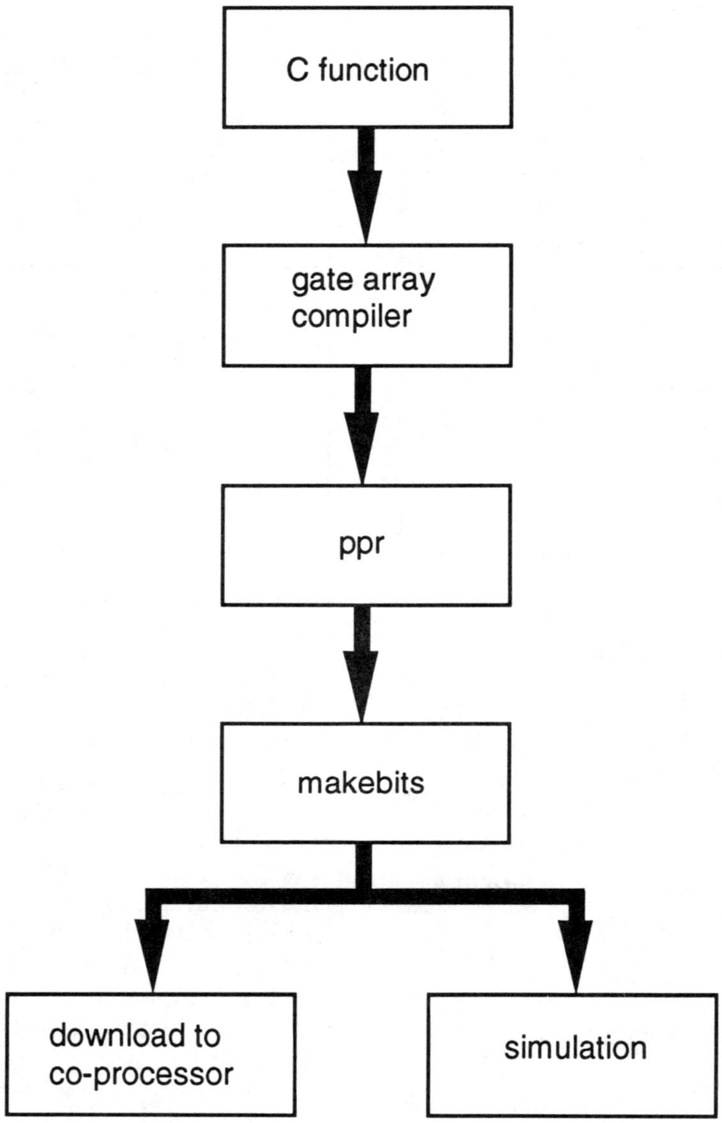

Figure 2. Design flow in the RECON programming environment

from each state are the resultant variables. A number of operations can be carried out in parallel within each state. The flow of the execution within the ASM is controlled by the sequencer and the control signal of the ASM.

Currently RECON is designed to support a single instruction single data computer model (SISD), but it can easily be extended to other computer models such as systolic arrays by increasing the number of reconfigurable processor units.

3. Programming the co-processor

The most elementary method of programming the co-processor is to translate the algorithm to a series of connected logic gates by the user using a schematic capture CAD program. This method is very time consuming and error prone. An automated programming environment would greatly enhance the user to program the co-processor. Figure 2 illustrates the basic steps used by RECON to program the co-processor. A

Xilinx net list file (XNF) [4] is generated from the source code by a gate array compiler. The net list file is then passed to a set of Xilinx tools to generate the configuration information or simulation information.

3.1 Gate Array Compiler

FPGA applications are usually implemented at the gate level using some logic description language [8] to describe a list of logic blocks and a list of interconnections, known as a net list, between these blocks. It has been the experience of their users that working at the gate level is a time consuming and tedious business.

The time required to program at the gate level strongly motivates the development of a gate array compiler (gacc) which automates the translation from a higher programming language to a net list. The source code is written in a subset of C which was chosen because of its popularity among today's programmers. The gate array compiler performs the basic tasks of a conventional compiler such as lexical, syntactic, and semantic analysis. However, rather than performing code generation straight away as in the conventional compiler, the gate array compiler will parallelise the source function to obtain an optimal equivalent logic circuit. During parallelisation, the compiler extracts the maximum amount of operations that can be executed concurrently in hardware, thus the average number of clock cycle per instruction is reduced. After parallelisation, a net list to represent the hardware logic is generated.

The first step in extracting parallelism is to perform a data dependency analysis on the function. This is best illustrated by an example. If a statement, S_2, requires data which is computed by another statement, S_1, then statement S_2 must execute after statement S_1 and hence the statement S_1 and S_2 cannot be executed concurrently. All statements which no data dependencies can execute concurrently. Polychrononopoulos [9] and Wolfe [10] suggested that data dependencies can be detected by using a data dependence graph. Here we show another method to detect dependence by utilising a list of variables kept in a table. Every time a variable is being assigned in the function, the table records all the necessary information. Each time that a variable is encountered by the compiler its status is checked by retrieving its corresponding data from the variable table. The data retrieved allows the compiler to see how the current statement depends on other statements.

The gate array compiler takes the source statements and classifies them into sequences of statement blocks where each block can be concurrently executed. On a conventional computer, each instruction is executed sequentially. Sometimes it is possible that a statement S_i will execute after statement S_n even though it could have been executed before it. In such a situation, the parallelisation process may re-order the statements. The gate array compiler has the ability to re-order the statements without altering the result which will be identical to that obtained using the original algorithm.

During data dependency analysis, the compiler searches the variable table for the variable which is being used in an assignment expression of the current statement. If the variable's entry is not in the table then the statement remains in the current sequence. If the variable's entry is found in the table, and its time of last update is greater than or equal to the current sequence, then the current statement will be classified into the next statement block. This simple data synchronisation strategy ensures the correct data flow of the algorithm. An example C function and its corresponding ASM is shown in Figure 3. Note that a number of operations can be executed concurrently in each ASM state, thus reducing the average number of clock cycles per instruction.

After the ASM is constructed, the compiler then converts the ASM to hardware logic. The gate array compiler first extracts the number of state variables needed in the circuit from the ASM, then a state transition table is built using the ASM. The transition table contains information such as current state, next state, and the condition for transition. After the transition table is built, the state controller is constructed by using combinational logic. The gate array compiler uses the multiplexer controller method to construct the state controller because it is a simple method as well as resulting in low gate count comparing to other method such as traditional JK flip-flop or one-shot method [7].

Once the controller circuit design is completed, the compiler synthesises the co-processor logic circuits. The compiler extracts each operation from the ASM, then searches Xilinx's logic gates/macros database for the appropriate gate or macro to carry out the task. The compiler also ensures that the input value to each Xilinx gate/macro is the right size, and each gate/macro's input and output are connected to

```
/* This function multiples two 8 bit numbers together */
extern char n, c;
char
mult8()
{
        char i, a;

        for (i = 0, a = 0; i < n; i++)
                a += c;
        return(a);
}
        IN      0xffff,c                @SEQ0
        IN      0xfffe,n                @SEQ1
        MOV     0,i                     @SEQ2
        MOV     0,a                     @SEQ2
        TLT     i,n,SIG1                @SEQ3
        ADD     a,c,SIG2                @SEQ3
        ADD     i,1,SIG3                @SEQ3
        ENB     SIG2,a,SIG1             @SEQ4
        ENB     SIG3,i,SIG1             @SEQ4
        ENB     SEQ5,COUNTER,*SIG1      @SEQ4
        ENB     SEQ3,COUNTER,SIG1       @SEQ4
        OUT     a,0xfeff,1              @SEQ5
        OUT     COMPLETE,1,1            @SEQ5
```

Figure 3. An example C function and its corresponding algorithmic state machine

the intended wires. These requirements are programmed into the gate array compiler. The macros, gates, and their interconnections are written out to a net list file as each operation is converted to hardware. Currently, multiplication, division, and modulus operations are not implemented by the gate array compiler.

After the creation of the net list file, the compiler will invoke the Xilinx partition, placement and route program (ppr) [4] to check if the circuit is able to fit into the co-processor. Once `ppr` has successfully partitioned, placed and routed the logic circuit, the compiler invokes a Xilinx utility (makebits) [4] to convert the circuit into a binary configuration file ready to be downloaded into the co-processor board.

3.2 Profiling

Since there is a limit of the number of gates that can be accommodated into the co-processor, the entire program may not fit in the FPGA, therefore a candidate routine has to be selected for conversion. For most computational intensive programs, 90% of their execution time are usually spent on 10% of the code [1]. A frequently called routine without any operating system calls will be the best candidate. However, first the RECON has to find a way to obtain the profile information about a given program.

Most C compilers running under Unix provide a `-pg` option which prepares the executable file to collect data for profiling [12]. When a given program is ran, a run-time recording mechanism is invoked which produces a profile file named `gmon.out` using the Unix utility `gprof`. `gprof` which produces an execution profile of a given program from its `gmon.out` file. The symbol table in the executable file is read and correlated with the `gmon.out` file. The output is divided into two listings. The first listing, the call graph profile, shows the functions sorted according to the percentage of the total time of the program accounted for by this function and its descendants. The second listing is simply a flat profile of the program. For each external function, the percentage of time spent executing that function and the next function is printed in descending order, together with the number of times the function was called and the number of millisecond per call. A sample call graph profile and flat profile are listed in Figure 4.

```
call graph profile:
                                        called/total        parents
index  %time     self descendants  called+self     name      index
                                        called/total        children
                                                            <spontaneous>
[1]    100.0     0.00        0.01                  start [1]
                 0.00        0.01          1/1         _main [3]
                 0.00        0.00          1/1         _on_exit [5]
                 0.00        0.00          1/1         _exit [4]
                 0.01        0.00        200/200       _main [3]
[2]    100.0     0.01        0.00        200       _mult8 [2]
                 0.00        0.01          1/1         start [1]
[3]    100.0     0.00        0.01          1       _main [3]
                 0.01        0.00        200/200       _mult8 [2]
                 0.00        0.00          1/1         start [1]
[4]      0.0     0.00        0.00          1       _exit [4]
                 0.00        0.00          1/1         start [1]
[5]      0.0     0.00        0.00          1       _on_exit [5]
flat profile:
   %    cumulative    self             self     total
 time     seconds    seconds    calls  ms/call  ms/call  name
100.0       0.01       0.01      200     0.05     0.05   _mult8 [2]
  0.0       0.01       0.00        1     0.00     0.00   _exit [4]
  0.0       0.01       0.00        1     0.00    10.00   _main [3]
  0.0       0.01       0.00        1     0.00     0.00   _on_exit [5]
```

Figure 4. The call graph and flat profile information

From the two profile listings, the user can select the most appropriate function for conversion in the program. There are two basic criteria for the selection:

- the function is to have no descendants, that is no function calls at all. Whenever a function is calling another function, it has to push its return address and parameters on the run-time memory stack respectively. To reduce the amount of memory bus traffic and memory delay, the co-processor cannot afford to call other functions;
- the function should be small enough to be implemented into the co-processor. This criteria is heavily depending on the FPGA used and on the user's judgment.

Profiling and determining the candidate function is currently done by the user manually inspecting the data. Development is under way at the moment to automate this process within RECON.

3.3 Configuration and Execution

Once the gate array compiler has generated the configuration file for the selected function, the host is ready to download it to the co-processor board's memory. A utility program was written to:

- handle the transferring of the configuration file to the co-processor board's memory;
- send a configuration signal to the co-processor board controller to start configuring the FPGA; and
- check the co-processor board status.

After the configuration, the original program needs a number of modifications. Firstly, the function which has been converted to hardware does not need to be compiled to object code again. Secondly, an initialisation function is called by the application program to initialise and set up the coprocessor's memory. Finally, each function call is invoked by a co-processor library routine. The co-processor library routine initiates the co-processor execution, and checks the status of the co-processor for errors after the execution is completed.

4. Results

To demonstrate the amount of speed up gained by implemented in hardware over software, the example function shown in Figure 3 was chosen. This simple function fits quite easily into the XC4010 FPGA, requiring 15% of the total CLBs [4]. Taking the clock frequency at 25 MHz, the simulation software, ViewSim [14], showed that the FPGA required 2.08 μs to carry out the function if the variables n and c are equal to 50 and 3 respectively. The simulation time included the time to transfer data to and from the FPGA and the coprocessor's memory. The time required for the host to read from and write to the coprocessor's memory is 40ns. In the test program, the example function was invoked 200 times. The test program execution time with the aid of the co-processor was 0.44 ms. On a SparcStation IPC running at 25 MHz with load average of 0.01 and one user, the same test program with the same data took 10 ms to complete. The time is obtained from the profiling information. The speed up gained was calculated as:

(program execution time without co-processor)/(program execution time with co-processor)

and it was a factor of 23 times. This result indicates that by changing the computational intensive portion of an application to hardware, its performance is greatly improved.

5. Conclusion

Conventional computer architecture has many limitations in the current world of computing. Computer architects have designed more ingenious architecture such as pipelined architecture, superscalar architecture, and multi-processors computer to gain better computational performance. With the advance in FPGA technology, a reconfigurable co-processor provides a cost effective and attractive means of achieving higher performance. Algorithms embedded in hardware can execute faster than software because of less memory access overhead. This paper presented a reconfigurable co-processor in which the architectures are tailored to each application by the user. It also outlined the operations of a compiler which translates an function written in higher level language such as C to logic gate level directly. The results showed that considerable speed up can be achieved for computationally intensively programs with the application of a reconfigurable co-processor.

6. References

[1] John Hennessy and David Patterson, "Computer Architecture: A Quantitative Approach", Morgan Kaufman, San Mateo, Calif., 1990.
[2] H.T.Kung, "Why Systolic Architecture?", IEEE Computer, Vol.15, No.1, Jan. 1982, pp 37-42.
[3] M.Gokhole, W.Holmes, A.Kopser, S.Lucas, R.Minnich, D.Sweely, D.Lopresti, "Building and Using a Highly Parallel Programmable Logic Array", IEEE Computer, Vol.24, No.1, Jan. 1991, pp 81-90.
[4] The Programmable Gate Array Data Book, Xilinx Inc, 1991.
[5] P.C.French, R.W.Taylor, "A self-reconfiguring processor", Proceedings of FPGAs for custom computing machines (1993), pp 50-59.
[6] L64853A SBus DMA Controller Technical Manual, LSI Logic Corp., 1992.
[7] David Winkel and Franklin Prosser, "The art of Digital Design", Prentice-Hall, Englewood Cliffs, New Jersey, 1980.
[8] Xilinx ABEL manual, Xilinx Inc, 1992.
[9] Constantine D. Polychronopoulos, "Parallel Programming and Compilers", Kluwer Academic, Norwell, Mass., 1988.
[10] Michael Wolfe, "Multiprocessor Synchronization for Concurrent Loops", IEEE Software, Vol.5, No.1, Jan. 1988, pp 34-42.
[12] SunOS Reference Manual, Sun Microsystems Inc, 1988.
[13] SBus Specification A.1, Sun Microsystem Inc, 1990.
[14] ViewSim User Manual, Xilinx Inc, 1992.

Finding Lines and Building Pyramids with Splash 2

A. Lynn Abbott, Peter M. Athanas, Luna Chen, and Robert L. Elliott

The Bradley Department of Electrical Engineering
Virginia Polytechnic Institute and State University
Blacksburg, Virginia 24061-0111

Abstract

This paper describes the design and implementation of two image-processing algorithms using the SPLASH 2 *custom computing platform.* SPLASH 2 *is a reconfigurable system that can be tailored to perform a wide variety of tasks. The particular tasks discussed here are the Hough transform, a well-known technique for detecting lines in an image, and pyramid generation, the process of transforming a single image into a set of filtered images with successively lower spatial resolution. This paper describes how these computationally intensive processes have been mapped onto* SPLASH 2 *hardware. Both processes have been designed to operate at high speed. In particular, the generation of both Gaussian (low-pass) and Laplacian (band-pass) pyramids can occur concurrently in real time using images from a video camera, assuming the standard frame rate of 30 images per second. Results are presented to illustrate the efficacy of reconfigurable FPGA-based machines to image processing applications.*

1 Introduction

General-purpose workstations can provide acceptable performance for many image-processing tasks when high speed is not required. However, for such applications as robotic control, visual tracking, and autonomous navigation, fast image processing is essential. Unfortunately, fast computation rates are difficult to achieve because of the large amount of data associated with images. General-purpose machines are overwhelmed not only by the numbers of computations required, but also by the I/O requirements of real-time image processing, which exceed 7 Megabytes per second for typical monochrome video cameras.

When high performance is needed, the traditional approach has been to develop application-specific hardware. The drawbacks of this approach are lengthy design cycles and costly redesigns when new algorithms are developed (or when mistakes are found in the original design). An attractive alternative is to utilize reconfigurable FPGA-based platforms that can be tailored to different applications without sacrificing performance.

This paper examines the computational benefits of the reconfigurable approach by presenting two case studies using the SPLASH 2 attached processor. A brief overview of SPLASH 2 is given in Section 2. The two tasks that are presented are well known in the image-processing community, and are substantially different in nature. The first of these, described in Section 3, is a 23-FPGA design to perform the Hough transform and related preprocessing functions. Section 4 describes two 10-FPGA designs for generating real-time (and near real-time) image pyramids at the standard video rate of 30 images per second. Section 5 is a comparison and summary of these designs.

2 The Splash 2 Architecture

SPLASH 2 is a second-generation reconfigurable attached processor designed by the Supercomputing Research Center in Bowie, Maryland. This section presents a brief overview of the system; refer to [Arno92] for more details.

A SPLASH 2 system consists of a Sun SPARC-2 host, an interface board, and one or more array boards. Up to 15 SPLASH 2 array boards are supported within a single system, and each contains 17 Xilinx XC4010 FPGAs arranged in a linear array and are fully connected through a 16x16 crossbar. (Refer to Figure 1.) The 17 FPGAs are designated X0 - X16, and each has a local 256Kx16 RAM. The principle data paths between FPGAs are 36 bits in width, and can therefore accommodate up to four 8-bit picture elements (pixels) simultaneously along with a 4-bit control word.

0-8186-5490-2/94 $03.00

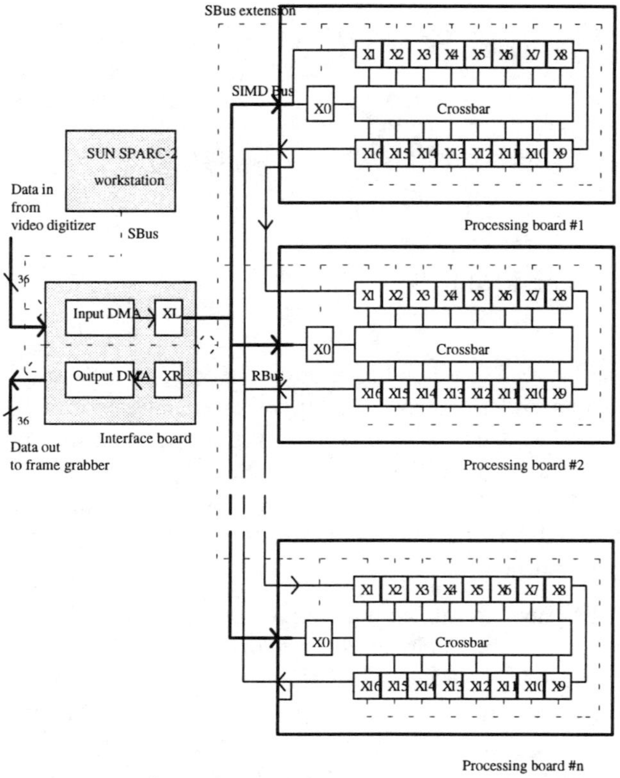

Figure 1. The SPLASH 2 *architecture. Up to 15 reconfigurable array boards can be placed in a system. Each board contains 17 Xilinx FPGAs that are connected as a linear array and through a crossbar.*

Applications are "programmed" for SPLASH 2 by creating a VHDL model which is simulated, refined, and synthesized to a gate list. An alternative method is to use schematic capture and supporting software such as XBLOX [Xili91]. The gate list is finally mapped onto the FPGA architecture using the Xilinx or the Synopsis synthesis tools. This design cycle is described more thoroughly in [Arno93].

3 Line Detection using the Hough Transform

3.1 The Hough Transform

The Hough transform is a procedure for detecting straight lines in an image [Houg62, Duda72]. Line detection is a very useful low-level operation, particularly for image analysis of scenes that may contain man-made objects such as buildings, roads, and manufactured goods. Extensions of the method may be used to detect curves or other objects of known shape.

The essence of the method is to transform edge points in an image to curves in *parameter space*. An accumulator array is maintained to contain these curves. After all edge points have been processed, peaks in the accumulator array (also called the "Hough array") indicate the parameters of the lines in the original image.

To see this, consider the following equation for a line: $d = x\cos\theta + y\sin\theta$. The variables x and y correspond to horizontal and vertical image dimensions, respectively. As illustrated in Figure 2a, the value d represents the perpendicular distance of the line from the origin, and θ is the angle of the perpendicular with the x-axis. (The standard slope-intercept equation is not used because of problems with vertical lines.) The problem of line detection is to recover the two parameters d and θ that pass through a significant number of edge points in the image. This is done by mapping each edge point (x_i, y_i) in the image to a sinusoid in d-θ parameter space, as illustrated in Figure 2b. For collinear edge points, all of the corresponding sinusoids will intersect at the single point (d_j, θ_j) which corresponds to the line through the edge points.

The standard Hough approach implements the parameter space as an accumulator array, where each quantized d-θ cell in the array corresponds to a single line in the image. Each cell in the array is initialized to 0. For each edge point, the corresponding sinusoid is traced within the Hough array, incrementing each cell that is visited. In effect, each edge point "votes" for all lines that pass through it. After all edge points have been processed in this manner, the array is examined. Any large values are good candidates for lines that may be present in the image.

3.2 Implementation

When detecting whether lines are present in a real visual data stream, only boundaries of objects within the visual field are of interest. In other words, if one wanted to characterize a gear or a wrench with a set of lines, the colors and textures of these objects are not relevant. In order to accentuate object boundaries, the image is first processed with a 3×3 Sobel edge detector[1]. The resulting high-pass data are

[1]This function, along with the other pre-processing operations, are also implemented on SPLASH on a separate processor board, and also operates in real-time on the input data stream.

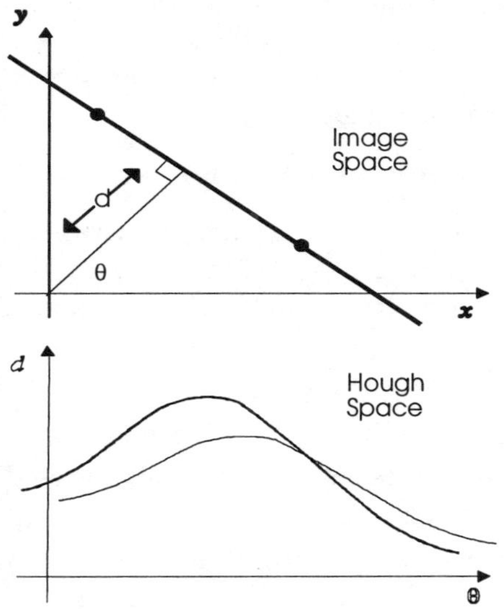

Figure 2. The Hough transformation to parameter space. Edge points (x_i, y_i) in the image (a) map to sinusoids in the d-θ *parameter space (b). In this example, the two sinusoids intersect at the values* d *and* θ *which determine the line that passes through* (x_1, y_1) *and* (x_2, y_2).

filtered and thresholded to eliminate outlyers. The digitized raster-scan video signal consists of 512×512 8-bit pixels, which is clocked into SPLASH 2 at a rate of 10 million pixels per second.

This filtered binary data stream tends to be relatively sparse in '1's, which are present only around object boundaries. Figure 3 provides a high-level overview of the complete tranformation process on the laboratory platform. The focus of this section is on the construction of parameter space (*BOARD 2* in Figure 3).

The operations that are to be realized in the SPLASH 2 platform are as follows: 1) extraction of *x* and *y* values for edge points; 2) derivation of values for θ; 3) computation of $x\cos\theta$; 4) computation of $y\sin\theta$; 5) calculation of *d* by adding the partial sums; 6) forming an address into the accumulator array for every *d*-θ pair; and 7) incrementing the value stored at that address. These operations have been mapped to SPLASH 2 devices X0-X16 as shown in Figure 4. The components of this are described below.

There are fourteen Hough processors on a SPLASH 2 processor board. In addition, one processing element (PE) serves to queue the frame data (since throughput is data dependent), and another PE serves as a task dispatcher. The task dispatcher examines each pixel value. If the pixel is an edge point, the pixel's column

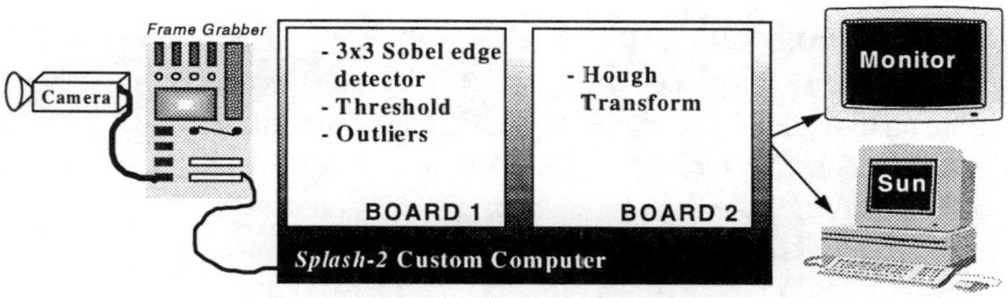

Figure 3. The laboratory system use for the Hough transform implementation.

and row within the image are passed to an available Hough processing element. The row and column serve as *x* and *y* values, respectively. This PE also serves to broadcast the appropriate *sine* and *cosine* factors to the slave PEs. All of the PEs are in lock-step.

Within each Hough PE, the generated Hough array is stored in a static RAM (attached to each PE), and is quantized to 512 values of θ (corresponding to the range [-90°, 90°) in steps of 180/512 degrees) and 512 discrete values of *d* (covering the range [-722, 721)). Each Hough processor performs the computations $x\cos\theta$ and $y\sin\theta$ in a four-step process. Each PE accepts the two 9-bit quantities *x* and *y* (indicating the address of the edge point in image space), uses a 9-bit counter to increment from 0 to 511 for each quantized value of θ, accepts broadcast values for $\cos\theta$ from the task dispatcher, and performs a 13×13-bit signed multiplication to compute $x\cos\theta$. Likewise, values for $\sin\theta$, are accepted from the task dispatcher, and another 13×13-bit multiplication is performed to compute $y\sin\theta$. An adder is used to generate $d = x\cos\theta + y\sin\theta$. An address into the Hough array is generated by concatenating the 9-bit quantity θ and a scaled 9-bit quantity *d*. This 18-bit value is used as an index into the attached RAM. A 4-clock read-modify-write operation is used to increment the indexed RAM location. As mentioned earlier, all of these operations are combined into a 4-clock pipeline.

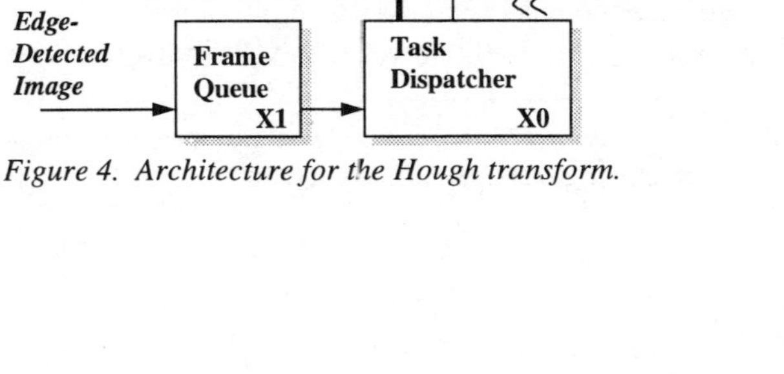

Figure 4. Architecture for the Hough transform.

3.3. Discussion

The amount of processing required by the Hough transform is data dependent. For each edge point in the image, a constant number of calculations are needed for tracing through the accumulator array. Post-processing is needed to combine separate Hough arrays from each PE, and to detect peaks in the composite array. Considering only arithmetic operations (disregarding internal data movement), and neglecting operations associated with input edge detection, this task performs approximately 310 million operations per second.[2] This application is easily extendible to multiple SPLASH processor boards for higher throughput.

A sample image processed by the Hough transform is provided in Figure 8.

4 Pyramid Generation

4.1 Image Pyramids

Multiresolution image processing techniques have emerged over the past decade as important components of advanced image analysis systems. Such computer vision tasks as stereo matching, motion analysis and object recognition routinely utilize image information at different levels of detail. This is done for reasons of efficiency and simplicity. For example, the photograph of a building may consist of large-scale objects such as walls, small-scale objects such as doorknobs and bricks, and medium-scale objects of intermediate size. These different entities can best be detected by using techniques that operate at the appropriate level of image resolution.

A standard data structure which contains image data at different levels of resolution is the *image pyramid*. An image pyramid is constructed by recursively filtering and subsampling an input image, creating a hierarchy of images of decreasing size and spatial resolution. Although a number of pyramid types have been developed, the most popular are the Gaussian and Laplacian pyramids [Burt82] which are illustrated in Figure 9. Each image in a Gaussian pyramid is formed by smoothing and subsampling the image at the previous level. Laplacian pyramids contain band-pass versions of the images, so that each level represents intensity edges at a particular resolution..

After a pyramid has been constructed for a given image, analysis can begin at the lower-resolution portion of the pyramid to guide processing at higher-resolution levels. For some tasks (such as surveillance and road following) this approach can greatly reduce the overall amount of processing required.

4.2 Gaussian Pyramid Generation

The standard technique for generating a Gaussian pyramid is described in [Burt82]. The original image g_0 is processed to generate the lower-resolution image g_1, which is in turn processed to generate the lower-resolution image g_2, etc. The sequence of images g_0, g_1, . . ., g_{N-1} is called the Gaussian pyramid. Each image g_k is at half the resolution (in both dimensions) as g_{k-1}, so that the number of pixels at each level is one quarter of the number at the previous level.

This is illustrated in Figure 5. Each pixel value in g_k is obtained by a weighted sum of pixels from g_{k-1}, computed over a 5x5 neighborhood as follows:

$$g_k(i,j) = \sum_{m=-2}^{2} \sum_{n=-2}^{2} w(m,n)\, g_{k-1}(2i+m, 2j+n).$$

For simplicity, this process is referred to as REDUCE when computed for all values *(i, j)* at level *k*:

$$g_k = \text{REDUCE}\,(g_{k-1})$$

To simplify computational requirements, the 5x5 filter w is typically made separable: $w(m,n) = w_x(n)\, w_y(m)$. In addition, it is usually normalized, symmetric, and unimodal so that it resembles the Gaussian function. The weighting patterns that have been chosen for SPLASH 2 are [1/16 1/4 3/8 1/4 1/16] for w_x and the transpose of this for w_y. Because w is separable, an image can be filtered by the one-dimensional (1D) filters w_x and w_y in sequence. The two 1D filters are considerably simpler to implement in hardware than the single 2D filter that they replace. Powers of 2 have been chosen for the denominators so that filtering can be accomplished using only shift-and-add circuitry.

4.3 Implementation for Gaussian Pyramids

A block diagram of the SPLASH 2 implementation for real-time Gaussian pyramid generation is given in Figure 6. The FPGA designated as X0 simply receives image pixels and passes them to FPGA X1 through the crossbar. Four 8-bit pixels are presented within each 36-bit word, and the input data is updated every four

---

[2]Formal definitions of MIP ratings (or other benchmarks) for custom computing machines remain undefined.

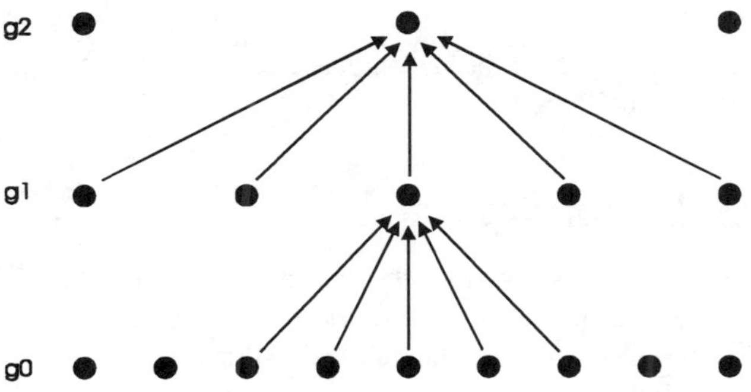

Figure 5. One dimensional representation of Gaussian pyramid generation. Each row of dots represents an image within one level of the pyramid. Each dot represents one pixel, which is computed as the weighted average of 5 pixel values from the level below it. Notice that the pixel spacing doubles from one level to the next, while the same weighting pattern is used to generate all new levels. (Adapted from [Burt82].)

SPLASH 2 clock periods. The processing steps, in sequence, are horizontal convolution by w_x, (X1), vertical convolution by w_y (X2 and X3), storage of g_1 (X4), generation and storage of g_2 through g_4 (X5-X8), and output selection (X9). Image resolutions are reduced from 512x512 (for g_0) to 32x32 (g_4). X1 performs the convolution by w_x, resamples to eliminate half of the pixels per image row, and passes the result to X2. Some buffering is required because each computation involves the weighted sum of *five* pixels, whereas only *four* are received at a time.

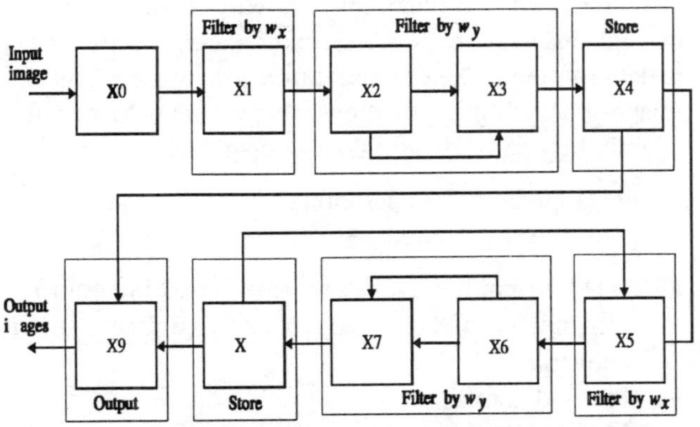

Figure 6. SPLASH 2 implementation of a 5-level Gaussian pyramid generator. This design can generate the upper 4 levels at video frame rates of 30 images/second. Xilinx chips X5-X8 duplicate the circuitry in X1-X4.

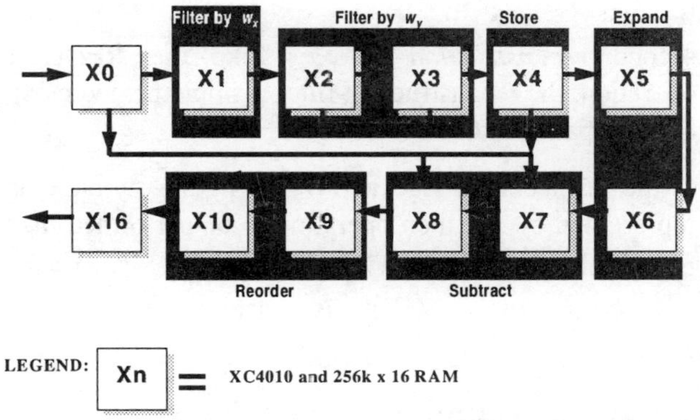

Figure 7. SPLASH 2 *implementation for simultaneous Gaussian and Laplacian pyramids.*

Devices X2 and X3 work together to perform the convolution by w_y. Each computation requires five image pixels from five successive rows. This requires that four previous rows must be stored and accessed simultaneously. To accomplish this, X2 and X3 redundantly store image rows in their respective RAMs. The crossbar is used to pass the untouched pixel stream. X2 computes three of the five partial sums, and passes this result to X3 directly. X3 adds this to the remaining two partial sums. This result is passed to X4, which resamples the image in the vertical dimension and stores the complete image g_1 in memory.

Xilinx devices X5-X8 generate the remaining three levels of the pyramid. The design is such that these devices duplicate the circuitry contained in X1-X4. Because of the reduction in image sizes, each successive level of the pyramid takes one forth of the time required at the previous level. Working at the same clock rate, X5-X8 are able to generate g_2 through g_4 (by recirculating from X8 to X5) in less than one third the time required to generate g_1. X9 multiplexes the results from X4 and X8 to deliver g_1 through g_4 as output, in sequence, simultaneously while the next image is entering the pipeline.

4.4 Laplacian Pyramid Generation

A Laplacian pyramid may be described as a sequence of "difference images," where each image is the difference between two successive levels of the Gaussian pyramid [Burt82]. To accomplish this, the resolution of the image at level *k+1* must be increased to the resolution at level *k* before subtraction can occur. This operation is known as EXPAND, and is accomplished by up-sampling the image produced at level *k+1* (by inserting zeros between each sample), and interpolating with a second *reconstruction* filter. Like the REDUCE operation, the reconstruction filter is implemented using a 5×5 separable window filter.

If the Laplacian image at level k in the pyramid is represented by h_k, then operation to be performed may be written as $h_k = g_k - \text{EXPAND}\ (g_{k+1})$. Since image g_N does not exist, it is customary to define $h_{N-1} = g_{N-1}$.

4.5 Implementation for Simultaneous Gaussian and Laplacian Pyramids

Additional circuitry is needed when the Laplacian pyramid is to be generated along with the Gaussian pyramid. The design discussed here requires six more FPGAs, placing the total above those available on one SPLASH 2 board. It was decided to reduce the computational speed to half of video frame rate by devoting X5-X8 to Laplacian pyramid generation (rather than to the Gaussian pyramid as in the earlier section).

This is illustrated in Figure 7. Devices X1-X4 operate as before, except that X4 can now feed back through the crossbar to X1 to permit recirculation of Gaussian pyramid levels. By adopting this approach, only alternate video frames will be processed. X5 and X6 are now devoted to the EXPAND operation. X7 and X8 accept data from X4 and X6 and perform pixel-by-pixel subtraction to generate a difference image. X9 and X10 reformat the images for output.

4.6 Discussion

The implementations described above compare favorably with a custom VLSI design developed at Sarnoff Research Center [vand92]. This chip, known as PYR, can produce both a Gaussian and Laplacian pyramid for a 512 x 480 image in 22.7 ms, using a clock rate of 15.7 MHz. The chip size is approximately 300x300 mil, and is packaged in an 84-pin PLCC.

The pyramid implementations described in this paper are *almost* as sophisticated. The SPLASH 2 designs are currently limited to a fixed input image size of 512×512 pixels, unlike the PYR chip, and the SPLASH 2 implementation is considerably larger. However, the processing speeds are comparable, particularly if a second SPLASH 2 board is used to accommodate both pyramid types at frame rate. Considering only arithmetic operations, this application performs in excess of 500 million operations per second. Example images that have been computed using SPLASH 2 are shown in Figure 9.

5 Summary

This paper has described the design and implementation of two nontrivial image-processing algorithms on the SPLASH 2 custom computing platform. The two algorithms -- the Hough transform and Gaussian/Laplacian pyramid generation -- are common in image analysis and are computationally intensive. Both may be described as mappings from an input image to data structures containing new images.

Gaussian pyramid generation has been designed for real-time operation at the standard video frame rate of 30 images/second. The processing rate for generating Hough arrays is more difficult to quantify. This is because Hough processing is linear in the number of edge points in the input image. The design given here can utilize a PE (consisting of one FPGA and one static RAM) that can be replicated over the number of SPLASH 2 boards that are available.

It is significant that SPLASH 2 can be configured to perform either task at performance levels that rival or equal those of dedicated, application-specific hardware. Furthermore, with a sufficient number of SPLASH 2 array boards, these two tasks (along with others) could be pipelined to operate concurrently.

Perhaps the major architectural limitation of SPLASH 2 for real-time image processing is the local FPGA-to-RAM interface. Since dual-port RAMs are not provided, a read-modify-write operation requires 4 clock cycles. This operation is used extensively in the designs discussed here. A secondary architectural issue is data routing. The crossbar offers great flexibility, but image-processing applications always seem to beg for slightly higher bandwidth than is available.

Other applications operational on the laboratory *VTSplash* system include:

- 2-D Fast Fourier Transform (using floating point).
- Expandable 8×8 convolver (online filter adjustment).
- Pan and zoom.
- Median filtering.
- Morphologic operators
- Histogram and graphical display.
- Region detection and labeling
- Profile classifier.

6 Acknowledgments

The entire VTSPLASH team at Virginia Tech contributed to the work described in this paper. In addition to the authors, the team includes Brad Fross, Jeff Nevits, Jim Peterson, Ramana Rachakonda, Nabeel Shirazi, and Adit Tarmaster. The authors are also indebted to Jeff Arnold and Duncan Buell of the Supercomputing Research Center, and to the Institute for Defense Analyses.

7 Bibliography

[Arno92] J. M. Arnold, D. A. Buell, and E. G. Davis, "Splash 2," *Proceedings: 4th Annual ACM Symposium on Parallel Algorithms and Architectures*, pp. 316-322, 1992.

[Arno93] J. M. Arnold, "The Splash 2 Software Environment," *Proceedings: 1st IEEE Workshop on FPGAs for Custom Computing Machines*, pp. 88-93, Apr. 1993.

[Burt83] P. J. Burt and E. H. Adelson, "The Laplacian Pyramid as a Compact Image Code," *IEEE Transactions on Communications*, vol. COM-31, no. 4, pp. 532-540, Apr. 1983.

[Duda72] R. O. Duda and P. E. Hart, "Use of the Hough Transform to Detect Lines and Curves in Pictures," *Communications of the ACM*, vol. 15. pp. 11-15, 1972.

[vand92] G. S. van der Wal and P. J. Burt, "A VLSI Pyramid Chip for Multiresolution Image Analysis," *International Journal of Computer Vision*, vol. 8, no. 3, pp. 177-189, 1992.

[Houg62] P. V. C. Hough, "A Method and Means for Recognizing Complex Patterns," US Pattent No. 3,069,654, 1962.

[Xili91] Xilinx, Inc., *The Programmable Gate Arrays Users Book,* San Jose, California, 1991.

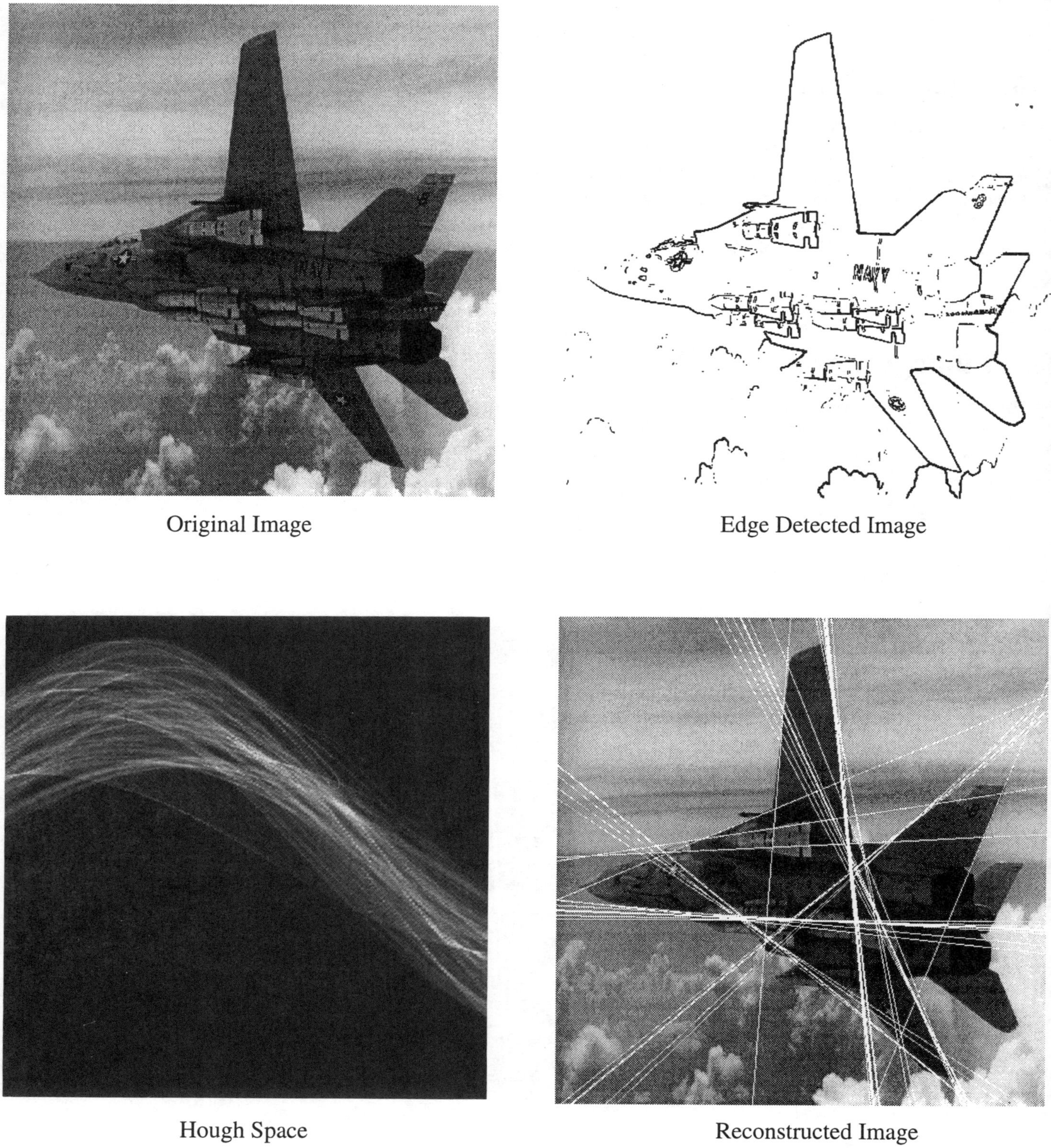

Figure 8. Hough transform example: a) input image, b) iput image after edge detection, c) Hough representation of input image, and d) overlay of detected lines onto the input image.

Figure 9. (a) Gaussian (low-pass) and (b) Laplacian (band-pass) pyramids. As one progresses toward higher levels of the Gaussian pyramid, increasingly larger image details are removed. The same is true for the Laplacian pyramid, except that edge information is represented. The top level of the Laplacian pyramid is missing in this example.

Comparing the Performance of FPGA-Based Custom Computers with General-Purpose Computers for DSP Applications

Neil W. Bergmann and J. Craig Mudge

CSIRO/Flinders Joint Research Centre in Information Technology
Flinders University, GPO Box 2100, Adelaide, SA 5001, AUSTRALIA
Tel: 61-8-201-3109; Fax: 61-8-201-3507
E-mail: neil@jrc.flinders.edu.au, jcmudge@jrc.flinders.edu.au

Abstract

When FPGA logic circuits are incorporated within a stored-program computer, the result is a machine where the programmer can design both the software and the hardware that will execute that software. This paper first describes some of the more important custom computers, and their potential weakness as DSP implementation platforms. It then describes a new custom computing architecture which is specifically designed for efficient implementation of DSP algorithms. Finally, it presents a simple performance comparison of a number of DSP implementation alternatives, and concludes that (i) the new custom computing architecture is worthy of further investigation, and (ii) that custom computers based only on FPGA execution units show little performance improvement over state-of-the art workstations.

1. Custom computing

Field Programmable Gate Arrays are now a popular implementation style for digital logic systems and subsystems [1]. Where the programming configuration is held in static RAM, the logic function implemented by those FPGAs can be dynamically reconfigured, in fractions of a second, by rewriting the contents of the SRAM configuration memory. When such FPGA logic circuits are incorporated within a stored-program computer, the result is a machine where the programmer can design both the software and the hardware that will execute that software. Such a machine, where the hardware can be reconfigured and customised on a program-by-program basis, is called a *custom computer* [2].

Several researchers report algorithm speed-up rates of hundreds or thousands of times compared to conventional desktop workstations, and often significantly greater than the best reported results using "conventional" super-computers, especially for those algorithms which can be decomposed into many, simple, parallel processing tasks. Many Digital Signal Processing (DSP) algorithms can be decomposed into parallel tasks, but each task often involves relatively complex operations such as a multiply-accumulate. DSP algorithms are therefore less clearly suitable candidates for efficient implementation on a custom computer.

This paper surveys some of the most important custom computers, presents the authors' work on a new custom computing architecture specifically designed to support DSP applications, and analyses the performance of various implementation alternatives for DSP algorithms.

2. Previous methods of customising computers for DSP

There is a constant tension in computer design between being general purpose, i.e., doing a wide range of computational tasks moderately well, and being application specific, i.e., doing a smaller range of computational tasks much better, usually at the cost of either increased system resources or of poorer "general purpose" performance.

There have been many different approaches investigated over the years for improving the performance of a general purpose computer for the implementation of DSP algorithms. Custom computers represent the latest technology which shows some promise for this task.

A common approach to improving the performance of a general purpose computer for specific applications is the addition of application specific hardware, such as

0-8186-5490-2/94 $03.00 © 1994 IEEE

graphics accelerators for computer displays, or image and video compression chips for multi-media workstations. These can provide excellent speedup for that specific application, but provide no performance improvement when other applications are run. This approach represents one extreme of the generality/cost spectrum.

Another common approach, at the opposite end of the spectrum, is the addition of a general-purpose parallel processing sub-system to a host processor. Such add-on parallel processing boards have seemed an obvious and attractive enhancement to desktop computers for some time, but they have achieved only limited success in the marketplace. It is our conjecture that this is because of difficulty of programming, and high cost resulting from low sales volumes. Additionally, such parallel processing systems have commonly been inefficient at implementing the fine-grain, communications-intensive parallel algorithms associated with DSP applications. Recently, general-purpose, Digital Signal Processor chips such as the TMS320C40 [3] have become available. These combine high speed, floating-point arithmetic performance with high speed interprocessor communication channels incorporating individual DMA controllers. Arrays of such chips provide a formidable challenge for other DSP implementation alternatives.

The idea of a computer which can be customised, under programmer control, on an application-by-application basis, is not new. A writable control store within a micro-programmed computer allows the programmer to design application-specific machine instructions, which can make better use of the existing functional units within the computer, and hence improve the performance of specific applications, including those within DSP [4]. Such performance improvement has been limited because of the interpretative nature of microprogramming.

A custom computer goes one step further than a writable control store by allowing design of new functional units, rather than simply making better use of existing functional units.

3. Some Existing Custom Computers

In this section, we examine three of the best known custom computers as examples of the current state of the art in this area.

3.1 SPLASH

SPLASH and SPLASH II [5] are custom computers which have been developed at the Supercomputer Research Corporation, Maryland. The SPLASH II processor consists of an extendable number of processor boards, with each board containing 16 Xilinx 4010 FPGAs [6], connected as a linear array, plus an extra Xilinx 4010 for control, with all of the FPGAs having some additional interconnections via a central crossbar switch. The SPLASH boards can communicate with a SUN Sparcstation host via input and output FIFOs, which are on an additional interface board connecting the SUN and SPLASH array.

Once configured, data is streamed through the SPLASH processor using the systolic array programming model, with results streaming back to the host. The SPLASH processor is most suited to simple streaming operations, and has shown significant speedups over conventional supercomputers for tasks such as text searching and genetic database searching.

SPLASH is usually programmed by specifying the function of the FPGAs using VHDL, which is then automatically translated into an FPGA configuration file. Current research [5] is examining the use of other programming languages, such as data parallel C.

3.2 Programmable Active Memory

The PAM (Programmable Active Memory) has been under development at DEC's Paris Research Labs for several years [7], [8]. The latest version, PeRLe-1, consists of a 5x5 array of Xilinx 3090 FPGAs, connected to local 32-bit wide RAM banks, and also, via a 100MB/s TURBOchannel interface, to a DEC desktop workstation. The workstation writes data to the RAM banks, which is processed by the Xilinx array and returned to the RAM banks, from where the host then retrieves the results.

Programming the PAM consists of designing software components for the host, and hardware components for the PAM array. The latter can be done by writing a program in a conventional programming language (Lisp, C++, and Esterel are used) using a specialised library. The program describes logic modules by their bit-level logic equations, or by using standard library modules such as adders, and registers.

Ten applications are described in [8], including long multiplication, RSA cryptography, data compression, string matching, heat and Laplace equations, a Boltzmann machine neural network, 3-D graphics acceleration, and the discrete cosine transform. Results are very encouraging; e.g., the PAM implementation of 512-bit RSA cryptography was faster than any other reported implementation in any technology as of February 1990, and 10 times faster than the next best reported implementation on a custom VLSI circuit.

3.3 The Virtual Computer

The Virtual Computer [9], from the Virtual Computer Corporation, provides approximately 500,000 programmable logic gates, using an array of 52 Xilinx 4010 FPGAs and 24 ICUBE Field Programmable Interconnect Devices, 8 megabytes of SRAM, and 16k x 16-bit 25ns dual-port RAMs. The system also has 3 x 64-bit I/O ports - one for hardware configuration / read-back, and two for general purpose I/O such as connection to a host workstation. The central processing array of 40 Xilinx FPGAs, called the Virtual Array, consists of four Virtual Pipelines, each with 10 FPGAs connected to dual-port RAMs at each edge of the pipeline, with the other port of these dual-port RAMs connected to a control FPGA with a RAM buffer.

The array is intended to be a flexible computing resource, with a typical application on a host processor loading data into SRAM, which is streamed through the pipeline under local control via the dual-port RAMs. Results would take the reverse route back to the host. All of the FPGAs are designed to be reprogrammed in parallel, so that the function of all 500,000 logic gates can be changed in 25 ms.

It is intended that programming could be at several levels. At the highest level, a run-time function library would be provided. Next would be translation of VHDL or C++ code into hardware implementations, and at the lowest level would be full-custom hand placement and routing. The Virtual Computer is interesting in that it is designed as a commercial product (initially targetted at the research community), rather than as a research vehicle.

4. CC-DSP: A New Custom Computer

4.1 Weaknesses of Existing Custom Computing Architectures for DSP

It is useful to examine those applications where custom computing has shown the greatest speedups. In general, such applications can be decomposed into many parallel computations, each of which can be implemented by a low-gate-count processing element. Thus many such elements are able to be implemented on the available FPGA resources of a custom computer. Typical applications in this category include text searching and genetic database matching.

DSP applications often exhibit a high degree of potential parallelism, but are less suitable for implementation on a custom computer because of the high gate count of the arithmetic operations (addition and multiplication) typically required for each parallel processing element. For this reason, we are now exploring a new custom computing architecture explicitly targetted at the efficient implementation of digital signal and image processing applications.

4.2 Our New Architecture

Our decision to concentrate our efforts on a custom computing architecture which is specifically designed for the support of DSP algorithms leads us naturally to the provision of specific hardware support for the arithmetic operations which dominate many DSP algorithms, but which are costly to implement using FPGA programmable gates.

Our proposed architecture has developed from previous work into the rapid prototyping of DSP algorithms [10]. An experimental system was built from an Algotronix CHS2x4 (Configurable Hardware System) [11] PC plug-in board containing 8 CAL1024 chips and 512 kbytes of RAM, plus a second plug-in board with 4 custom VLSI chips, each containing four 16-bit, bit-serial multiply-accumulate units. The major drawback of our initial architecture is its reliance on a custom-designed arithmetic resource chip. Our limited design and fabrication budget means that such chips have only moderate arithmetic performance, and even a small array of such chips will at best be able to match the arithmetic performance of modern CPU chips. Attempts to code up simple DSP algorithms for this system, such as FIR filters, have also demonstrated weaknesses in the data transfer capability of the CHS2x4 system for communications-intensive applications.

We have therefore commenced work on a more ambitious architecture [12], which more closely couples an arithmetic chip, static RAM, and reconfigurable logic within a processing node as shown in figure 1. This node is then replicated a number of times to produce a complete custom-computing co-processor for a workstation. It seems likely that this architecture will use commercially available arithmetic chips, providing of the order of 20 MFLOPS each. Eight such processing nodes would give some 160 MFLOPS of processing power. The architectural and algorithmic challenge then becomes to ensure that the reconfigurable logic chips and static RAM chips can store, communicate and organise operands for these arithmetic chips to allow such a peak processing performance to be sustained.

It is useful to review our progress in the design of such a custom computer in the light of the other custom computing projects underway internationally. In particular, this paper examines whether such an architecture does give some performance advantage compared to the more general-purpose custom computing

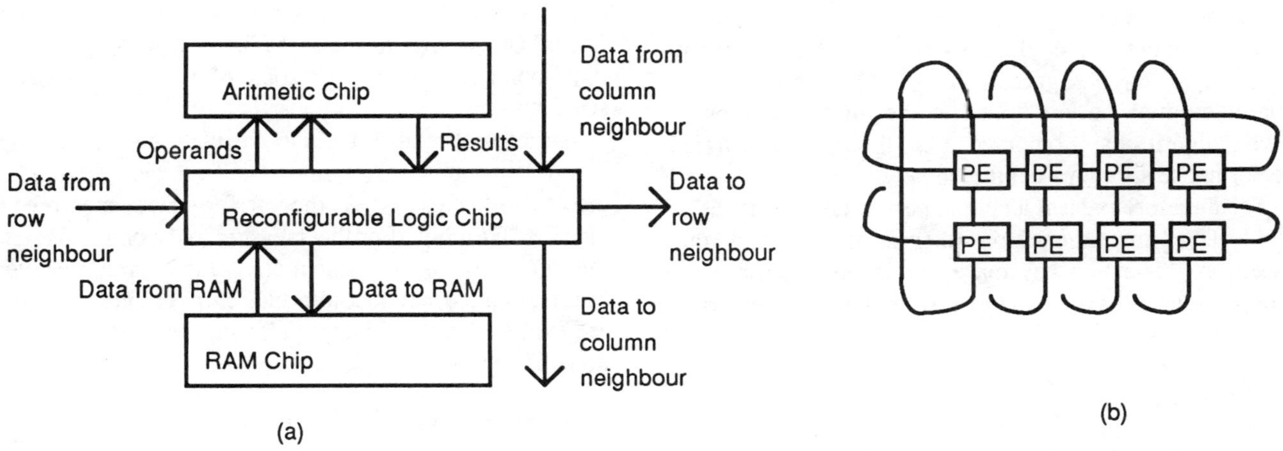

Figure 1: A new custom computing architecture showing (a) processing node structure, and (b) processing node interconnection.

architectures described above, for the specific application area of digital signal processing.

5. Other Computing Architectures for DSP

To use for later comparison two more conventional DSP implementation methods are briefly described below.

5.1 Alpha-based workstation.

Digital Equipment Corporation's Alpha 21064 processor chip [15], with a system clock rate of 200 MHz, is indicative of the current state of the art in desktop workstation performance. The 21064 chip also forms the basis for the recently announced massively-parallel processing (MPP) supercomputer from Cray Research, Inc [15].

Of particular interest here is the excellent arithmetic performance of the processor. The 21064's pipelined ALU can accept new operands on every clock cycle, with a ten-cycle latency before results appear. It is reasonable to assume that careful coding of DSP inner loops to maximise pipeline occupancy is no more difficult than custom computer hardware design. The peak floating-point (or integer) computation rate is then 200MFLOPS. This rate would require operands to be available in registers, and instructions to be available in the cache to be sustained. Assumptions about a suitable sustained computation rate for comparison with custom computing approaches are given later.

5.2 TMS320C40 Parallel Processing Development System

The TMS320C40 [3], with a clock rate of 40MHz, is indicative of the current state-of-the-art in software-programmable digital signal processor chips. Important features of the TMS320C40 are the ALU design, and the interprocessor communications design.

The ALU is based on a single-cycle floating-point unit, which has separate multiplication and addition units to allow these two operations to be done in parallel. Single-cycle operation eases programming of inner loops compared to the Alpha's highly-pipelined unit. Peak arithmetic performance is then 80 MFLOPS, with a 40 MHz clock.

The TMS320C40 also has six, byte-wide, bi-directional interprocessor communications ports with a transfer rate of 20 Mbytes/s each. Each port has a dedicated DMA controller, which relieves the CPU of much of the burden associated with the high interprocessor communications in fine-grained, parallel DSP algorithms.

Texas Instruments market a parallel processing board based on the TMS320C40, called the Parallel Processing Development System (PPDS) [3], which can be attached to a general purpose workstation. The TMS-PPDS contains 4 interconnected TMS320C40 chips, plus global and local memory banks. Its peak arithmetic computation rate is then 4 * 80 MFLOPS = 320 MFLOPS. The PPDS will be used as an element of the performance comparison in the next section.

6. Performance comparison of programmable DSP Architectures

As mentioned previously, the high logical complexity of the arithmetic operations which are central to many DSP algorithms suggests that FPGA-based custom computers may be less suited to the implementation of such algorithms compared to their demonstrated performance speedups in other areas.

We therefore present a simple performance analysis of some DSP implementation alternatives, to test this assertion. The two key questions in any performance comparison are what to compare, and how to compare them.

6.1 What to Compare?

We have chosen to compare DSP implementation systems which are of the order of a single printed circuit board, and which might be used to improve the DSP performance of a desktop computer workstation. The following six systems will be compared.

State-of-the-Art Custom Computers

(i) *A single SPLASH II processor board.* Results for multiboard systems can be extrapolated from this result.

(ii) *The DEC PeRLe-1 system*

(iii) *The Virtual Computer*

Specialised DSP Custom Computer

(iv) *CC-DSP*: The new (yet to be built) custom computer described in section 4.2 above is used, referred to as CC-DSP in this paper. We assume it consists of 8 PE's, each containing one RAM chip, one arithmetic chip, and one reconfigurable logic chip. For the arithmetic chip, we assume an arithmetic performance of one floating-point multiply-accumulate every 100ns can be sustained, which is consistent with existing state-of-the-art ALU chips (e.g. [16]).

General-Purpose Processors

(v) *A TMS-PPDS consisting of four TMS320C40s.*

(vi) *A workstation using a 200MHz DEC Alpha 21064 processor.*

6.2 How to Compare Them?

The goal of this analysis is to give some ballpark figures for the various DSP implementation alternatives to give some insight into their relative merit.

A very straightforward analysis has been undertaken, based on a number of assumptions which are listed below. The performance analysis is a static analysis based on the stated performance of various components. We have not implemented any benchmark algorithms on the various alternatives and we have not measured the actual performance of any of the systems.

Performance is described in terms of millions of multiply-accumulate operations per second (megaMAC/s) for the case of both floating-point and fixed-point arithmetic, for each of the "single-board"-sized systems.

An attempt is also made to calculate the cost of each board, using a simple measure of "number of chips" as the cost. This gives the performance measure of megaMAC/s/chip. For this measure, only processing and interprocessor communication chips are counted. Memory chips, and host-interface chips are not counted.

Details of the individual performance calculations are given in section 6.4, below.

6.3 Assumptions

Assumption 1. The limiting factor in DSP performance is the computation of multiply-accumulate operations, which dominate many DSP algorithms, such as digital filters, linear transforms, matrix multiplications, and artificial neural networks.

Assumption 2. For the previously-mentioned conventional custom computing architectures, which all use Xilinx FPGA's, the cost of a fixed-point multiplication is based on a recent design by Casselman [13]. This 24-bit fractional multiplier requires 48 CLBs (configurable logic blocks) within a 4000 series Xilinx FPGA, and produces a result in 16 clock cycles at 16 MHz. We assume that a fixed-point addition can be done in the same time using an extra 2 CLB's for a total of 50 CLB's for a fixed-point multiply-accumulate operation, at 1 million operations per second.

Assumption 3. For the same conventional custom computing architectures, the cost of a floating-point multiplication is based on the same design by Casselman [13]. A single-precision floating point multiplier requires 60 CLBs within a 4000 series Xilinx FPGA, and produces a result in 16 clock cycles at 16 MHz. We estimate, given some experience with previous floating-point operator designs [14], that a floating-point adder requires a similar-sized circuit to a floating-point multiplier, which would give a total of 120 CLB's for both. We can assume some saving for a combined floating-point multiply-accumulate operator, and so we will assume 100 CLB's are required. Operating speed is again 1 million operations per second.

Assumption 4. For the same conventional custom computing architectures, it is assumed that 25% of chip area is required for control, and other overhead hardware such as multiplexers and registers. Most of the systems described use Xilinx 4010 FPGA's, with 400 CLB's.

Accounting for the 25% overhead leaves 300 CLB's for the multiply-accumulate operations. Hence we assume that a Xilinx 4010 can provide a performance of 6 megaMAC/s (fixed-point) or 3 megaMAC/s (floating-point). We further assume that the Xilinx 3090s used in the DEC PeRLe-1 can provide the same performance.

Assumption 5. For our new CC-DSP architecture, we assume 8 processing nodes, where each node is provided with a custom arithmetic support chip providing 10 million multiply-accumulate operations per second (80 million multiply-accumulate operations per second for the system). We assume that the reconfigurable logic chips in the system are used to control data flow to ensure that the FPU's are kept busy, but do not provide any additional multiply-accumulate resources.

Assumption 6. For the DEC Alpha 21064 workstation, Linpack 1000x1000 results [15] suggest a best-case sustained computation rate of 75% of the peak rate. Reducing this to 50% to account for general algorithm and system overheads, this gives 50 million multiply-accumulate operations per second. A nominal chip count of 10 is assigned to the Alpha-based workstation to account for the support chips needed for this processor.

Assumption 7. The TMS-PPDS has a peak processing rate of 4 * 80MFLOPS (each chip can do parallel floating-point multiply and add operations at 40 MHz). Since the processors have to deal with overhead instructions, as well as the floating-point operations, we suggest the same average floating-point computation rate as in assumption 6, i.e., 50% of the peak.

6.4 Performance and Cost Estimates

SPLASH II: A SPLASH II board consists of 16 Xilinx 4010 chips, a crossbar switch controlled by another Xilinx, plus some memory and interface circuitry. The 16 Xilinx chips provide 16*6 = 96 megaMAC/s fixed-point, and 16*3 = 48 megaMAC/s floating-point. The cost of the system is considered to be the 16 FPGAs plus another 16 chips for the crossbar switch and its control, giving a total cost of 32 chips. Performance/cost is 96/32 = 3 megaMAC/s/chip (fixed-point) and 48/32 = 1.5 megaMAC/s/chip (floating-point).

DECPeRLe-1: The DEC PeRLe-1 co-processor board consists of 25 Xilinx 3090 chips for the programming core, four RAM banks, plus additional FPGAs and logic circuits to control the RAM banks and general purpose interconnect. The 25 Xilinx chips provide 25*6 = 150 megaMAC/s fixed-point, and 25*3 = 75 megaMAC/s floating-point. We assign a total cost of 40 chips, giving performance/cost of 150/40 = 3.75 megaMAC/s/chip (fixed-point) and 75/40 = 1.9 megaMAC/s/chip (floating-point).

Virtual Computer: The Virtual Computer contains a total of 52 Xilinx 4010 FPGAs and 24 ICUBE FPICs, 8 megabytes of SRAM, and 16k x 16-bit 25ns dual-port RAMs. 40 Xilinx chips are available for arithmetic operations, giving 40*6 = 240 megaMAC/s fixed-point, and 40*3 = 120 megaMAC/s floating-point. The cost of the system is considered to be 52+24 = 76 chips, giving performance of 240/76 = 3.1 megaMAC/s/chip (fixed-point) and 120/76 = 1.6 megaMAC/s/chip (floating-point).

CC-DSP: Our new custom computing architecture for DSP has 8 nodes, with each node consisting of one FPGA, one arithmetic chip of 10 megaMAC/s performance, and one RAM chip. Total performance is then 80 megaMAC/s, fixed- or floating-point. Cost, excluding RAM, is 16 chips, giving 5 megaMAC/s/chip, fixed- or floating-point.

TMS-PPDS: The peak performance of the 4-processor system is 4 * 40 = 160 megaMAC/s. With a sustained rate of 50% of the peak this gives 80 megaMAC/s. Examination of the PPDS shows about four extra support chips (excluding RAM) for each processor chip, giving a total cost of 20 chips, and hence 4 megaMAC/s/chip fixed- or floating-point.

Alpha 21064 Workstation: The peak performance of this system is 200MFLOPS = 100 megaMAC/s. With a sustained rate of 50% of the peak this gives 50 megaMAC/s. With a nominal workstation motherboard cost of 10 chips (excluding RAM), this gives 5 megaMAC/s/chip fixed- or floating-point.

These calculations are summarised in Table 1 below.

6.5 Conclusions

Two conclusions can be drawn from the above, simple analysis.

The first is that our CC-DSP architecture gives a moderate performance improvement over other custom computing approaches for floating-point DSP applications, on a computation-per-chip basis, and so is worthy of further investigation. There is an insignificant (in terms of the resolution of this analysis) performance improvement for fixed-point DSP operations.

The second conclusion is that, for DSP applications, single-board custom computing approaches (including our CC-DSP) do not give any performance/cost

System	# of chips (# of Xilinx)	megaMAC/s (fixed-point) sustained/max	megaMAC/s/ chip (fixed-point) sustained	megaMAC/s (floating-point) sustained/max	megaMAC/s/chip (floating-point) sustained
SPLASH II board	32 (16)	96 / 96	3	48 / 48	1.5
DECPeRLe-1	40 (25)	150 / 150	3.75	75 / 75	1.9
Virtual Computer	76 (40)	240 / 240	3.1	120 / 120	1.6
Our CC-DSP	16	80 / 80	5	80 / 80	5
TMS-PPDS	20	80 / 160	4	80 / 160	4
Alpha Workstation	10 {nominal}	50 / 100	5	50 / 100	5

Table 1: Relative performance of DSP implementation solutions

improvement over the conventional parallel processing and uniprocessor approaches. The major reason for this is that both the TMS320C40 and Alpha 21064 have high-performance hardware support for floating-point arithmetic. Custom computers provide the best speedups compared to conventional workstations when they can implement in parallel hardware what the workstation needs to implement in serial software. DSP does not immediately appear to be such an application area.

The reason for the poor performance of the CC-DSP architecture is the unavailability of single chip ALU's which can match the floating-point performance of modern processors. The single-chip ALU's are largely limited by their ability to transfer operands and results to and from the chip, compared to the processors whose ALUs transfer data to and from local registers.

Finally, a general comment on the long-term sustainability of special purpose, or custom, architectures can be made. The TMS-PPDS and the Alpha workstation described here are both general purpose systems. Hence their technology progress functions will approximate that of logic technology. The new custom computing architecture presented here, because it is special purpose, will be manufactured in lower volumes and hence will tend to have a less steep technology progress function. Thus, it will be challenging for the custom architecture to sustain a competitive position. It is necessary that the arithmetic, SRAM and FPGA operand-handling components have the same slope of progress function as the general purpose systems. Furthermore, we require that the operand handling architecture built from FPGAs be scalable, so as to avoid a data communications bottleneck which will prevent full utilisation of the technology progress functions of these individual components.

We plan further work in this area to:

(a) get better performance measures than those used in the simple analysis presented in Table 1,

(b) decide on the best method to provide arithmetic resources for DSP within a custom computing architecture, and

(c) discern a demonstrably scalable design which can utilise the technology progress function of the individual components of our CC-DSP architecture.

7. Acknowledgments

This work is supported by the Australian Research Council under Grant A49132307. Thanks to Lui Cirocco for his assistance in the design of our next generation CC-DSP architecture.

8. References

[1] J. Rose, A. El Gamal, and A. Sangiovanni-Vincentelli, "Architecture of Field-Programmable Gate Arrays," *Proceedings of the IEEE*, 81(7), July 1993, pp 1013-1029.

[2] *Proceedings of IEEE Workshop on FPGA's for Custom Computing Machines*, Napa, April, 1993.

[3] *TMS320C4x Technical Brief*, Texas Instruments, 1991, pp 6.5-6.8

[4] L. R. Morris, and J.C. Mudge, "Speed Enhancement of Digital Signal Processing Software via Microprogramming a General Purpose Minicomputer," *Proceedings of ICASSP '77*, 1977.

[5] M. Gokhale, R. Minnich, "FPGA Computing in Data Parallel C," *Proceedings of IEEE Workshop on FPGA's for Custom Computing Machines*, Napa Valley, April, 1993.

[6] The XC4000 Data Book, Xilinx, Inc., San Jose, 1992.

[7] P. Bertin, D. Roncin, J. Vuilemin, "Introduction to Programmable Active Memories", *DEC Paris Research Labs, Research Report #3*, June, 1989.

[8] P. Bertin, D. Roncin, J. Vuilemin, "Programmable Active Memories: a Performance Assessment", *DEC Paris Research Labs, Research Report #24*, 1993.

[9] S. Casselman, "Virtual computing", *Proceedings of IEEE Workshop on FPGA's for Custom Computing Machines,* Napa Valley, April, 1993.

[10] N.W. Bergmann, H. Wong, P. Sutton, "A Rapid Prototyping and Implementation Method for Systolic Array Digital Signal Processors", *Proceedings of 1991 Microelectronics Conference,* Melbourne, pp 91-93, 1991.

[11] *CHS2x4 User Manual,* Algotronix Ltd, Edinburgh, Scotland, February, 1992.

[12] N.W. Bergmann, J.C. Mudge and L.R. Cirroco, "FPGA-Based Custom Computers", *1993 Australian Conference on Microelectronics*, Gold Coast, October 1993.

[13] S. Casselman, "FPGA multiplier", *info-fpga electronic mail posting from sc@vcc.com,* October, 1993.

[14] D. Giarola & N.W. Bergmann, "Design and Testing of a Bit-Serial Floating Point Adder", & "Design and Testing of a Bit-Serial Floating Point Multiplier", *University of Queensland, Electrical Engineering Dept., Internal Reports No. EE89/5 & EE89/9*, May, 1989.

[15] E. McLellan, "The Alpha AXP Architecture and 21064 Processor", *IEEE Micro, 13(3)*, June 1993, pp36-47.

[16] M. Birman, A. Samuels, G. Chu, T Chuk, L. Hu, J. McLeod, J. Barnes, "Developing the WTL3170/3171 Sparc Floating-Point Coprocessors", *IEEE Micro, 10(1),* pp. 55-65, February, 1990.

An FPGA-based Custom Coprocessor for Automatic Image Segmentation Applications

Greg J. Gent, Scott R. Smith, and Regina L. Haviland

Department of Electrical Engineering
Southern Illinois University
Edwardsville, IL

Abstract

This paper describes a customized computing platform we are developing to accelerate a computer vision application. An FPGA-based coprocessor solution is derived which accelerates most of the compute-intensive calculations of a template deforming image segmentation algorithm. Design issues are identified and performance results reported. The results are parameterized so that alternative solutions can be evaluated according to technological advances.

We discuss how implementing such a design with available reconfigurable logic platforms can be a worthwhile tool for the development of customized FPGA-based computing solutions.

1. Introduction

We have designed a special-purpose computing system to accelerate an image segmentation algorithm. The system consists of a host computer augmented with an FPGA-based attached processing machine. A systolic array which performs the majority of the algorithm's computations was designed and implemented using a commercially available logic emulation board (the CAT-12 Virtual ASIC board developed and marketed by Integrated Circuits Applications, Ltd. [1]). The array was integrated into the overall system via a "data feeder" unit which provides operands to the array, retrieves results from it, and provides memory to hold constants and other values required by the computations. We are implementing the data feeder using the AnyBoard developed by Van den Bout, et al at NCSU [2].

We were able to design the systolic array so that it could be applied to several different transformations called for by the algorithm. The algorithm is an iterative one in which the transformations use a different number of terms as the iterations progress. The coprocessor arrangement allowed for each of these variations that we wanted the systolic array to perform. This flexibility was possible in part by virtue of a sophisticated data feeder circuit.

Design issues are identified and performance results reported. The results are parameterized so that alternative solutions (involving differing numbers and types of FPGAs) can be evaluated according to technological advances in both FPGAs and high-performance microprocessors. These evaluations allow one to determine the cost-effectiveness of an FPGA-based custom solution when comparing the performance obtainable from workstation, or even parallel processor, solutions.

Several groups have demonstrated the benefits of using FPGAs to create customized, application-specific processing machines, e.g., [3],[4]. To fully realize the potential of this implementation strategy requires design methodologies that address the unique set of issues involved when utilizing FPGAs. In particular, designers cannot fit as much logic into a single IC as with gate arrays and full-custom ICs. Exact logic utilization and circuit timing figures cannot be ascertained until the design is actually placed and routed. Additionally, the number of ICs that a design must be partitioned across is several times that of non-programmable technologies. This increases the difficulty of optimally splitting up a design while working within each IC's I/O pin constraints.

In implementing our design, we are finding that the use of available reconfigurable logic platforms can lead to a more efficient design and development cycle for customized computing machines. The ability to quickly implement a design allows one to better identify and understand the above implementation issues earlier in the design process. Even if initial solutions are not optimal, they allow iterative improvements to be made. To a point, these improvements can be made while working with the "prototyping" hardware. After this, they become specifications for a customized FPGA solution. With these benefits the designer is in a better position to create a special purpose FPGA-based custom computing machine which is optimized for the targeted applications and that will meet the performance criteria.

The rest of the paper is organized as follows. Section 2 describes the segmentation algorithm. Section 3 provides details on the systolic array we designed. Section 4 discusses how the array is

0-8186-5490-2/94 $03.00 © 1994 IEEE

integrated into the total computing system, including a description of the data feeder. Results concerning the size and speed of the coprocessor are given in Section 5, followed by discussions and conclusions in Section 6.

2. Description of deformable template image segmentation algorithm

The algorithm for which we have designed a customized hardware solution performs image segmentation. This entails automatic identification of distinct objects within an image. The deformable template algorithm used here was proposed and detailed in [5]. It automatically segments novel images by deforming a template image so that it looks like the novel image. This template image has been manually segmented so that areas of interest are identified; it is also similar to and representative of the images that will be automatically processed (in our case MRI brain images). Automatic segmentation of the novel image is accomplished by applying the same deformations to the template's segmentation information. The idea is that, as the template image is made to look more like the image under study, the contours and edges of specific, identified areas also deform and move to the appropriate locations. Thus the manual segmentation data is mapped onto the new image.

Mathematically, this process can be expressed using the following equation, which expresses the error between a novel image, D, and the template image, T:

$$E(\Gamma) = \int | T(\mathbf{x} + \Gamma(\mathbf{x})) - D(\mathbf{x}) |^2 \, d\mathbf{x} \qquad \text{Eqn. 1}$$

Notice that the template's coordinates can undergo a mapping, Γ. The overall idea is to find a mapping which minimizes the error between the images. This mapping is the result of running the template deformation algorithm. To prevent the algorithm from dramatically changing the template (and thus losing the basic structural information of interest), an additional term is added to the error as shown:

$$I(\Gamma) = \alpha(\Delta\Gamma^1, \Delta\Gamma^2) + \int | T(\mathbf{x} + \Gamma(\mathbf{x})) - D(\mathbf{x}) |^2 \, d\mathbf{x} \qquad \text{Eqn. 2}$$

with Δ representing the Laplacian operator, α being a scale factor, and the superscripts on Γ identifying the dimensions of the image. It is this equation which is actually minimized. The minimization is accomplished using a gradient descent technique which iteratively updates the mapping and computes the resulting change in error.

The new term of Eqn. 2 is based on the change in the template displacements. Its magnitude increases the more the template is rearranged. This results in a penalty for trying to match the template to the image without maintaining the structure of the template. This mechanism disallows severe deformations thus preserving basic anatomical properties while still allowing subject to subject variations.

To evaluate $I(\Gamma)$, $\alpha(\Delta\Gamma^1, \Delta\Gamma^2)$ is expressed in the spectral domain using an orthonormal series expansion. The eigenvectors of $\alpha(\Delta\Gamma^1, \Delta\Gamma^2)$ are

$$\phi^1_{mn}(x_1, x_2) = \{ 2 \sin(\pi m x_1) \cos(\pi n x_2), 0 \} \qquad \text{Eqn. 3a}$$

$$\phi^2_{mn}(x_1, x_2) = \{ 0, 2 \cos(\pi n x_1) \sin(\pi m x_2) \} \qquad \text{Eqn. 3b}$$

with eigenvalues

$$\lambda_{mn} = \alpha \pi^2 (m^2 + n^2)$$

Therefore, $I(\Gamma)$ can be rewritten as

$$I(\Gamma) = \sum_{m,n=-\infty}^{\infty} \lambda_{mn}(\gamma^1_{mn} + \gamma^2_{mn}) + \int | T(\mathbf{x}+\Gamma(\mathbf{x})) - D(\mathbf{x}) |^2 d\mathbf{x} \qquad \text{Eqn. 4}$$

where

$$\gamma^k_{mn} = \int \Gamma^k(\mathbf{x}) \, \phi^k_{mn}(\mathbf{x}) \, d\mathbf{x}$$

The gradient descent updates mentioned above are done in the spectral domain. The error between the [deformed] template image and the novel image is still computed in the spatial domain. So, as the gradient descent iterations are performed, there is a need to transform certain values back and forth between domains. This makes up a large portion of the total computations required by the algorithm [6]. Some of the burden is relieved by using fewer expansion terms in the transformations for early iterations (m and n range just from 0 to h). As the iterations progress, and a solution approached, more and more terms are added (up to 7 for our applications). Even with this, approximately half of the computation time for the algorithm is spent doing the transformations. The hardware solution presented next has been designed to perform these transformations.

3. Design and Implementation of the Systolic Array

We were able to design a systolic array [7] that could be applied to the transform equations shown below:

$$\text{xdispl}(i,j) = \Gamma^1(i,j) = \qquad \text{Eqn. 5a}$$

$$2/\pi^2 \; \Sigma_{m=1,h} \Sigma_{n=0,h} \text{xcoeff}(m,n) \sin(\pi m j \Delta) \cos(\pi n i \Delta)/(n^2 + m^2)$$

$$\text{ydispl}(i,j) = \Gamma^2(i,j) = \qquad \text{Eqn. 5b}$$

$$2/\pi^2 \; \Sigma_{m=1,h} \Sigma_{n=0,h} \text{ycoeff}(m,n) \sin(\pi m i \Delta) \cos(\pi n j \Delta)/(n^2 + m^2)$$

$$\text{Vx}(m,n) = \qquad \text{Eqn. 6a}$$

$$1/(\sigma^* \pi^2) \; \Sigma_{i=0,siz-1} \Sigma_{j=0,siz-1} \text{Ex}(i,j) \sin(\pi m j \Delta) \cos(\pi n i \Delta)/(n^2 + m^2)$$

$$\text{Vy}(m,n) = \qquad \text{Eqn. 6b}$$

$$1/(\sigma^* \pi^2) \; \Sigma_{i=0,siz-1} \Sigma_{j=0,siz-1} \text{Ey}(i,j) \sin(\pi m i \Delta) \cos(\pi n j \Delta)/(n^2 + m^2)$$

where xcoeff(m,n) and ycoeff(m,n) are names given to $\gamma1_{mn}$ and $\gamma2_{mn}$, respectively. The terms Ex, Ey, Vx, and Vy are the gradients of the "energy" between the data image and displaced template, and their transforms. Images are "siz" by "siz" pixels; the Δ factor scales the image to unit squares for the computations.

These equations show that there are two basic transformations called for by the algorithm, and that for each, results are computed for two separate dimensions (corresponding to the image's horizontal and vertical directions). The number of spectral coefficients (xcoeffs and ycoeffs) involved in the computations is a function of h which changes with the iteration number as the algorithm progresses. To design an array handling all of these cases, we rearranged the equations so that they all became a summation of three multiplied terms. This entailed pulling out constants and proper multiplication of some of the terms with other values in other steps of the algorithm. Once these changes were verified, our task was to create a systolic array that could perform the calculations of any of the following equations:

$$xdispl(i,j)=\Sigma_{m=1,h}\Sigma_{n=0,h}xcoeff(m,n)\sin(\pi mj\Delta)\cos(\pi ni\Delta) \quad \text{Eqn. 7a}$$

$$ydispl(i,j)=\Sigma_{m=1,h}\Sigma_{n=0,h}ycoeff(m,n)\sin(\pi mi\Delta)\cos(\pi nj\Delta) \quad \text{Eqn. 7b}$$

$$Vx(m,n) = \Sigma_{i=0,siz-1}\Sigma_{j=0,siz-1}Ex(i,j)\sin(\pi mj\Delta)\cos(\pi ni\Delta) \quad \text{Eqn. 8a}$$

$$Vy(m,n) = \Sigma_{i=0,siz-1}\Sigma_{j=0,siz-1}Ey(i,j)\sin(\pi mi\Delta)\cos(\pi nj\Delta) \quad \text{Eqn. 8b}$$

The systolic array design thus became a generic 3-term multiply-and-accumulator (MAC). Handling each of the above equations was essentially a matter of feeding the array with the correct ordering of operands and retrieving and interpreting the results in the appropriate manner. The array design is presented (using Eqn. 7a as an example) after discussing the issues and criteria we considered.

Knowing that we wanted to implement the array using multiple FPGAs constrained the optimal design to be one that 1) did not exceed the available logic and I/O resources, 2) allowed the most processing elements (PEs) to fit in an FPGA, and 3) kept each PE as fully utilized as possible. These factors led to the following guidelines. The systolic array should be as free from dependencies on h as possible; this motivated selection of particular projection vectors when mapping the dependency graph (DG) to a signal flow graph (SFG). The projection vector selection was also motivated by the desire to obtain a rectangular array which would ease problem partitioning (discussed below). Scheduling vector selection was motivated by the desire to present operands to the array in as few places as possible (to satisfy I/O constraints) and to avoid diagonal edges in the SFG (which may adversely affect signal routing within FPGAs, and thus the amount of usable logic obtainable).

To derive a dependency graph for Equation 7a, it was rewritten in a locally recursive form:

$$xdispl_{i,j}^{(k+1)} = xdispl_{i,j}^{(k)} + xcoeff_{i,j}^{(k)}sin_{i,j}^{(k)}cos_{i,j}^{(k)} \quad \text{Eqn. 9}$$

where $xdispl_{i,j}^{(0)} = 0$

$$sin_{i,j}^{(k)} = sin_{i-1,j}^{(k)}, \qquad sin_{0,j}^{(k)} = \sin(\pi mj\Delta),$$

$$cos_{i,j}^{(k)} = cos_{i,j-1}^{(k)}, \qquad cos_{i,0}^{(k)} = \cos(\pi ni\Delta),$$

and $xcoeff_{i,j}^{(k)} = xcoeff_{i,j-1}^{(k)}, \quad xcoeff_{i,0}^{(k)} = xcoeff(m,n).$

Note that a new summation index, k=(m-1)*(h+1)+n, has been introduced which incorporates both the m and n indices (m and n values can be regained using integer and modulo division). This allows a three dimensional DG to be constructed (vs. the four dimensions implied by the original equation). The DG is shown in Figure 1. The variables have been abbreviated to facilitate labelling this and following graphs as:

$xdispl(i,j) = X_{i,j}$ $\qquad$ $xcoeff(m,n) = F_{m,n}$

$\sin(\pi mj\Delta) = S_{j,m}$ $\qquad$ $\cos(\pi ni\Delta) = C_{i,n}$

Each node of the DG performs a three term multiplication and an accumulate (as well as transmitting sine and cosine values to the next node). The $F_{m,n}$ arcs are not shown, but each must be distributed to its corresponding k plane of the DG. We chose to do this by feeding them into the graph just as the cosine terms are.

To obtain a signal flow graph from the DG, a projection vector, d^T=[001], and schedule vector, s^T=[111], were used. This collapses the DG along the vertical (k, or m and n) direction, and minimizes the pipelining period of the SFG. Figure 2 shows the resulting SFG. All arcs have a delay of one. For this graph, the second index on the sine and cosine values are in terms of k, the F values are also indexed with k.

In Figure 2, the xcoeff terms and the cosine terms are transmitted side by side through the array. Cosine and xcoeff terms that are presented to a boundary cell at the same time are multiplied by each other inside each cell along that column of the array. Therefore, the xcoeff terms can be multiplied by the cosine terms in

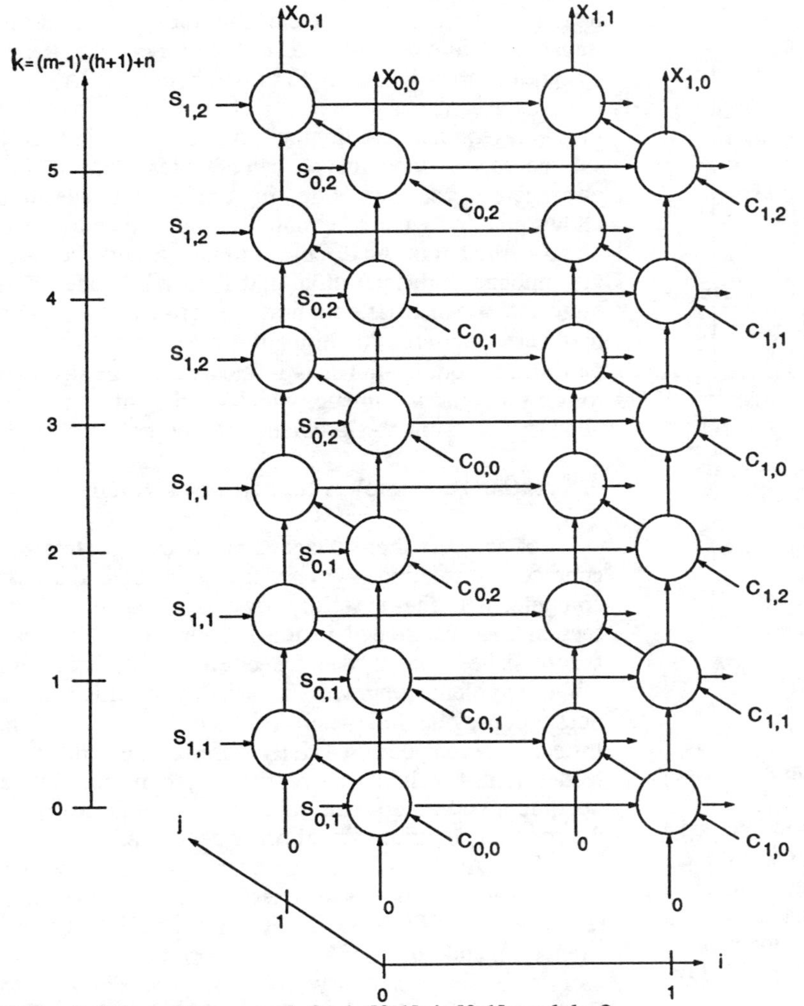

Figure 1. Dependency graph for i=[0,1], j=[0,1], and h=2.

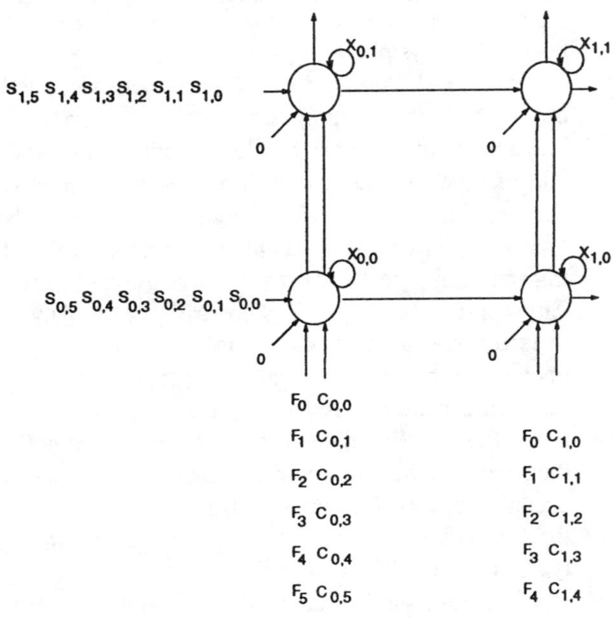

Figure 2. Signal flow graph corresponding to Fig. 1.

separate multipliers and the result can subsequently be propagated through the array. This reduces the number of data paths necessary in the array, as well as reducing the number of terms to be multiplied in each cell from three to two. The introduction of these extra multipliers requires that the xcoeff and cosine terms be provided one time unit earlier. The SFG containing the extra multipliers is shown in Figure 3. The xcoeff terms are transmittent data, being passed unchanged to the adjacent multiplier. The cosine terms are not passed along to another unit. Only the result of the cosine and xcoeff multiplication is passed vertically into the array of MACs. Once again, all arcs have a delay of one. All references to k have been replaced with references to m and n to clarify how the design relates to the original equation. This also explicitly shows that the same sine and cosine values need to be introduced to the array at more than one time.

The derivation of the SFG for the calculation of V.(m,n) is very similar. The array has the same structure as the array for xdispl(i,j), although the size is different and the data being fed into it also differs. Also, the variable h changes throughout the iterative process, which means that the array size must change as well.

We have determined the general structure of the systolic array. For the transformations of Eqns. 7, each processing element computes the displacement value at a particular image pixel. The summation over index k of Eqn 9 occurs over time in each PE. For the other transformations (Eqns 8), each PE finds a spectral coefficient (and the summing over all pixels occurs in time).

Once the basic systolic array design was completed, several implementation details needed to be resolved. After analyzing and experimenting with the numeric values used in the algorithm, we determined that 16 bit fixed point numbers could adequately represent them and thus be used in the array. The limited resources of a single FPGA (in terms of both logic and I/O) motivated the use of bit-serial arithmetic processing for the PEs. We used Booth's algorithm [8] to implement the multipliers, and obtained the accumulate function by presenting the term to be added to the

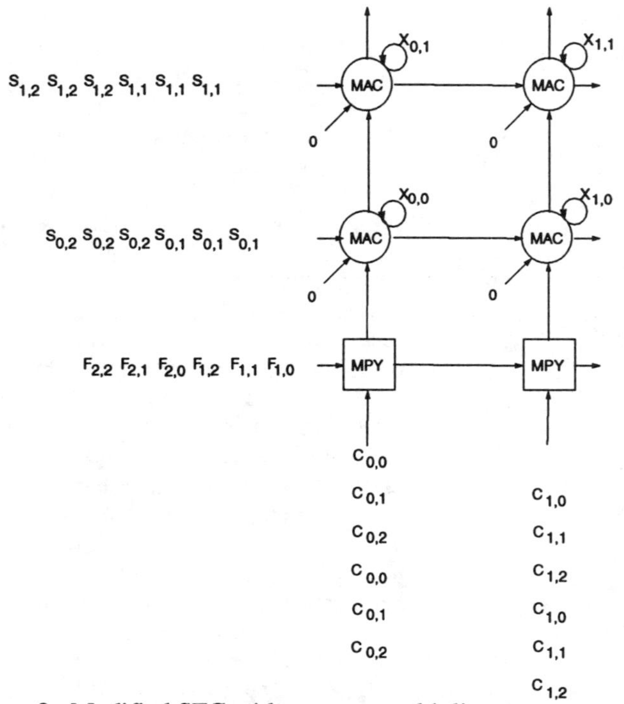

Figure 3. Modified SFG with separate multipliers.

multiplier as the initial running sum. We experimented with two designs for the basic "bit-cell" of these multipliers. The first was specifed using VHDL, followed by logic synthesis using Viewlogic, Inc.'s ViewSynthesis package [9]. We also manually configured 3 XC3000 configurable logic blocks (CLBs) to obtain the bit-cell design [10].

We wished to take advantage of the systolic array when processing images up to 128 by 128 in size. The inability to create such a large number of PEs (especially when using programmable logic), forced us to partition the problem for the transformation direction of Eqns 7. Note that the computations for each pixel, and for each subimage, are independent; thus enabling straightforward partitioning. The primary issue in partitioning the problem was to make the array size a multiple of the image size so that "boundary effects" did not severely degrade utilization. (Large values of h can motivate similar partitioning reasons and issues for the other transform direction.)

The array which we implemented has a 4 by 8 set of MACs. Figure 4 depicts a portion of the systolic array which shows the PE blocks that make it up. The "CTRLUNIT" block produces signals that propagate through the array and instruct each PE when to start computing a new product, or a new summation (these timings, as well as operand presentation windows, are more complex due to the bit-serial nature of the array's operation). The other blocks are essentially the basic MAC PE. The bottom row of multipliers has the accummulate function disabled. The leftmost column of PEs accepts the sine operands in serial (for the boundary of the array). Note that these operands are transmitted in parallel once in the array (a horizontal strip of the array is meant to fit within one FPGA).

To use the above array on a 128 by 128 image requires partitioning the problem into 512 subimages. Each subimage can be presented to the array before the last one is totally complete, this allows pipelining the subproblems which increases the array's utilization. As discussed in the results section, the amount of this partitioning that must be done is a large factor when determining the effectiveness of a hardware solution. Additionally, the time for each partition's computations is influenced by the decision to use bit-serial arithmetic; which on the other hand, allows partitioning the problem into bigger parts.

4. Creating the complete coprocessor solution

To achieve the advantages of our customized coprocessor solution, we needed to couple the host computer with the systolic array described in the last section. As mentioned in the Introduction, this was accomplished using a "data feeder" unit which we are initially implementing with the AnyBoard. This section does not provide full details of the data feeder design. Instead, its intent is to briefly describe how the data feeder unit fits into the entire system, the unit's operation, and how it can affect the overall utility of the coprocessor arrangement being developed.

The AnyBoard is a PC plug-in card which contains a fixed host interface circuit plus five reconfigurable FPGAs (XC3020s through XC3090s are supported) and three 128Kbyte memories to implement user specified circuitry. We use the FPGAs to implement the circuits described below. The memories hold sine and cosine values and act as a buffer for transferring data and results between the host and the systolic array.

The host computer (a 33 MHz 486-based PC, in this case) runs a program that performs user interaction and image display functions as well as all of the segmentation algorithm's calculations except for the transformations described above. When a tranformation calculation is needed, the host transfers all the data to be transformed into the AnyBoard's memory. It then triggers the AnyBoard to feed the array with the data and the sine/cosine operands. The host then waits for the array to execute the tranformations. As results are obtained from the array, the AnyBoard collects them in its memory. It then signals the host which reads the results. This scenario occurs four times during each iteration of the algorithm. A complete segmentation task typically takes 120 iterations.

The following circuitry was put on the AnyBoard: 1) a memory interface to allow the host PC to read and write AnyBoard memory, 2) The "CTRLUNIT" circuit

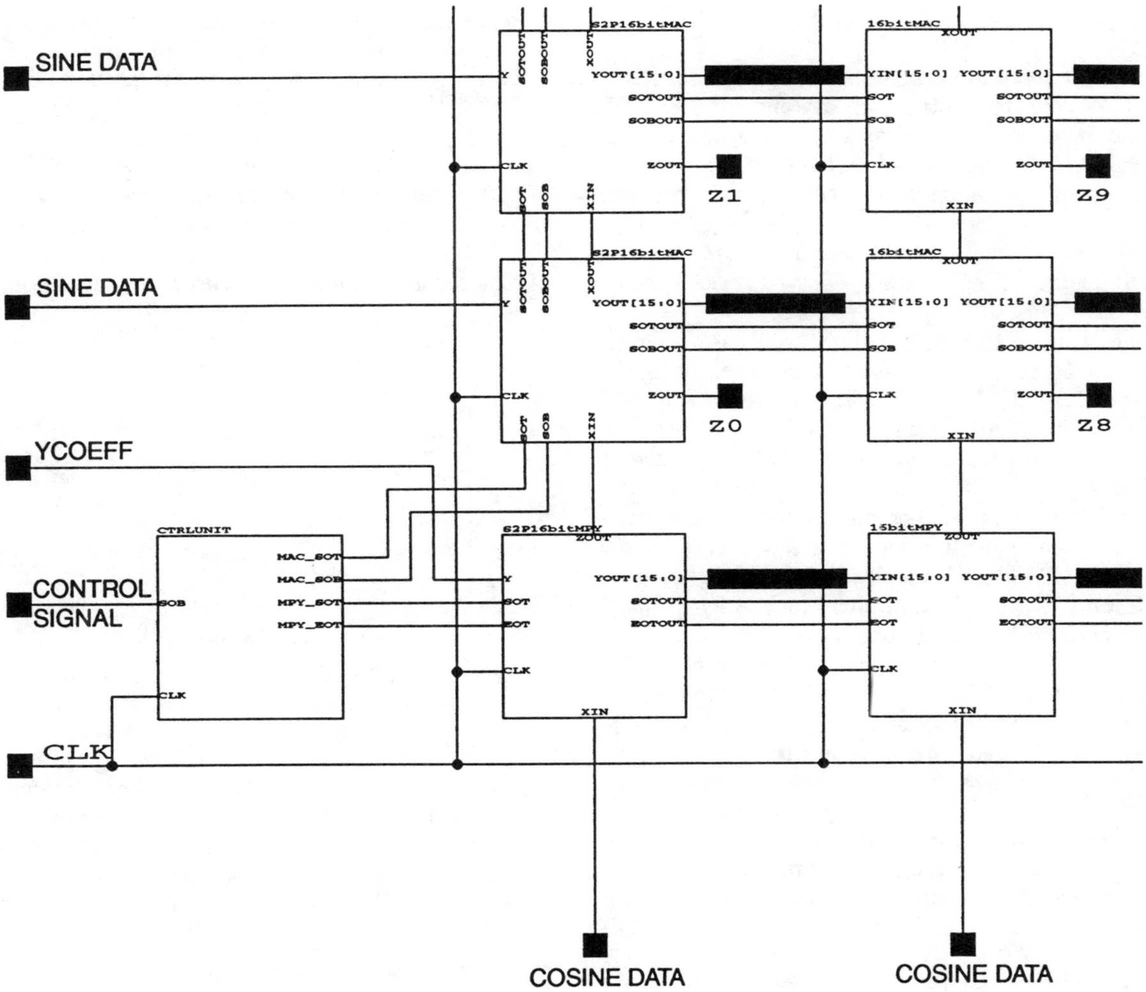

Figure 4. Partial View of Transformation Systolic Array Schematic. The entire array is 8 MACs high and 4 MACs wide, plus the 4 multipliers. Z terms are the displacement results.

shown in Figure 4, and 3) circuits to provide bit-serial operands to the array, and to accept bit-serial results from it. These latter circuits consist mainly of several shift registers that perform serial-to-parallel (or vice versa) data conversions. For the 4 by 8 PE array, 45 16-bit shift registers are needed (4 for cosine values, 8 for sine values, 1 for the data input operand, and 32 for the results). The interface to the AnyBoard memories incorporates mechanisms to correctly retrieve and store the parallel data from the shift registers. The CTRLUNIT circuit was modified to provide the correct timing signals required by each of the shift registers. These signals control when parallel data is moved between memory and shift register, and when the shift register shifts. Each shift register typically performs these functions at slightly different times.

In general, the overall scheme and particular design of the data feeder unit can greatly affect the overall speed (and thus effectiveness) of the coprocessor arrangement under development. For example, in determining the "bit" clock speed of the coprocessor, one needs to consider not only the operating frequency of the systolic array (reported in the next section), but also the frequency at which the data feeder can operate. The operating scheme described above in which either the host or systolic array is not being used while the other is, and in which neither is doing useful work during data transfers between the host and AnyBoard, can potentially severely degrade overall performance. Our main goal to this point has been to implement a working system. Experience with the initial implementation is providing suggestions for improving the data feeder design. For example, we found that the shift registers for transferring the transform results could be better put onto the Virtual ASIC board without changing the I/O requirements between the two FPGA boards. Further ways and ideas to enhance the data feeding function are discussed in Section 6.

5. Results

This section reports logic utilization and performance results for the transformation systolic array. We determine the array size and speed one can obtain with certain FPGA parts. With this information, cost/performance comparisons are made between software only implementations of the segmentation algorithm and the customized hardware scheme described here.

Figure 4 shows that the systolic array's basic building block is the MAC cell. We found that, when using the MAC bit-cell synthesized from VHDL, a 16-bit MAC PE used 72 CLBs. The Virtual ASIC board used to implement the array has 12 XC3090-100 FPGAs, each of which has 320 CLBs. Thus, we were able to put 4 MAC PEs per FPGA; this number corresponds to the array width when implementing each horizontal strip of the array with one FPGA. Using all 12 FPGAs allows a 4 by 11 MAC array plus the 4 multipliers (or a 4 by 8 subset when power of two sizes are desired). Using the Xilinx timing analysis tools, we determined that the MAC PE could be clocked at 14.9 MHz (for the -100 speed grade parts). In general, an entire array made up of these PEs could run at this speed. When using the Virtual ASIC board, though, a slower frequency was necessary since four of its FPGAs were not directly connected to the board's interface connector. This forced us to route these FPGAs' I/O signals through intermediate FPGAs, halving the maximum speed obtainable. This penalty could be avoided by pipelining the path of these I/O signals.

When creating the MAC PE using the manually mapped bit-cell, each took 49 CLBs. This enables 5 MACs per FPGA which leads to a 5 by 11 MAC array. Although this size does not lead to as straightforward partitioning of "power-of-two sized" images, it does reduce the number of partitions and thus total processing time. It also benefits the transformations of Eqns. 8 which require an h by h+1 sized array. In addition to decreasing the logic consumed by each MAC, the manually mapped implementation allows increasing the operating speed to 22.1 MHz. (Preliminary analyses indicate that up to 35 MHz operation may be achieved with further optimizations.)

One of our main goals was to develop a basic array design and to characterize it as above. Further, we wanted to determine how the 4 by 8 Virtual ASIC-based array and other implementations compared to the performance expected from workstations equipped with high-performance microprocessors. The performance of alternate implementations built with different numbers and speeds of FPGAs can be easily evaluated using the above results and the following performance analyses.

To allow the comparisons, we determined the total number of clock cycles the systolic array takes to execute transform computations throughout an entire segmentation run. In particular, approximately 130,000 clock cycles are needed to evaluate Equation 7a when running a 64 by 64 image through 20 iterations for each h ranging from 1 to 7 (140 total iterations). This is true only if no partitioning of the problem is needed (ie., a 64 by 64 array is available). When partitioning the problem onto a 4 by 8 array, about 14 million cycles are required (there are 128 subproblems). Figure 5 graphs the reduction in cycles required as larger arrays are used. (Each of Equations 7

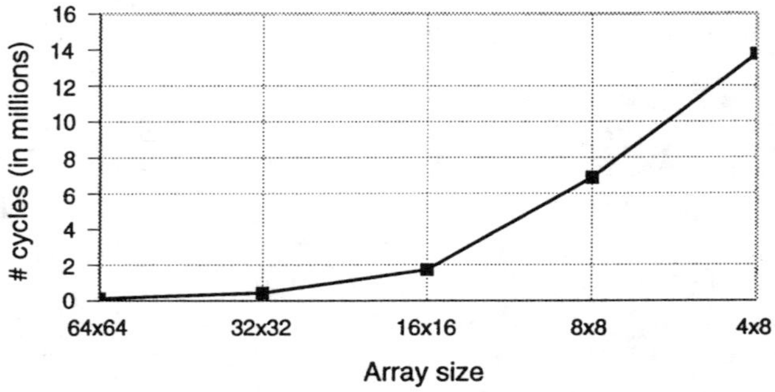

Figure 5. Total # of Cycles vs. Array Size for the calculation of 'xdispl' for 64 by 64 images when doing 20 iterations each for h ranging from 1 to 7.

and 8 require about the same number of calculations; thus the total number of cycles to execute all of the transforms scales by a factor of 4.) The total time spent doing the computations is the product of these numbers and the clock period, and can be expressed as:

T = (# sec/cycle) (# cycles) Eqn. 10
= (# sec/cycle) (# cycles/partition) (# partitions)

The number of cycles per partition is approximately 107,000 (over the range of reasonable array sizes). Knowing this and the speed and array size enabled by a particular multi-FPGA board allows calculating the board's performance capabilities.

If a processor was programmed to perform the same task, approximately 41.5 million instructions would have to be executed. This assumes one add, one multiply, and one "looping" instruction in the tightest loop of the algorithm, plus one more multiply every time through the second tightest loop (giving approximately 13.8 million of each instruction). The total time a processor would take to perform these operations can be given as:

T = (# sec/cycle) (# cycles/instruction) (# instructions) Eqn. 11

The first term in the above equation represents the processor's operating frequency. The second term can be used to differentiate different processor architectures. For example, some microprocessors may take 5 or more cycles/instruction, pipelined microprocessors may allow 1 cycle/instruction, a fully utilized superscalar CPU may be able to achieve 1/3 to 1/2 cycles/instruction, and a large parallel processor may have a very small cycles/instruction factor.

When using the above equations to compare solutions, one should realize that "system-wide" issues such as data transfer bandwidth, cacheability of data (for a processor solution) and data feeding (for the systolic array) have not been taken into account. Equations 10 and 11 actually give approximate upper limits on the potential performance realizable from each computing engine. For example, if it is possible to provide operands to a 4 by 8 systolic array as fast as needed, the "xdispl" calculations will take .68 seconds. This is about ten times faster than a 33 Mhz processor able to execute an instruction in 5 cycles, the same as a 1 instruction/cycle processor running at 66 Mhz, and six times as slow as 4 fully utilized superscalar processors running at 50 MHz and executing 2 instructions per cycle. These three processor solutions roughly correspond to a 486-like microprocessor (doing floating point operations), to a Pentium processor, and to 4 i860s. As another example, a 100 MHz superscalar microprocessor executing three instructions/cycle can achieve maximum performance in the same range as an 8 by 8 systolic array clocked at 50 MHz.

6. Discussion and Conclusions

We have described the general arrangement for an FPGA-based coprocessor system which can increase throughput for an image segmentation algorithm. The system consists of a systolic array to perform a major portion of the computations, plus a data feeder unit to transfer data between the array and host computer. Depending on the logic resources available, various size systolic arrays can be implemented. The performance analyses indicate that even fairly small arrays can offer a cost-effective acceleration technique. When seeking to further increase performance, predictable advances in FPGA density, speed, and architecture appear to offer more promise than expected advances in single processor solutions.

Fully realizing the array's computation potential requires solving the data transfer problem. Even for the 4 by 8 array operating at 20 MHz, a bandwidth of approximately 20 Mbytes/sec must be maintained. For a 33 MHz 32 by 32 array, the rate increases to about 350 Mbytes/sec. So, even if raw computing power may be most easily improved with the custom hardware solution, the bandwidth required by larger arrays limits realization of the promised increases. Experience with our initial data feeding scheme and its AnyBoard implementation indicates that pipelining data movement and computations along with higher bandwidth data paths are needed for an efficient overall system. We plan to try connecting the systolic array directly to a 32-bit processor's bus. High bandwidth transfers could be achieved if data movements were primarily between the array and the processor's cache memory using burst transfer cycles.

This paper has illustrated a process of rapidly prototyping application-specific computing elements with available reconfigurable logic platforms. For the example application, we have shown how this process is enabling a better optimized solution. We believe the method to be a worthwhile tool when developing FPGA-based computing solutions. This is particularly true as multi-FPGA partitioning software continues to improve and become increasingly capable of handling arbitrary multi-FPGA boards. The ability to quickly implement and then iteratively optimize several distinct designs should prove advantageous when designing customized multi-FPGA boards meant to be reconfigurable for a set of applications.

Acknowledgements

We wish to thank Lance Kendrick for his assistance throughout this project. We are grateful for the support obtained from Integrated Circuits Applications, Ltd., Xilinx, Inc., Dr. Van den Bout of North Carolina State University, and Stealth Technologies, Inc.

REFERENCES

[1] Integrated Circuits Applications, Ltd., Concept Silicon User's Manual, 1993.

[2] D. Van den Bout, J. Morris, D. Thomae, S. Labrozzi, S. Wingo, and D. Hallman, "Anyboard: An FPGA-based, reconfigurable system," IEEE Design & Test of Computers, September, 1992.

[3] M. Gokhale, W. Holmes, A. Kopser, S. Lucas, R. Minninch, D. Sweely, and D. Lopresti, "Building and using a highly programmable logic array," IEEE Computer, January 1991.

[4] P. Bertin, D. Roncin, J. Vuillemin, "Introduction to programmable active memories," Technical Report No. 3, DEC Paris Research Laboratory, June 1989.

[5] Y. Amit, U. Grenander, and M. Piccioni, "Structural image restoration through deformable templates," J. American Statistical Association, 1989.

[6] L. Kendrick, Deformable template image models: application to segmenting magnetic resonance images, M. S. Thesis, Southern Illinois University, Edwardsville, 1993.

[7] G. Gent, Systolic array implementation of template deformation algorithm using field programmable gate arrays, M. S. Thesis, Southern Illinois University, Edwardsville, 1994.

[8] J. P. Hayes, Computer Architecture and Organization, McGraw- Hill, 1988.

[9] Viewlogic, Corp., ViewSynthesis User's Manual, 1992.

[10] Xilinx Corp., The Programmable Logic Data Book, 1993.

Density Enhancement of a Neural Network Using FPGAs and Run-Time Reconfiguration

James G. Eldredge and Brad L. Hutchings
Dept. of Electrical and Computer Eng.
Brigham Young University
Provo, UT 84602
Tel: (801) 378-2667
Email: hutch@ee.byu.edu

Abstract

Run-time reconfiguration is a way of more fully exploiting the flexibility of reconfigurable FPGAs. The Run-Time Reconfiguration Artificial Neural Network (RRANN) uses run-time reconfiguration to increase the hardware density of FPGAs. The RRANN architecture also allows large amounts of parallelism to be used and is very scalable. RRANN divides the backpropagation algorithm into three sequentially executed stages and configures the FPGAs to execute only one stage at a time. The FPGAs are reconfigured as part of normal execution in order to change stages.

Using reconfigurability in this way increases the number of hardware neurons a single Xilinx XC3090 can implement by 500%. Performance is effected by reconfiguration overhead, but this overhead becomes insignificant in large networks. This overhead is made even more insignificant with improved configuration methods. Run-time reconfiguration is a flexible realization of the time/space trade-off. The RRANN architecture has been designed and built using commercially available hardware, and its performance has been measured.

1 Introduction

In many cases, reconfigurable Field Programmable Gate Arrays (FPGAs) are used as an easy way to prototype digital logic circuits and as a way to achieve cheap, low-volume, custom VLSI. The ease with which a designer can develop a circuit and then configure an FPGA to implement that circuit is the primary reason. This flexibility comes at the cost of decreased performance due to the overhead involved in making a device fully programmable. Because of this overhead, an FPGA provides less functionality per unit area of silicon and longer communication delay times than gate-array or full-custom implementations [1]. In a conventional *static* design (one where the FPGA's configuration does not change) this flexibility is wasted, while its overhead remains.

The efficient use of FPGAs beyond prototyping and low-volume production requires that the FPGA's flexibility be used directly. One way of exploiting this flexibility is through run-time reconfiguration. Run-time reconfiguration divides an algorithm into sequentially executed stages; at run-time, only one stage is configured on the FPGAs at a time. When one stage completes, the FPGAs are reconfigured with the next stage. This process of "configure and execute" is repeated until the algorithm has completed its task. Because only one stage of the algorithm is actually using hardware at any given time, there are more hardware resources available for use by each stage. These additional hardware resources can be used to improve the performance of the active stage.

This paper describes the Run-Time Reconfiguration Artificial Neural Network (RRANN). RRANN uses run-time reconfiguration to increase the number of hardware neurons implemented on a single Xilinx XC3090. It does this by dividing the backpropagation algorithm into three stages, feed-forward, backpropagation, and update and configuring the FPGAs for only one stage at a time. Because of run-time reconfiguration, RRANN was able to increase the number of available hardware neurons by 500% per FPGA.

As the RRANN architecture uses the backpropagation algorithm for learning, we begin by describing the basics of the backpropagation algorithm for neural networks. Then, the RRANN architecture is presented and explained in some detail. Next, the performance of the RRANN architecture is given, and then some conclusions are made about the project.

2 The Backpropagation Algorithm

The backpropagation learning algorithm [2] provides a way to train a multilayered feed-forward neural network such as the one shown in Figure 1.

It begins by feeding input values forward through the network according to (1) and (2).

$$net_i = \sum_{j \epsilon A} O_j W_{ji} \quad \forall\, i :\ i \epsilon B, \tag{1}$$

where A is the set of all neurons in a layer, B is the set of all neurons in the next layer, O_j is the output (or activation) for neuron j, and W_{ji} is the weight assigned to the connection between neurons j and i. Equation (1) takes the output values (or activations) from a layer and feeds them forward to the next layer through weights. This operation is performed for each neuron in the next layer producing a *net* value for it. The *net* value is the weighted sum of all the activations of neurons in the previous layer, and each neuron's *net* value is then applied to (2), known as the activation

0-8186-5490-2/94 $03.00

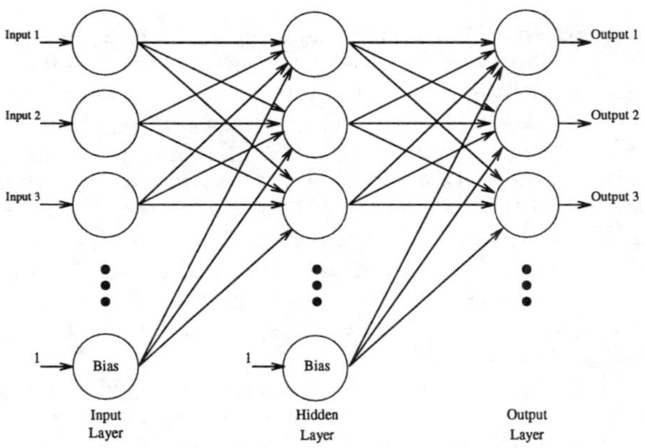

Figure 1: A Multilayer Feed-Forward Neural Network.

function, to produce that neuron's activation.

$$O_i = f(net_i) = \frac{1}{1 + e^{-net_i}}. \qquad (2)$$

After all neurons in the network have an activation value associated with them for a given input pattern, the backpropagation algorithm continues by finding errors for every non-input neuron. This process begins by finding the error for the neurons on the output layer according to (3).

$$\delta_i = f'(net_i)(T_i - O_i) \quad \forall\, i : i \in C, \qquad (3)$$

where C is the set of all output neurons, T_i is the target output for neuron i, $f'()$ is the first derivative of (2), and δ_i is the error for neuron i. The errors found for the output neurons are then propagated back to the previous layer so that errors can be assigned to neurons contained in hidden layers. This calculation is governed by (4).

$$\delta_i = f'(net_i) \sum_{j \in E} \delta_j W_{ij} \quad \forall\, i : i \in D, \qquad (4)$$

where D is the set of all neurons in a non-input layer and E is the set of all neurons in the next layer. This calculation is repeated for every hidden layer in the network.

After every non-input neuron has an activation and error associated with it, the network's weights can be updated. First, the amount by which each weight should be changed is found by calculating (5).

$$\Delta W_{ij} = C_l O_i \delta_j \quad \forall\, i,j : i \in A,\ j \in B, \qquad (5)$$

where C_l, known as learning rate, is a constant controlling the size of weight changes, and ΔW_{ij} is the weight change between neuron i and j. The weight is changed by evaluating (6).

$$W_{ij_{t+1}} = W_{ij_t} + \Delta W_{ij}. \qquad (6)$$

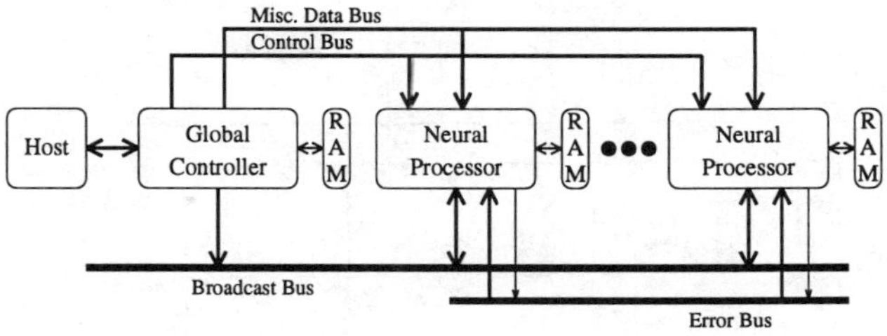

Figure 2: The General RRANN Architecture.

3 The RRANN Architecture

The RRANN architecture divides the backpropagation algorithm into the sequential execution of three stages known as feed-forward, backpropagation, and update. The feed-forward stage is responsible for taking input patterns and propagating them through the network assigning an activation (output) to every neuron according to Equations (1) and (2). The backpropagation stage (expressed by Equations (3) and (4)) finds the output errors and propagates them backward through the network in order to find errors for neurons contained in hidden layers. After every non-input neuron has been assigned an error value, the update stage (Equations (5) and (6)) begins operation. The update stage uses activation and error values found by the previous two stages to compute the amount by which weights should be changed and updates all weights with these changes. The completion of the update stage marks the end of the evaluation of one training pattern. This process is then repeated for all training patterns until the network is sufficiently trained.

RRANN contains a global controller occupying one FPGA and many neural processors occupying the balance of the available FPGAs (Figure 2). The global controller is mainly responsible for sequencing the execution of local hardware subroutines on the neural processors and for supplying key data to the neural processors (such as input patterns). Each neural processor contains six hardware neurons and local hardware subroutines implemented with state machines. The neural processors are responsible for performing all computations needed for the backpropagation algorithm. Each neural processor also has a local RAM associated with it. This RAM is used to store weight and target output data and as a scratch pad to buffer *net* and error values.

In order to use hardware efficiently, RRANN utilizes bit-serial hardware to do mathematical computations. Also, as with other projects [3, 4], RRANN uses look-up tables to implement the activation function (Equation (2)) and its derivative.

3.1 The Feed-Forward Stage

The feed-forward stage computes Equations (1) and (2), and the feed-forward neural processor, shown in Figure 3, contains the hardware for these computations. The feed-forward neural processor contains six hardware neurons that compute the activation-weight $(O \cdot W)$ products and accumulate these products. The

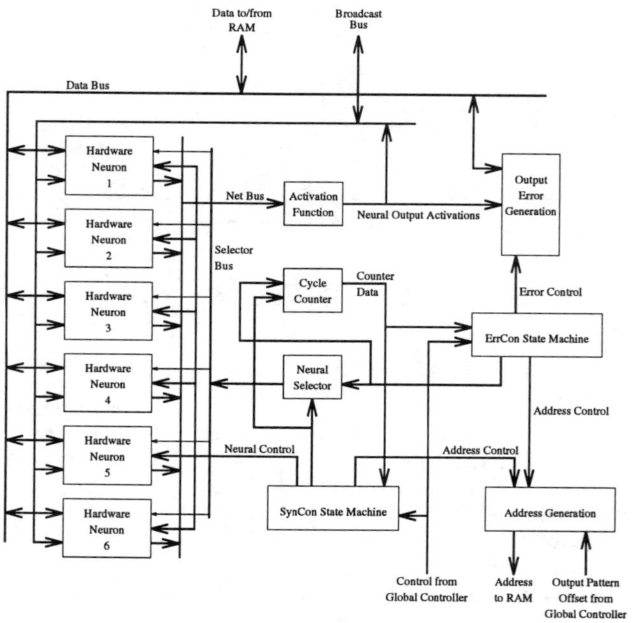

Figure 3: The Feed-Forward Neural Processor.

neural selector decides which hardware neuron and neural processor is currently supplying activation data to the broadcast bus. The block labeled *activation function* in the figure produces Equation (2). It does this by using a *net* value supplied by a hardware neuron as an index into a look-up table. The cycle counter is used by the state machines to sequence events, and the address generation unit produces the addresses needed to access the local RAM. The output error generation unit finds the difference between target outputs and the network's outputs. This is technically part of the backpropagation stage (Equation (3)), but it is done here for convenience. Finally, the SynCon and ErrCon state machines implement subroutines that control the evaluation of the network equations.

To begin the feed-forward stage, the global controller broadcasts an input value to the neural processors. This broadcast is done over a time-multiplexed bus one input value at a time [4]. As each input value is placed on the bus, the neural processors read it and do the appropriate weight multiplication for neurons in the first hidden layer. After the multiplication is complete, the product is accumulated with those from previous input iterations (Equation (1)), and the next input is broadcast over the bus. This method of interconnection allows for a large amount of parallelism to occur as all hardware neurons perform a multiply concurrently. It also allows for a large amount of scalability because hardware neurons can be added to the network by simply connecting them to the bus. Also, each hardware neuron only requires one multiplier; this allows for the development of one generic neuron that can be used with networks of arbitrary size.

After the evaluation of the first hidden layer is completed, the neural processors become responsible for broadcasting activation values to be used as inputs to the next layer. Before the evaluation of another layer begins, the hardware neurons buffer the *net* values calculated for the first hidden layer. Then, each hardware neuron in turn evaluates (2) for its buffered *net* value and broadcasts the result over the broadcast bus to all other hardware neurons including itself. This process iterates as the hardware neurons evaluate (1) and buffer the new *net* values as was done for the first hidden layer.

If the network has four layers, the above process is again repeated for the output layer. After the *net* values for the output layer have been found, they are used to evaluate (2), and the results are compared with the input pattern's target outputs (T_i). These compare operations ($T_i - O_i$) are computed in parallel, and the differences are buffered for use by the backpropagation stage.

3.2 The Backpropagation Stage

The backpropagation stage computes Equations (3) and (4), and the backpropagation neural processor, shown in Figure 4, contains the hardware to do these computations. The hardware neurons find the error-weight products ($\delta \cdot W$) during the evaluation of (4) and also buffer error values. The input and output sum blocks compute the summation of (4). The output register provides an index (a *net* value) into the activation function derivative look-up table, and the activation function derivative look-up table supplies f' to the multiplier. This multiplier finds ($f' \cdot \sum$) to complete the computation of (4). This final product is check for overflow and underflow by the overflow/underflow block. The neural selector determines the hardware neuron and neural processor Equation (4) is being computed for. The cycle counter aids the state machines in sequencing operations, and the address generation unit supplies addresses to the local RAM. Two multiplexors are also used to direct data to their proper locations. The GetErr, OutErr, and ErrComp state machines control this hardware to correctly calculate (3) and (4).

The backpropagation stage begins by finding the errors for the output layer using the differences found during the feed-forward stage according to (3). This operation can be executed with a large degree of parallelism, is purely local, and, therefore, does not require any communication of data between hardware neurons.

Erdogan and Hong [5] point out a stumbling block to parallelism in the calculation of (4). This problem occurs when error values are broadcast back through the network in a similar manner as activation values during the feed-forward stage. The weight values needed for the multiplication after the broadcast are not locally available to the hardware neuron that needs it. Erdogan and Hong suggest weight value duplication as a possible solution. RRANN solves the problem in a fundamentally different way that avoids weight duplication and error broadcasting.

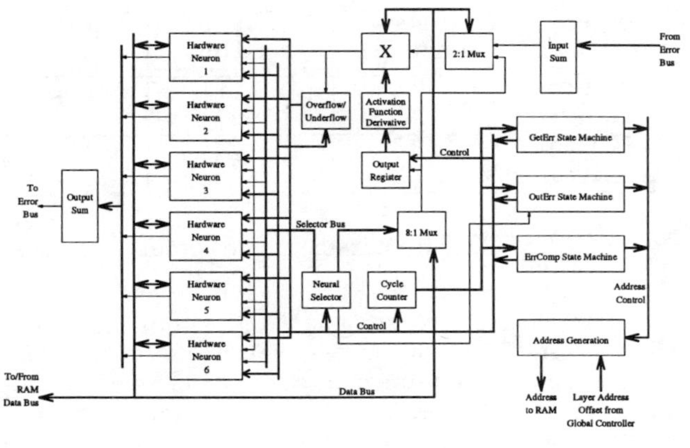

Figure 4: The Backpropagation Neural Processor.

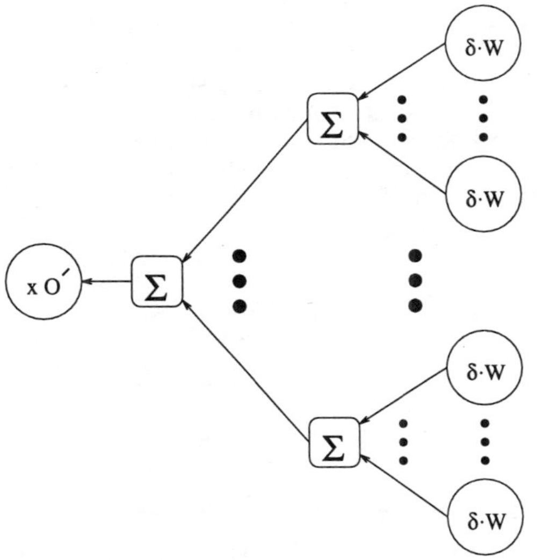

Figure 5: Computing Errors for Hidden Neurons.

RRANN completes the computation of Equation (4) for each hidden neuron in the network (including the summation) before beginning (4) for another hidden neuron. This operation is illustrated by Figure 5. It begins as each output neuron calculates the error-weight product ($\delta \cdot W$) in parallel. Each neural processor then sums the products generated by its hardware neurons, and this partial sum is then communicated to the targeted neural processor. This target neural processor receives these partial sums and completes (4) by adding the partial sums together and then multiplying by the appropriate activation derivative.

Computing Equation (4) in this manner achieves the same level of parallel execution as the feed-forward and update stages. This is an important advantage that overcomes the problem of non-local weight distribution discussed by Erdogan and Hong [5] without requiring weight duplication or broadcasting. However, a small amount of scalability is lost as each neu-

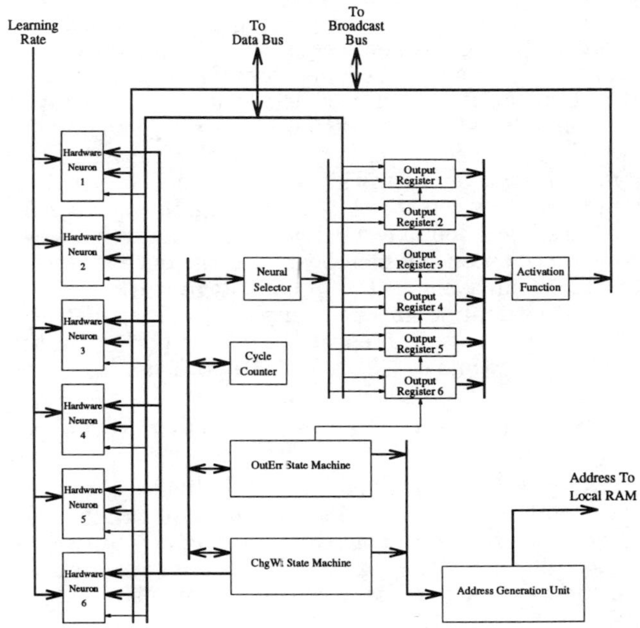

Figure 6: The Update Neural Processor.

ral processor requires its own line of communication. As the number of neural processors grow, the number of error communication lines grow. This increase in communication lines also necessitates an increase in adder circuitry for merging the partial sums. These requirements are minimized, however, by the use of bit-serial data representations. The communication lines are only one bit wide, and bit-serial adders only require one Xilinx Combinational Logic Block (CLB).

3.3 The Update Stage

The update stage computes Equations (5) and (6), and the update neural processor, shown in Figure 6, contains the hardware needed for these calculations. The update hardware neurons compute (5) using error (δ) values retrieved from local RAM, activation (O) values supplied over the broadcast bus, and learning rate (C_l) supplied by the global controller. After finding the ΔWs, the update hardware neurons immediately use these data to update the corresponding weights. The output registers hold *net* data retrieved from local RAM and supply these data as indexes into the activation function look-up table. The neural selector decides which neural processor supplies activation data to the broadcast bus and which output register supplies input to the look-up table. The cycle counter supplies sequencing information to the state machines, and the address generation unit produces addresses for the local RAM. The OutErr and ChgWt state machines control the above hardware to achieve the proper execution of (5) and (6).

The update stage begins in a similar manner to the feed-forward stage with the global controller broadcasting input values to the first hidden layer. The hardware neurons then use the activation and error values found by the first two stages to compute (5). The ΔW produced is immediately used in the calculation of (6), and the new weight value is copied over the old value. This process is repeated for every weight in the hidden layer in a parallel fashion as each input presents its value. Then RRANN begins changing the weights between the first hidden layer and the output (in a three layer network) or the second hidden layer (in a four layer network). This is again repeated, in the case of a four layer network, for the weights between the second hidden layer and the output layer.

The completion of the update stage marks the end of the evaluation of one complete training pattern. The three stages are repeated for each pattern in the training set (*one epoch*), and new epochs are run until the network is sufficiently trained.

3.4 Run-Time Reconfiguration Between Stages

As was just explained, RRANN divides the backpropagation algorithm into three sequentially executed stages, and then configures only one of the stages on the FPGAs at a time. This process is shown in Figure 7 for one *pass* through all three stages.

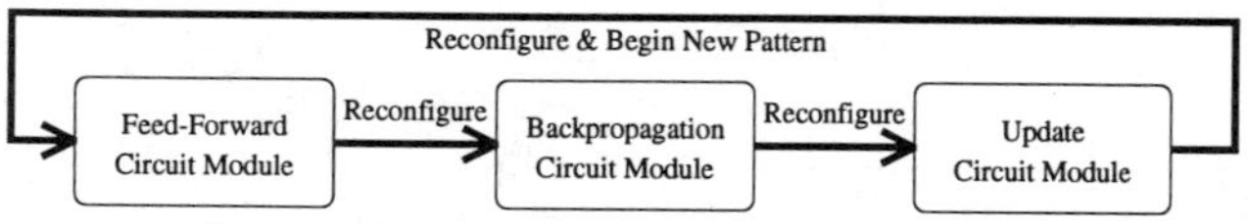

Figure 7: RRANN's Run-Time Reconfiguration.

A separate circuit module was developed for each stage of execution. Each circuit module followed the general architecture shown in Figure 2 consisting of a global controller and many nearly identical neural processors. As one circuit module finished (indicating the completion of the corresponding stage), all FPGA hardware was reconfigured with the next stage's circuit module.

4 Implementation and Evaluation

The RRANN architecture has been built and tested using a commercially-available FPGA board (the X12 board, previously referred to as the SCA board) produced by National Technology Inc. The X12 board is an ISA compatible expansion board that can be used in a host IBM-compatible PC, and it can be populated with up to 12 Xilinx XC3000 series FPGAs. The host PC stores all configuration information for the FPGAs, monitors the progress of each stage of execution, and supplies the appropriate configuration data to the X12 board.

With the X12 board populated with Xilinx XC3090s, reconfiguration time was measured at approximately 30 ms. Compare this to the minimum reconfiguration time for an XC3090 of approximately 7 ms. The reason for the X12 board's longer reconfiguration time is due to the host's low bus bandwidth. In a newer version of the X12 board, this problem is solved through bus mastering and configuration data caching. Therefore, the following analysis will assume the 7 ms reconfiguration time.

	Feed-Forward	Backpropagation	Update
Neural Processor	260	253	224
Global Controller	97	62	98

Table 1: The CLB Requirements of Circuit Modules.

All circuitry was designed and simulated using Mentor Graphics' schematic capture software, and these circuits were implemented on FPGAs using Xilinx's XACT software. Using run-time reconfiguration, six hardware neurons were implemented on each Xilinx XC3090 FPGA. The RRANN circuitry successfully simulated at 10 MHz and operated at 14 MHz. With improved pipelining, especially between the neural processor and local RAM, it is estimated that the circuitry could operate in excess of 40 MHz. Part utilization (in Xilinx XC3000 CLBs) for the feed-forward, backpropagation, and update stages are summarized in Table 1. The RRANN circuitry was tested on neural networks requiring four XC3090s. For these networks, weight convergence was observed, and the networks made useful generalizations about the training patterns presented them [6].

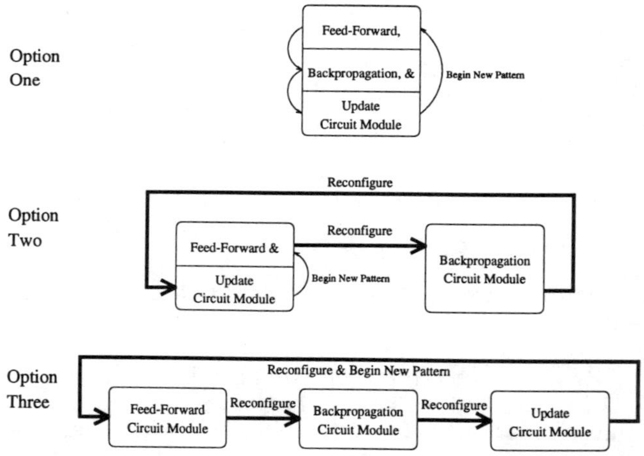

Figure 8: Other Run-Time Reconfiguration Options.

For comparison, two other options for implementing the RRANN architecture have been investigated. The first option combines all three stages of execution into the same circuit module, and this circuit module is then configured onto the FPGAs. Reconfiguration is not required for this option as all stages are present in the one configuration. The second option combines the feed-forward and update stages into one circuit module and the backpropagation stage into another. Reconfiguration is needed after the completion of the feed-forward and backpropagation stages but not after the update stage. These two options have been studied theoretically, and no hardware has been developed for them. The design explained in the previous section is referred to as option three in the proceeding text. Figure 8 shows these additional two options compared with option three (Figure 7). Again, this third option was implemented and tested using the X12 board and XC3090 FPGAs.

Run-time reconfiguration improves hardware utilization allowing more hardware neurons to be implemented per FPGA. It is estimated that one hardware neuron per FPGA is possible for option one, and four hardware neurons per FPGA for option two. Six hardware neurons per FPGA were attained for option three, yielding a 500% increase in hardware neuron densities over option one. This increase in hardware neuron density is made possible because inactive circuitry is not using FPGA resources. As an example of this, consider the input sum, output sum, and activation derivative blocks of the backpropagation stage (Figure 4). The feed-forward and update stages do not need this circuitry, and, through run-time reconfiguration, they do not implement it. The FPGA resources freed in this example are then used to implement more hardware neurons.

The cost of this improved utilization is the time it takes to reconfigure the FPGAs with a different circuit module. As stated previously, option one requires no FPGA reconfigurations adding 0 ms to overall execution time. Option two requires two reconfigurations adding 14 ms per pass to execution time. Option three requires three reconfigurations adding 21 ms per pass to execution time. Execution time t_E for one pass through all three stages of the RRANN architecture is given by

$$t_E = t_C + t_R, \tag{7}$$

where

$$t_C = \frac{(n \times 148 + (l-1) \times 13 + 282)}{f_C}$$

is the time spent doing computations, n is the number of non-output neurons, l is the number of layers, f_C is the clock frequency (14 MHz), and t_R is the reconfiguration time for the given option. The reconfiguration time t_R remains constant for each option regardless of the network's size. However, computation time t_C grows linearly with n and, therefore, with the number of FPGAs. For option one, t_E is dominated only by t_C because $t_R = 0$ ms. However, t_E for options two and three is dominated by t_R for small numbers of FPGAs. As the number of FPGAs is increased, t_C begins being more significant to t_E. The reconfiguration overhead is, therefore, more dominant for smaller networks.

The Performance of the RRANN architecture for all three options is shown in Figures 9 and 10. Figure 9 shows how the total computational power of the network, measured in weight updates per second (WUPS), grows as a function of XC3090s used. Options two and three are clearly dominated by reconfiguration overhead for small numbers of FPGAs. For larger numbers (> 23) of FPGAs, computational time begins to be more dominant, and run-time reconfiguration begins to pay off with better performance.

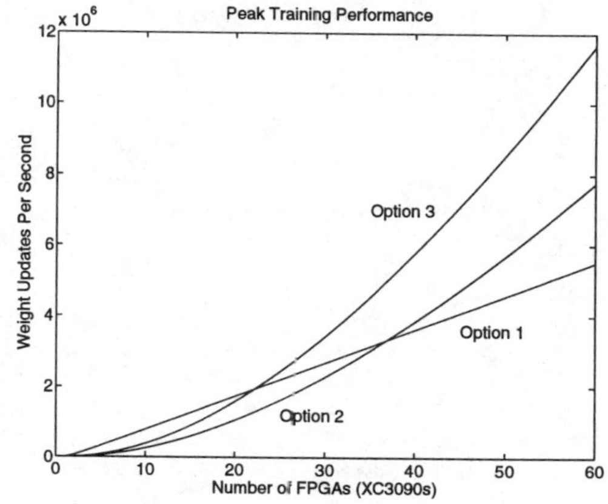

Figure 9: RRANN's Performance (14 MHz).

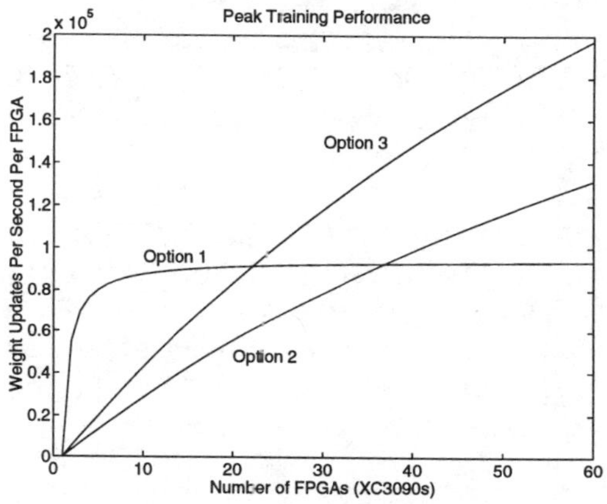

Figure 10: RRANN's Performance per XC3090 (14 MHz).

Figure 10 shows the computational power that each XC3090 is providing as a function of the total number of XC3090s used. Option one reaches peak output per FPGA of 94.6×10^3 WUPS relatively quickly. Again because of reconfiguration overhead, options two and three require larger networks before higher performance is possible. The performance of each FPGA continues to grow asymptotically for these two options until reaching 378×10^3 WUPS for option two and 568×10^3 WUPS for option three.

After the backpropagation algorithm completes operation and the neural network has been sufficiently *trained*, the network is then used to compute outputs for new input patterns. This is known as *operational mode*, and it requires the computation of Equations (1) and (2) only. These equations are totally implemented by the feed-forward stage, and thus, in operational mode, the backpropagation and update stages can be totally discarded. Also, because only one stage is used, no FPGA reconfigurations are needed. This again emphasizes run-time reconfiguration's main advantage: Only that hardware presently needed uses

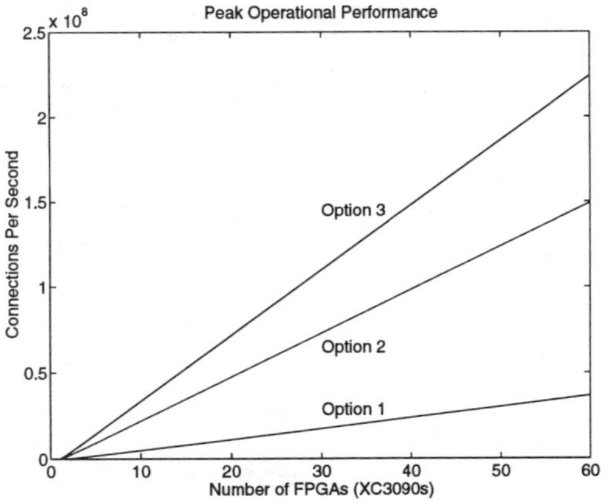

Figure 11: RRANN's Operational Performance (14 MHz).

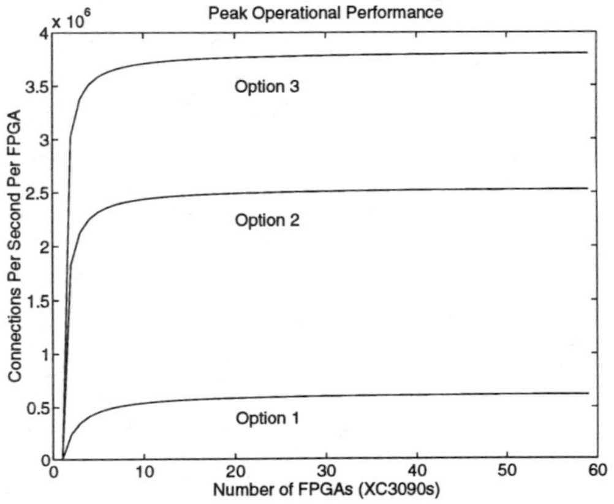

Figure 12: RRANN's Operational Performance per XC3090 (14 MHz).

valuable FPGA resources.

The operational mode performance is shown in Figures 11 and 12. This performance is measured in connections per second (CPS), and the figures show that option three is clearly better. This result is not surprising because only the feed-forward stage is needed, and reconfiguration overhead is eliminated. Also, option three implements more neural processors per XC3090 allowing it to do more neural computations.

In order to make run-time reconfiguration more feasible, the significance of reconfiguration overhead needs to be reduced. One way of doing this is by making computation time more significant at a faster rate. As previously noted, RRANN's implementation of the backpropagation algorithm causes computational time t_C to grow linearly with the number of hardware neurons and, hence, FPGAs. If, for a different algorithm, this rate of growth were $n \log n$ or n^2, t_C would dominate t_R much sooner.

Another way of decreasing the significance of reconfiguration overhead is by finding faster methods for reconfiguring FPGAs (i.e. reducing t_R directly). Using Xilinx parts as an example, the internal data path used to load configuration data could be widened from one to eight bits, and the maximum configuration clock rate could be increased from 10 MHz to perhaps 50 MHz. Negligible reconfiguration times could be realized through an FPGA that is capable of storing multiple configurations. Configuration data for several configurations would be loaded and stored on the FPGA at the beginning of execution. The active configuration could be selected by a few dedicated external pins, and, after its execution is complete, another configuration could be activated by manipulating the select lines and waiting a few microseconds. Of course, internal configuration memory is not free, and an FPGA containing enough memory to hold four configurations might otherwise be able to have four times as many CLBs instead. This is the case with any configuration improvement; the improvement probably increases the part's programmability overhead and reduces the part's functionality. Issues such as these should be studied in order to find out what improvements can be made and the amount of additional overhead they would create.

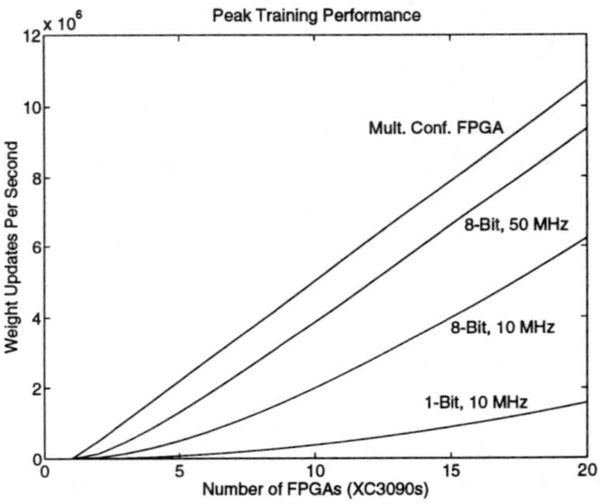

Figure 13: Effect of Configuration Improvement on Option Three Performance.

The performance results of these possible modification are summarized in Figures 13, 14, and 15 for option three. Figure 13 shows that the amount of computational power increases at a much faster rate when improved reconfiguration is used. Figure 14 shows that the performance of each FPGA becomes significantly larger in smaller networks. Figure 15 shows that reconfiguration times are not as dominant for even small networks. Comparing Figures 13 and 14 to Figures 9 and 10 respectively, it can be seen that reconfiguration improvements cause option three performance to be superior for networks using as little as three XC3090s. Note that in Figures 13, 14, and 15 all four configuration possibilities shown asymptotically arrive at the same values in the limit (> 1000 XC3090s). It is no surprise that improved reconfiguration time would increase the feasibility of run-time

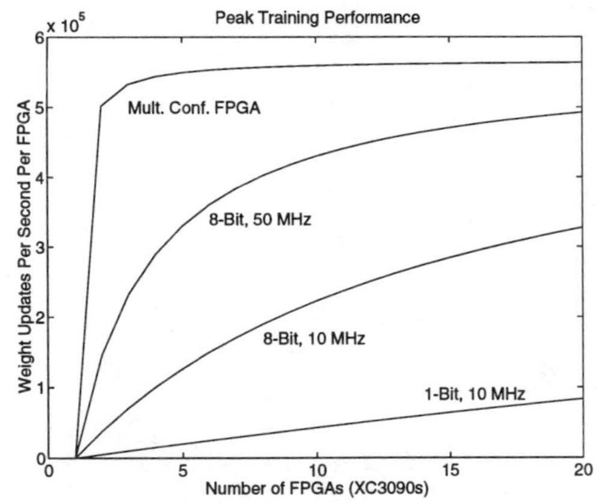

Figure 14: Effect of Configuration Improvement on Option Three Performance per XC3090.

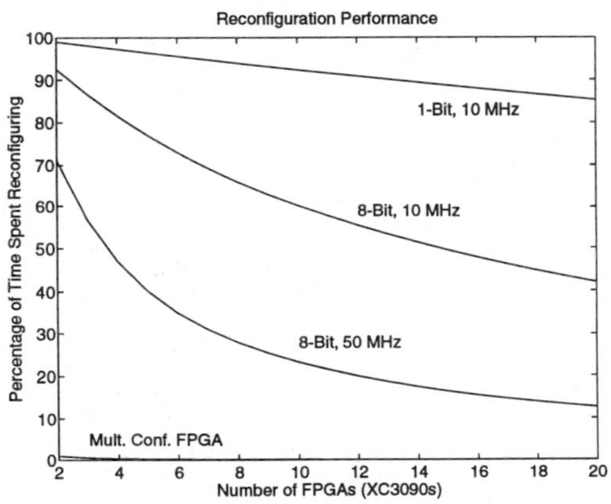

Figure 15: Effect of Configuration Improvement on Option Three's Percentage of Time Spent Reconfiguring.

reconfiguration.

5 Conclusion

The catalyst for this project was to find ways to use the FPGA's flexibility beyond prototyping. The focus was on exploiting reconfigurability–the biggest advantage a reconfigurable FPGA has over other forms of ASICs. Specifically, neural networks were used as an application, and run-time reconfiguration was used to improve neuron densities.

The Run-Time Reconfiguration Artificial Neural Network is an original neural network architecture designed and built by the authors to exploit the reconfigurability of FPGAs. RRANN implements the backpropagation algorithm by dividing it into three separate stages of execution and executing one of these stages at a time. Each stage is implemented with its own circuit module, and only one circuit module is configured onto the FPGAs at a time. When one stage completes, the FPGAs are reconfigured with the next stage's circuit module. Because circuitry from inactive stages are not using FPGA resources, the active stage's circuitry has more resources available to it. These extra resources are used to increase the number of hardware neurons on each neural processor.

This increase in available FPGA resources comes with the overhead of reconfiguration time (about 21 ms per pattern). This overhead dominates execution time when small numbers of FPGAs are being used. Two other options for implementing the backpropagation algorithm have been investigated and used for comparison. These other options require less reconfiguration overhead and achieve lower neuron densities.

Option three is able to implement 500% more hardware neurons per FPGA compared to option one. Because the computation time of the RRANN architecture increases linearly and reconfiguration time remains constant, reconfiguration overhead becomes increasingly less significant as the number of FPGAs grows. In the limit (> 1000 FPGAs), this overhead becomes insignificant, and the increased FPGA utilization becomes dominant. Moreover, in the limit, a given FPGA provides 500% better performance (WUPS) with run-time reconfiguration. If better methods for reconfiguring FPGAs were used, this better performance would be possible for even small numbers of FPGAs.

Run-time reconfiguration is another realization of the time/space trade-off common in computer engineering. This trade-off normally allows increases in performance at the cost of additional hardware or reductions in hardware at the cost of degraded performance. This trade-off applies to FPGAs and run-time reconfiguration in a slightly different sense. When more hardware is needed, the same space on an FPGA can be reused many times through reconfiguring, but doing so reduces the amount of time that the FPGA can spend executing. For example, if ten XC3090s are available, ten neurons per layer are the limit for option one. If more are needed, the same FPGAs can be reused for different stages creating more *space* for hardware neurons, but less *time* is available for computation due to reconfiguration overhead.

This new dimension to the time/space trade-off provided by the reconfigurability of FPGAs is also flexible. This trade-off does not have to be made at manufacture-time, but can be made optimally at run-time. For example, let's say a neural network with 25 neurons per layer is needed, and seven XC3090s are available. Option one is clearly insufficient providing only seven hardware neurons, and option three leaves 17 hardware neurons unused. However, option two provides 28 hardware neurons leaving only three unused, and it requires less reconfiguration overhead than option three. Since option two seems to be the optimal choice for this particular network, the decision to execute option two is made at run-time. After the completion of this 25 neuron per layer network, suppose a six neuron per layer network is needed. The run-time decision to execute option one (being clearly better for this job) can be made, and the same FPGA hardware can be reused. The flexibility of the reconfigurable FPGA can therefore be exploited on a case-by-case basis at run-time to achieve optimal performance.

References

[1] N. H. E. Weste and K. Eshraghian, *Principles of CMOS VLSI Design, A Systems Perspective*, 2nd ed., pp. 399-403, Reading, MA, Addison-Wesley Publishing Co., 1993.

[2] D. E. Rumelhart, G. E. Hinton, and R. J. Williams, "Learning Internal Representations by Error Propagation," in *Parallel and Distributed Processing*, Vol. 1, Cambridge, MA, MIT Press, 1986.

[3] T. Watanabe, et. al., Neural Network Simulation on a Massively Parallel Cellular Array Processor: AAP-2, *IEEE International Joint Conference on Neural Networks*, 2:155-61, Washington DC, 1989.

[4] D. Hammerstrom, A VLSI Architecture for High-Performance, Low-Cost, On-chip Learning, *IEEE International Joint Conference on Neural Networks*, 2:537-544, San Diego CA, 1990.

[5] S. S. Erdogan and T. H. Hong, Massively Parallel Computation of Back-Propagation Algorithm Using The Reconfigurable Machine, *World Congress on Neural Networks '93*, 4:861-4, Portland OR, 1993.

[6] J. Eldredge, *FPGA Density Enhancement of a Neural Network Through Run-Time Reconfiguration*, Masters Thesis, Dept. Electrical and Computer Engineering, Brigham Young University, Dec. 1993.

FPGA-Based Stochastic Neural Networks –Implementation

Stephen L. Bade and Brad L. Hutchings
Dept. of Electrical and Computer Eng.
Brigham Young University
Provo, UT 84602
Email: hutch@ee.byu.edu
Tel: (801) 378-2667

Abstract

Reconfigurable Field-Programmable Gate Arrays (FPGAs) provide an effective programmable resource for implementing hardware-based Artificial Neural Networks (ANNs). They are low cost, readily available and reconfigurable –all important advantages for ANN applications. However, FPGAs lack the circuit density necessary to implement large parallel ANNs with many thousands of synapses. This paper presents an architecture that makes it feasible to implement large ANNs with FPGAs. The architecture combines stochastic computation techniques with a novel lookup-table-based architecture that fully exploits the lookup-table structure of many FPGAs. This lookup-table-based architecture is extremely efficient: it is capable of supporting up to two synapses per Configurable Logic Block (CLB). In addition, the architecture is simple to implement, self-contained (weights are stored directly in the synapse), and scales easily across multiple chips.

1 Introduction

Reconfigurable Field-Programmable Gate Arrays (FPGAs) provide a reprogrammable hardware resource that can be exploited to great advantage for Artificial Neural Networks (ANNs). In contrast with custom Very Large Scale Integration (VLSI), they provide many important advantages. They are readily available at reasonable cost and have a reduced hardware development cycle. In addition, FPGA-based ANNs can be tailored to specific ANN configurations; there is no need for worst-case fully-interconnected designs as in full-custom VLSI design.

The fundamental problem limiting the size of FPGA-based ANNs is the high cost of implementing multiplication. High-speed, i.e., fully-parallel, ANNs require a tremendous number of multipliers –each synaptic connection in an ANN requires a single multiplier and the number of synaptic connections typically grows as the *square* of the number of neurons. For example, a fully-interconnected, 10-neuron ANN requires 100 multipliers (10 synapses per neuron x 10 neurons); the same network with 100 neurons would require 10,000 multipliers.

Practical implementations of ANNs are possible only if the amount of circuitry devoted to multiplication is significantly reduced. This can be accomplished in two ways: 1) reduce the number of multipliers, and/or 2) reduce the complexity of the multiplier. Most digital, hardware-based ANNs reduce *both* multiplier complexity and the total number of multipliers. For example, digital ANNs typically allocate a single bit-serial multiplier per neuron and use time-division multiplexing (TDM) to share it across all neuron inputs [3]. Performance is reduced but this multiplexed approach is much more practical for moderately sized ANNs.

Another way to reduce the circuitry necessary for multiplication is to use bit-serial *stochastic* computing techniques. Stochastic computing uses relatively long, probabilistic, bit-streams where the numeric value is proportional to the density of "1"s in the bit-stream. The main advantage of stochastic computing is that the multiplication of two probabilistic bit-streams can be accomplished with a single 2-input logic gate. This makes it feasible to implement large, dense, fully-parallel networks with digital techniques that achieve a high-level of performance.

Our paper presents new and original work in the following areas of application and theory:

- *Architecture.* This paper presents a lookup-table-based architecture that fully exploits the table-lookup organization of many FPGAs. This architecture can achieve densities (neurons per FPGA component) that are at least an order of magni-

0-8186-5490-2/94 $03.00 © 1994 IEEE

tude higher than the architecture presented in [6]. Moreover, it uses the FPGA resources such that it is optimal in the number of logic-block outputs used. This makes it feasible to implement very large ANNs with FPGAs. For example, it is possible to implement 480 synaptic connections on a single Xilinx 4010 part with this architecture.

- *Activation function.* A simple and effective activation function can be computed by thresholding a stochastic sum.
- *ANN Implementation.* A single-chip ANN is implemented using which can process 181K patterns per second.

2 Stochastic ANNs: A Brief Review

In general, all ANN architectures consist of a set of inputs and interconnected neurons, some of which are output neurons. This is shown in Figure 1. Each

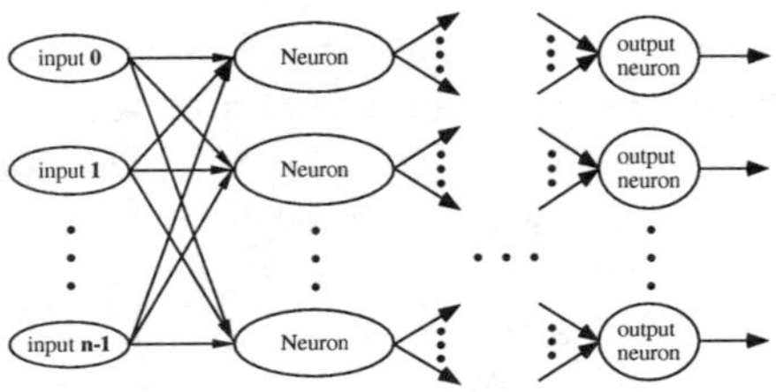

Figure 1: Overall Network Architecture

neuron contains a set of synapses and an activation function (see Figure 2). The function of the synapse is to multiply its input by a weight value to produce an output. A neuron's activation function is a non-linear thresholding function on the sum of the output of it's synapses.

A stochastic ANN uses the same general organization described above; the primary difference is that

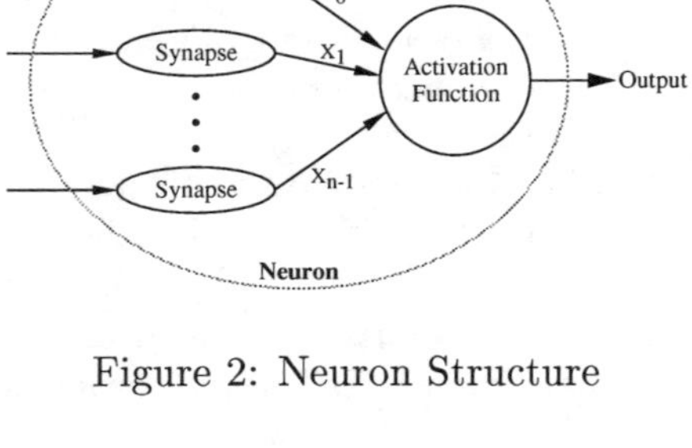

Figure 2: Neuron Structure

it uses stochastic techniques for signal representation and computation. Signals are represented as relatively long bit-streams where the actual signal value is encoded as a statistical distribution of the "1"s in the bit-stream. Computation is then based upon principles of statistics and uses simple boolean functions to perform the otherwise complex operations of multiplication, thresholding, and activation. The main advantage of the stochastic technique is that it can dramatically reduce the circuitry required to implement a synapse and neuron, and in turn, an entire neural network.

The stochastic ANN will be presented in two parallel sections: a conceptual view and an implementation view. The conceptual view presents the general theory and organization behind the stochastic ANN architecture. The implementation view discusses the specific details of ANN implementation with lookup-table FPGAs, specifically, the Xilinx FPGA. Finally, simulation results of an entire network are presented.

3 The Stochastic ANN : Conceptual View

This section presents the inputs first, followed by the synapse and the activation function.

3.1 Inputs

The first step toward stochastic processing is to convert real-valued inputs into a stochastic bit-streams[1]. The converted bit-streams are produced by a *bit-stream generator*. For a description of bit-stream generators, see [5, 6]. For the purposes of this paper, a bit-stream generators is circuit elements that uses a Linear Feedback Shift Register (LFSR).

3.2 The Synapse

The function of the synapse is to multiply some input by an internally stored weight value. This multiplication is performed using stochastic bit-streams. A stochastic bit-stream is simply a sequence of equally weighted bits where the probability of each bit being set is proportional to the value the bit-stream represents. More formally, let A be a Bernoulli random variable, and $A(t)$ be the value of A at time t. Then the sequence of values $[A(0), A(1), \ldots, A(n-1)]$ is a

[1] This conversion need only occur at the interface between the world and the ANN; within the ANN itself, *all* signals are represented as stochastic bit-streams.

stochastic bit-stream. In this paper, capital letters are used to represent both Bernoulli random variables and the bit-streams they generate.

There are two common mappings of a real number e to a Bernoulli random variable. These mappings directly affect the synapse circuitry, and so are presented here.

Representation I. Unipolar: The unipolar representation maps rational number e in the interval $(0, v)$ to the random variable A with generating probability:

$$p = P(A = 1) = e/v \tag{1}$$

Thus the maximum value ($e = v$) would be when every bit of the bit-stream is 1, and the minimum ($e = 0$) when each bit is 0. Stochastic multiplication with this representation is a simple bitwise "and" of the input bit-streams. For example, given the real values x, y, and z, $(0 \leq x, y \leq v)$, where $xy = z$, the value z/v can be obtained by the "and" of the bit-streams that represent x and y. Let the generating probabilities for the bit-streams that represent these values be p_x, p_y, and p_z respectively. The "and" operation defines

$$p_z = p_x p_y \tag{2}$$

Since $p_i = e_i/v$, this gives

$$z/v = xy \tag{3}$$

Note the product of the multiplication is scaled by $1/v$. This scaling keeps the range the same for of numbers in the ANN.

Representation III. Bipolar: A more compact bipolar representation is to map a rational number e $(-v \leq e \leq v)$ to the binary random variable B with generating probability:

$$p = p(B = 1) = e/2v + \frac{1}{2} \tag{4}$$

Thus the maximum value ($e = v$) is reached when every bit of the bit-stream is 1, and the minimum ($e = -v$) when each bit is 0, and zero when exactly half the bits are 1. The inverse transform is $e/v = 2p - 1$. Multiplication of bipolar bit-streams is the bitwise "x-nor" of the input bit-streams. In this representation, given the real values x, y, and z, $(-v \leq x, y \leq v)$, where $xy = z$, the value $z/2v$ can be obtained by the "x-nor" of the bit-streams that represent x and y. Again let the generating probabilities for the bit-streams

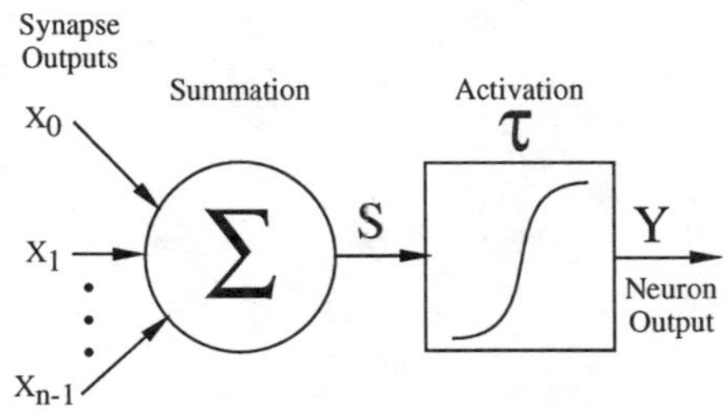

Figure 3: Activation Function

that represent these values be p_x, p_y, and p_z. The "x-nor" operation defines

$$p_z = p_x p_y + (1 - p_x)(1 - p_y) \tag{5}$$

Substituting $p_i = e_i/2v + \frac{1}{2}$,

$$z/v = xy \tag{6}$$

Thus synaptic multiplication of two bit-streams can be performed with a single boolean logic function. The following chapter on implementation presents an approach in which the synapse stores a compact representation of the weight, and then *generates the actual weight bit-stream during computation.*

3.3 Activation Function

The second stage of neural processing consists of summation and activation. During summation, the sum $s(t)$ is computed from the weighted inputs from the synapses. The activation function, $\mathcal{T}$, maps $s(t)$ to Y, the neuronal output. For this architecture, the activation function, is a continuous sigmoid-like function that is achieved by simply outputting a "1" if the sum of the synapses is above a threshold value, and a "0" if it is not.

Assume that at clock cycle t, a Bernoulli random variable (or bit-stream) B takes the value $B(t) \in \{0, 1\}$. Let the synapse outputs be variables $X_0, X_1, \cdots X_{m-1}$, and the neuron output be Y, then the neuronal output is written as:

$$Y(t) = \mathcal{T}(s(t)) = \mathcal{T}\left(\sum_{i=0}^{m-1} X_i(t)\right) \tag{7}$$

where

$$\mathcal{T}(s(t)) = \begin{cases} 1 & \text{if } s(t) > \frac{m}{2} \\ 0 & \text{otherwise} \end{cases} \tag{8}$$

The simple threshold function above depends on the stochastic nature of $s(t)$ to generate a sigmoid-like output. Notice that the value of $s(t)$ is an integer between 0 and m (number of neuron inputs), so $s(t)$

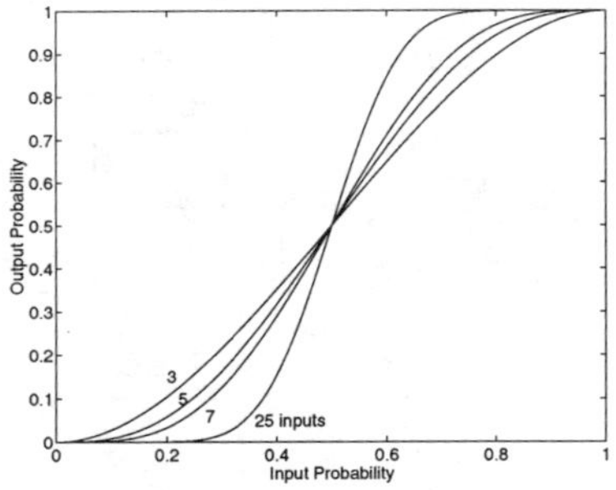

Figure 4: Binomial Activation Function

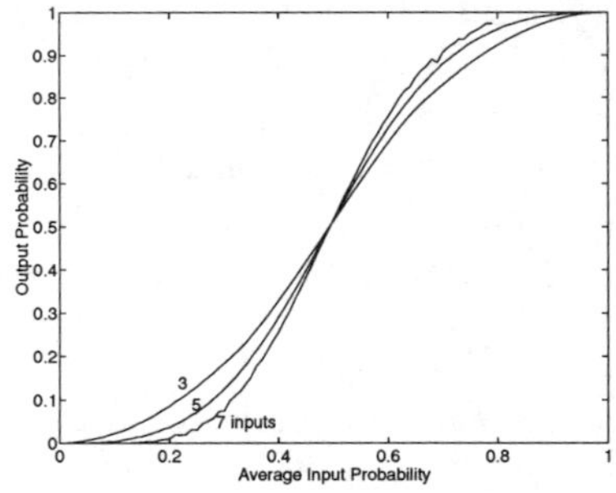

Figure 5: Actual Threshold function

cannot be represented by a Bernoulli random variable. We have chosen to represent the random vector $[X_0, X_1, \ldots, X_{m-1}]$ as $\mathbf{S}$, which has a value of s (number of ones in $\mathbf{S}$). At each clock cycle t, $\mathbf{S}(t)$ is the m length vector $[X_0(t), X_1(t), \cdots X_{m-1}(t)]$.

To describe the activation function, it is necessary to explain the distribution of $\mathbf{S}$. Assume for the moment that all the bit-streams X_i have the same generating probability (p). Then the vector $\mathbf{S}$ will have a binomial distribution described by p and m (length of $\mathbf{S}$), so the probability that $\mathbf{S}$ will have k bits set is:

$$P(s(t) = k) = \binom{m}{k} p^k (1-p)^{m-k} \tag{9}$$

The probability value of the output Y is:

$$P(Y(t) = 1) = \mathcal{T}(s(t)) = \sum_{k=\lceil \frac{m}{2} \rceil}^{m} \binom{m}{k} p^k (1-p)^{m-k} \tag{10}$$

Figure 4 gives a graphical view of this function for a 3, 5, 7, and a 25 input neuron. The function becomes more non-linear as the number of inputs increases. The threshold function is continuous, and is very easy to realize in hardware. It is continuous because the independent variable (p) is continuous, even though the actual values represented by a finite length bit-stream are quantized. The quantization depends on the length of the output bit-stream $Y(t)$.

Now drop the assumption that each input bit-stream to the activation function has the same probability. Then $\mathbf{S}(t)$ *no longer has a binomial distribution.* Thus Equation 10 no longer accurately describes the threshold function. This is obvious by noting that Equation 10 is a function of one probability only, whereas each random variable in $\mathbf{S}$ has a *separate* probability. Thus the activation function is not a function of one input, i.e., the average probability of all m inputs, but is a function of m *distinct* inputs.

The actual function is:

$$P(Y(t) = 1) = \mathcal{T}(s(t)) = \sum_{j=0}^{2^m-1} \mathcal{T}(j) \prod_{i=0}^{m-1} P(X_i = \Phi_{ji}) \tag{11}$$

where

$$\Phi_{ji} = \begin{cases} 1 & \text{if bit i in j is set}^2 \\ 0 & \text{otherwise} \end{cases} \tag{12}$$

and

$$\mathcal{T}(j) = \begin{cases} 1 & \text{if} > \frac{m}{2} \text{ bits in } j \text{ are set} \\ 0 & \text{otherwise} \end{cases} \tag{13}$$

Simulations have shown the actual function to be in general slightly more non-linear than the approximation, which should work well for a neural network. This function is shown in Figure 5.

4 The Stochastic ANN : Implementation

As stated in the introduction, the ANN implementation works well with custom VLSI, but is optimized for dynamically reconfigurable FPGAs. The architecture was developed specifically for Xilinx FPGAs, but should work well with any lookup-table-based FPGA. A brief overview of the Xilinx FPGA architecture is given so that implementation details can be discussed. Following this the implementation of each part of the ANN will be presented.

4.1 Xilinx FPGA Organization

The basic building block of a Xilinx FPGA is the Configurable Logic Block, or CLB. A CLB has two D flip-flops, can implement two logic functions of four

[2] treating j as a binary number.

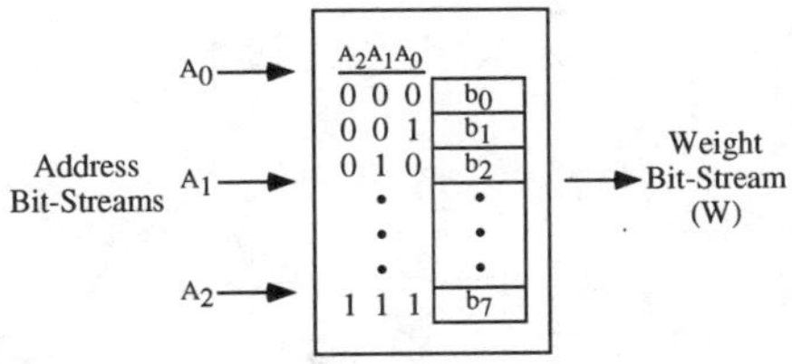

Figure 6: Lookup Table to Generate Synapse Weight

variables or one function of five variables, and has two outputs. These logic functions are implemented as 32-bit lookup tables. Because the logic functions are implemented with table lookup, there is no penalty for complicated logic functions as opposed to simple ones. Circuits are implemented by programming and interconnecting the CLBs. CLB utilization is typically limited by the number of flip-flops available, by the number of logic functions, or by the number of outputs available. Currently, Xilinx FPGAs have from 64 to 480 CLBs per chip [?]. Functionality per CLB will be our metric for circuit density.

4.2 Synapse

As stated in section 3.2, the synapse not only does a multiply, but it also stores a weight value and generates a weight bit-stream. Because synapse multiplication is a simple logic function of 2 inputs, the size of the circuitry that generates the weight bit-stream determines the size of the synapse.

The architecture described here proposes a novel approach to weight bit-stream generation and stochastic multiplication. This approach minimizes the synapse circuitry and maps very efficiently to lookup-table-based FPGA architecture. Rather than treating bit-stream generation and multiplication as discrete operations, this approach implements the entire synapse as *a single boolean function of four variables.* This approach provides several distinct advantages over other implementations. First, the required circuitry is drastically reduced because it exploits the lookup-table architecture common to FPGAs, and second, no control circuitry is required which further reduces circuit requirements. These advantages make it possible to construct practical implementations of large self-contained ANNs with FPGAs.

4.2.1 Generating the Weight Bit-Stream

Consider the problem of generating a synapse weight bit-stream. This can be performed as a boolean function of three variables. This function is implemented with an eight by one lookup table (eight locations of one bit each) that encodes both the weight value and the logic for generating the weight bit-stream (see figure 6). Three *address bit-streams* serve as inputs to the lookup table, represented by the Bernoulli random variables A_0, A_1, and A_2.

These address bit-streams determine the precision with which the weight can be represented. With n lookup table bits, $\log_2 n$ to n bits of precision can be achieved. The weight bit-stream (W) is made of the bits $(b_7, b_6, \ldots, b_0)$ in the table that are addressed by the address bit-streams, as shown in Figure 6. Let the triplet $A_2A_1A_0$ represent a three digit binary number, then the probability that bit i will be addressed is $P(A_2A_1A_0 = i)$. The weight bit-stream can be described by:

$$P(W=1) = \sum_{i=0}^{7} b_i P(A_2A_1A_0 = i), \qquad b_i \in \{0,1\} \tag{14}$$

Thus the available weight values are dependent on the probability values of the lookup table bits. For example, if each bit had an equal probability of being addressed (of $\frac{1}{8}$), then only nine distinct weights $(0, \frac{1}{8}, \frac{2}{8}, \ldots, \frac{7}{8}, 1)$ could be generated. This would correspond to 3 bits of precision. The optimal bit-probability of being addressed is $\frac{2^n}{2^m-1}$ where n is the bit position, and there are m total bit positions. With this bit probability, the lookup table could be thought of as an unsigned binary number with an implied decimal point before it's most significant bit. This would allow 256 weight bit-streams to be generated $(0, \frac{1}{255}, \frac{2}{255}, \ldots, \frac{254}{255}, 1)$. Choosing values for the synapse address bit-streams is discussed in [1, sect 4.3].

The address bit-streams are easily generated by the same method used for the input bit-streams. This is done by hard-coding the bit-stream generator to produce only one value. In addition, multiple uncorrelated sets of synapse address bit-streams may be derived by using delayed versions of a single set of address bit-streams. This is possible because Bernoulli values $A(i)$ and $A(j)$ are uncorrelated for $i \neq j$ [4].

4.2.2 Multiplying the Input with the Weight Bit-Stream

The synapse output is the product of the weight bit-stream, W, and the synapse input, I. This multiplication is a logic function of two variables (W and I), and the weight is a function of three variables (A_0, A_1, and A_2). These can be combined as one function of four

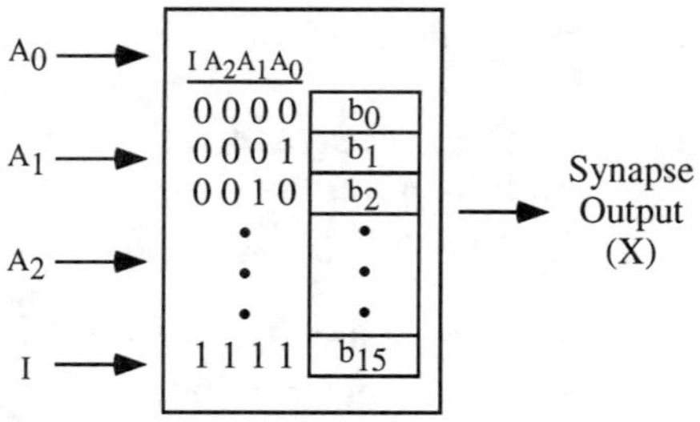

Figure 7: Complete Synapse

variables (A_0, A_1, A_2, and I), as shown in Figure 7. The next step is to determine the lookup-table value for the synapse. Let I be the most significant address bit for the lookup table, and the contents of the 8-bit lookup table that generates the desired weight be the vector $\mathbf{B} = [b_7, \ldots, b_0]$. The synapse lookup table is then the 16-bit vector $[\mathbf{B}|\mathbf{0}]$ for the unipolar representation, and $[\mathbf{B}|\bar{\mathbf{B}}]$ for the bipolar representation. This corresponds to an "and" of W and I for the unipolar representation, and a "x-nor" for the bipolar representation.

4.3 Activation Function

In this architecture, the summation and activation functions for an m-input neuron are implemented directly as a boolean function of m inputs. This is possible due to the simple way in which the activation function thresholds the synapse outputs. Like the synapse, this approach has important advantages: 1) it maps very well to lookup-table based FPGAs, 2) the activation function operates at the same speed as the synapse, so that neither becomes a bottleneck for the other, and 3) no control circuitry is required. Unlike the synapse implementation, the size of the activation function hardware varies with the number of inputs to the neuron.

For small numbers of inputs, the activation function can be implemented directly in a lookup table with m inputs, 2^m lookup table bits, and one output. For five or fewer inputs, this can be implemented with a single CLB. For large numbers of inputs, this direct implementation quickly becomes impractical because of the size of the required lookup table. For large numbers of inputs, we approximate the activation function by partitioning the function of m inputs ($m > 5$) into a set of smaller thresholding functions of 5 or less inputs[3]. The outputs of these smaller functions are then thresholded to produce the neuronal output. Figure 8 depicts how this would be done for a 25 input neuron. With up to five inputs per CLB, the size of the activation function using this approximation tends towards $1/4m$ CLBs for an m-input neuron.

[3] Functions are limited to five variables or less because a single Xilinx CLB can directly implement functions of up to five inputs.

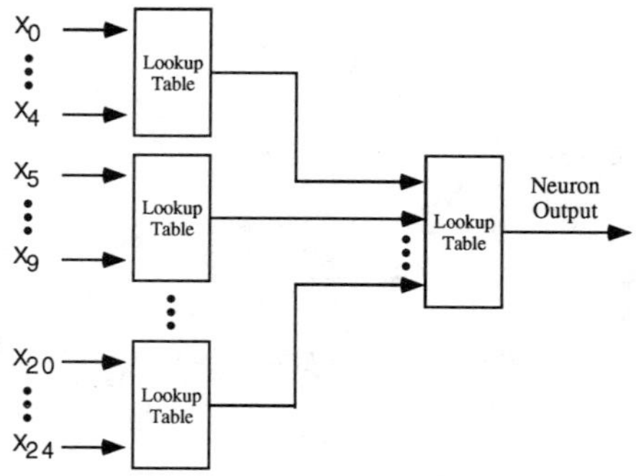

Figure 8: 25-Input Activation Function

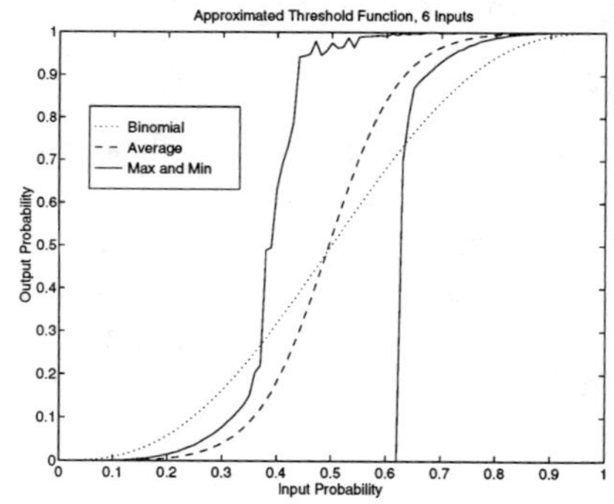

Figure 9: Approximated Activation Function

This approximation does introduce some error into the activation function. Figure 9 shows the average and bounding paths that the activation function can take for an 6-input neuron. The error is minimized when the inputs to the activation function assume a binomial distribution.

5 The Complete Network

A complete ANN using this architecture consists of the following:

- One Linear Feedback Shift Register to provide the random carrier bit-streams for both the inputs and the synapse address bit streams.
- One bit-stream generator for each input to the system.

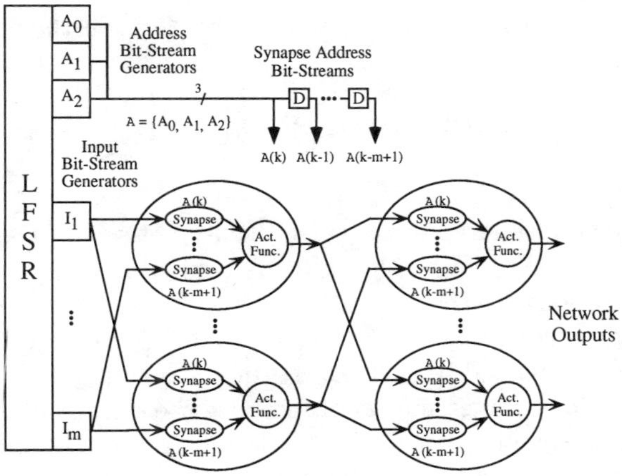

Figure 10: Complete Network

- Three bit-stream generators to provide the address-bit-streams used by all the synapses in weight generation.
- Delay elements (flip-flops) used to provide delayed versions of the inputs and address bit-streams to reduce correlation.
- Neurons, which consist of synapses and activation functions, and
- Circuitry to convert the output bit-streams to usable values. This can be provided with a simple counter or integrator, depending on the application.

Figure 10 gives a complete view of the network. Notice that each synapse has four inputs, one from the previous layer, and three address bit-streams. A network can be configured with any number of layers; the figure depicts a two-layer network for the sake of brevity.

The variable that most affects the size of the network is the amount of correlation allowed in the network. Correlation introduces error in the neural processing, but eliminating it entirely greatly increases the network's size. Correlation can be eliminated completely by providing each synapse a unique delayed version of the address bit-streams, and a unique delayed version of it's input. These four delays add a cost of two CLBs (four flip-flops) to each synapse, making the total synapse size two and one-half CLBs rather than only one-half CLB. Reasonable accuracy may be obtained while heavily reusing bit-streams. We found that using a total of m synapse address bit-streams works well (one for each input), as shown in Figure 10.

5.1 Accuracy

Given a Bernoulli sequence of length n from a random variable with generating probability p, it is shown by [2, pg. 58] that the standard deviation of the estimated value of p is

$$\sigma(\hat{p}) = \left[\frac{p(1-p)}{n}\right]^{\frac{1}{2}} \tag{15}$$

Thus the average error of a sequence is at a maximum for $p = 0.5$ and it decreases with the square root of the length of the sequence sampled. Thus for the worst case, to achieved b bits of accuracy, you need a sequence of length 2^{2b-2}. [6]

An important observation is that all of the operations performed in the network produce Bernoulli sequences if they have Bernoulli sequences as inputs. The only errors in excess of that discussed above in the network are due to the correlation of input bit-streams.

6 Implementation

We had three implementation goals: First, a working software model which simulated the architecture *bit-for-bit* as it would run in hardware, second, to show that the dense ANNs could be built using this architecture, and third, to build and test a working "proof of concept" circuit. The hardware implementations will be presented first, followed by some results from the software simulator. To demonstrate the density that could be achieved, an ANN was completely routed. The individual CLBs were not programmed, as the goal was simply to show that routing was possible.

This was implemented on a smaller Xilinx part from the 4000 series, the 4003PG120-5, which has 100 CLBs laid out in a 10x10 array. The 4000 series was chosen over the 3000 series because of the far superior routing resources of 4000 series. An attempt was made at using the 3000 series (using the 3090pc84), but the limitations in routing resources did not allow as dense of a layout as had been hoped.

6.1 Circuit Description

The circuit implemented a single layer ANN. The layer is fully connected with 12 inputs and 10 outputs. More layers could be added by simply cascading this circuit. This circuit consists of 120 synaptic connections (120 stored weights, with weight bit-stream generation and 120 multipliers), and 10 activation functions. The inputs to the chip are the neuron inputs

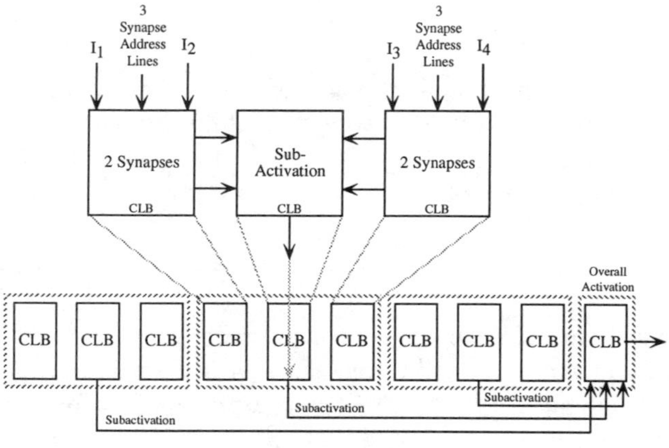

Figure 11: One row of the Physical Layout

(as bit-streams) and the synapse address bit-streams. The inputs could be generated either on or off-chip. As our intent is to show the neural processing circuitry, we will assume the input bit-streams are generated off-chip. The outputs are the ten bit-streams from the activation functions. Because the activation function has more than 5 inputs, the function is computed in two steps, as discussed in section 4.3 (see Figure 11). Three sub-activations of four inputs each are computed, and then they are run through an activation function to produce the neuronal output.

In the physical layout, each neuron with it's 12 synaptic connections occupies one row on the chip, or 10 CLBs. This is depicted in Figure 11. Aside from the synapse weights each row is identical, all receiving the same inputs and synapse address bit-streams. Each row consists of three identical blocks each containing four synapses and sub-activation circuitry. These blocks occupy three CLBs each, two for the synapses and one for the sub-activation function. This uses nine of the 10 CLBs per row. The 10th CLB is used to compute the overall activation function for the row. Figure 11 shows a row of the physical layout.

As shown by Figure 11, each of the synapse address bit-streams are shared by two synapses. Sharing address lines was done simply to reduce pin and routing requirements. This does cause some correlation, which was computed in software simulations of the circuit. [1, Sect. 6]. The correlation of the inputs to the activation function was measured both with separate and shared synapse address bit-streams. The correlation of the bit-streams entering an activation function was found by taking the difference of the observed joint probability and the product of the marginals. An overall sum squared error was then computed using each of the joint probabilities. For example, if an activation function had two inputs, A and B, then the sum squared error would be:

$$\sum_{i=0,1} \sum_{j=0,1} [P(A=i, B=j) - P(A=i)P(B=j)]^2 \tag{16}$$

The sum squared error was typically between .01 and .06 as computed by the software simulator.

As long as the synapse weights are not too similar, the correlation does not noticeably increase when the synapse address lines are shared. Nor did sharing address lines noticeably impact the output of the activation function. The correlation may cause accuracy problems if the inputs and synapse weights are too similar, and there may be correlation problems with multi-layer networks. This is an area of future research.

This design allows 120 synapses on only 100 CLBs. Every CLB on the chip is fully utilized. 60 CLBs are used to implement the synapses, and 40 CLBs are dedicated to activation function circuitry. This approaches the upper limit of synapse-density that is possible on this style of FPGA.

In order to make the best use of the resources on the chip, it was necessary to have more control over the physical routing than is normally available with high level design tools. The design was routed using XDE (an interactive physical layout design tool by Xilinx). XDE allowed hand routing which was necessary to place and route the circuit. One of the most useful routing resources for this design was the long lines that run the width and length Xilinx FPGAs. The long lines enabled the input and synapse address lines to run the length of the chip to all the synapses. The problem with routing this design on the 3000 series is that there are only a few long lines with limited connections, which made routing impossible. A hierarchy of macros were used to route the entire chip.

One difficulty we observed in routing this design is that the design tools currently available do not provide good support for allowing the designer to specify the physical layout. Such a tool would be very helpful if one was to try and do very much work designing layouts such as this.

6.2 Timing and Circuit Speed

Since the output of each CLB is gated through a flip-flop, the determining factor for the speed of the device is the routing delays. The main factor for the delay through a net is the number of "switchboxes" the net goes through. The nets that went through the most switchboxes had the greatest delays, with the longest delay being 27.6 ns (timing calculated using xdelay). Nets with the same fan-out (20 outputs) that used long-lines rather than going through switch-boxes had delays of up to 6ns. A more careful route could avoid the longer delays by using long-lines rather than switch-boxes, and operate at much higher speeds. With delays of up to 27.6ns, the part can operate at 36Mhz.

The speed measurement of Connections Per Second (cps) is not a good measure of parallel machines such as this, since the number is so dependent on the size of the network. For example, if assuming a bit-stream length of 200 bits (3.5% error), one input vector (pattern) could be processed in 5.5μs, or about 22 Mcps. A larger network using the same architecture (say 12000 synapses) would run at 2.2 Gcps. Thus a better metric for a parallel ANN is the number of patterns it can process per second (PPS), regardless of pattern size or network size. Using this metric, our design can operate at 181 KPPS.

6.3 Proof of Concept Circuit

The second goal was to produce a small working proof of concept circuit. This circuit implemented a three input, one output, single layer network. The circuit was implemented in a Xilinx 3090-pc84 FPGA, and installed in the National Technology Inc. Gips-II board, which allows the FPGA to be configured and tested with a PC. The longest routing delay for this circuit was 16ns. The circuit was tested with random input patterns and generated the expected outputs.

6.4 Simulation Results

The software simulator was mainly a test-bed for developing this architecture. It was designed to collect error and correlation statistics. This section presents findings concerning neuron output error and the correlation of the weighted inputs to neurons. The bit-stream error is calculated by taking the absolute value of the difference of the expected probability and the observed bit-stream probability, for example, given a bit-stream A of length n with expected value of p, the error is calculated by:

$$error = \left| p - n^{-1} \sum_{i=0}^{n-1} A(i) \right| \qquad (17)$$

Thus an error of .08 would correspond to the bit-stream value being 8% different than expected. The error is caused by both the variance of the binomial distribution (Section 5.1) and by correlation. The correlation reported in the following graphs is found by taking the sum squared of the differences of the joint probability and the product of the marginals for each joint probability.

For these simulations, a fully-connected three-layer, feed-forward network with five inputs was simulated. The network configuration had five neurons per layer with five inputs per neuron, for a total of 15 neurons and 75 synapses. Simulations were run with bit-stream lengths of 100, 250, 500, 1000, and 2500. 100 trials were run with each of these bit-stream lengths, 50 with a unipolar representation, and 50 bipolar. Each trial had a new random set of synapse weights. Simulation time (for all 500 trials) was under an hour on an i486-50MHz PC.

Figure 12 shows the maximum and average error values for all 15 neurons in the network. The two dashed lines are the maximum errors for each bit-stream length, one line for the unipolar representation, and one for the bipolar representation. The knees in the graph are due to sparce data points on the x axis. The average neuron error is represented by two dotted lines on top of each other, one for each number representation. This shows that the number representation does not significantly affect the neuron output error. The solid line is the predicted maximum error assuming no correlation, as given by equation 15, with $p = 0.5$.

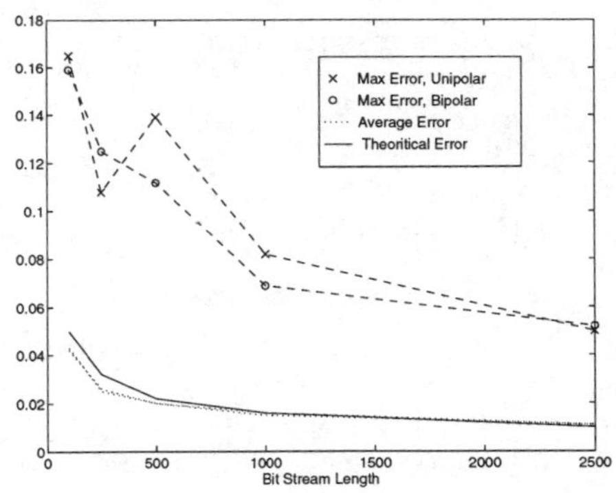

Figure 12: Maximum and Average Error of Neuron Output

As explained earlier, correlation is introduced only to reduce the hardware required to implement the ANN. Thus the tradeoff is network size v.s. loss of accuracy due to correlation. For a specific application, the network could be designed with as much or as little correlation in order to achieve the required accuracy. Defining this tradeoff more formally could be addressed in further research.

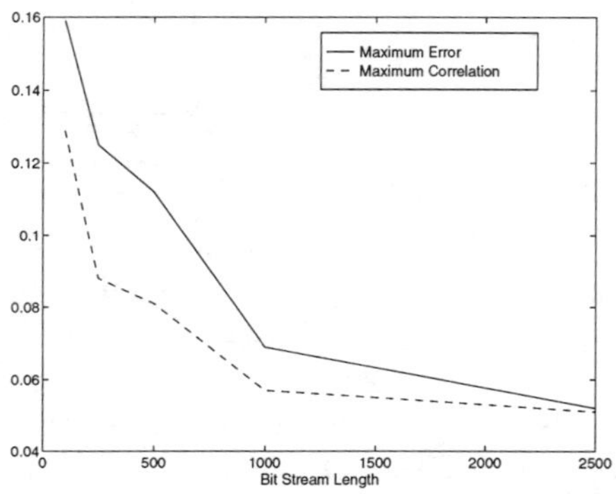

Figure 13: Relationship between Error and Correlation

7 Conclusions

This paper has presented a lookup-table-based architecture for stochastic ANNs that maps efficiently to FPGAs. It exploits all of the advantages inherent to FPGAs: low cost, availability, reconfigurability, the ability to support arbitrary network architectures, lowered development costs, all while providing a level of density that makes it feasible to implement large ANNs with FPGAs. This architecture provides the following distinct advantages:

- The entire network is self-contained, there is no need for supporting circuitry to store weights or aid in computations.
- The structures are very regular and repeated.
- There is no control logic except the clock.
- There are no bus lines and delays for reading weight values, since each synapse stores it's own weight.
- The architecture is fully parallel, resulting in O(1) operation.
- The architecture scales easily, and can be scaled across multiple chips to form large networks.

This architecture also provides the greatest possible synapse density on the above described Xilinx FPGA architecture. Circuits implemented with Xilinx FPGAs, for example, are often output limited because each CLB provides only two outputs, one per function generator. This architecture uses one function generator and one output per synapse, making it possible to implement two synapses with a single CLB. Even if the function generator could be eliminated, one output per synapse would still be required, therefore two synapses would still consume an entire CLB.

8 Future Work

The main issue which needs to be addressed is network learning algorithms. Learning is complicated in stochastic networks because the number representation is such that it is hard to store a number with enough precision to perform standard learning calculations. We would also like to study the ability of the architecture to support very large networks, for example, networks with 10,000 - 100,000 synapses or more. Networks of this size could be constructed with Multi-Chip Modules (MCMs) or Wafer-Scale Integration (WSI). The reprogrammability of FPGAs is strong advantage for WSI implementations because it makes it possible, in many cases, to program *around* defects in the wafer. Another important area of study is the effects that correlation has on accuracy. Allowing some correlation provides a denser network at the cost of some accuracy. It will be important to understand the tradeoffs between correlation and accuracy so that the accuracy of a given network can be predicted.

References

[1] Stephen L. Bade. Lookup table based neural network using FPGAs. *Thesis, Brigham Young University*, 1994.

[2] B. R. Gaines. Stochastic computing systems. *Advances in Information Science*, 2(1):37–172, 1969.

[3] Dan Hammerstrom. VLSI architecture for high performance, low cost, on-chip learning. *IJCNN-9-Wash-DC*, 2:537 – 544, January 1990.

[4] Xilinx Inc. *The Programmable Logic Data Book.* 1993.

[5] Robert J. McEliece. *Finite Fields for Computer Scientiists and Engineers.* Kluwer Academic Publishers, 1987.

[6] M. van Daalen, P. Jeavons, J. Shawe-Taylor, and D. Cohen. Device for generating binary sequences for stochastic computing. *Electronic Letters*, 29(1):80 – 81, 1993.

[7] Max van Daalen, Peter Jevons, and John Shawe-Taylor. A stochastic neural architecture that exploits dynamically reconfigurable fpgas. *Proceedings IEEE Workshop on FPGAs for Custom Computing Machines*, pages 202–211, April 1993.

Author Index

Abbott, A.L. 155
Agarwal, A. 14
Agarwal, L. 101
Arnstein, L. 125
Athanas, P.M. 155
Babb, J. 14
Bade, S.L. 189
Banâtre, J.P. 119
Bellec, P. 49
Bergmann, N.W. 164
Bertin, P. 133
Borriello, G. 11
Box, B. 40
Chen, L. 155
Cowen, C.P. 59
Dahl, M. 14
Dai, W.W.-M. 1
Darnauer, J. 1
DeHon, A. 31
Dhaussy, P. 72
Eldredge, J.G. 180
Ellervee, P. 111
Elliott, R.L. 155
Filloque, J.-M. 72
Forward, K. 147
Garay, P. 1
Gent, G.J. 172
Ghosh, S. 101
Gilson, K.L. 23
Hanono, S. 14
Hartenstein, R.W. 139
Hauck, S. 11
Haviland, R.L. 172
Hemani, A. 111
Hoki, D. 14
Hutchings, B.L. 23, 180, 189
Isshiki, T. 1
Jantsch, A. 111
Kraljić, I.C. 91
Kress, R. 139
Lagnese, E. 125
Lavenier, D. 119
Luk, W. 82
Marchal, P. 66
Monaghan, S. 59
Mudge, J.C. 164
Öberg, J. 111
Page, I. 82
Pottier, B. 72
Quénot, G.M. 91
Ramirez, J. 1
Reinig, H. 139
Rubini, S. 72
Sanchez, E. 66
Schmit, H. 125
Sérot, J. 91
Singh, S. 49
Smith, S.R. 172
Tessier, R. 14
Thomas, D. 125
Touati, H. 133
Vieillot, M. 119
Wazlowski, M. 101
Wirthlin, M.J. 23
Wo, D. 147
Wu, T. 82
Zavidovique, B. 91

IEEE Computer Society

IEEE Computer Society Press Publications

Monographs: A monograph is an authored book consisting of 100-percent original material.
Tutorials: A tutorial is a collection of original materials prepared by the editors and reprints of the best articles published in a subject area. Tutorials must contain at least five percent of original material (although we recommend 15 to 20 percent of original material).
Reprint collections: A reprint collection contains reprints (divided into sections) with a preface, table of contents, and section introductions discussing the reprints and why they were selected. Collections contain less than five percent of original material.
Technology series: Each technology series is a brief reprint collection — approximately 126-136 pages and containing 12 to 13 papers, each paper focusing on a subset of a specific discipline, such as networks, architecture, software, or robotics.
Submission of proposals: For guidelines on preparing CS Press books, write the Managing Editor, IEEE Computer Society Press, PO Box 3014, 10662 Los Vaqueros Circle, Los Alamitos, CA 90720-1264, or telephone (714) 821-8380.

Purpose

The IEEE Computer Society advances the theory and practice of computer science and engineering, promotes the exchange of technical information among 100,000 members worldwide, and provides a wide range of services to members and nonmembers.

Membership

All members receive the acclaimed monthly magazine *Computer*, discounts, and opportunities to serve (all activities are led by volunteer members). Membership is open to all IEEE members, affiliate society members, and others seriously interested in the computer field.

Publications and Activities

***Computer* magazine:** An authoritative, easy-to-read magazine containing tutorials and in-depth articles on topics across the computer field, plus news, conference reports, book reviews, calendars, calls for papers, interviews, and new products.
Periodicals: The society publishes six magazines and five research transactions. For more details, refer to our membership application or request information as noted above.
Conference proceedings, tutorial texts, and standards documents: The IEEE Computer Society Press publishes more than 100 titles every year.
Standards working groups: Over 100 of these groups produce IEEE standards used throughout the industrial world.
Technical committees: Over 30 TCs publish newsletters, provide interaction with peers in specialty areas, and directly influence standards, conferences, and education.
Conferences/Education: The society holds about 100 conferences each year and sponsors many educational activities, including computing science accreditation.
Chapters: Regular and student chapters worldwide provide the opportunity to interact with colleagues, hear technical experts, and serve the local professional community.